Wordplay and Metalinguistic / Metadiscursive Reflection

The Dynamics of Wordplay

Edited by
Esme Winter-Froemel

Editorial Board
Dirk Delabastita, Dirk Geeraerts, Raymond W. Gibbs, Alain Rabatel,
Monika Schmitz-Emans and Deirdre Wilson

Volume 1

Wordplay and Metalinguistic / Metadiscursive Reflection

—

Authors, Contexts, Techniques, and Meta-Reflection

Edited by
Angelika Zirker and Esme Winter-Froemel

DE GRUYTER

Die Tagung und die Publikation dieses Bandes wurden gefördert von der Fritz Thyssen Stiftung für Wissenschaftsförderung, der Deutschen Forschungsgemeinschaft (DFG) und dem Sonderforschungsbereich 833 „Bedeutungskonstitution – Dynamik und Adaptivität sprachlicher Strukturen" der Eberhard Karls Universität Tübingen.

Peter Koch (1951–2014) in memoriam

ISBN 978-3-11-057871-3
e-ISBN (PDF) 978-3-11-040671-9
e-ISBN (EPUB) 978-3-11-040684-9

Library of Congress Cataloging-in-Publication Data
A CIP catalog record for this book has been applied for at the Library of Congress.

Bibliographic information published by the Deutsche Nationalbibliothek
The Deutsche Nationalbibliothek lists this publication in the Deutsche Nationalbibliografie; detailed bibliographic data are available on the Internet at http://dnb.dnb.de.

© 2015 Walter de Gruyter GmbH, Berlin/Boston
This volume is text- and page-identical with the hardback published in 2015.
Printing: CPI books GmbH, Leck

♾ Printed on acid-free paper
Printed in Germany

www.degruyter.com

Contents

Angelika Zirker and Esme Winter-Froemel
Wordplay and Its Interfaces in Speaker-Hearer Interaction: An Introduction —— 1

I Authors and Contexts

Martina Bross
"Equivocation will undo us"? Wordplay and Ambiguity in Hamlet's First and Second Line —— 25

Thomas Kullmann
Wordplay as Courtly Pastime and Social Practice: Shakespeare and Lewis Carroll —— 47

Maik Goth
***Double Entendre* in Restoration and Early Eighteenth-Century Comedy —— 71**

Sheelagh Russell-Brown
The Serious Work of Play: Wordplay in the "Dark Sonnets" of Gerard Manley Hopkins —— 95

II Linguistic Techniques of Wordplay

Vincent Renner
Lexical Blending as Wordplay —— 119

Pierre J. L. Arnaud, François Maniez and Vincent Renner
Non-Canonical Proverbial Occurrences and Wordplay: A Corpus Investigation and an Enquiry Into Readers' Perception of Humour and Cleverness —— 135

Sebastian Knospe
A Cognitive Model for Bilingual Puns —— 161

Ian Duhig
Interview: A Perspective from Practical and Professional Experience – Wordplay in Poetry — 195

III Genre and Meta-Reflection

Johannes Kabatek
Wordplay and Discourse Traditions — 213

Svea Schauffler
Wordplay in Subtitled Films – An Audience Study — 229

Monika Schmitz-Emans
Plays around Surfaces and Depths: Transitions between Two- and Three-Dimensionality Reflected by Wordplays and Puns — 245

Matthias Bauer
Secret Wordplay and What It May Tell Us — 269

Appendix

List of Contributions and Abstracts — 291

List of Contributors — 301

Index — 309

Angelika Zirker and Esme Winter-Froemel
Wordplay and Its Interfaces in Speaker-Hearer Interaction: An Introduction

Abstract: Taking the ubiquity and variety of wordplay in both everyday communication and literary texts as a starting point, this contribution sets out to present two different perspectives that allow for a profound interdisciplinary approach. Firstly, the metalinguistic / metadiscursive point of view helps us analyze how wordplay is used and interpreted in various communicative situations. This metalinguistic / metadiscursive perspective reflects on both the linguistic code (or linguistic codes in cases of multilingual wordplay) and on the act of communication itself. Secondly, we are looking at various interplays of wordplay, including linguistic, cognitive, social, etc. forms of such interplay. Our approach foregrounds not only the complexity of wordplay as an interface phenomenon but also allows for a better understanding of wordplay as employed in speaker-hearer interaction and thus also unravels fundamental aspects of language and communication.

Keywords: auto-referentiality, everyday communication, fraternization, interdisciplinary approach, interfaces, interplay, metalinguistic function, poetic function, Roman Jakobson, speaker-hearer interaction

1 Introductory Remarks

Wordplay is a genuine interface phenomenon to be found both in everyday communication and in literary texts and is thus part of various discourse traditions. It may fulfil a wide range of functions and be entertaining and comical, it may be used to conceal taboo, and it may influence the way in which a speaker's character is perceived. The interdisciplinary approach to the study of wordplay proposed here thus combines literary and linguistic analysis and integrates various kinds of text types, genres as well as contexts of usage. For instance, linguistics is interested in the semantic connections between the lexical units involved and, more generally, in linguistic motivation / transparency as illustrated by wordplay, as well as in its pragmatic use in communication. Literary studies analyzes autoreferentiality of wordplay, for example in nonsense literature. Methods and tools of analysis may therefore be combined and lead to broader perspectives with regard to functions, effects and the systematics of wordplay. Literary studies hereby provides a corpus of highly complex phenomena, while linguistics offers criteria of description and analysis for these: The reference to linguistic categories results in the more precise analysis and classification of forms and functions of wordplay and thus allows for a refinement of tools of analysis in the field of literary studies. The approaches and material complement each other in that both the aesthetic quality of wordplay in everyday communication is foregrounded and the linguistic analysis of literary wordplay proves to be fruitful.

The two opening volumes in the series *The Dynamics of Wordplay* go back to an interdisciplinary research project on "Wordplay in Speaker-Hearer Interaction" and a conference which took place at Tübingen University in 2013. The conference aimed at bringing about an interdisciplinary dialogue and at joining researchers from different linguistic and academic backgrounds. At the same time, we wished to bring together academic perspectives and "practical" perspectives of comedians, authors, directors, etc., who use or deal with wordplay in their professional life. Thus, the conference programme included also a performance by Christian Hirdes (comedian, singer and poet) and contributions by Marc Blancher (author), Valia Sakkou (media director), Sam Lesser (actor), and Phillip Breen (director).

The conference languages were English and French, which has resulted in the bilingual publication as now presented. The volumes show that the conference not only managed to bridge differences in the realm of language, but also provided manifold interdisciplinary insights which are reflected in cross-references within the individual contributions. They should therefore be regarded as a joint project, and the reader is invited to approach them as such. We have provided a French version of this introduction (see *The Dynamics of Wordplay* 2), and in the concluding parts of the volumes we also assemble the abstracts and contributors' notes in both English and French in order to emphasize the links between the volumes.

The following interdisciplinary analyses of wordplay focus on two main aspects: firstly, a conception of wordplay as a metalinguistic / metadiscursive phenomenon (see the topic of the conference where most of the papers published here were presented, "Wordplay and Metalinguistic Reflection – New Interdisciplinary Perspectives / Les jeux de mots et la réflexion métalinguistique – nouvelles perspectives interdisciplinaires"), and, secondly, a communicative approach with a particular focus on speaker-hearer interaction (see Winter-Froemel and Zirker 2015), which permits us to approach various kinds of interplays in concrete uses of wordplay. This means that the definition of wordplay is not based on formal criteria alone, but on regarding wordplay as a dynamic and multifaceted phenomenon in concrete communicative settings.

2 The Ubiquity of Wordplay in Everyday Language and Literature – and Its Fugacity

Wordplay can be seen as being part of our everyday linguistic experience. It may turn up in spontaneous face-to-face communication (1) as well as in Twitter messages (2), on road signs and posters as well as in advertising slogans and brand names (3), in jokes (4) and nursery rhymes (5) as well as in literary language (6). In these various contexts (and many more), we can find a broad range of manifestations of playful language use that we may intuitively categorize as wordplay, although they may differ considerably with regard to formal and functional aspects.

(1) Germ. *Schittebön. – Schankedön.* (wordplay on German *Bitteschön.* [Here you are.] – *Dankeschön.* [Thank you.])

(2) i dont remember much about my dream with zayn but i remember he pushed me into an elevator and things escalated quickly (Twitter message by "a loves baby bean," 22 October 2014, 11:39)

(3) Germ. *haargenau* (name of a hairdresser playing on German *haargenau* [to a hair] and *Haar* [hair])

(4) Deux poules discutent:
– Comment vas-tu ma cocotte?
– Pas très bien. Je crois que je couve quelque chose!
[Two hens are talking to each other. – How are you doing, my dear? – Not so well. I think that I am incubating / coming down with something.]

(5) En passant dans un petit bois,
Où le coucou chantait,
Où le coucou chantait.
Dans son joli chant il disait:
"Coucou, coucou,
Coucou, coucou."
Et moi je croyais qu'il disait:
"Coupe-lui le cou!
Coupe-lui le cou!"
Et moi de m'en cour,' cour,' cour'
Et moi de m'en courir.

[...]
[Walking through a small forest where the cuckoo was singing. And he said in his nice chant "Cuckoo, cuckoo! Cuckoo, cuckoo!" And I thought that he was saying "Cut off his neck, cut off his neck!" And I ran, ran, ran, and I ran away.]

(6) SAMPSON. Gregory, on my word, we'll not carry coals.
     GREGORY. No, for then we should be colliers.
     SAMPSON. I mean, and we be in choler, we'll draw.
     GREGORY. Ay, while you live, draw your neck out of collar.

(Shakespeare 2012: 1.1.1–4)

The wordplay in (1) is based on a permutation of two sounds in each word ([b] and [ʃ], and [d] and [ʃ], respectively), leading to nonsense items that may make us laugh if we recognize the formal deviation, successfully undo the permutation, and "retranslate" the words. In (2), by contrast, the pun is based on two conventional meanings of the English verb *elevate* ('rise,' 'get out of control'), the latter, figurative meaning suggesting a sexual interpretation, so that the play alludes to a taboo. In (3), we can also find a play on the lexicalized German expression *haargenau* and the conventional literal meaning of one of the elements of the compound, German *Haar*. In this case, however, the wordplay is much more innocent, and its main achievement consists in remotivating the compound by stressing what would be its literal meaning. In (4) we can also observe a play on the polysemy of French *couver* 'to incubate (an egg)' / 'to come down with (an illness),' and (5) narrates a comical misunderstanding of the cuckoo's chant in a much more threatening sense ([cut off his neck]; the nursery rhyme continues with a series of other misunderstandings of real-world sounds as threatening acts). For an analysis of the complex wordplay in (6), see below.

In that sense, all the examples cited require a certain additional effort of interpretation, reflecting on various senses of the linguistic items or on certain formal manipulations. At the same time, however, in spite of its eye-catching or ear-catching nature, wordplay can be seen as a somewhat ephemeral phenomenon. On the one hand, as we have seen with the advertising slogan in (3), wordplay is often used in order to attract the hearer's or reader's attention and enhance the memorization of the message; on the other hand, the ultimate aim of the advertising message is a different one, and the producer of the advertising campaign does not intend us to remember the wordplay as such, but the product and the advertising message. Similarly, in social contexts of telling jokes to each other (see (4)), it is common to deplore one's own lack of memory concerning good jokes once heard. Here again, in a certain sense, the ultimate function of communication in joke-telling is not the message of the wordplay itself; rather wordplay is a means for the speaker (and the hearer) to present him- / herself as being linguistically competent, witty as well as quick-witted to pass a subtle underlying social battle – and once this message has passed, the wordplay itself is no longer important (unless one tries to remember it in order to use it again in a later context of joke-telling with a different audience).

Let us therefore dwell on the phenomenon of wordplay itself, which, as we will see, permits us to approach very fundamental aspects of language and communication and explore interdisciplinary bridges between linguistics, literary studies and various other disciplines.[1] Which perspectives can be gained by departing from a large conception of wordplay including very different contexts of use and very different perspectives of analysis? And what can the different disciplines and previous studies on wordplay in various contexts contribute to a more comprehensive approach of this multifaceted phenomenon?

3 Interdisciplinary Perspectives on Wordplay in Speaker-Hearer Interaction

Many previous linguistic approaches have focused on various types of wordplay based on formal analyses, aiming at a comprehensive classification (see e.g. Guiraud 1976; Vittoz Canuto 1983; for an overview see also Winter-Froemel 2009). Other approaches, by contrast, have focused on the use of wordplay in specific authors (e.g. Kemmner 1972) or specific settings, e.g. in publicity (see e.g. Vittoz Canuto 1983; Grunig 1990; Tanaka 1992, 1999), in newspaper language (see e.g. Carstensen 1971; Hausmann 1974), in new media (Chovanec and Ermida 2012), or in specific elements within texts, e.g. headlines (see e.g. Dittgen 1989). Special attention has also been directed to specific text types involving wordplay (e.g. jokes, see Ulrich 1977), and still other approaches have focused on the challenges that translating wordplay and multilingual wordplay involve (see Rauch 1982; Grassegger 1985; Heibert 1993; Paton, Powell and Wagg 1996; Delabastita 1997; Ulrich 1997; Stefanowitsch 2001; Schröter 2010; and Valero-Garcés 2010; Kharkhurin 2012, respectively).

Moreover, we may also refer to an important tradition of humour research (Raskin 1985; Attardo and Raskin 1991; Attardo 1994, 2006; Goatly 2012; see also

---

[1] The collection of linguistic jokes provided by Koch, Krefeld and Oesterreicher (1997), together with the authors' linguistic comments, has been a first source of inspiration leading to our interest for this topic.

Preisendanz and Warning 1976; Hesbois 1986) which immediately relates to the topic of wordplay but adopts a much wider perspective, including various forms of non-linguistic humour and emphasizing further aspects of analysis, e.g. the psychological and / or anthropological dimension of wordplay (see, e.g. the works of Sigmund Freud 1905; Helmuth Plessner [1941] 1950; G. B. Milner 1972; Johan Huizinga [1938] 1987; and Henri Bergson [1940] 1993). Finally, wordplay has also been analyzed in the context of linguistic motivation (Gauger 1971, 1976; Käge 1980; Rettig 1981; Cuyckens, Dirven and Panther 2003; Partington 2009; on figurative language see also Gibbs and Colston 2012) and from cognitive linguistic perspectives (Veale 2009).

In the realm of literature (and literary studies) wordplay has so far been studied as a category related to larger interpretive contexts and to particular authors, genres, and periods. One focus of research is the function of wordplay in puns (see Culler 1988; Delabastita 2001), in literary riddles (cf. Cook 2006), modernist poetry (see Cook 1998) as well as an expression of wit, for instance, in order to draw conclusions concerning the truth value of language (cf. Mahood 1957). Wordplay furthermore is a key to the discovery of language as a heuristic tool, for example religious knowledge in metaphysical poetry during the 17th century (see Bauer forthcoming). This leads us immediately to the metalinguistic dimension of wordplay (see Schmitz-Emans 1997, especially 49–105; Delabastita 2001, 2005), which will be explored in more detail below.

Wordplay in literary texts may also serve as a means of characterization – and very often so with some comical intent. In Charles Dickens's *A Tale of Two Cities*, we read about one character:

(7) Mr Cruncher himself always spoke of the year of our Lord as Anna Dominoes: apparently under the impression that the Christian era dated from the invention of a popular game, by a lady who had bestowed her name upon it. (Dickens [1859] 2003: II.1, 57)

"Anna Dominoes" is a comic wordplay based on a mishearing or misunderstanding of the expression Anno Domini (for comic misunderstanding as a specific use of ambiguity see Winter-Froemel and Zirker 2010) – but as the character does not know any Latin, he has reinterpreted the expression (somewhat playfully) and situated it in a context that is identifiable to him, namely the game of dominoes. The wordplay here represents an instance of bilingual wordplay.

Wordplay thus playfully questions the functioning of language and makes creative use of its limits. But wordplay does not necessarily only serve a comic effect; it may also be subversive and it may have a poetic function, especially if one thinks of Huizinga's situating poetry in the realm of play (cf. Huizinga

[1938] 1987: 133). This link of poetry and play initiates the reflection of poetry as play (see Zirker 2010: 220).

The examples so far have addressed the ubiquity of wordplay in everyday language as much as in literary texts; they have, however, not addressed the aspect of speaker-hearer interaction nor the benefits of an interdisciplinary approach. A first example to illustrate possible interdisciplinary links suggested by wordplay is the following advertising slogan by the tea company Twinings:

(8) Twinings – L'amour avec un grand thé.

This TV slogan alludes to the expression *l'amour avec un grand a* [the big / true love] and replaces the initial letter of the word *amour* by the sounds [te]. This sequence of sounds is disambiguated at the level of spelling, where it is transcribed as French *thé* [tea] which, of course, immediately relates to the conceptual frame (or scenario) of HAVING A CUP OF TEA. On the phonic level, however, [te] generates an additional interpretation in the sense of 'the letter T,' i.e. the initial of both the word *thé* and the name of the company Twinings, a proper name and therefore written with a capital T. Like example (3) cited in section 2, this wordplay is clearly based on speaker strategy: it is aimed at directing the hearer's attention to the message and in this way, to make him / her memorize the slogan and the brand name Twinings and, eventually, be more inclined to buy the products of this company (see Tanaka 1992). At the same time, the wordplay can be explained as an attempt of the speaker to present him- / herself in a positive, creative way. In this sense, wordplay is a manifestation of an aesthetic use of language, which is condensed in order to achieve an aesthetic effect (even if, of course, this effect is subordinate to the dominant, commercial function in the example cited here). The strategy used – a play on homophony (*thé / t*) and an allusion to the expression *l'amour avec un grand a*, or its variation by manipulating one single sound – recalls manipulations of language in literary texts, see e.g. Dylan Thomas's "Once below a time" (Thomas 2000).

Turning to literary texts, drama is one of the genres where speaker-hearer interaction is most evidently foregrounded. Shakespeare's *Romeo and Juliet* opens with an exchange between two characters that is based on wordplay:

(6) SAMPSON. Gregory, on my word, we'll not carry coals.
    GREGORY. No, for then we should be colliers.
    SAMPSON. I mean, and we be in choler, we'll draw.
    GREGORY. Ay, while you live, draw your neck out of collar.
                                            (Shakespeare 2012: 1.1.1–4)

Sampson begins the dialogue with a refusal to "carry coals," which is a proverbial expression and means as much as "allow ourselves to be insulted" (Shakespeare 2012: 124n1), Gregory immediately takes up Sampson's utterance and answers with an instance of wordplay in referring to their not being "colliers," i.e. a literal 'carrier of coals.' The interplay at first is between the figurative and literal meanings of the words coal and collier. Sampson's retort that they "be in choler" continues the paronymic play on *coals* and *collier*, albeit with a completely different meaning: *choler* refers to their anger (see Shakespeare 2012: 124n1). Again, Gregory joins the verbal game and answers with a reference to "collar," which is a homophone of "choler" and refers to a halter; Gregory's "draw your neck out of collar" thus means to "keep clear of the hangman's noose" (Shakespeare 2012: 124n4): "Gregory cautions Samson against committing a capital offence by drawing his weapon too eagerly."

Overall, the meaning of the dialogue between these two characters is rather serious: they talk about doing dirty work, anger, avoiding being hanged. But they do so on the basis of paronymic wordplay which invites the audience or reader to deciphering the meaning. The effect on the theatre audience (or the reader, for that matter), therefore, is, at least to a certain degree, comic: wordplay here serves comic relief in a play that is identified to be a tragedy already in the prologue. The characters onstage thus communicate with each other, but, at the same time, the author of the play also communicates with the audience; they learn something about the overall atmosphere in the play, but also about the two characters who open it: tragedy will be interspersed with scenes of comic relief, and the two servants onstage are not to be taken too seriously.

Linguistic categories, such as homophony and paronymy in the example, help analyze literary texts, while the literary text provides the linguist with highly complex examples. The examples thus illustrate the great interdisciplinary potential of studying wordplay.

Summing up, we could say that wordplay invites to and is expressive of metalinguistic reflection. It directs the hearer's / reader's attention to the message and the language itself, as it often functions as a riddle that has to be solved, and, in order to be solved, requires the hearer's reflection about the meanings and ambiguities involved as well as about the structures of language that are playfully manipulated (for linguistic, literary and rhetoric perspectives on ambiguity, see also Fuchs 1996; Bauer, Knape, Koch and Winkler 2010; Winter-Froemel 2013; Winter-Froemel and Zirker 2015). This leads us to a first approach to analysing wordplay that can be explored in an interdisciplinary perspective, as both linguistic and literary methods may contribute to a better understanding of this metalinguistic / metadiscursive and poetic function.

Moreover, the use of wordplay in both everyday language and literary texts is influenced by the speaker's and hearer's knowledge, communicative intentions and, more generally, by the communicative setting. Here again, an interdisciplinary approach that goes beyond an analysis of the formal features of wordplay and stresses its use in speaker-hearer interaction provides fruitful insights. It is thus these two aspects that we would like to explore in the following sections of this paper and in the first two volumes of this book series.

4 The Metalinguistic Dimension of Wordplay

The metalinguistic component is central to wordplay, but has, so far, only rarely been explicitly foregrounded (see e.g. Koch, Krefeld and Oesterreicher 1997; Miorița Ulrich 1997). The term 'metalinguistic' immediately leads us to Jakobson's (1960) approach, where the metalinguistic function is defined as one of the six basic functions of linguistic messages. More specifically, it is related to the code in Jakobson's model, and thereby opposed to other functions as the referential function, which is in turn related to the context, and the poetic function, which again is related to the message itself. In spite of various critiques that have been stated,[2] Jakobson's approach still represents a key reference in both linguistics and literary studies, and we therefore decided to take it as a heuristic starting point for both the conference and the first two volumes of the series *The Dynamics of Wordplay*, in order to explore this specific dimension of wordplay. However, we do not intend to assume that wordplay is restrained to its metalinguistic dimension. Indeed, in many cases, specific realizations of wordplay seem to oscillate between a metalinguistic and a poetic function, and still other functions may be of even greater importance for certain cases of

---

2 Many of these critiques concern the poetic function, its special role in Jakobson's model, and the concept of literature and literary language that it implies. They cannot be discussed in detail here; concerning the metalinguistic function, however, it seems important to mention that its delimitation from the referential function can be put into question, as language or the code can be seen as just one special subtype of referent or one specific element of the context, so that the metalinguistic function could also be regarded as a subtype of the referential function (see Coseriu 2007, 76–92 and the contribution by Kabatek, this volume; cf. also other semiotic models such as Karl Bühler's, who proposes only three basic functions of linguistic signs, namely the expressive, the appellative, and the referential function [Germ. *Ausdrucks-, Appell-, Darstellungsfunktion*], Bühler 1934).

wordplay (e.g. the conative or appellative function of wordplay in advertisements, see the examples discussed above).

Altogether, the metalinguistic dimension of wordplay is part of its functional characteristics. At the same time, it can be realized in quite different ways: wordplay can be employed creatively in a wide range of uses but it may also be referred to only subtly. The creation of unexpected links between linguistic units often has a comic effect (e.g. the advertisement slogans "Have a break, have a kit-kat," and "Il n'y a que Maille qui m'aille" [There is only Maille that suits me], with a homonymic play on French *Maille* and *m'aille*) and may be expressive of wit (i.e. of the speaker's wit). In literary communication it may furthermore be one of the indicators of double communication, i.e. on the internal level of the text as well as on the external one, between the author and reader / audience; a telling name like Mrs. Malaprop in Sheridan's *The Rivals* (first performed in 1775) is directed at the audience as a metacommentary about this character and her language use. Wordplay in these cases thwarts mimesis and, thus, the illusion (see Warning 1976).

Moreover, the focus on the metalinguistic dimension of wordplay proposed here can be linked to discourse and communication: in speaker-hearer interaction, wordplay may be regarded as an invitation to metalinguistic reflection directed at the addressee of the utterance as much as an intentional expression on behalf of the speaker. Wordplay reflects on language and communication and unravels characteristics of literary language in everyday communication as much as it opens up the possibility to analyze literary texts from a linguistic perspective.

In the first section of *The Dynamics of Wordplay* 1, contributors focus on authors and contexts. Martina Bross reflects on the prominence of "Wordplay and Ambiguity in Hamlet's First and Second Line" and especially on its protagonist's eagerness to play with words. She analyzes two examples of wordplay in the two first lines spoken by Hamlet: both lines – "A little more then kin, and lesse then kind" and "Not so much my Lord, I am too much in the sonne" – allegedly contain ambiguities, but in the second line the pun is more problematic than often acknowledged. Bross therefore shows in how far ambiguity serves as a basis for wordplay in *Hamlet*, but does so in various ways with regard to the internal and external level of communication. As a metalinguistic and metadiscursive device, ambiguity and wordplay feed into characterization and help to recognize character constellations but they also involve the audience who, in this case, is never fully allowed to disambiguate Hamlet's lines. Patricia Oster follows a similar approach in her essay (see *The Dynamics of Wordplay* 2) in studying the metalinguistic aspect of neologisms in the theatre of Marivaux and their playful dimensions. In his plays, innovative wordplay often is linked to ambiguity and thus points to metalinguistic reflection but also to the unconscious dimension of both the production and the perception of wordplay.

Thomas Kullmann in his contribution on "Wordplay as Courtly Pastime and Social Practice: Shakespeare and Lewis Carroll" focuses on one of Shakespeare's comedies, *Much Ado About Nothing,* and links wordplay as a communicative practice to Lewis Carroll's *Alice* books (published in 1865 and 1872). He takes his starting point from Grice's maxims and regards wordplay not so much as a violation of these rather than being functional in the texts examined with regard to communication and social interaction. Whereas in Shakespeare's comedy the main characters use wordplay to show their verbal and courtly superiority and thus create an atmosphere of humour and playfulness, wordplay in Carroll's *Alice* books proves to be a challenge both for the heroine and for the reader. But even in this context, wordplay serves as a means to further social practices, and Alice, in the course of her adventures, learns to use and react to wordplay and develop a certain degree of "courtliness." Kullmann thus looks at wordplay as an indicator of metalinguistic awareness that allows for integration into particular social and communicative contexts.

Maik Goth turns "*Double Entendre* in Restoration and Early Eighteenth-Century Comedy" to reassess the notion of *double entendre* by placing it at the intersection of dramatic text, theatrical performance and contemporary criticism. He develops a theory of *double entendre* that takes into account the particular communicative situation and double address in the theatre; he bases his analysis on a taxonomy that takes into account various forms of structures and the interaction of meaning. This taxonomy is then applied to the interpretation of Wycherley's *The Country Wife* (1675) and Steele's *The Funeral* (1701 / 02), thus juxtaposing double entendre as a play about sexual and intellectual prowess with its non-bawdy variety and showing that wordplay may link different comic modes with one another.[3]

While the focus so far has been on the comic effect(s) of wordplay, Sheelagh Russell Brown reads it in the sense of *serio ludere* and addresses it as "The Serious Work of Play" in the "Dark Sonnets" of Gerard Manley Hopkins. While Hopkins's use of wordplay has been widely studied in most of his poetry and in his philosophy of words, the so-called "Dark Sonnets" are more difficult to tackle in this respect: these six untitled poems (composed in 1885 and 1886) express a

---

[3] For further functions of wordplay in drama in the specific context of the Parisian fairground theatres in the eighteenth century, see also the contribution by Pauline Beaucé (in *The Dynamics of Wordplay* 2).

sense of isolation and, hence, resist a reading that focuses on linguistic playfulness. Rather, Hopkins here uses wordplay to be able to "utter" the landscape of his mind: wordplay becomes a means to distance himself from normal speech and thus echoes the distance he himself was experiencing in his life.

Vincent Renner turns to linguistic techniques of wordplay and "Lexical Blending as Wordplay," i.e. mechanisms of word-formation in the following section on "Linguistic Techniques of Wordplay." Renner draws on various languages in order to show that the formation process of blending can in itself be regarded as a form of wordplay and offers an overview of features that increase wordplayfulness in blending. Jean-François Sablayrolles' contribution (in *The Dynamics of Wordplay* 2) takes up and broadens these issues by investigating wordplay in the more general context of neology, focusing on specific types of lexicogenic matrices and their communicative and pragmatic functions. Moreover, Michelle Lecolle's contribution (also in *The Dynamics of Wordplay* 2) presents an in-depth reflection about various kinds of formal processes in their relation to linguistic motivation.

The contribution by Pierre Arnaud, François Maniez and Vincent Renner provides a corpus investigation of "Non-Canonical Proverbial Occurrences and Wordplay."[4] The authors collected a set of 303 instances of six English proverbs and analyzed as well as classified their non-canonical occurrences. Most of these turned out to be contextual adaptations, while only a few qualified as instances of wordplay. On the basis of a questionnaire they have been able to establish that the simple contextual adaptation of proverbs does not create wordplay, but that wordplay requires semantic complexity combined with humour.

Both humour and semantic complexity feed into Sebastian Knospe's article on "A Cognitive Model for Bilingual Puns," in which he presents examples of German / English bilingual puns in German press texts. His focus is on both the linguistic make-up of bilingual puns and on their cognitive processing in their contexts of use. Readers have to invest cognitively in order to decode the meaning, while particular discursive effects may be achieved by means of bilingual puns.

In an interview with Angelika Zirker, contemporary British poet Ian Duhig reflects on his perspective on wordplay in poetry and discusses how poetry can express more in fewer words than other texts do. In his view, wordplay is one of the most important means to intensify literary language. His main examples

---

4 Cf. also Sylvia Jaki's contribution on phraseological modification and punning (in *The Dynamics of Wordplay* 2).

comprise Laurence Sterne's *Tristram Shandy* (1759–1767) as well as his own poetry. This contribution foregrounds a special feature of our previous reflection on the topic of wordplay as well as of the conference: not only do we wish to transcend disciplinary boundaries, but we also would like to enter into a dialogue with experts on wordplay from various domains, i.e. literary authors, comedians, directors, etc.

Finally, issues of genre and meta-reflection are addressed. Johannes Kabatek in his paper on "Wordplay and Discourse Traditions" shows that wordplay is determined not only by a particular language and its use, but also by traditional and culture-specific patterns. He advocates the importance of a distinction between the different levels of analysis that may be involved in wordplay, including discourse traditions and translation.

Svea Schauffler's contribution "Wordplay in Subtitled Films – An Audience Study" is situated in the field of (audiovisual) translation studies and presents an experimental study that investigates the reception of two different strategies for subtitling English wordplay into German on the basis of the short film *Wallace and Gromit in a Matter of Loaf and Death*. The subtitled versions were presented to audiences in two renditions, one prioritizing the transfer of humour, the other adhering to the original dialogue. Audience reactions to both versions were documented in questionnaires.

In her investigation into "Plays Around Surfaces and Depths: Transitions Between Two and Three-Dimensionality Reflected by Wordplays and Puns," Monika Schmitz-Emans once again turns to Lewis Carroll's *Alice* books and focuses not so much on strategies of wordplay as such but rather on the preconditions of wordplay as developed by their author, the mathematician Dodgson. She regards concepts derived from mathematics as the stage on which words are enabled to play games and roles and links the *Alice* books to their author's mathematical writings, for example *Euclid and His Modern Rivals* (1879). Two- and three-dimensional objects as well as surfaces and depths turn into semantic spaces, concepts of surface and depths into means of language reflection.

Matthias Bauer considers "Secret Wordplay and What It May Tell Us" and its wider implications for the study of wordplay. "Secret wordplay" is defined as a kind of wordplay which stays unnoticed for some time and / or by a part of the hearers. Wordplay is thus read in a communicative context: whereas open wordplay flouts the cooperative principle, secret wordplay does not do so. Bauer moreover regards wordplay as a scalar phenomenon and develops four parameters of analysis that take into account linguistic features as well as context, social and communicative functions. Secret wordplay is thus shown to be related, for instance, to word knowledge and world knowledge when it comes to reading literary texts.

5 Wordplay and Its Interplays – Playing on Different Levels of Language and Communication

As we have seen in the previous section an important function of wordplay is to orient the speaker and hearer towards language and / or the message and the discourse event itself. The latter aspect leads us immediately to another dimension of analysis, namely to the relation of wordplay to the concrete communicative setting in which it is used. As we have already seen above, it seems helpful to study not only the formal characteristics of wordplay, but also the ways in which it is used in different situations of communication, where it functions as a social practice (as Kullmann explicitly stresses in his contribution).

Wordplay involves certain rules not only concerning formal features, but also with regard to legitimate uses of wordplay or of specific instances of wordplay in certain situations. This functional aspect leads to a dynamics in which wordplay interacts with a broad range of contextual factors, which can be related to the participants of the communicative exchange, their social roles, their knowledge etc. In a sense, wordplay can therefore have a (anti-)social function in that it may create a gap between various groups of hearers, e.g. between hearers who appreciate a certain playful use of language and others who do not, between hearers who participate in the social practice and master it, and others who do not, or at a more basic level, between hearers who understand (i.e. successfully decode) the wordplay and others who fail to do so.

The contribution by Alain Rabatel, "Points de vue en confrontation substitutifs ou cumulatifs dans les contrepèteries (*in absentia*)" (in *The Dynamics of Wordplay* 2) illustrates several of these aspects: it presents a study on a specific subtype of wordplay which is characteristic for French, the tradition of the *contrepèteries*. On a purely formal level, these are characterized by a permutation of letters or sounds, which is also characteristic for the German tradition of the *Schüttelreim* and the English tradition of the spoonerism, but there are additional restrictions for the French tradition. *Contrepèteries* are never explicit, i.e. they are wordplays *in absentia*, where the second possible interpretation remains hidden, and this hidden interpretation is strongly related to a taboo (in most cases the domain of sexuality). This additional characteristic implies that this type of wordplay can be hard to decode, and the successful interpretation of a *contrepèterie* will therefore lead to a strong sense of gratification (on an indiviual level) and fraternization / *connivence* (on a social level). As a side-note, it seems interesting to observe that similar processes of fraternization and effects of *connivence* always (explicitly or implicitly) not only imply a strategy of inclusion and constitution of social groups, but also an exlusion (at least potentially) of others. This complex social setting is also reflected in the cases of *double entendre* studied by Maik Goth: although it is based on a very different kind of linguistic strategy on a formal level, it also involves this double game of inclusion and exclusion by virtue of the successful decoding vs. failure of additional hidden messages; the additional, secret message is also very often related to sexual taboo.

In other cases, the interactional functions of wordplay are accentuated even more explicitly. The contribution of Pauline Beaucé, "Les jeux de mots dans le répertoire des théâtres de la Foire à Paris au XVIIIe siècle: de la publicité à la satire" (in *The Dynamics of Wordplay* 2) offers insights into this aspect by studying the use of wordplay in the plays of the French *théâtres de la Foire*, where wordplay can be used to parody other theatre institutions and to mock legal measures that restrict the liberty and success of these popular manifestations of dramatic play. At the same time, the contribution reveals commercial motives underlying the use of wordplay, which has also an advertising function in order to attract the audience.

Moreover, in the domain of literary texts, we can observe a systematic multiplication of levels of communication. Studying wordplay in drama invites us to analyze its functioning not only on the level of the communication between the characters and the actors on stage, but also include the audience as a further group of hearers. This aspect is also stressed in Patricia Oster's contribution on the theatre of Marivaux, "'Ne nous tutoyons plus, je t'en prie': Jeux de mots et enjeu du langage dans le théâtre de Marivaux" (*The Dynamics of Wordplay* 2). As Patricia Oster shows, Marivaux's plays make use of the specific communicative setting of dramatic texts in order to manipulate language, or to put language itself on stage in order to invite the audience to reflect about consciousness and unconsciousness in communication.

These observations are complemented by the study of the narrative texts of Balzac provided by Laélia Véron, "Jeu de mots et double communication dans l'œuvre littéraire: l'exemple de la *Comédie humaine* de Balzac." The multiplication of communicative levels – the intradiegetic and the extradiegetic level – also proves central here, and, again, Véron's examples illustrate that wordplay can be used on both levels for different pragmatic and interactional functions, such as social critique; she furthermore shows how the narrator comments on the uses of wordplay. Additionally, Véron stresses the distinction between various groups of readers in a historical perspective, which becomes fundamental when we study wordplay in everyday language as well as in literary texts from earlier periods. As a corollary of language change, we may not necessarily have the linguistic and cultural knowledge required in order to successfully decode wordplay of previous times.

This immediately leads us to a second aspect concerning the social functions of wordplay and inclusion / exclusion of hearer groups: the various types of knowledge that the use of a certain instance of wordplay requires. We have already seen that this dimension becomes relevant in the case of French *contrepèteries* studied by Alain Rabatel, and in the *double entendre* studied by Maik Goth; the same goes for the multilingual puns studied by Sebastian Knospe and the cases of multilingual play in the texts of the Luxembourgian author Roger Manderscheid (see the contribution by Julia Genz in *The Dynamics of Wordplay* 2), which require a certain amount of knowledge of several linguistic codes.

However, we can also observe that the various uses of wordplay themselves are not necessarily directed towards a uniform group of hearers / readers, as the case of *Astérix* illustrates (cf. the contribution on *Astérix* by Marc Blancher, in *The Dynamics of Wordplay* 2). The success of the series can at least be partially explained by the fact that it can be read and enjoyed on various levels. Sophisticated uses of wordplay and allusions requiring extensive historical and linguistic knowledge will increase the gratification of certain groups of readers, but will not lead to an exclusion of others, as there are still enough other manifestations of wordplay that can be decoded in a more direct and explicit way.

The importance of a certain level of linguistic knowledge is also taken up by Marc Blancher's contribution "De l'auteur de jeux de mots aux jeux de mots d'auteur," in which he presents some practical examples of motives and restrictions on the use of wordplay in detective stories written for language learners who only have limited knowledge of the foreign language (L2). Again, this contribution provides insights from a practical perspective, thereby illustrating pragmatic constraints on the use of wordplay in specific text types and communicative settings.

The texts of Roger Manderscheid likewise point to interlinguistic aspects of wordplay in a very specific communicative context which is strongly shaped by an interaction of different languages. The relations between plurilingualism and wordplay in this specific context are analyzed by Julia Genz in her contribution "'*Il wullte bien, mais il ne puffte pas*' – de la polyglossie à la polyphonie dans le roman *Der sechste Himmel* (*Feier a Flam*) de Roger Manderscheid" (*The Dynam-*

ics of Wordplay 2). With the aid of Ferguson's concept of diglossia as well as Ducrot's concept of linguistic polyphony, she investigates the functions of wordplay in the novel and with regard to the shaping of the narrator's identity.

The fact that wordplay involves playing with certain elements and structures of a specific language also implies, in a general way, that its translation poses a challenge. Perec's novel *La Disparition* (1969) represents a somewhat extreme case, as argued by Federica Di Blasio in her paper "*La Disparition* de Georges Perec et les jeux de mots: l'ambiguïté du métatexte et la négociation de la traduction" (*The Dynamics of Wordplay* 2). On the one hand, on a formal level, the challenge of translating this text which is based on the technique of the lipogram depends on the structures of the target language and, more, specifically, on the rate of recurrence of the most frequent vowel. On the other hand, Di Blasio shows that the lipogram also has a thematic function in the source text, which creates additional restrictions for the translation, but also opens up certain possibilities of developing functionally analogous instances of wordplay in different target languages.

The interplays of wordplay can furthermore be studied from a semiotic perspective. An important question in this context concerns the relationships between wordplay and linguistic innovation. The contribution by Jean-François Sablayrolles, "Néologismes ludiques: études morphologique et énonciativo-pragmatique" (*The Dynamics of Wordplay* 2) shows that wordplay is based on certain techniques which can also be found in other cases of neology / innovation, but that wordplay predominantly makes use of extragrammatical techniques, whereas "regular" techniques such as suffixation and composition, which are central to linguistic innovation in general, are less frequent. Moreover, Sablayrolles investigates the various functions that wordplay may have and explores the diachronic development of ludic neologisms, which may become conventionalized or, in contrast, fall into oblivion.

The essay by Michelle Lecolle, "Jeux de mots et motivation: une approche du sentiment linguistique" (*The Dynamics of Wordplay* 2) stresses a particular aspect of the manipulation of language effectuated by wordplay, which is the linguistic competence (the knowledge of the language system, which the speakers may not be explicitly aware of), and, more specifically, the motivatedness of the linguistic items played with. As Lecolle shows, the motivation or remotivation of linguistic items can be seen as a fundamental function of many cases of wordplay, and here again, we touch upon other types of innovation which are no longer ludic, but involve similar processes of (re-) motivation, e.g. popular etymology and learners' errors.

The contribution by Sylvia Jaki, "Détournement phraséologique et jeu de mots: le cas des substitutions lexicales dans la presse écrite" (*The Dynamics of Wordplay* 2), focuses on newspaper language and on specific structures that may be playfully manipulated, namely phraseologisms in which one specific element is substituted by another lexeme. The issue of defining the boundaries of wordplay equally becomes relevant here. Jaki argues that manipulations of phraseologisms should not automatically be considered to be genuine manifestations of wordplay in the narrow sense, and she proposes to distinguish between true cases of wordplay on the one hand and cases of playing with language on the other hand.

Finally, wordplay may involve not only a play on language or languages, but also on other semiotic systems. This aspect is addressed by Marc Blancher in his contribution "'Ça est un bon mot!' ou l'humour (icono-)textuel *à la Goscinny*" (*The Dynamics of Wordplay* 2), where he examines the interplay of language and the drawings in *Astérix*. He shows that the overall "quality" of the wordplays contained in the text is enhanced if the wordplay is also reflected on at the level of the drawings, and only this joint use of the various semiotic systems at hand means that the true potential offered by the comic strips is explored. Concurrently, this interplay offers a broad range of possibilities to create highly sophisticated wordplays which rely on intertextual and intermedial allusions and which may require a complex process of decoding.[5]

The various contributions that deal with the various possibilities of playing with different semiotic devices that may be accessible in specific communicative settings leads us back to the metalinguistic and metadiscursive dimension of wordplay, stressing once more the complexity and multifaceted character of this evidence of linguistic and aesthetic mastership.

6 Final Remarks and Acknowledgements

We are grateful for the financial support we received from the Fritz Thyssen Foundation (Fritz Thyssen Stiftung), the German National Research Foundation (Deutsche Forschungsgemeinschaft, DFG) the Collaborative Research Centre

---

[5] Another study that provides interesting insights into the interplays of various semiotic systems is Svea Schauffler's study on strategies of subtitling wordplay. And, on a more theoretic level, Monika Schmitz-Emans's paper stresses the ways in which wordplay in Lewis Carroll's texts reflects the "semiotic event" (discourse) itself.

(SFB) 833 "The Constitution of Meaning" (Tübingen) and the University of Tübingen to prepare the conference and also the publication of the proceedings. We also received lots of practical help, and our thanks goes to Eva Rettner, Beate Starke and Reinhild Steinberg as well as all student assistants who helped before and during the event (Julie Anhorn, Assata Frauhammer, Kathrin Luzius, Nora Menzel, Lena Moltenbrey, Tanita Salerno) and particularly Nathan Houstin, who was involved in helping to organize the event from an early stage. Without their support the conference would not have taken place the way it finally did; nor would it have without the participants. They proved to be especially open not only to a multilingual but also an interdisciplinary, if not even transdisciplinary, approach to analyzing wordplay, which resulted in very stimulating discussions during the three days of the conference.

Against this background of the multilingual and -disciplinary perspectives, each of the contributions has been read and evaluated by several reviewers, representing the fields of both linguistics and literary studies, thus ensuring an interdisciplinary reflection and approach. As organizers of the conference and editors of these volumes, we have encouraged all authors to write their contributions with a heterogenic readership in mind. We have also asked them to make disciplinary and theoretical presuppositions and notions evident that might otherwise be difficult to grasp for readers outside of the respective field of research.

The conference was prepared with the help of a reviewing committee that helped select papers out of over 80 submissions. We are grateful to Heidi Aschenberg (Tübingen), Matthias Bauer (Tübingen), Hans-Martin Gauger (Freiburg), Johannes Kabatek (Zürich), Peter Koch† (Tübingen), Burkhard Niederhoff (Bochum), Margit Peterfy (Mainz), Britta Stolterfoht (Tübingen), and Richard Waltereit (Newcastle upon Tyne). They also helped with the reviewing for publishing the proceedings, alongside further reviewers – Dennis Sobolev (Haifa University), Eline Zenner (KU Leuven) and members of the scientific network "The Dynamics of Wordplay," Georgia Christinidis (Rostock), Barbara Frank-Job (Bielefeld), Bettina Full (Bochum), Bettina Kluge (Hildesheim), Alexander Onysko (Venice), and Verena Thaler (Mannheim) – as well as the editorial board of this book series, who has accompanied the publication in an efficient and helpful way.

Our thanks also go to those who were involved in preparing the publication of these volumes: Véronique Featherston-Lardeux, Sophia Fünfgeld, Mirjam Haas, Birgit Imade, Anne Klein, Daniela Küster, Nora Menzel, Carlotta Posth, and Timo Stösser. The editorial team at De Gruyter's, Ulrike Krauß, Daniel Gietz,

Olena Gainulina, and Christine Henschel, were supportive and helpful all the way through.

Last but not least, we would like to thank Matthias Bauer and Peter Koch for their unfaltering support in all matters concerned with wordplay, ambiguity and speaker-hearer interaction. We will always remember Peter Koch as an academic inspiration. He closely accompanied our research and activities and supported us in every possible manner and thus furthered research in a domain which permits to discuss very basic issues of linguistic theory and literary studies, and which becomes accessible to and attractive for a wide readership. The present two volumes are dedicated to his memory.

7 References

Attardo, Salvatore. 1994. *Linguistic Theories of Humor*. New York: Mouton.
Attardo, Salvatore. 2006. Cognitive Linguistics and Humor. *Humor* 19(3). 341–362.
Attardo, Salvatore & Victor Raskin. 1991. Script Theory Revis(it)ed: Joke Similarity and Joke Representation Model. *Humor* 4(3–4). 293–347.
Bauer, Matthias. Forthcoming. *Mystical Linguistics: George Herbert, Richard Crashaw, and Henry Vaughan*. Münster: LIT.
Bauer, Matthias, Joachim Knape, Peter Koch & Susanne Winkler. 2010. Dimensionen der Ambiguität. *Zeitschrift für Literaturwissenschaft und Linguistik* 158. 7–75.
Bergson, Henri. [1940] 1993. *Le rire: Essai sur la signification du comique*, 10th edn. Paris: Quadrige / Presses Universitaires de France.
Bühler, Karl. 1934. *Sprachtheorie: Die Darstellungsfunktion der Sprache*. Jena: Gustav Fischer.
Carstensen, Broder. 1971. *Spiegel-Wörter, Spiegel-Worte: Zur Sprache eines deutschen Nachrichtenmagazins*. München: Hueber.
Chovanec, Jan & Isabel Ermida (eds.). 2012. *Language and Humour in the Media*. Newcastle upon Tyne: Cambridge Scholars Publishing.
Cook, Eleanor. 1998. *Against Coercion: Games Poets Play*. Stanford: Stanford University Press.
Cook, Eleanor. 2006. *Enigmas and Riddles in Literature*. Cambridge: Cambridge University Press.
Coseriu, Eugenio. 2007. *Textlinguistik: Eine Einführung*, 4th edn. Tübingen: Narr.
Culler, Jonathan (ed.). 1988. *On Puns: The Foundation of Letters*. Oxford: Blackwell.
Cuyckens, Hubert, Thomas Berg, René Dirven & Klaus-Uwe Panther (eds.). 2003. *Motivation in Language: Studies in Honor of Günter Radden*. Amsterdam: Benjamins.
Delabastita, Dirk (ed.). 1997. *Traductio: Essays on Punning and Translation*. Manchester: St. Jerome; Namur: Presses Universitaires de Namur.
Delabastita, Dirk. 2001. Aspects of Interlingual Ambiguity: Polyglott Punning. In Paul Bogaards, Johan Rooryck & Paul J. Smith (eds.), *Quitte ou double Sens*, 45–64. Amsterdam: Rodopi.
Delabastita, Dirk. 2005. Cross-Language Comedy in Shakespeare. *Humor* 18(2). 161–184.
Dickens, Charles. [1859] 2003. *A Tale of Two Cities*. Ed. Richard Maxwell. London: Penguin.

Dittgen, Andrea Maria. 1989. *Regeln für Abweichungen: Funktionale sprachspielerische Abweichungen in Zeitungsüberschriften, Werbeschlagzeilen, Werbeslogans, Wandsprüchen und Titeln*. Frankfurt a. M.: Lang.

Freud, Sigmund. 1905. Der Witz und seine Beziehung zum Unbewussten. In *Gesammelte Werke*, vol. 6. Frankfurt a. M.: Fischer.

Fuchs, Catherine. 1996. *Les ambiguïtés du français*. Paris: Ophrys.

Gauger, Hans-Martin. 1971. *Durchsichtige Wörter: Zur Theorie der Wortbildung*. Heidelberg: Winter.

Gauger, Hans-Martin. 1976. *Sprachbewußtsein und Sprachwissenschaft*. München: Piper.

Gibbs, Raymond W. & Herbert L. Colston. 2012. *Interpreting Figurative Meaning*. Cambridge: Cambridge University Press.

Goatly, Andrew. 2012. *Meaning and Humour: Key Topics in Semantics and Pragmatics*. Cambridge: Cambridge University Press.

Grassegger, Hans. 1985. *Sprachspiel und Übersetzung: Eine Studie anhand der Comic-Serie Asterix*. Tübingen: Stauffenburg.

Grunig, Blanche-Noëlle. 1990. *Les mots de la publicité: L'architecture du slogan*. Paris: Presse du CNRS.

Guiraud, Pierre. 1976. *Les jeux de mots*. Paris: Presses Universitaires de France.

Hausmann, Franz Josef. 1974. *Studien zu einer Linguistik des Wortspiels: Das Wortspiel im Canard enchaîné*. Tübingen: Niemeyer.

Heibert, Frank. 1993. *Das Wortspiel als Stilmittel und seine Übersetzung: Am Beispiel von sieben Übersetzungen des* Ulysses *von James Joyce*. Tübingen: Narr.

Hesbois, Laure. 1986. *Les jeux de langage*. Ottawa: Éditions de l'Université d'Ottawa.

Huizinga, Johan. [1938] 1987. *Homo ludens: Proeve eener bepaling van het spel-element der cultuur*, 3rd edn. [Homo Ludens: Versuch einer Bestimmung des Spielelementes der Kultur]. Basel: Akad. Verl. Anst. Pantheon.

Jakobson, Roman. 1960. Linguistics and Poetics. In Thomas A. Sebeok (ed.), *Style in Language*, 350–377. New York: Wiley.

Käge, Otmar. 1980. *Motivation: Probleme des persuasiven Sprachgebrauchs, der Metapher und des Wortspiels*. Mainz: University of Mainz dissertation. Göppingen: Kümmerle.

Kemmner, Ernst. 1972. *Sprachspiel und Stiltechnik in Raymond Queneaus Romanen*. Tübingen: University of Tübingen dissertation. Tübingen: TBL.

Kharkhurin, Anatoliy Vladimirovich. 2012. *Multilingualism and Creativity*. Bristol: Multilingual Matters.

Koch, Peter, Thomas Krefeld & Wulf Oesterreicher. 1997. *Neues aus Sankt Eiermark: Das kleine Buch der Sprachwitze*. München: Beck.

Mahood, Molly M. 1957. *Shakespeare's Wordplay*. London: Methuen.

Milner, G. B. 1972. Homo Ridens: Towards a Semiotic Theory of Humour and Laughter. *Semiotica* 5(1). 1–30.

Partington, Alan. 2009. A Linguistic Account of Wordplay: The Lexical Grammar of Punning. *Journal of Pragmatics* 41(9). 1794–1809.

Paton, George E. C., Chris Powell & Stephen Wagg. 1996. *The Social Faces of Humour: Practices and Issues*. Aldershot: Ashgate.

Plessner, Helmuth. [1941] 1950. *Lachen und Weinen: Eine Untersuchung der Grenzen menschlichen Verhaltens*. München: Lehnen.

Preisendanz, Wolfgang & Rainer Warning (eds.). 1976. *Das Komische*. München: Fink.

Raskin, Victor. 1985. *Semantic Mechanisms of Humor*. Dordrecht: D. Reidel.

Rauch, Bruno. 1982. *Sprachliche Spiele – spielerische Sprache: Sammlung, Erklärung und Vergleich der Wortspiele in vier ausgewählten Romanen von Raymond Queneau und in den entsprechenden Übersetzungen von Eugen Helmlé*. Zürich: University of Zürich dissertation.
Rettig, Wolfgang. 1981. *Sprachliche Motivation: Zeichenrelationen von Lautform und Bedeutung am Beispiel französischer Lexikoneinheiten*. Frankfurt a. M. & Bern: Lang.
Schmitz-Emans, Monika. 1997. *Die Sprache der modernen Dichtung*. München: Wilhelm Fink.
Schröter, Thorsten. 2010. Language-Play, Translation and Quality – with Examples from Dubbing and Subtitling. In Delia Chiaro (ed.), *Translation, Humour and The Media*, 138–152. London & New York: Continuum.
Shakespeare, William. 2012. *Romeo and Juliet*. Ed. René Weis. London: Methuen.
Stefanowitsch, Anatol. 2001. Nice to *Miet* You: Bilingual Puns and the Status of English in Germany. *Intercultural Communication Studies* 11(4). 67–84.
Tanaka, Keiko. 1992. The Pun in Advertising: A Pragmatic Approach. *Lingua* 87(1-2). 91–102.
Tanaka, Keiko. 1999. *Advertising Language: A Pragmatic Approach to Advertisements in Britain and Japan*. London: Routledge.
Thomas, Dylan. 2000. Once Below a Time. In *The Dylan Thomas Omnibus: Under Milk Wood, Poems, Stories and Broadcasts*, 94–96. London: Orion.
Ulrich, Miorița. 1997. *Die Sprache als Sache: Primärsprache, Metaprache, Übersetzung; Untersuchungen zum Übersetzen und zur Übersetzbarkeit anhand von deutschen, englischen und vor allem romanischen Materialien*. Tübingen: Narr.
Ulrich, Winfried. 1977. Semantische Turbulenzen: Welche Kommunikationsformen kennzeichnen den Witz? *Deutsche Sprache* 5. 313–334.
Valero-Garcés, Carmen. 2010. *Dimensions of Humor: Explorations in Linguistics, Literature, Cultural Studies and Translation*. Valencia: Universitat de València.
Veale, Tony. 2009. Hiding in Plain Sight: Figure-Ground Reversals in Humour. In Geert Brône & Jeroen Vandaele (eds.), *Cognitive Poetics: Goals, Gains and Gaps*, 279–286. Berlin: Mouton de Gruyter.
Vittoz Canuto, Marie-B. 1983. *Si vous avez votre jeu de mots à dire : Analyse de jeux de mots dans la presse et dans la publicité*. Paris: A.-G. Nizet.
Warning, Rainer. 1976. Elemente einer Pragmasemiotik der Komödie. In Wolfgang Preisendanz & Rainer Warning (eds.), *Das Komische*, 279–333. München: Fink.
Winter-Froemel, Esme. 2009. Wortspiel. In Gert Ueding (ed.), *Historisches Wörterbuch der Rhetorik*, vol. 9, 1429–1443. Tübingen: Niemeyer.
Winter-Froemel, Esme. 2013. Ambiguität im Sprachgebrauch und im Sprachwandel: Parameter der Analyse diskurs- und systembezogener Fakten. *Zeitschrift für französische Sprache und Literatur* 123(2). 130–170.
Winter-Froemel, Esme & Angelika Zirker. 2010. Ambiguität in der Sprecher-Hörer-Interaktion. Linguistische und literaturwissenschaftliche Perspektiven. *Zeitschrift für Literaturwissenschaft und Linguistik* 158. 76–97.
Winter-Froemel, Esme & Angelika Zirker. 2015. Ambiguity in Speaker-Hearer Interaction: A Parameter-Based Model of Analysis. In Susanne Winkler (ed.), *Ambiguity: Language and Communication*, 283–339. Berlin & New York: de Gruyter.
Zirker, Angelika. 2010. *Der Pilger als Kind: Spiel, Sprache und Erlösung in Lewis Carrolls Alice-Büchern*. Münster: LIT.

I Authors and Contexts

Martina Bross
"Equivocation will undo us"? Wordplay and Ambiguity in Hamlet's First and Second Line

Abstract: Wordplay is a prominent feature in William Shakespeare's *Hamlet*, and particularly the protagonist is famous for his eagerness to play on words. These instances of wordplay draw our attention to the ambiguous nature of language and help to depict Hamlet as a character who is highly aware of ambiguity and of its effects on communication. In this article, two well-known examples of wordplay found in Hamlet's first two lines are analyzed to explore the nature and function of ambiguity used by Shakespeare. Hamlet's first line, "A little more then kin, and lesse then kind," contains structural and lexical ambiguities, and his second line, "Not so much my Lord, I am too much in the sonne," is said to contain an obvious pun. A closer examination of the second line, however, suggests that this pun is more problematic than often acknowledged. The analysis of both lines shows that, as the basis for Hamlet's wordplay, ambiguity serves several functions on both the internal and the external level of communication in *Hamlet*. It contributes to characterization and helps to reveal character constellations. This article traces the processes of disambiguation triggered and influenced by the interdependence of verbal context and the communicative situation depicted in the play. It argues that this interdependence creates a range of possible interpretations of Hamlet's first two lines. The combination of verbal context and communicative situation never fully allows the audience to disambiguate Hamlet's play on words. Ambiguity thus serves to link and emphasize themes, topics and motifs which become important throughout the play.

Keywords: ambiguity in literature, communication in drama, communicative situation, disambiguation, dramatic character, early modern drama, homophony, lexical ambiguity, pun, speaker-hearer interaction, strategic use of ambiguity, structural ambiguity, verbal context, William Shakespeare, wordplay in drama

1 Introduction

Hamlet is Shakespeare's tragedy with the most instances of wordplay (cf. Mahood 1957: 112), not least because of its protagonist, Prince Hamlet himself. His frequent use of wordplay and particularly of puns draws our attention to the ambiguous nature of language and at the same time helps to depict Hamlet as a character who is highly alert to ambiguity. He feels compelled to highlight each potential ambiguity in his play on homonyms, homophones and polysemes and is shown to be fully aware of the impact this may have on communication. "We must / speak by the card or equivocation will undo us" (Shakespeare [1604] 1982: 5.1.133–134), Hamlet tells Horatio somewhat sarcastically when he has found his match in the Gravedigger, whose failure, or rather refusal, to disambiguate Hamlet's words correctly generates pun after pun:

> *Ham.* [...] Whose grave's this, sirrah?
> *Grave.* Mine sir, [...].
> *Ham.* I think it be thine indeed, for thou liest in't.
> *Grave.* You lie out on't, sir, and therefore 'tis not yours.
> For my part, I do not lie in't, yet it is mine.
> *Ham.* Thou dost lie in't, to be in't and say 'tis thine. 'Tis for the dead, not for the quick: therefore thou liest.
> *Grave.* 'Tis a quick lie, sir, 'twill away again from me to you.
> (Shakespeare [1604] 1982: 5.1.115–125)

The example of Hamlet and the Gravedigger reminds us that wordplay based on instances of ambiguity can have several functions on different levels of communication in drama. In this case the lexical ambiguity of the homonyms "to lie" meaning "[t]o be in a prostrate or recumbent position" (*Oxford English Dictionary* 2014: "lie" $v.^1$ I.1.a.) and "to lie" meaning "[t]o tell a lie or lies; to utter falsehood; to speak falsely" ("lie" $v.^2$ 1.a.) is used by the characters in the world of the play to demonstrate their wittiness. It also serves a function in the communication between playwright and audience[1] because it enables the playwright to create a comic effect through Hamlet's and the Gravedigger's punning.[2] As so often in this play, the exploitation of ambiguity in wordplay not only becomes a challenge for the characters but also for the audience. As soon as we think we have successfully disambiguated an utterance, the meaning slips away from us and we are prompted to look and think again.

This multiplicity of meaning which emerges from the use of ambiguity in the drama's wordplay, and which elicits ever new annotations from editors

---

[1] "Audience" is used to refer to both a theatre audience and readers of the play throughout this article.
[2] For an analysis of the role of ambiguity in speaker-hearer interaction, particularly on different levels of communication in literary texts, see Winter-Froemel and Zirker (2010). See also Bauer, Knape, Koch and Winkler (2010: 31–32).

exploring and listing every possible meaning, surely contributes to *Hamlet*'s undiminished popularity. But it also raises the question how and to what end exactly Shakespeare incorporates ambiguity into his play and at the same time ensures that "equivocation" does not "undo us." Does the wordplay he creates for his protagonist really invite us to spot and list every possible meaning and to read each line in as many ways as possible? Or does it leave us with clues which help to illuminate how the different meanings are generated and how the particular communicative situation represented in the play foregrounds different meanings and might make some of them more obvious than others? Ultimately, these questions are of course linked to the larger question of the function of ambiguity in literature (cf. Bauer, Knape, Koch and Winkler 2010: 27–28, 39–40). Is it really desirable to find the greatest number of possible meanings of a literary text, or do we need strategies to identify readings which are more plausible than others (cf. Jannidis 2003: 309–310)?

Wordplay based on instances of ambiguity invites us to think about these questions because it deliberately draws our attention to the fact that ambiguity is an inherent quality of language. Two examples of wordplay in *Hamlet* which are particularly striking in this context because they seem to generate ever new combinations of possible readings are found in the first two lines spoken by Hamlet in the play:

> KING. [...] But now my Cosin *Hamlet*, and my sonne.
> HAM. A little more then kin, and lesse then kind.
> KING. How is it that the clowdes still hang on you.
> HAM. Not so much my Lord, I am too much in the sonne.
>
> (Shakespeare 1604: 244–247)[3]

Both of Hamlet's lines have been subject to many annotations in editions of the play which attempt to capture the multiple meanings emerging from his play on words.

---

[3] In order to retain the original spelling, this passage is quoted from the Second Quarto text available online at *Internet Shakespeare Editions* (Shakespeare 1604). All other quotations from *Hamlet* are taken from the Second Arden edition by Harold Jenkins (Shakespeare [1604] 1982).

2 Hamlet's First Line

The play on words in Hamlet's first line rests on the similar sounding words "kin" and "kind." The lexical ambiguity of "kind" as well as the omission of subject and verb in the conjoined comparative clause uttered by the Prince opens up a number of possible interpretations. Hamlet's line is a reaction to, or rather interruption of, Claudius's address "But now my Cosin *Hamlet*, and my sonne." The exchange between Hamlet and Claudius occurs in the second scene of the play. Claudius has become King after his brother's – Hamlet's father's – death and has married his brother's widow, Hamlet's mother Gertrude. In his address, Claudius solves the problem of characterizing his and Hamlet's relationship by assigning two roles to Hamlet which are, under normal circumstances, mutually exclusive. The play offers no reason to believe that Hamlet is not cooperating in this exchange, and we can therefore assume that his reaction to Claudius will adhere to the Gricean Maxim of Relation (cf. Grice [1975] 1991: 308). The first part of Hamlet's utterance, "A little more then kin," seems to meet audience expectations: It can be read as taking up the notion of an unusual family relationship. The noun "kin" denotes "[t]he group of persons who are related to one; one's kindred, kinsfolk, or relatives, collectively" (*OED* 2014: "kin" $n.^1$ I.3.).[4] The subject of the first part of the line can either be Claudius, Hamlet, or both of them together. In each case Hamlet's answer to Claudius suggests that they are related in more than one or in more than the usual way. It is the second part of Hamlet's line which makes us stumble and reflect on our attempt to disambiguate.

The syntax of Hamlet's line allows for "kind" to be either an adjective or a noun. The reading as an adjective is syntactically more plausible since it requires us to supplement the line with less than the reading as a noun does. The *OED* lists "kind" as adjective meaning "[e]xhibiting a friendly or benevolent disposition by one's conduct *to* a person" ("kind" $adj.^1$ II.5.c.), and "[o]f persons: Naturally well-disposed; having a gentle, sympathetic, or benevolent nature; ready to assist, or show consideration for, others; †generous, liberal, courteous (*obs.*). Also of disposition" ("kind" $adj.^1$ II.5.a.). The parallel construction of

---

4 The *OED* lists several uses of "kin" $n.^1$ I.3. from Shakespeare's plays: "[W]ith possess. pron. (rarely *the*)" ("kin" $n.^1$ I.3.a.): "[O]ne of thy kin has a most weak *pia mater*" (*Twelfth Night*: 1.5.115–116); "Without article or pronoun. Now *rare*, exc. in kith and (or) kin: see kith n." ("kin" $n.^1$ I.3.b.): "One only daughter have I, no kin else" (*Timon of Athens*: 1.1.124); "Used of a single person: Kinsman, relative" ("kin" $n.^1$ I.3.c.): "Of charity, what kin are you to me?" (*Twelfth Night*: 5.1.228).

this conjoined comparative clause encourages the assumption that the subject and verb of the second part of the line are the same as in the first part. For a reading with both Hamlet and Claudius as the subject of both parts of the line this entails that neither of the two men is kindly disposed towards the other despite their relationship which now exceeds that of nephew and uncle. Or, if we follow the suggestion made by Thompson and Taylor in the Third Arden edition that there is a connection of Hamlet's line to the contemporary proverb "The nearer in kin the less in kindness" (cf. Thompson and Taylor 2006: 170n65; Tilley 1950: K38), they dislike each other *because* of their close relationship. As part of the external level of communication between the playwright and the audience, the line can be read as serving the expository function of establishing the relationship between Hamlet and Claudius.

Hamlet's dislike of Claudius is foregrounded if we assume that he is referring to himself with "lesse then kind." This again evokes a causal relationship between the two parts of his line. The reason why Hamlet is feeling "lesse then kind[ly]" disposed towards Claudius is of course Claudius's marriage to his own brother's widow, Hamlet's mother, which makes him "more then kin" to Hamlet. Hamlet's remark raises expectations in an audience as to how his dislike will become manifest in his behaviour towards Claudius. If we follow this reading, the line also constitutes a relatively bold statement directed at a king in front of his court, which might be a reason for an actor to play the line as an aside.[5] In these cases, the line is unambiguously hostile towards Claudius. The play on sounds in this line which links "kin" with "kind" might serve to soften Hamlet's "piece of rudeness" (Thompson and Taylor 2006: 170n65).[6]

Another possibility is that "lesse then kind" refers to Claudius. After all, up to this point Claudius has been very eager to establish himself as a firm but kind ruler. The scene opens with a speech in which Claudius addresses his court and expresses his gratitude for their support of both his ascension to the throne and his marriage. He then proceeds to deal with the looming threat of an army raised by the young Norwegian Prince Fortinbras. Claudius's resolve and verve in political matters is juxtaposed with a display of kindness when he grants his

---

5 Thompson and Taylor point out that "[m]any editors mark this speech as an aside [...], and the fact that the King continues with his sentence structure supports this. But it could also be a deliberate piece of rudeness or confrontation" (2006: 170n65). A recent example of an actor playing the line as an aside is Jonathan Slinger in the 2013 RSC production of *Hamlet* directed by David Farr.

6 Kökeritz lists the line as a "jingle" (1953: 77–78). Leech points out that "the likeness of sound [in a jingle] leads one to look out for a connection in sense as well" (1969: 212).

councillor Polonius's son Laertes his suit to return to France: "Take thy fair hour, Laertes, time be thine, / And thy best graces spend it at thy will" (1.2.62–63). And to make it really clear that he is a monarch who not only thinks about state affairs but also values family ties he does not neglect to ask Laertes's father to give his opinion first: "Have you your father's leave? What says Polonius?" (1.2.57). To underline the personal dimension of the matter, Claudius switches from the more distant form of address "you" (cf. 1.2.42, 43, 44) to the more familiar "thou" when he talks to Laertes (cf. 1.2.45, 50). Hamlet's claim that Claudius is "lesse then kind" can be read as an attempt to undermine the new King's efforts to create a certain image of himself. It also suggests that Hamlet is understandably hurt by Claudius addressing him as son, which is rather untactful seeing that he is still mourning his late father.

So far, the analysis shows that the structural ambiguity caused by the missing subject in Hamlet's line makes several interpretations of the line possible which depend on the meaning of "kind" as adjective as well as on different aspects of the situational context presented in this scene. However, the parallel construction of Hamlet's line together with the parallelism in Claudius's preceding line also prompts us to consider "kind" as noun meaning either "[t]he family, ancestral race, or stock from which one springs" (*OED* 2014: "kind" *n.* II.12.), or "[a] race, or a natural group of animals or plants having a common origin" ("kind" *n.* II.10.a.), even though the examples listed in the *OED* show that both meanings require us to supplement the line with a preposition.[7]

If "kin" and "kind" are both considered to be nouns and near synonyms, with "kind" meaning "[t]he family, ancestral race, or stock from which one springs" ("kind" *n.* II.12.), Hamlet's line presents a paradox. It seems hardly plausible under normal circumstances that two people are related more than usual and less than usual at the same time; however, the play sets up such an unusual family situation and Claudius's previous line presents this in a particularly poignant way: Hamlet is both his cousin[8] and son.

As Hamlet's first line follows the binary structure of Claudius's line, the question arises whether the pairs "Cosin" / "sonne" and "kin" / "kind" can be assigned to one another. One possibility is that Hamlet's line is a paraphrase of Claudius's attempt to put their relationship in a nutshell. "A little more then

---

7 "kind" *n.* II.10.a.: "myself / (One of their kind)" (*The Tempest*: 1.5.22–23); "kind" *n.* II.12.: "She's such a one that, were I well assured / Came of a gentle kind and noble stock, / I'd wish no better choice and think me rarely wed" (*Pericles*: 5.1.60–62).
8 As Harold Jenkins points out, "cousin" could refer to "any kinsman more distant than a brother" and was "often used of a nephew" (1982: 182n64).

kin" can be read as meaning "our relationship exceeds that of belonging to the same family, ancestral race, or stock." It is interesting to note that Hamlet uses the quantifier "a little," which already indicates some reservation about Claudius's claim on his part. "Lesse then kind" can be read as an ellipsis of "less than of your kind," which means that Hamlet is not directly descended from Claudius. Thus, "Cosin" / "sonne" and "kin" / "kind" can, strictly speaking, not directly be assigned to one another. Rather, *both* parts of Hamlet's line capture the meaning of Claudius's line.

If we choose to read the line in this way, it can, unlike in a reading which is based on "kind" as adjective, even be regarded as a sympathetic reaction to Claudius's address. It might be seen as Hamlet's attempt at helping the new King to characterize their relationship by making it a matter of degree and by establishing a third category besides cousin and son that lies somewhere in the middle of the two, instead of choosing the option of assigning two mutually exclusive roles to Hamlet, which seems unnatural. The play on the similar sound of "kin" and "kind" helps to add a light tone to this attempt. For a reader who is not familiar with Shakespeare's *Hamlet* this is a viable reading. The playtext has so far not given any indication as to how Claudius and Hamlet are disposed towards each other. Of course, the usual reading of this line is that of carrying a tone of hostility. The editors of the Third Arden edition read it as a reaction to Claudius's claim of "an excess of kinship in designating himself father as well as uncle," which would make his "[a] little more then kin" an ironic comment on this claim. But the playtext itself does not necessarily foreground such a reading if we look at the passage up to this point. The fact that Hamlet's line mimics the structure of Claudius's line also seems to suggest that it affirms Claudius's claim. Claudius's rhetoric earlier on in this scene is clearly aimed at reconciling contradictory notions and at conveying a sense of harmony to his subjects when he tells them that he has married his brother's widow "[w]ith an auspicious and a dropping eye, / With mirth in funeral and with dirge in marriage, / In equal scale weighing delight and dole" (1.2.11–13). In order to unite opposites, Claudius heavily relies on internal rhyme (e.g. "With *mirth* in funeral and with *dirge* in marriage"; emphasis mine), alliteration (e.g. "delight and dole") and parallelism (cf. 1.2.3–4, 11–12) in his oration. His address of Hamlet as "Cosin, and [...] sonne" shows that he is eager to continue his "play of equally balanced clausal structures" (Hopkins 1994: 156). Hamlet's choice of a similarly parallel construction, which incorporates alliteration and internal rhyme as well, might indicate that he mimics Claudius's rhetoric.

If we do not only know what comes before the line but are also aware of what lies ahead because we have read or seen the play before, the common reading of the line as hostile is the more plausible one. In performance, an actor playing Hamlet who bases his interpretation of the character on his knowledge of the entire play might narrow down possible implications of Hamlet's line and make it clear that he does not like Claudius via intonation, facial expressions etc. But one could imagine an actor choosing to play this line as an attempt on the part of Hamlet to at least shield his dislike for his mother's marriage with his uncle from public view and to maintain the impression of respect towards the new King before growing increasingly irritated with him as the scene progresses.

We have to interpret Hamlet's line as a negative reaction to Claudius, however, if we read "and lesse" as meaning "but lesse." This is a viable interpretation and depends on how we reconstruct the ellipsis in the second half of Hamlet's line. A tone of hostility between the two men is more obvious if "lesse then kind" is read as an ellipsis of "less than of a kind," drawing on the meaning of "kind" as "[a] class of individuals or objects distinguished by attributes possessed in common; a genus or species" (*OED* 2014: "kind" *n.* II.13.a.). Hamlet's reaction to Claudius would thus acknowledge their being related in a way that exceeds usual kinship but at the same time point out that they are not alike. The fact that the line does not read "[a] little more then kin, and lesse then kin" invites us to consider the possibility that "kin" and "kind" are not near-synonyms.

A reading of the line as a rejection of likeness between uncle and nephew is supported by Hamlet's rejection of likeness between his late father and Claudius later on in the play. His father is to Claudius as "Hyperion to a satyr" (1.2.140). Again, we are required to read or watch the entire play to see the connection, or we need an actor to deliver the line with a tone of resentment or even a gesture to underline this meaning. By choosing the same construction with "and" as Claudius does, although he actually means "but," Hamlet adds a mocking tone to his imitation of Claudius's rhetoric. What he really means is: "We are a little more than kin, *but* less than alike." Hamlet tries to describe not only their relationship but also their differences in terms of personality. Jenkins includes both aspects in his note on the line: "more than kinsmen in our actual relationship and less than kinsmen in our likeness to one another and in our mutual feelings and behaviour" (1982: 183n65).

Another meaning of "kind" as noun, which might not be obvious to a modern day audience, is that of "[n]ature in general, or in the abstract, regarded as the established order or regular course of things (*rerum natura*). Rarely with *the*.

Freq. in phr. law or course of kind" (*OED* 2014: "kind" *n.* I.4.†a.).⁹ The *OED* lists an example from *Merchant of Venice*: "[T]he doing of the deed of kind" (1.3.80). To an Elizabethan audience the idea of a man marrying his brother's widow would have seemed unnatural,¹⁰ and Claudius's paradoxical address of Hamlet as cousin and son would have evoked this meaning of "kind" as noun.

As to the structural ambiguity of Hamlet's line Jenkins concedes that it "is perhaps not greatly material" to whom the line refers and suggests that it "is therefore best applied [...] to both [...] [Hamlet] and Claudius, or rather to the relation in which they stand to one another" (1982: 434–435). While the analysis of the line with "kind" as adjective has shown that this is definitely not the case, I agree that the structural ambiguity is less problematic for "kind" as noun. If we read "kind" as "[n]ature in general, or in the abstract, regarded as the established order or regular course of things (*rerum natura*)," the entire line refers to the relationship of Hamlet and Claudius. It can then be read as follows: "Our relationship exceeds normal kinship and this is less than kind, i.e. unnatural because it exceeds a natural relationship." This reading is particularly intriguing if we consider that Claudius later on in this scene goes to great lengths to show Hamlet that he considers the grief he still bears for his deceased father, and thus the relationship he still has with him, to be "a fault to heaven, / A fault against the dead, a fault to nature" (1.2.101–102). Jenkins notes that Claudius sees Hamlet's grief as an "offence against the natural order of things" (1982: 185n102). Claudius's speech can be read as a reaction to Hamlet's condemnation of their relationship as unnatural, and at the end of his speech Claudius there-

---

9 Jenkins comments that a similar meaning arises if we read "kind" as adjective: "[T]he adjective *kind*, in its Elizabethan use, included the modern sense ('benevolent'), but often retained the strong primary meaning of 'natural,' and especially 'showing feelings natural among blood relations'" (1982: 435). The *OED* lists "[t]hat is, or exists, in accordance with nature of the usual course of things" as one meaning of "kind" ("kind" *adj.* I.†1.a.). The last quotation for this entry is from 1579. The annotation provided in the Third Arden edition seems to pick up on both meanings of "kind" referred to by Jenkins but does not distinguish between the two: Claudius is "acting in a way which could be construed as 'unkind' or unnatural" (Thompson and Taylor 2006: 170n65).

10 The question of whether or not it was natural for a man to marry his brother's widow was highly relevant to the play's first audiences. Queen Elizabeth I, who ruled from 1558 to 1603, was the daughter of King Henry VIII and his second wife Anne Boleyn. In order to marry Anne, Henry had had the marriage to his first wife, Catherine of Aragon, annulled in 1533 on the grounds that she had already been married to his elder brother Arthur, who had died in 1502 shortly after the marriage. The legitimacy of Henry's marriage with Anne and, consequently, the legitimacy of Elizabeth's reign rested on the assumption that the marriage between Henry and Catherine had been unnatural and that the annulment was justified.

fore establishes a link between Hamlet overcoming his grief and him reevaluating their relationship: "We pray you throw to earth / This unprevailing woe, and think of us / As of a father" (1.2.106–108). The situation which is set up in this scene would definitely make a comment plausible which deems Claudius's and Hamlet's relationship unnatural. Of course, a twenty-first century spectator, or even a reader who does not consult the *OED*, might not pick up on this.

The analysis of Hamlet's first line has shown that his play on words opens up a host of possible meanings and interpretations based on the lexical ambiguity of the word "kind" and the structural ambiguity of the entire line. The syntax makes it difficult to determine who and what exactly Hamlet's line refers to. An audience is faced with several plausible options none of which can be considered a definitive reading. Different meanings are foregrounded by different aspects of the line itself as well as by the verbal and situational context. This interdependence of verbal and situational context generates a possible spectrum of readings. Depending on how much we know about the play, we can read the line as either a friendly or a hostile reaction to Claudius. What has also become clear is that, even if we find some meanings made more plausible than others, none of them can be fully excluded from our reading of the line. Ambiguity is used to evoke and emphasize different themes which have come up before in the play or will be of importance later on. We get the impression that we are not meant to ever fully disambiguate the line or to isolate one meaning. And while it is quite obvious that this is a strategy the playwright Shakespeare uses, we at least suspect that it is also a strategy which Hamlet uses (or, rather, which Shakespeare makes Hamlet use). It seems likely that we are meant to understand that Hamlet wants Claudius to pick up on some meanings while he does not want the other courtiers to do so; or, at least he wants them to remain uncertain as to which meaning he actually intends. Hamlet's first line raises expectations for his next line. Is he going to take up one or several of the aspects brought up so far and thus foreground particular readings? Is he going to continue his play on words and possibly confirm our suspicion that this is a strategy?

3 Hamlet's Second Line

Hamlet's second line is particularly striking because it is often acknowledged to contain a pun. Harold Jenkins in the Second Arden edition, for example, comments: "There is an obvious pun on son" (1982: 435). But the pun is more complex than this widely held assumption suggests.

The pun that editors and critics point out in Hamlet's second line is based on the homophony of "sun," referring to "[t]he brightest [...] of the heavenly bodies, the luminary or orb of day" (*OED* 2014: "sun" *n.*¹ 1.a.), and "son," referring to "[a] male child or person in relation to either or to both of his parents" ("son" *n.*¹ 1.a.). John Dover Wilson, in the 1934 Cambridge edition, notes: "Another quibble [...]: 'too much in the son' refers to the insult of being called 'son' by Claudius." In the most recent, Third Arden edition, Ann Thompson and Neil Taylor refer to other examples of puns on "sun" and "son" in Elizabethan and Jacobean plays to explain Hamlet's pun in their footnote on this line. In fact, the pun on these two words is one of the most common in Shakespeare and possibly in the English language (cf. Kökeritz 1953: 147). We find examples in *The Taming of the Shrew* (4.5.3-7), *Richard III* (1.1.1–2), *Henry IV Part 1* (1.2.185–193), and *Romeo and Juliet* (3.5.126–128), to name but a few. It is therefore not unreasonable to assume that we can find the pun in *Hamlet* too.[11]

Hamlet's second line has been variously discussed before. Edward Le Comte draws up the most extensive list of readings; he comes up with forty-three in his essay "Hamlet's Second Utterance: Forty-Three Interpretations" (1975). Le Comte, like many of his fellow critics, simply assumes that the line contains a pun without discussing the nature of this pun. His list consists of his own readings as well as of readings he finds in editors' annotations of the play. Some are interpretations such as "I am too much in the presence of royalty" (Le Comte 1975: 4), and "[o]n the contrary, I am not mourning for my father enough" (Le Comte 1975: 5). Other readings spell out implicatures of the line: "My word play shows that I am attempting a forced cheerfulness" (Le Comte 1975: 7). Although Le Comte provides explanations for his readings in his notes, he does not attempt an in-depth analysis of how the different readings emerge and how (and if) they relate to one another.

The assumption that there is a pun in this line rests on a pair of homophones, an ambiguity created by means of sound. The line certainly does meet one "condition for pun perception," namely "multiple and disparate meanings

---

[11] Some non-Shakespearean and post-*Hamlet* examples which underline the popularity of the pun can be found in Thomas Middleton's *Michaelmas Term* ([1604] 2000: 5.1.4–7) as well as in Middleton and Dekker's *The Roaring Girl* ([1610] 1999: 3.3.21–25), and in Chapman, Jonson and Marston's *Eastward Ho* ([1605] 1999: 3.2.122–125). George Herbert uses the pun in his sonnet "The Sonne" to praise the English language above all others as it "neatly doe[s] [...] give one onely name / To parents issue and the sunnes bright starre!" ([1633] 2007: 5–6). The poem culminates in the image of Christ, the "*Sonne of Man*," who is both "the son" and "the sun" (2007: 14). See also Matthias Bauer's comments on the "son" / "sun" pun in his contribution to this volume.

for the pun word" (Brown 1956: 14–15). However, only one of these does make sense in the syntactical construction the word occurs in, even though Hamlet's line is not what Leech calls an "'asyntactic' pun" in which "one of the meanings does not actually fit into the syntactic context" (Leech 1969: 211).[12] Both words fit the syntax in our example: a noun is needed, and both words are nouns. But the noun "son" meaning "male child" is usually not used after the preposition "in" or after the verb "to be" in combination with the preposition "in." Even though both words are nouns, the ambiguity created by sound is resolved by the syntax in this line. "To be in the sun" is not a phrase that is or was commonly used to invoke the meaning of "son" as a "male child." The line presents an example of local ambiguity (cf. Bauer, Knape, Koch and Winkler 2010: 40) as the syntax disambiguates the homophones and makes it difficult to see or hear the pun.

None of the relevant editions of *Hamlet* discusses the syntax in connection with the pun.[13] One aspect editors cite as an indication of a pun in this line is the spelling found in the Second Quarto edition of 1604, which is believed to be either based on Shakespeare's foul papers or at least rather close to them (cf. Jenkins 1982: 18–19, 64).[14] The Second Quarto (Q2) has "too much in the sonne," taking up the spelling of Claudius's "my Cosin *Hamlet*, and my sonne" earlier on in this passage. John Dover Wilson (1934) bases his annotation of the line, and his assumption that we are to detect a pun, on the spelling in Q2, and

---

12 Leech cites Mercutio's play on the word "grave" in *Romeo and Juliet* as an example of the asyntactic pun. Mercutio, fatally wounded by Tybalt, tells his friends: "Ask for me tomorrow and you shall find me a grave man" (3.1.98–99). "The sinister meaning of *grave* hinted at here," Leech comments, "is that of *grave* as a noun, although in the given construction 'a grave man,' it can only be an adjective" (1969: 211). It is not correct that "grave" can only be an adjective in this syntactic construction. For a discussion of Mercutio's pun, also in relation to Hamlet's description of the dead Polonius as "most still, most secret, and most grave" (3.4.216), see Matthias Bauer's article in this volume.

13 Neither John Dover Wilson in the Cambridge edition (1934) of *Hamlet* nor Jenkins in the Second Arden edition (1982) or Thompson and Taylor in the Third Arden edition (2006) discuss the syntax in connection with the pun. Other editors pointing out a pun but not discussing the syntax are Edward Dowden in the First Arden edition (1899), George Rylands in the New Clarendon Shakespeare (1947), Horace Howard Furness in the New Variorum (1963), Philip Edwards in the New Cambridge Shakespeare (1985), G. R. Hibbard in the Oxford edition (1987), and Jonathan Bate and Eric Rasmussen in the RSC edition (2008). The 1963 Variorum edition lists two editors, G. Wilson Knight and Caldecott, who dismiss the notion of a pun and state that there is no quibble as the meaning of the line can be explained with respect to an old proverb.

14 In the Folio text of *Hamlet* (1623c), the line reads "Not so my Lord, I am too much i'th' Sun" (1.2.247; original spelling). The text of the First Quarto of 1603 neither contains this line nor Hamlet's "A little more then kin, and lesse then kind."

Thompson and Taylor (2006) follow him in that. However, the *OED* lists both "sunne" and "sonne" as variants of the word "sun" for the sixteenth century. Shakespeare's spelling of "sun" in *Hamlet* as well as in his other plays is usually "sunne" (cf. for example *The Comedy of Errors* 2.2.425, *As You Like It* 2.5.928, *Love's Labor's Lost* 4.3.1358, 1595, *Troilus and Cressida* 2.1.975), not "sonne," so the spelling in Hamlet's line, if we assume the meaning of "brightest [...] of the heavenly bodies" to be the intended meaning, is indeed an exception. But given the fact that people very much spelled as they pleased at the time – and this is also one reason why there are no homographic puns in Shakespeare – a certain way of spelling a word would not necessarily cause a pun to be recognized even if it was intended to be (cf. Delabastita 1993: 81). Trying to argue in favour of a pun in this line based on spelling alone is difficult. Yet, modern editions often attempt to make the pun more visible by finding particular ways of spelling it (for the necessity to mark puns in spelling after it had become standardized see Read 2009: 86). John Dover Wilson (1934) and Thompson and Taylor (2006), for example, opt for "in the 'son'" to make the pun more obvious. Is this an indication that the sense of "male offspring" would not come to mind if the word just read "sun"? To argue that there is supposed to be a pun because spelling suggests there is does neither advance our understanding of the pun nor of the play. It is more interesting to see what the pun does to the line and what the line does without the pun. As Rubinstein states: "One way of determining whether Shakespeare intended a pun is to see if meaning is enhanced [...]. They act as signposts that Shakespeare stopped here and so should we. They alert us to larger metaphors or themes we might otherwise overlook" (1984: x; cf. also Brown 1956: 15).

In order to determine whether meaning is indeed enhanced by a pun in this line it is necessary to consider more closely the verbal context and the communicative situation set up by the play and to see whether they evoke both "sun" and "son." After all, Delabastita suggests that "the strength of [...] syntactic constraints must not be overestimated, as considerations of syntactic well-formedness can sometimes be seen to give way under the pressure of other [...] contextual constraints" (1993: 71). As he points out, verbal and situational context both matter for a pun (cf. 1993: 70–73): "On the one hand, contexts may reduce potential ambiguities and filter out irrelevant associations. [...] On the other hand, the context may equally force potential ambiguities to be realized and trigger particular apt associations. [...] [P]uns may be more or less plausible contextually" (1993: 73–74).

The following analysis of the verbal and situational context of the line will begin with readings which draw on the meaning of the pun word as "[t]he brightest [...] of the heavenly bodies." As an answer to Claudius's metaphorical question "How is it that the clowdes still hang on you" (246), Hamlet's line can either be read metaphorically or literally. Hamlet is on stage before he utters his first lines, silent until addressed by Claudius. His mother, Queen Gertrude, later asks him to "cast [...] [his] nighted colour off" (1.2.68), and he himself refers to his "inky cloak" (1.2.77), which suggests that he is wearing black and is in a state of mourning for his late father. Given Hamlet's attire in this scene and the circumstances, Claudius's question can be read as meaning: "Why are you still in mourning?" Claudius's following speeches underline this meaning as he tells Hamlet to suspend his "unmanly grief" (1.2.94). A literal way to read Hamlet's answer with the first meaning of the pun word as "brightest [...] of the heavenly bodies" is that of an accidental or deliberate misunderstanding of Claudius's question as being meant literally. Hamlet's phrase then literally means: "I spend too much time exposed to the actual sun." If we interpret the misunderstanding as deliberate, Hamlet's answer implies a degree of mockery of his uncle's use of metaphor. This reading supports the interpretation of Hamlet's previous line as hostile.

If we read the phrase as a metaphorical answer to the metaphorical question, it offers a number of possible meanings. The *OED* lists two meanings for the phrase "in the sun" ("sun" *n.* 4.b. (a) *fig.*, chiefly in phr. in the sun): the obsolete meaning of "free from care or sorrow" and the meaning of "exposed to public view." With the first of these meanings, Hamlet's line can be read as follows: "I am too free from care or sorrow, that is, I am not grieving enough." Of course, Hamlet does not really lack in grief. His line is meant hyperbolically in the sense of "not even I am grieving enough." A possible implicature of the line is that Hamlet accuses Claudius, Gertrude and the rest of the court of not showing any grief. They are like the sun with whom he is faced and which appears too bright for him. Again, he rejects the notion that he is hung over by clouds. This interpretation of Hamlet's answer is emphasized by the verbal context because it corresponds with the meaning of Claudius's question. As with the meaning of "kind" as "[n]ature in general, or in the abstract, regarded as the established order or regular course of things (*rerum natura*)" ("kind" *n.* I.4.†a.), this is another case in which one meaning made plausible by the verbal context is not obvious to a twenty-first century audience.

With the second meaning for "in the sun" cited by the *OED* the line can be read as: "I am too much exposed to public view, that is there is too much attention on me." Hamlet would then interpret Claudius's question as metaphorical and meaning "Why are you concealed from the public?" Both answers can, but do not necessarily, carry an undertone of hostility. The meaning revolving around the topic of receiving too much attention might be more obvious to a modern-day spectator than that of being too carefree; however, as the scene has so far not brought up the notion of being in the public eye, Hamlet's line would introduce a new topic. Hamlet referring to his grief for his father seems more plausible since the topic of Old Hamlet's death dominates the scene from the start.

Another metaphorical reading of the line, commonly noted by editors, rests on the Elizabethan proverb "out of God's blessing into the warm sun," listed in Tilley's *Elizabethan Proverb Lore* (1926: 287). In general, the proverb refers to a situation in which someone or something is going from good to bad or from bad to worse (cf. Tilley 1926: 171). Jenkins reads the line as meaning that "Hamlet [...] [has] been turned out from the place Heaven gave him and deprived of the throne" (1982: 436), which brings up the question of succession. This is indeed a topic referred to by Claudius later on in the scene, when he declares Hamlet to be "the most immediate to [...] [his] throne" (1.2.109), so Hamlet's line might be read as prompting Claudius's reaction. Tilley refers to an example from Lyly's *Euphues*: "If thou wilt follow my advice [to leave the court and go into the country] and prosecute thine own determination, thou shalt come out of a warm sun into God's blessing" (Lyly [1578] 2003: 148–149; cf. Tilley 1926: 287). The use of the proverb in the example from Lyly implies that leaving the court is positive because one comes into God's blessing, while staying at court means being in the warm sun and has a negative connotation. The link of Hamlet's line to the proverb is surely a rather faint one; after all there is no reference to being under God's blessing, and it remains unclear what this would mean in Hamlet's case. However, the proverb shows that "being in the sun" would potentially have a negative connotation for Elizabethan audiences, and the usage of this metaphor in Hamlet's line would have underlined his miserable situation.

Yet another meaning emerges when we read "sun" as a metaphor for the King and thus for Claudius. After all the sun is a symbol of royalty.[15] The line can be read as meaning: "I am too much in your, that is the King's presence." This entails that Hamlet misunderstands Claudius's question as implying that Hamlet does not get enough attention from the King. Le Comte comments on this reading: "On the surface – unless delivered sarcastically – this is a courtierly response. Underneath, it is a barb" (1975: 3). Mahood explains that with his pun

---

15 See for example *Henry V*, where the King's gaze and thus the King himself is likened to the sun: "A largess universal, like the sun, / His liberal eye doth give to every one, / Thawing cold fear, that mean and gentle all / Behold, as may unworthiness define, / A little touch of Harry in the night" (4.0.43–47).

Hamlet "wraps inside a compliment about the King's favour the statement that he is insulted to be called Claudius's son" (1957: 114). Again, different interpretations could be emphasized by means of tone of voice, intonation, gestures or facial expression in a stage performance. Even without taking the homophony of "son" and "sun" into consideration, there are plenty of readings for the line as a play on the literal and figurative meanings of "sun," the "brightest [...] of the heavenly bodies."[16]

As stated earlier, the phrase "to be in the son" does not normally evoke the notion of "male child" for syntactical reasons, but it is, of course, possible to construct a communicative situation in which this would be fitting and make sense. A father who sees his own character traits or qualities – too much for his own liking – in his son could say "I am too much in the son." He would probably say "my son," but in this context the line would work equally with the definite article. This constitutes a figurative use of the phrase. However, the line is not spoken by a father, but by a son in *Hamlet*. Another communicative situation drawing on the one just mentioned, one which, however, generates a slightly different meaning, can be found in the Bible, in 1 John 5: 20: "[W]e are in him [...], *even* in his Son Jesus Christ" (*The Bible* [1611] 2008). That is, we are in God and in Christ. The phrase refers to a notion of identity or belonging to, but, again, the context in *Hamlet* does not fit.

In order to read the line as containing a pun, we need to read it as an ellipsis of "I am too much in the position / role of the son." Or, as Philip Edwards suggests in his note on the line, we assume that the contraction of the line in the First Folio of 1623 as "i'th' Sun" helps to underline the pun on stage, as the pronunciation of this contraction could hover between "i'th' sun" and "o'th' sun" (Edwards 1985: 86n67) and prompt us to read the line as "I am too much of a son."

Jenkins offers yet another interpretation: "Hamlet finds this relationship 'too much' for him and Claudius is making 'too much' of it (making him more his 'son' than he really is)" (1982: 435–436). Another way to read it would be "I am the son of too many fathers." This suggests that Hamlet does not answer Claudius's question in the previous line but reacts to being addressed as

---

16 Altick suggest an added meaning of the sun as "a powerful agent of corruption" (1954: 168), which would make Hamlet's line a comment on Claudius's corrupting and corrupted nature (cf. Altick 1954: 168–169). Altick notes, however, that "only looking back, especially from the point where Hamlet envisions the sun breeding maggots in a dead dog, do we realize that he is characterizing the King more truly than he can, at this point" (1954: 169).

cousin and son earlier on in the exchange and, as in his first line, rejects the notion of being "more then kin, and lesse then kind."

No matter which reading of the line we choose, Hamlet does not simply answer Claudius's question, a question that asks for an explanation; he rejects the premise of that question. If we take the meaning of "in the sun" as "free from care or sorrow" as an example, which would be Hamlet answering the question "Why are you still grieving?," Hamlet answers "I am not grieving so much as your question implies, I am too careless."

To sum up: the homophony of the two words "son" and "sun" can trigger pun perception. However, Hamlet's line is not phrased in a way that would immediately make both meanings obvious. A look at the wider verbal as well as the situational context is necessary to determine the workings and function of the pun in this line. Also, the question arises whether the line can be read as a strategic use of ambiguity both on the part of Shakespeare and his protagonist.

Hamlet utters a line that has the potential to contain a pun, but the syntax makes it difficult to perceive the pun. Looking at the communicative situation, it is clear that Hamlet cannot openly insult Claudius in this scene. This is the reason why most editors mark Hamlet's first line (cf. Edwards 1985; Furness 1963; Rylands 1947; Dowden 1899; Dover Wilson 1934), in which the exploitation of ambiguity as part of wordplay is more obvious, and some even the second line, with the more concealed pun (cf. Bate and Rasmussen 2008), as possible asides. Shakespeare has Hamlet make a pun but does not quite have him make it at the same time. The material for and convention of punning on these homophones is there; Hamlet could, like he has done in his first line, strategically use the ambiguity created by the homophones but he does not quite use it. This can be linked back to the question why the pun does not work grammatically; it does not because it cannot in this communicative situation. This is not only a pun that disguises something, it is a hidden pun. It does not so much work as "a signpost" which "alert[s] us to larger metaphors or themes we might otherwise overlook" (Rubinstein 1984: x); on the contrary, the themes and metaphors which dominate the immediate and wider verbal context alert us to the possibility that there is a pun.

The verbal context of the line, its situational context and the communicative situation of its occurrence in the world of the play support both meanings of the pun word in different ways. The meaning of "sun" is supported by Claudius's metaphorical use of the clouds to enquire about Hamlet's mood. The meaning of "son" is supported by Claudius's address of Hamlet as "Cosin [...], and [...] sonne," as well as by Hamlet's first line with the play on "kin" and "kind" that takes up the notion of relationship. Claudius's speech that follows this exchange, in which he again calls Hamlet his "son" twice (1.2.111, 117), underlines the meaning of "son" in Hamlet's second line.

What is the function of this concealed pun? We can see that it is important with regard to the internal communication between characters in the play as well as with regard to the external communication between play(wright) and audience. On the internal level, we have Hamlet as a character who uses wordplay, and puns in particular, to express his dislike of his uncle, which he cannot reveal openly in front of the court. The concealment of the pun also provides Claudius with the opportunity to show Hamlet that he has indeed understood the hidden insult by calling him "son" repeatedly as the scene goes on (1.2.111, 117). The rivalry between the two men has thus been established within four lines before Hamlet even knows that Claudius is the murderer of his father. On the external level, the line affects the perception of Hamlet's situation as well as his relationship with Claudius. It provides the audience with information they need to follow the action, namely that Hamlet dislikes his uncle, and thus fulfills its function as part of the play's exposition. With their multiple functions, both of Hamlet's lines point to what Redfern calls "[t]he economy of puns" (1984: 9).

Hamlet's pun is not necessarily a pun that can only be grasped on the external level, that is by the audience, while its meaning is obscure to characters in the play. However, its hidden nature can serve to conceal its meaning from some characters on stage, for example the members of the court, while its meaning is clear to others, for example Hamlet and Claudius.

4 Conclusion

The wordplay in both of Hamlet's lines incorporates instances of ambiguity. While his first line contains structural and lexical ambiguities which become apparent in both written and spoken language, his second line contains a case of local ambiguity which entirely rests on sounds. Both cases illustrate how the interdependence of verbal context and the communicative situation depicted in the play triggers a process of disambiguation which fulfills its function precisely because it fails to yield a definitive reading of the passage. At the same time, this interdependence ensures that, rather than to generate an unlimited scope of meaning, the passage presents us with a range of possible interpretations highlighting and linking different topics, themes and motifs found in this scene and later on in the play. Hamlet's first line evokes the antipathy between Hamlet and Claudius, their supposed unlikeness in personality and character as well as their unnatural relationship caused by Claudius's marriage. Each of these topics is brought up by a particular combination of certain elements of verbal context and communicative situation, and each of these combinations, in turn, points to the next possible combination and leads us to see the other topics as well.

The use of local ambiguity in Hamlet's second line leaves us, and the characters in the play, uncertain whether the line does indeed contain a pun. While the immediate verbal context seems to prompt us to overlook the homophony of "sun" and "son," the wider verbal context, as well as the communicative situation depicted in the scene, makes it impossible to ignore it. Shakespeare has spun a fine web of references and contexts in this passage which makes us see and hear the pun in Hamlet's second line although it is not quite there. In both lines, wordplay helps to draw our attention to these instances of ambiguity and encourages us to engage with different meanings which influence our understanding not only of Hamlet as a character but of the entire play.

5 References

Altick, Richard. 1954. *Hamlet* and the Odor of Mortality. *Shakespeare Quarterly* 5(2). 167–176.
Bate, Jonathan & Eric Rasmussen (eds.). 2008. *Hamlet*. Basingstoke: Macmillan.
Bauer, Matthias, Joachim Knape, Peter Koch & Susanne Winkler. 2010. Dimensionen der Ambiguität. *Zeitschrift für Linguistik und Literaturwissenschaft* 158. 7–75.
The Bible: Authorized King James Version with Apocrypha. [1611] 2008. Robert Carroll & Stephen Prickett (eds.). Oxford: Oxford University Press.
Brown, James. 1956. Eight Types of Puns. *PMLA* 71. 14–26.
Chapman, George, Ben Jonson & John Marston. [1605] 1999. *Eastward Ho*. R. W. Van Fossen (ed.). Manchester: Manchester University Press.
Delabastita, Dirk. 1993. *There's a Double Tongue: An Investigation into the Translation of Shakespeare's Wordplay, with Special Reference to* Hamlet. Amsterdam: Rodopi.
Dowden, Edward (ed.). 1899. *Hamlet*. London: Methuen.
Edwards, Philip (ed.). 1985. *Hamlet, Prince of Denmark*. Cambridge: Cambridge University Press.
Furness, Horace Howard (ed.). 1963. *Hamlet*. New York: Dover.
Grice, H. P. [1975] 1991. Logic and Conversation. In Steven Davis (ed.), *Pragmatics: A Reader*, 305–315. Oxford: Oxford University Press.
Herbert, George. [1633] 2007. The Sonne. In Helen Wilcox (ed.), *The English Poems of George Herbert*, 572–574. Cambridge: Cambridge University Press.
Hibbard, G. R. (ed.). 1987. *Hamlet*. Oxford: Clarendon Press.
Hopkins, Lisa. 1994. Parison and the Impossible Comparison. In Mark Thornton Burnett & John Manning (eds.), *New Essays on* Hamlet, 153–164. New York: AMS Press.

Jannidis, Fotis. 2003. Polyvalenz – Konventionen – Autonomie. In Fotis Jannidis, Gerhard Lauer, Matías Martínez & Simone Winko (eds.), *Regeln der Bedeutung: Zur Theorie der Bedeutung literarischer Texte*, 305–328. Berlin: de Gruyter.
Jenkins, Harold (ed.). 1982. *Hamlet*. London: Methuen.
Kökeritz, Helge. 1953. *Shakespeare's Pronunciation*. New Haven: Yale University Press.
Le Comte, Edward. 1975. Hamlet's Second Utterance: Forty-Three Interpretations. In *Poets' Riddles: Essays in Seventeenth-Century Explication*, 3–9. Port Washington, NY: Kennikat Press.
Leech, Geoffrey N. 1969. *A Linguistic Guide to English Poetry*. Harlow: Longmans.
Lyly, John. [1578] 2003. *Euphues: The Anatomy of Wit*. In Leah Scragg (ed.), Euphues: The Anatomy of Wit *and* Euphues and His England, 25–152. Manchester: Manchester University Press.
Mahood, M. M. 1957. *Shakespeare's Wordplay*. London: Methuen.
Middleton, Thomas. [1604] 2000. *Michaelmas Term*. Gail Kern Paster (ed.). Manchester: Manchester University Press.
Middleton, Thomas & Thomas Dekker. [1610] 1999. *The Roaring Girl*. Paul A. Mulholland (ed.). Manchester: Manchester University Press.
Oxford English Dictionary, 2nd edn. 2014. http://www.oed.com (17 July 2015).
Read, Sophie. 2009. Puns: Serious Wordplay. In Sylvia Adamson (ed.), *Renaissance Figures of Speech*, 81–94. Cambridge: Cambridge University Press.
Redfern, Walter. 1984. *Puns*. New York: Basil Blackwell.
Rubinstein, Frankie. 1984. *A Dictionary of Shakespeare's Sexual Puns and Their Significance*. London: Macmillan.
Rylands, George (ed.). 1947. *Hamlet*. Oxford: Clarendon Press.
Shakespeare, William. 1598. *Love's Labor's Lost*. Timothy Billings (ed.). http://internetshakespeare.uvic.ca/Annex/Texts/LLL/Q1/ (17 July 2015).
Shakespeare, William. 1604. *Hamlet Q2*. http://internetshakespeare.uvic.ca/Annex/Texts/Ham/Q2/default/ (17 July 2015).
Shakespeare, William. 1609. *Troilus and Cressida*. W. L. Godshalk (ed.). http://internetshakespeare.uvic.ca/Library/Texts/Tro/Q1/ (17 July 2015).
Shakespeare, William. 1623a. *As You Like It*. David Bevington (ed.). http://internetshakespeare.uvic.ca/Library/Texts/AYL/F1/default/ (17 July 2015).
Shakespeare, William. 1623b. *The Comedy of Errors*. Matthew Steggle (ed.). http://internetshakespeare.uvic.ca/Annex/Texts/Err/F1/ (17 July 2015).
Shakespeare, William. 1623c. *Hamlet Folio 1*. http://internetshakespeare.uvic.ca/Library/Texts/Ham/F1/default/ (17 July 2015).
Shakespeare, William. [c. 1600] 1964. *The Merchant of Venice*. John Russell Brown (ed.). London: Arden Shakespeare.
Shakespeare, William. [1623] 1969. *Timon of Athens*. H. J. Oliver (ed.). London: Arden Shakespeare.
Shakespeare, William. [c. 1601] 1975. *Twelfth Night*. John Maule Lothian & T. W. Craik (eds.). London: Arden Shakespeare.
Shakespeare, William. [c. 1597] 1980. *Romeo and Juliet*. Brian Gibbons (ed.). London: Thomson Learning.
Shakespeare, William. [c. 1591] 1981. *The Taming of the Shrew*. Brian Morris (ed.). London: Thomson Learning.
Shakespeare, William. [1604] 1982. *Hamlet*. Harold Jenkins (ed.). London: Thomson Learning.

Shakespeare, William. [c. 1599] 1995. *King Henry V*. T. W. Craik (ed.). London: Thomson Learning.
Shakespeare, William. [c. 1610] 1999. *The Tempest*. Virginia Mason Vaughan & Alden T. Vaughan (eds.). London: Arden Shakespeare.
Shakespeare, William. [c. 1597] 2002. *Henry IV Part 1*. David Scott Kastan (ed.). London: Thomson Learning.
Shakespeare, William. [c. 1607] 2004. *Pericles*. Suzanne Gossett (ed.). London: Arden Shakespeare.
Shakespeare, William. [c. 1592] 2009. *Richard III*. James R. Siemon (ed.). London: Methuen.
Thompson, Ann & Neil Taylor (eds.). 2006. *Hamlet*. London: Cengage Learning.
Tilley, Morris Palmer. 1926. *Elizabethan Proverb Lore in Lyly's* Euphues *and Pettie's* Petite Pallace: *With Parallels from Shakespeare*. New York: Macmillan.
Tilley, Morris Palmer. 1950. *A Dictionary of the Proverbs in England in the Sixteenth and Seventeenth Centuries: A Collection of the Proverbs Found in English Literature and the Dictionaries of the Period*. Ann Arbor: University of Michigan Press.
Wilson, John Dover (ed.). 1934. *Hamlet*. Cambridge: Cambridge University Press.
Winter-Froemel, Esme & Angelika Zirker. 2010. Ambiguität in der Sprecher-Hörer-Interaktion: Linguistische und literaturwissenschaftliche Perspektiven. *Zeitschrift für Linguistik und Literaturwissenschaft* 158. 76–97.

Thomas Kullmann
Wordplay as Courtly Pastime and Social Practice: Shakespeare and Lewis Carroll

Abstract: Communicative utterances which involve wordplay violate the Gricean maxims and evidently privilege the "metalingual" function (Jakobson) of language over the conative, emotive and referential ones. The prominence of wordplay in literary works like Shakespeare's *Much Ado About Nothing* (set at a prototypical Renaissance court) and Lewis Carroll's *Alice's Adventures in Wonderland* (which appears to depict the Victorian drawing-room world from a child's point of view), however, suggests that wordplay might have a communicative and social function which is not quite covered by Jakobson's categories. In *Much Ado About Nothing* Beatrice and Benedict demonstrate their courtly superiority by using wordplay to provoke and tease their interlocutors. *Much Ado* thus testifies to the use of wordplay as a courtly practice, as outlined theoretically in Castiglione's *Courtier*, in which *facezie* belong to the conversational skills an ideal courtier should possess. The functions of wordplay obviously lie in a display of wit, in showing a mastery of language and in the creation of an atmosphere of humour and playfulness. Jonson's *Cynthia's Revels*, by contrast, features uncourtly uses of wordplay, such as ridiculing other characters' courtly ineptitude. In Carroll's *Alice* books, instances of wordplay in the speeches made by the Wonderland creatures constitute a major challenge for the heroine and the reader. In mastering this challenge, Alice displays and develops her social skills. As can be seen by the example of wordplay, Victorian drawing-room culture seems to imitate Renaissance courtliness, with children admitted as 'courtiers.' In these 'courtly' communities, metalinguistic awareness as displayed by a mastery of words and of wordplay allows initiates to keep their ground in an environment whose internal rules are terrifyingly complex.

Keywords: Baldassare Castiglione, Ben Jonson, children, communicative principle, courtliness, Lewis Carroll, ludic function (of language), metalinguistic function, Paul Grice, politeness, Renaissance, Roman Jakobson, Victorian Age, William Shakespeare, wordplay in drama

1 Introduction

Why do people play with words? From the communicative point of view, wordplay – as a rule – appears to be detrimental to the purposes of conveying information or appealing to the interlocutor to act in a certain way. It is obvious that utterances involving wordplay violate the "Cooperative Principle" established by Paul Grice with regard to at least two of Grice's four categories: "relation" and "manner" (Grice 1975: 45–47).[1] Given the arbitrariness of the sounds used in language, drawing attention to phenomena like homophony and polysemy (in a non-linguistic context) can hardly be considered to conform to the maxim of relevance. Concerning the category of manner, utterances involving wordplay are likely to be ambiguous and obscure[2]; at any rate, they demand a higher degree of language awareness than statements which do not involve wordplay. Applying the functional model established by Roman Jakobson (1981: 25), we notice that wordplay obviously has a "metalingual" (or metalinguistic) function while the conative, emotive and referential functions seem to lose their prominence.[3]

In order to examine possible communicative uses of wordplay, I should like to take a look at two literary authors whose works depict acts of communication involving wordplay, and who have often been considered masters of this device: William Shakespeare and Lewis Carroll. At first sight the two authors do not seem to have much in common; according to Molly Mahood (1968: 11), the fact that wordplay occurs in a children's book somehow testifies to the low prestige of wordplay in Victorian literary consciousness: "[...] their [the Victorians'] own wordplay," Mahood claims, "[...] had to hide in the nursery. Jabberwocky could be enjoyed only at seven and a half exactly."[4] I would like to contest the impli-

---

1 Grice (1975: 54–55) actually discusses the wordplay involved in the English translation of Latin "peccavi," ascribed to Major-General Napier on his conquest of the country of Sind (in 1843) by the *Punch* magazine, as an example of flouting the maxim of perspicuity.
2 As Molly Mahood (1968: 10) points out, wordplay and other "delicacies of wit" were rejected by poets, preachers and rhetoricians in the late seventeenth and the eighteenth century because they endanger the perspicuity of language. On *double entendre* as a form of wordplay in the late seventeenth and early eighteenth century, see Goth, this volume.
3 On the relation of punning to Jakobson's poetic function of language, cf. Culler (1988: 9).
4 While it is true that wordplay is avoided by novelists like Dickens, Thackeray and George Eliot, it is often found in Victorian letters, including texts revised for publication. A fine example occurs in a letter written from India in 1838, in which Julia Maitland ([1843] 2004: 105) discusses gentlemen meeting at her house and talking about their chances of becoming "collectors," i.e. district administrators: "[...] if left to themselves, they sit and conjugate the verb

cation that wordplay in the Victorian Age is restricted to 'insignificant' contexts, and I would also like to contend that the wordplay the Wonderland characters engage in has quite a few similarities with the puns some of Shakespeare's characters habitually fling at one another. While there may not be a direct connection between Shakespeare and Carroll,[5] both authors certainly stand out from their contemporaries with respect to the prominence of wordplay in their works and the interest they take in the social mechanisms of communications involving wordplay.

My paper will focus on Shakespeare's *Much Ado About Nothing* and Lewis Carroll's *Alice's Adventures in Wonderland*. After discussing pertinent examples of wordplay from *Much Ado* I propose to show the courtly quality of this social practice by placing it into the context of Castiglione's discussions of wordplay in *Il cortegiano* (1528, translated into English in 1561). Wordplay (and the related phenomenon of malapropism), of course, could be put to other than courtly uses, which will be outlined by references to the Dogberry and Verges scenes in *Much Ado*, as well as to a contemporaneous play, Ben Jonson's *Cynthia's Revels* (1600). The phenomenon of Elizabethan courtly wordplay will then be compared to the functions of wordplay in *Alice's Adventures in Wonderland*, on the basis of an interpretation of "Wonderland" as a reflection of the child readers' social lives: In *Much Ado*, I should like to contend, characters try to outdo one another in (playfully or aggressively) disturbing their interlocutors' attempts at communication, while in *Alice's Adventures*, the heroine's attempts at communication are disturbed by the wordplay apparent in the words of the Wonderland creatures, whose habits are often reminiscent of those of real-life adults, seen from a child's point of view. While *Alice* differs from *Much Ado* in that the Wonderland creatures may not use wordplay consciously (so that only the readers become conscious of it), I believe that this phenomenon can be related to social practices prevalent in Victorian drawing-rooms. As I will argue in a final chapter, these practices can well be compared to those of Renaissance courts.

'to collect': 'I am a collector – He was a collector – We shall be collectors – You ought to be a collector – They might, could, should, or would have been collectors,' so, when it comes to that, while they *conjugate* 'to collect,' I *decline* listening."

5 Lewis Carroll, however, was a lover of the theatre, and familiar with Shakespeare's plays, cf. below, note 21.

2 Wordplay in *Much Ado About Nothing*

In *Much Ado About Nothing*, wordplay appears as a pastime practised by the ladies and gentlemen at the court of Messina.[6] When in the first scene a messenger announces the imminent arrival of Don Pedro and his suite, Beatrice introduces herself by twisting around the pieces of information provided. In reply to the messenger's statement that Benedick "hath done good service [...] in these / wars" (1.1.45–46), she avers that "he is a very valiant trencher-man: he hath an / excellent stomach" (48–49), implying that Benedick might be better at eating food served on trenchers or platters than at fighting courageously in trenches dug in a battle-field. Beatrice, in fact, produces a series of elaborate puns, punning on the literal and a metaphorical meaning of *valiant* (*Oxford English Dictionary* 2014: "valiant" *adj*. 2.a. and 4.), a metaphorical and a metonymic meaning of *stomach*, i.e. 'courage' and 'appetite' (*OED* 2014: "stomach" *n*. 8.a. and 5.a.), and the phonetic similarity (and etymological connection) of *trench* and *trencher*.[7] The messenger, who has obviously understood the literal meaning of Beatrice's reply, stands his ground by reiterating his message: "And a good soldier too, lady" (50); this, in turn, is grammatically twisted by Beatrice in a way which belittles Benedick's military qualities: "And a good soldier to a lady; but what is he to / a lord?" (51–52). To some extent the messenger (who is certainly a courtly gentleman himself) now catches up with the game, by making use of parallelism and metaphor: "A lord to a lord, a man to a man, stuffed

---

[6] In view of the plethora of studies on Shakespeare, it is amazing how little critical attention the phenomenon of wordplay (in Shakespeare in general, and *Much Ado About Nothing* in particular) has received. Mahood's *Shakespeare's Wordplay* (published in 1957 but still the study on wordplay quoted most often) focuses on plays "in which the wordplay appears [...] to offer a valuable means of access to the heart of the drama" (1968: 55); these plays include *Hamlet* and *Macbeth* but not *Much Ado*; on this choice of plays cf. Mahood (1996 / 97). Norbert Kohl (*Das Wortspiel in der Shakespeareschen Komödie* 1966) was one of the first scholars to draw attention to Shakespeare's wordplay as a courtly display of wit, but bewilderingly concentrates on the 'early comedies' and 'late plays,' thus passing by *Much Ado*.

[7] Beatrice's puns belong to the categories of polysemy (*valiant, stomach*) and paronomasia (*trench / trencher*), i.e. the two categories of wordplay mentioned by Castiglione (who distinguishes between "facezie [...] che nascono dalla ambiguità" (which of course include instances of homonymy) and "un' altra sorte [...] che chiamiamo bischizzi, e questa consiste nel mutare ovvero accrescere o minuire una lettera o sillaba"; cf. below, p. x). Castiglione may be following Cicero's categories of "ambigua" and "paronomasia"; cf. Kohl (1966: 26–27). On polysemy cf. Leech (1969: 209–214); on paronomasia and related phenomena cf. Wolfgang G. Müller (1996). I thank my colleague Alexander Bergs for his advice on the linguistics of wordplay.

with / all honourable virtues" (53–54); "stuffed" simply meaning 'provided' (*OED* 2014: "stuffed" *adj.* 1.a.). The image of stuffing now provides Beatrice with an opening to produce another multilayered pun: "It is so indeed, he is no less than a stuffed man, / but for the stuffing – well, we are all mortal" (55–56), where "stuffed" involves the meanings of being well-fed (*OED* 2014: "stuffed" *adj.* 1.b.), being rich ("stuffed" *adj.* 1.c.), being a scarecrow ("stuffed" *adj.* 2. and 3.), and, apparently, having been the object of sexual aggression.[8] It may be this piece of obscenity which finally floors the messenger and induces Leonato to come to his rescue:

> "You must not, sir, mistake my niece; there is a / kind of merry war betwixt Signor Benedick and her. / They never meet but there's a skirmish of wit between them" (57–60).

The messenger gets to know that Beatrice is licensed to speak as she does: in Leonato's eyes, there is nothing wrong with Benedick's and Beatrice's "kind of merry war" and "skirmish of wit." The objective of Beatrice's playing with words is obviously to engage in teasing the messenger, perhaps provoking him to defend Benedick. It also appears to be a kind of game intended to amuse the other ladies and gentlemen present. On another level, the dialogue aptly introduces Beatrice's character to the audience.

The "skirmish of wit" mentioned is resumed when Benedick actually appears. The playful abuse Beatrice and Benedick heap upon one another is wound up by Benedick's comparison of Beatrice's tongue to his horse, Beatrice's tongue having greater speed. This pun on the literal and metaphorical meaning of *speed* is taken up by Beatrice's remark: "You always end with a jade's trick" (1.1.138). Benedick is provocatively compared to a female horse, and his rhetorical skills to the horse's antics – punning on two meanings of *tricks*, as skilful performances and instances of capricious misbehaviour (*OED* 2014: "trick" *n.* 3. and 2.).

After this welcoming scene, Claudio wishes to talk to Benedick in private, to consult him on his chances of marrying Hero. Benedick now takes up the role Beatrice played before when answering the messenger. When Claudio opens the case with the question: "Benedick, didst thou note the daughter of Signor / Leonato" (154–155), Benedick answers: "I noted her not, but I looked on her" (156), taking issue with the term *note*, which, apart from "notice, perceive" (*OED* 2014: "note" $v.^2$ II.5.b.), could mean "put a mark on" ("note" $v.^2$ I.3.). Similarly

---

[8] Cf. *Much Ado About Nothing*, ed. Claire McEachern, ([1600] 2007: 1.1.55n); cf. *OED* (2014: "stuffed" *adj.* 6. ["get stuffed"]).

when Claudio confesses: "In mine eye, she is the sweetest lady that ever I / looked on" (177–178), his reply deliberately focuses on the literal meaning of Claudio's statement: "I can see yet without spectacles, and I see no / such matter" (179–180). Claudio, of course, as the synaesthesia involved in the term "sweetest lady" indicates, did not just refer to Hero's good looks; he wishes to 'taste' her, not only to look at her. Even when asked for his "sober judgement" (162), Benedick resorts to a series of puns: "Why, i'faith methinks she is too low for a high / praise, too brown for a fair praise and too little for a / great praise" (163–165). As with Beatrice and the messenger, Benedick is teasing his interlocutor, provoking him into being more explicit and, perhaps, trying to reduce the tension by dissolving the seriousness of the information given or of the appeal made.

Benedick continues to play this part in the ensuing conversation with Don Pedro, who is willing to support Claudio, deflecting Claudio's discourse of passion by a series of puns which again involve polysemy and paronomasia. He prides himself on giving a short answer by mentioning Leonato's short daughter (200–201), he states that it would take an earthquake to make him quake with love (252–254), and he sums up his attitude about marrying by saying: "And the fine is – for the which I may go / the finer – I will live a bachelor" (229–230), implying that he can spend more money on dress if he does not have to support a wife. In scene 2.1 Beatrice answers suggestions about marrying in a similar vein.

What all of these puns have in common is their provocative quality. They twist around the rhetorical openings of a speaker, provoking him to defend his way of speaking. They reduce the impact of serious messages and appeals and serve to create an atmosphere of leisure, humour and playfulness. You can only engage in puns if the messages to be conveyed aren't all that urgent.[9] What is more important is the "skirmish of wit" involved, and perhaps the evidence given of a mastery of language and thus of a good education. In Jakobson's model puns thus relate to the language and the sender, and partake of the metalingual and emotive functions (Jakobson 1981: 21–27). What appears to be most important, however, is the teasing element. Most of the puns somehow force the interlocutor to go on talking; they serve as an appeal not to take some action[10]

---

9 Inexperienced courtiers, however, might interpret provocative puns as acts of aggression. As an anonymous reviewer of this article pointed out, puns can indeed be indicative of aggression in other Shakespearean plays, as in *Henry V* ([c. 1599] 2007: 1.2.260–298).
10 This is why, I think, the conative function does not apply. Moreover, the appeal is not conveyed by the words' meaning but by their form or phonetic quality.

but to continue sending messages, to go on with a social game. This purpose is certainly similar to that of phatic utterances, but I wonder if this appellation can really do justice to the phenomenon. Wordplay does not just function to establish "contact" as, according to Jakobson, baby talk or "ritualized formulas" do, but fulfils more specific functions of interaction between two interlocutors, functions which are not related to any "message" and cannot easily be related to either "addresser" or "addressee" alone; the relationship to the "code" is an indirect one. I would therefore like to suggest supplementing Jakobson's model by the factor of 'situation' and to posit another function of language, which might be a 'ludic' or 'provocative' one.[11] By playing with words, Benedick and Beatrice, "this pair of master linguists" (Bauer 2010: 49), are playing with the courtiers and ladies around them, not just for fun but for the serious purpose of creating a harmonious and relaxed environment which can 'contain' (or stem) potential sources of conflict like war, rivalry, passion, jealousy and marriage.[12]

3 Wordplay as Courtly Practice in Castiglione's *Cortegiano*

Wordplay as practiced by the courtiers of *Much Ado About Nothing* perfectly corresponds to a practice recommended to courtly ladies and gentlemen in Castiglione's famous treatise *Il cortegiano* (1528), *The Courtier* (cf. Kohl 1966: 24–28). According to Sir Frederick, one of the participants of the debate recorded in this book, a courtier should "with merry conceites and jestes [...] provoke" his hearers "to solace and laughter, so that without being at any time lothsome or

---

11 These appellations are used rather tentatively. By using the term 'ludic' I would like to refer to parlour games which allow several persons to interact in a way which may or may not be competitive. Phenomena other than wordplay may, of course, also belong to this category. Cf. Keir Elam's notion, based on Wittgenstein, of "language-games" which in Shakespeare's comedies are marked out "by their own unmistakable dramatic or comic conspicuousness" (1984: 18). Wordplay based on homophony and polysemy is considered to belong to a "predicating game," as a "drastic form of predicative upset" (1984: 99–100).
12 Benedick and Beatrice could be considered as courtiers who, as Harry Berger, Jr., puts it (2001: 226–227), "master the technology of sprezzatura and submit to its normative demand," which involves "a regime of self-surveillance" and the "repression" of "an 'original' private self." Berger's negative attitude with regard to courtliness would have been lost on Shakespeare's contemporaries. Beatrice and Benedick emerge as the mainstay of the courtly community of Messina, and they are doing a great job.

satiate, he may evermore delite" (133); "con motti piacevoli e facezie discretamente indurgli a festa e riso, di sorte che, senza venir mai à fastidio o pur a saziare, continuamente diletti" (Castiglione II.41; [1528] 1910: 200).[13] These *facezie*, or jests, may contain "some litle byting" ("né senza quel poco di puntura") and could also be termed *arguzie* (II.43; [1528] 1910: 202), "Privie tauntes" (134). Concerning wordplay another courtier (Bernardo Bibbiena) points out:

> Delle facezie adunque pronte, che stanno in un breve detto, quelle sono acutissime, che nascono dalla ambiguità: benché non sempre inducono a ridere, perché piú presto sono laudate pre ingeniose che per ridicule: como pochi dí sono disse il nostro messe Annibal Paleotto ad uno che gli proponea un maestro per insegnar grammatica a' suoi figlioli, e poi che gliel' ebbe laudato per molto dotto, venendo al salario disse, che oltre ai denari volea una camera fornita per abitare e dormire, perché esso non avea letto: allor messer Annibal subito rispose: E come po egli esser dotto, se non ha letto? – Eccovi come ben si valse del vario significato di quel *non aver letto*. Ma perché questi motti ambigui hanno molto dell'acuto, per pigliar l'omo le parole in significato diverso da quello che le pigliano tutti gli altri, pare, come ho detto, che piú presto movano maraviglia che riso [...].
>
> (II.58; [1528] 1910: 225–226)

> Of those readie jeastes therefore that consist in a short saying, such are most lively that arise out of doubtfulnesse, though alwaies they provoke not laughing: for they bee rather praysed for wittie, than for matters of laughter. As few dayes it is that our maister Anniball Palleotto saide to one that appointed him a maister to teach his children the Grammer, and after that hee had praysed him, to be a man very well learned, coming to wages, saide, that besides the money he would have a chamber furnished to dwell and sleepe in, for that he had not *letto*, that is a bedde.
>
> Then maister Anniball answered presently: and how can he be learned, if he have not *letto*, that is, read.
>
> See how well he tooke a vantage at the diverse signification of *haver letto* (which is interpreted both to have a bedde, and to have read.) But because those doubtfull wordes have a pretie sharpness of wit in them, being taken in a contrarie signification to that all other men take them, it appeareth [...] that they rather provoke a man to wonder than to laugh [...].
>
> (148–149)

After having provided examples of homophonic wordplay, Bibbiena goes on to define another kind, puns based on paronomasia:

> Un' altra sorte è ancor, che chiamiamo *bischizzi*, e questa consiste nel mutare ovvero accrescere o minuire una lettera o sillaba; come colui che disse: Tu dei esser piú dotto nella

---

[13] The English versions are taken from Thomas Hoby's translation (1561, revised version of 1588), which was probably known to Shakespeare.

lingua *latrina* che nella greca. – Ed a voi, Signora, fu scritto nel titolo d'una lettera: Alla signora Emilia Impia.

(II.61; [1528] 1910: 228–229)

There is yet an other sorte called in Italian *Bischizzi* and that consisteth in chaunging or increasing, or diminishing of a letter or sillable. As he that said: Thou shouldest be better learned in the Latrine tongue than in the Greeke.[14]

And to you (madam) was written in the superscription of a letter, To the Ladie Emilia Impia.

(150)

As the puns on "Latrine / Latin" and "Impia / Pia" show, one of the attractions of wordplay is certainly the opportunity of being playfully irreverent.

While Castiglione's courtiers show their awareness of the mechanisms of wordplay, it is their courtly function which mainly interests them. Wordplay, as Sir Frederick points out in the end, is a game played by a courtier on his partner in conversation:

[...] la principal cosa è lo ingannar l' opinion, e rispondere altramente che quello che aspetta l'auditore; ed è forza, se la facezia ha d'aver grazia, sia condita di quello inganno, o dissimulare o beffare o riprendere o comparare, o qual altro modo voglia usar l'omo. [...] Avendo adunque il Cortegiano nel motteggiare e dir piacevolezze rispetto al tempo, alle persone, al grado suo, e di non essere in ciò troppo frequente [...] potrà esser chiamato faceto [...].

(II.83; [1528] 1910: 271)

[...] the chiefe matter is to deceive opinion, and to answere otherwise than the hearer looketh for: and (in case the jeast shall have any grace) it must needs be seasoned with this deceite, or dissimulation, or mocking, or rebuking, or comparison, or what ever other kinde a man will use.

[...] In case therefore the Courtier in jesting and speaking merry conceites have a respect to the time, to the persons, to his degree, and not use it too often [...] hee may be called pleasant and feate conceited.

(168)

To wordplay, the same precautions apply as to other courtly practices: a courtier must take care not to overdo it and to consider its appropriateness in a particular situation. Castiglione, we see, appreciates the provocative function of

---

14 The word "Latrine" is provided by the Tudor Translations edition, ed. Walter Raleigh (Castiglione [1561] 1900), which evidently reproduces the 1561 text of Hoby's translation. The Everyman edition (which is based on the 1588 edition of the Hoby text) prints "Latin," thus making the *latrina / latina* pun disappear.

wordplay, as well as that of a game which requires two people to play it. By bewildering his interlocutor, a punning courtier makes sure courtly interaction goes on, i.e. he ultimately contributes to the social stability of his environment. Wordplay thus becomes one of the practices which furthers harmony among a large group of aristocratic ladies and gentlemen – which in Castiglione's treatise certainly emerges as the central objective of courtly behaviour.[15]

4 Uncourtly Uses of Wordplay

One of the less pleasant aspects (from today's point of view) of the courtly practice of wordplay is that – like other courtly practices – it can be used by members of the courtly aristocracy for the purpose of setting themselves apart from people of lower rank and / or courtly competence.[16] In the passages discussed, Beatrice and Benedick definitely show their superiority to their interlocutors, i.e. the messenger and Claudio, by poking fun at them, often in order to amuse other courtiers. On Shakespeare's stage, they certainly amuse the educated among the audience, who, in case they understand the wordplay, may take pride in their own courtly qualifications.[17]

Benedick and Beatrice prove to be perfect courtiers by exercising full control over the jokes they produce.[18] As members of the audience we laugh with

---

15 Cf. the praise accorded to "Courtesie" in Spenser's *Faerie Queene* (VI.1.1-3; [1590, 1596] 1978: 878).

16 Having fun at the expense of base-born people was apparently considered quite acceptable in Renaissance courtly circles. While Castiglione's courtiers are told to respect and reverence a lady's honour, this privilege is clearly not extended to servants. In the *Cortegiano*, Bernardo Bibbiena tells the story of a Bergamask cowherd who involuntarily poses as a Spanish nobleman. The reactions of the ladies who are not in the secret are recorded in detail, while nothing is said about the poor cowherd's feelings (II.85; [1528] 1910: 273–275, transl. Hoby 170–171). A trick which involves an inferior is also found in Sir Philip Sidney's *Old Arcadia*, where Musidorus, disguised as Dorus the shepherd, pretends to be in love with Mopsa, a real shepherdess, in order to gain access to Pamela, the princess who lives with the shepherd's family. Mopsa appears rather flattered by Dorus's attentions; we are not informed of her feelings when she is undeceived (Sidney [1580 / 1912] 1999: 87–93).

17 It is true that in Shakespeare wordplay is also practised by 'inferior' characters, but even those are often attached to a court or a courtier, like Feste in *Twelfth Night* and Speed in *Two Gentlemen of Verona*.

18 They will, of course, become victims of an intrigue, but as this intrigue is a perfectly playful and courtly one, a *burla* or "merrie prancke" in Castiglione' sense (II.84; [1528] 1910: 272, transl. Hoby 169), it does not lower their courtly prestige or dignity.

them, not at them; and we share their laughter at the discomfiture of their interlocutors. Punning, however, may also occur unintentionally, and, as with malapropisms, listeners are provoked into laughing at those who produce them. This is what happens to the low-born characters of *Much Ado*, Constables Dogberry and Verges. Both of them display their erudition by indulging in polysyllabic terms of Latin origin, which they usually get wrong: Verges exclaims that the watchmen "should suffer / salvation, body and soul" (3.3.2-3) if they are not "good men and true" (3.3.1); similarly, Dogberry warns Borachio that he will be "condemned into / everlasting redemption" (4.2.58–59). They tell Leonato that they have "comprehended two aspicious [sic] persons" (3.5.44). Grammatical polysemy is found when Dogberry advises the watch to "let" a thief "show / himself what he is, and steal out of your company" (3.3.57–58), and when he describes himself and Verges as "the poor duke's officers" (3.5.19). The constables are distinguished from the aristocrats by their inadequate way of speaking (which may, of course, sometimes convey an unintended truth).[19]

The motif of unintentional wordplay as a sign of courtly inadequacy is also found in another Elizabethan play about courtly life: Ben Jonson, *Cynthia's Revels* (first performed in 1600). Unlike *Much Ado About Nothing*, *Cynthia's Revels*, while staged in front of a court audience, is highly critical of courtly practices. A number of foppish, inane and badly educated young ladies and gentlemen, who frequent the court of Cynthia, the moon goddess, instruct one another in the art of courtly behaviour and courtly language. As their names indicate, they are allegorical representations of the various vices associated with courts and courtliness: Amorphus ('shapeless'), Phantaste ('fantastic'), Asotus ('past recovery'), Argurion ('silver'), Hedon ('voluptuous'), Philautia ('self-love'), Anaides ('shameless'), Moria ('folly'), Prosaites ('beggar'), Cos ('whetstone,' as a symbol of liars), Morus ('simpleton'), Gelaia ('laughter') (443–444, and notes). In many cases their behaviour might serve as an illustration of what courtliness, according to Castiglione, should not be like. This critical point of view is represented on stage by the gods Cupid and Mercury, who act as pages and comment on the follies they witness.

One of the uncourtly practices criticized is boasting. When Philautia, Self-Love personified, prides herself on her dancing: "And did I not dance movingly last night?" (2.4.38), Moria answers: "Movingly! Out of measure, in troth, sweet lady" (2.4.39), meaning that her dancing was excellent. It is up to Mercury, the god disguised as a page, to highlight the verbal ambiguity of Moria's praise: "A

---

19 Cf. *Much Ado About Nothing*, ed. Claire McEachern, ([1600] 2007: 3.3.3n*)*; and Margreta de Grazia (2001: 59). Cf. also Margaret Schlauch (1987: 97–98 *et passim*).

happy commendation, to dance out of measure" (2.4.40). Moria's unintentional pun, made explicit by Mercury, is characteristic of her courtly ineptitude.

Another unintentional pun occurs when Asotus tries to repeat what he considers a courtly speech:

> *Asotus:* More than most fair lady, let not the rigour of your just disdain thus coarsely censure of your servant's zeal. I protest you are the only and absolute unapparelled –
> *Amorphus:* Unparalleled.
> *Asotus:* Unparalleled creature, I do adore, and admire, and respect, and reverence in this court, corner of the world, or kingdom.
>
> (3.5.53–58)

Asotus has difficulties using the learned and stylish new word "unparalleled," and while he is labouring at addressing a lady, his mind already turns to the idea of seeing her naked. The malapropism (and unintentional paronomasia) can be seen as a Freudian slip.

When one of the courtiers does manage to use an intentional pun, it is grossly indecent: Speaking of his page, Mercury in disguise, who has just supplied his master with gold, Hedon remarks: "'Sheart, I'd geld him; I warrant he has the philosopher's stone" (2.2.8), punning on two meanings of *to geld*, to 'charge with land-tax' and 'to castrate,' as well as on *stone*, meaning 'testicle.'

Wordplay is used to make the audience laugh at the courtiers (or rather, would-be courtiers), rather than with them. It is only Mercury, the god and observer, who can skilfully manipulate wordplay, and when he does, it is to highlight courtly incompetence: When Prosaites and Cos announce to him that they "are going in quest of a strange fountain lately / found out" by Amorphus, "the great discoverer," Mercury remarks: "Thou hast well entitled him, Cos, for he will discover all he / knows" (2.5.37–40). The ladies and gentlemen who actually attended a Blackfriars performance were put in a position to laugh with the god, and feel superior to courtly inadequacy.[20]

---

[20] Performances of this play in front of courtly ladies and gentlemen certainly constituted some kind of courtly practice: Jonson as author and the child actors of Her Majesty's Chapel mean to tease and provoke courtiers and would-be courtiers in the audience, in order to playfully elicit protest and to emphasize Queen Elizabeth's idea of her court as a seat of virtue. The play can be seen as an early instance of children acting as courtiers; their childlike ways, staged in a "praeludium" in which three boy actors quarrel about who is to speak the prologue (445–452), evidently serve a courtly purpose, that of providing a relaxed environment in which the serious issues of courtly hypocrisy and rivalry can be discussed.

5 Functions of Wordplay in *Alice's Adventures in Wonderland*

As in *Much Ado About Nothing*, one of the outstanding features of wordplay in Lewis Carroll's *Alice's Adventures in Wonderland* is its teasing or provocative function.[21] Wordplay, on the one hand, appears as a narrative strategy of teasing the reader: When the Wonderland creatures, after having had a swim in the pool of Alice's tears, listen to the mouse's "dry" account of English history in order to be made dry (see Carroll [1865 / 1871 / 1876] 1992: 21), the reader is certainly more bewildered than Alice herself, but might be provoked into reflecting on the relationship between the literal and a metaphorical meaning of a word. A similar effect will be reached by the character of the Mock Turtle, according to the Queen of Hearts "the thing Mock Turtle Soup is made from" (73). The reader who suspects that mock turtle soup has other ingredients will be confused,[22] the more so as two illustrations (75, 79) actually show this non-existent species; and provoked into examining the rules of making up composite noun phrases.[23]

On the other hand, wordplay is central to the relationship between Alice and the Wonderland creatures. Unlike the characters in *Much Ado About Nothing*, however, Alice only gradually becomes aware of the ambiguities involved in certain phrases or clauses, and the creatures do not seem to be aware of them at all.[24] It is only the readers who are able to interpret the misunderstandings between Alice and the Wonderland creatures as instances of wordplay. At the beginning of Alice's contacts with the creatures she makes a few social mistakes, such as praising her cat Dinah when speaking to the mouse (18–19), and telling the caterpillar that "three inches is such a wretched height to be" (41).

---

21 Lewis Carroll, incidentally, knew *Much Ado About Nothing* well, as shown by a letter to Ellen Terry, which, characteristically, contains a pun: "Now I'm going to put before you a 'Hero-ic' puzzle of mine [...] My difficulty is this: Why in the world did not Hero (or at any rate Beatrice when speaking on her behalf) prove an 'alibi,' in answer to the charge?" (1979, vol. 1: 489).
22 Readers who know about the 'right' ingredients may enjoy their superiority over Alice, who is apparently taken in by the Queen of Hearts' explanation.
23 Using the example of mock turtle soup, Jean-Jacques Lecercle (1994: 42) remarks that "nonsense only practises what language normally practices. The morphological monsters of false composition are the mirror-images of analytic monsters of folk etymology."
24 We cannot be sure, though. The narrative point of view is restricted to Alice throughout the books; neither Alice nor the reader knows about what goes on in the Wonderland creatures' minds. This uncertainty appears to be a central part of the 'Wonderland experience.'

When listening to the mouse Alice misinterprets it twice: When the mouse announces her "long and sad" *tale*, she understands *tail*, and in her mind the mouse's tale takes the form of a tail, as shown to the reader by means of a graphic, tail-like printing (25). When, however, she remarks that the tale has proceeded to the fifth bend, she is snubbed by the mouse:

> "I had *not*!" cried the Mouse, sharply and very angrily.
> "A knot!" said Alice, always ready to make herself useful, and looking anxiously about her. "Oh, do let me help to undo it!"
> "I shall do nothing of the sort," said the Mouse, getting up and walking away. "You insult me by talking such nonsense!"
>
> (25–26)

The conversation with the caterpillar is not much smoother, but now Alice can to some extent stand her ground. The wordplay found here is based on a conventional conversational phrase that is taken literally. The first one is produced by Alice herself: When the Caterpillar asks: "What do you mean by that? [...] Explain yourself!" she answers: "I ca'n't explain *myself*, I'm afraid, Sir," said Alice, "because I'm not myself, you see." The 'wrong' interpretation of *to explain oneself* may be unintentional but it makes sense and appears rather witty. The caterpillar then flouts conversational rules (and, in turn, takes a conventional phrase literally) by replying: "I don't see" (35). Similarly, when Alice states that "one doesn't like changing so often, you know," he retorts: "I *don't* know" (41). By the time Alice takes part in the Mad Tea Party, she has got the feel of the game (or rather interprets the Mad Hatter's words as part of a game): when the Mad Hatter warns Alice that she knows Time and that you can't waste *it,* she replies that she has "to beat time when I learn music" (56). The Hatter then tells the story of having been accused by the Queen of Hearts of murdering the time, whereupon the Queen said "Off with his head!" (58). The tea party is brought to a close by another flouting of conversational, and linguistic, rules: Alice begins a sentence with the words: "I don't think –" to be interrupted by the Hatter: "Then you shouldn't talk" (60), whereupon Alice "got up in great disgust, and walked off" (60). The ambiguity of "I don't think" could be considered as an instance of grammatical polysemy: there is a play on two meanings of "think," as well as on the opposition of its use in a full sentence and its use as an expression which introduces an object clause. The Mad Hatter's wordplay provokes Alice into keeping her ground and gaining self-confidence.[25]

---

[25] Cf. Angelika Zirker's (2010: 251) suggestion concerning another part of Alice's conversation with the Mad Hatter: "[...] sie nimmt nicht einfach Tee, sondern geht auf seine Aussage ein,

It is in *Through the Looking-Glass*, the sequel to *Alice's Adventures in Wonderland*, that the practice of taking conversational phrases literally assumes a more playful form. When Humpty Dumpty mentions an "un-birthday present," Alice isn't sure she got this correctly: "I beg your pardon?" Humpty Dumpty retorts: "I am not offended" (162). This joke actually corresponds to a courtly one recommended in Castiglione's *Courtier*:

> [...] un d'essi, dapoi che ebbe mangiato tutto un minestro, disse: Signor Marchese, perdonatemi; – e così detto, cominciò a sorbire quel brodo che gli era avanzato. – Allor il Marchese subito disse: Domanda pur perdono ai porci, ché a me non fai tu ingiuria alcuna.
>
> (II.71; [1528] 1910: 250–251)

> [...] one of them after he had eaten up his dish of broth, saide: by your leave my Lorde marquesse. And when he had so saide, he began to suppe up the rest that remained in the dish. Then saide the marquesse by and by: Aske leave of the swine, for thou doest me no wrong at all.
>
> (159)

Both in *The Courtier* and in *Through the Looking-Glass*, the conventional phrase "perdonatemi" / "I beg your pardon" is taken literally by the respective interlocutor; there is a play on the different pragmatic functions an expression can have in different contexts.

After leaving the Mad Hatter's Tea Party Alice is confident enough to endure the game of croquet with the Queen of Hearts and to listen to the Mock Turtle's story. This story contains a series of puns, and now Alice is placed, like the reader, in a consumer's position, in that she is neither the victim nor the inno-

---

womit sie sich schon wie die Bewohner des Wunderlandes verhält: an dieser Stelle ist sie Teil der Welt des Wunderlandes geworden." Jean-Jacques Lecercle (1994: 111) argues that nonsense in the *Alice* books does not just violate Grice's Cooperative Principle but calls into question Geoffrey N. Leech's "Politeness Principle." As Lecercle (1994: 106) points out, the Wonderland creatures' lack of politeness might work cathartically: "On the one hand, nonsense shows us that politeness is a veneer protecting us from the violence of agon which is always threatening to erupt [...]. On the other hand, such exaggerated agon becomes, because of its very exaggeration, innocuous. From the rules of this discursive catastrophe a new linguistic cosmos will soon emerge. Such pervading violence can only have a cathartic effect. We identify with Alice, who still believes in the rules of cooperation, and the pathos of her experience purges our antagonistic passions, so that politeness will appear not as an unattainable ideal, but as a reasonable proposition." I should like to add that the dialectic process traced by Lecercle does not just apply to nonsense as found in the *Alice* books, but also to real-life courtly conversation (as in *Il Cortegiano*). The rules of politeness have to be tested continually, through playful forms of 'agon' (competition), in order not to become rigid and meaningless.

cent perpetrator of punning. As the Mock Turtle explains, his school master was called Tortoise "because he taught us" (75). The pun is based on accidental homophony but poses as an etymology – and certainly provokes reflection in Alice and the reader as to the relationship between sound and meaning. Of course, this false etymology also alludes to the famous philosophical paradox about Achilles' inability ever to catch up with the tortoise – which was taken up by Lewis Carroll later in his dialogue "What the Tortoise Said to Achilles" (1895), in which Achilles is renamed "A Kill-Ease" (1230). The list of subjects given by the Mock Turtle may strike the reader as a crossword puzzle: "Reeling," "Writhing," "Mystery, ancient and modern," "Seaography," "Drawling" (76), can easily be connected to the respective human school subjects. The four "branches of Arithmetic – Ambition, Distraction, Uglification and Derision" continue the puzzle, but at the same time bewilder Alice and the reader with regard to the literal meanings of these four words.

When finally an "old crab" is mentioned who "taught Laughing and Grief," Alice is "in a hurry to change the subject" (77). Why? I suspect that a private joke is at work here. Alice changes the subject because her real-life original, Alice Pleasance Liddell, would have done; Alice Liddell's father, of course, was the eminent Greek scholar Henry George Liddell, co-author of the *Greek-English Dictionary*, and his daughter would have taken pains to deflect any conversation about Greek masters she might have overheard, in order to prevent any embarrassment to the parties concerned. A reference to her father as an "old crab" would have been particularly embarrassing. What I think is striking is that the fictional Alice is confident enough to interrupt the conversation of the Gryphon and the Mock Turtle – just as I think Alice Liddell in real life may have been up to interfere in a conversation of adults if reasons of drawing-room diplomacy required this interference.

The fictional Alice goes on to display her conversational qualities by playing along with another game based on wordplay:

> "And how many hours a day did you do lessons?" said Alice, in a hurry to change the subject.
> "Ten hours the first day," said the Mock Turtle: "nine the next, and so on."
> "What a curious plan!" exclaimed Alice.
> "That's the reason they are called lessons," the Gryphon remarked: "because they lessen from day to day."
> This was quite a new idea to Alice, and she thought it over a little before she made her next remark. "Then the eleventh day must have been a holiday?"
> "Of course it was," said the Mock Turtle.
> "And how did you manage on the twelfth?" Alice went on eagerly.

"That's enough about lessons," the Gryphon interrupted in a very decided tone. "Tell her something about the games now."

(77)

We do not know, of course, if the Gryphon, like Castiglione's courtiers, is deliberately provoking Alice, or if he is dead serious about his etymologies. Alice cannot be sure about this either, but by now she is diplomatic, or courtly, enough not to doubt the etymology which is based on a pun. She develops the idea further until the Gryphon and the Mock Turtle can no longer follow her, and then the Gryphon has to make a diplomatic interruption to introduce a new topic.

Throughout *Alice's Adventures in Wonderland*, wordplay functions as a teaser. While at first Alice as the target of twisted language which can be interpreted as wordplay cannot defend herself, she is increasingly provoked to protest, and finally protest gives way to taking part in a game. In *Much Ado About Nothing* the 'victims' of wordplay react in similar ways: At first the addressee, like the messenger and Claudio, is nonplussed, then he starts to protest. Neither the messenger nor Claudio, however, fully reach the third stage, the acceptance of wordplay as a game to take part in. This is left to experienced courtiers, like Don Pedro, and Benedick and Beatrice themselves. The latter, of course, have also mastered what I would suggest is the fourth stage, i.e. the competence of producing wordplay themselves. This stage Alice never reaches; it is doubtful, though, if the Wonderland creatures do, or if the Wonderland wordplays are to be understood as the author's tricks, or perhaps as tricks produced by Alice's subconscious mind. In both literary works, though, wordplay, somewhat aggressively, provokes the interlocutors into continuing the conversation. By accepting and taking part in this game, the 'targets' or 'victims' of wordplay manage to become part of a courtly, or Wonderland, community.

At Renaissance courts, wordplay was certainly a real-life practice, functioning as a game among well-educated ladies and gentlemen who enjoyed spending time together. Taking part in court life was not pure enjoyment, of course: Often you wished to become acquainted with people who might further your career, help establish a trade connection or furnish you with a partner in marriage. The point was, as expounded at length by Castiglione, that you displayed your qualifications by not being too open about them, and therefore engaged in pastimes which appeared to be quite relaxed. The term used by

Castiglione to describe this attitude is *sprezzatura*, translated by Thomas Hoby as "disgracing" and "recklessness."[26]

I should like to suggest that the world of Alice as well as of the implied readers of the *Alice* books can in a number of ways be compared to the world of Renaissance courts. For one thing, wordplay was certainly practiced a lot by adults who wished to entertain children, in the upper circles of polite society at least, as can be seen, for example, from the letters written by Lewis Carroll to his many little-girl friends.[27] This form of entertaining, like Castiglione's courtliness, involves acts of teasing and provoking the children. A letter written to eleven-year-old Mary MacDonald on 14 November 1864 may serve as an illustration:

> My dear Mary,
> Once upon a time there was a little girl, and she had a cross old Uncle – his neighbours called him a Curmudgeon (whatever that may mean) – and this little girl had promised to copy out for him a sonnet Mr. Rossetti had written about Shakespeare. Well, and she didn't do it, you know: and the poor Uncle's nose kept getting longer and longer, and his temper getting shorter and shorter, and post after post went by, and no sonnet came – I leave off here to explain how they sent letters in those days: there were no gates, so the gate-posts weren't obliged to stay in one place – consequence of which, they went wandering all over the country – consequence of which, if you wanted to send a letter anywhere, all you had to do was to fasten it on to a gate-post that was going in the proper direction (only they sometimes changed their minds, which was awkward). This was called "sending a letter by the post." They did things very simply in those days: if you had a lot of money, you just dug a hole under the hedge, and popped it in: then you said you had "put it in a bank," and you felt quite comfortable about it. And the way they travelled was – there were railings all along the side of the road, and they used to get up, and walk along the top, as steadily as they could, till they tumbled off – which they mostly did very soon. This was called "travelling by rail." Now to return to the wicked little girl. The end of

---

26 In the *Cortegiano* Count Ludovico famously advises courtiers to "usar in ogni cosa una certa sprezzatura, che nasconda l'arte, e dimostri, ciò che si fa e dice, venir fatto senza fatica e quasi senza pensarvi" (I.26; [1528] 1910: 63), "to use in everye thing a certaine disgracing to cover arte withall, and seeme whatsoever he doth and saith, to doe it without paine, and (as it were) not minding it" (46); "Questa virtú adunque contraria alla affettazione, la qual noi par ora chiamiamo sprezzatura [...]" (I.28; 2010: 68), "This vertue therefore contrarie to curiositie, which we for this time terme Recklesnesse [...]" (48). Concerning "favori" (II.19; [1528] 1910: 167), "favor and promotions" (109), Federico Fregoso recommends a modest attitude: "Dee ben l'omo satar sempre un poco più rimesso che non comporta il grado suo" (II.19; [1528] 1910: 167); "Yet ought a man alwaies to humble him selfe somewhat under his degree" (109).
27 As some of their answers show, the recipients were not always sure if Carroll's provocative jokes were to be taken seriously or not. Their position resembles that of Alice who does not know what to make of the Wonderland creatures' remarks.

her was, that a great black WOLF came, and – I don't like to go on, but nothing was found of her afterwards, except 3 small bones.
I make no remark. It is a rather horrid story.
   Your loving friend,
   C. L. Dodgson

(1979, vol. 1: 73–74)

C. L. Dodgson / Lewis Carroll, after inventing fictional counterparts of himself and Mary, the addressee, turns to playing on literal and metaphorical meanings of 'long' / 'short' and then takes the cue from "post" to engage in a series of puns, telling ludicrous stories on false etymologies (based on homonymy or polysemy) of "post," "bank" and "rail." There is an obvious motive for doing so, a courtly one in Castiglione's sense, as it deflects the severity (or 'face-threatening act,' cf. Brown and Levinson 1987: 59–84) inherent in reprimanding Mary for failing to copy the sonnet. Dodgson still makes his appeal but at the same time establishes an easy-going atmosphere, displaying *sprezzatura* or "recklessness."[28]

What matters more, however, is that Victorian upper-class children belonged to the drawing-room and its cultural life to an extraordinary extent. The letter quoted provides an apt example: Dodgson / Carroll makes use of his friendship with an eleven-year-old girl to get hold of a copy of an unpublished poem by one of the leading poets of the day.[29] In the upper classes of society children were taken along on visits, displayed to visitors and entrusted with the task of entertaining them. When Queen Victoria and her family visited Christ Church College on 12 December 1860, it was the Dean's children who had to stage several *tableaux vivants*, which Dodgson / Lewis Carroll, who was present, found "very successful," as he pointed out in a letter to his family:

> Lady Williamson [a cousin of the Dean's, Henry George Liddell] was there, and supplied the costumes, and herself appeared in one scene. One of the prettiest was Tennyson's The Sleeping Princess, acted entirely by the children. The grouping was capital, I believe by

---

28 The puns, of course, are not the only instances of the ludic function of language found in this letter; when Dodgson / Carroll calls his fictional alter ego "a curmudgeon," he not only ironically exaggerates his own greed and unfriendliness, but also provokes Mary into enquiring for the meaning of a rare word (The *OED*, following Johnson, defines "curmudgeon" as "an avaricious churlish fellow, a miser, a niggard"; "curmudgeon" *n.*) and certainly also plays on the phonetic similarity to his own name, Dodgson. Concerning the invalidation or containment of threats through playing in the *Alice* books, cf. Zirker (2010: 353).
29 As Morton N. Cohen points out, the poem by Dante Gabriel Rossetti is obviously "On the Site of a Mulberry-Tree," written in 1853 and printed privately, but not published before 1871 (Carroll 1979, vol. 1: 73n2).

> Lady W. I was sure it could not be by Mrs. Liddell, of whose taste in that line I have already had melancholy experience in my photographs.
>
> (1979, vol. 1: 45)

At this reception and in producing *tableaux vivants*, the Liddell children were obviously acting as diplomats, or courtly entertainers, smoothing the relations between the high-ranking adults present. The Liddell children[30] also took part in the celebration of the wedding of the Prince of Wales to Alexandra, Princess of Denmark, on 10 March 1863, as recorded in Dodgson's diary:

> Afterwards Edwin and I went into the Broad Walk to see the three Deanery children plant three trees along the Cherwell in memory of the day. Each delivered a short speech over her tree "long life to this tree, and may it prosper from this auspicious day," and they named them Alexandra, Albert and Victoria.
>
> (Carroll [1954] 1971, vol. 1: 193)

When on 16 June the Prince and Princess of Wales visited Oxford, the Liddell children conducted a bazaar which was attended by the royal couple.[31]

A more typical instance of the Liddell children's participation in social life seems to be reflected by a diary entry of 16 February 1863 when Dodgson / Carroll was invited to dinner:

> Dined at the Deanery, and met Wall, whom I sat next, and had a good deal of talk with, Pattison, Max Müller etc. The children remained through the whole evening, which was devoted (as there was no music) to games in the gallery.
>
> ([1954] 1971, vol. 1: 192)[32]

We do not know about the effect of this treatment on the children, but we may guess it gave them confidence and helped develop their social skills.[33] Before this level of courtly competence was reached, however, there must have been many setbacks, toils and tears. I should like to propose that the Wonderland of

---

30 The children referred to were Lorina, Alice and Edith Liddell, aged 13, 10 and 8.
31 The Princess actually bought a white kitten from Lorina Liddell, as Alice had obviously been too shy to offer her one (see Carroll [1954] 1971, vol. 1: 198); cf. Anne Clark (1981: 83–84).
32 On the social life of the Liddell family cf. Clark (1981: 96–97, 120–122, 131 *et passim*). Cf. also Max Müller's remark: "The Deanery of Christ Church [...] under Dr. Liddell, with his charming wife and daughters, became a social centre not easily rivalled anywhere. There one met not only royalty, the young Prince of Wales, but many eminent writers, artists, and political men from London, Gladstone, Disraeli, Richmond, Ruskin, and many others" (Müller 1901: 258).
33 It may also have made them conceited and class-conscious. On Alice P. Liddell's adult life, cf. Cohen (1995: 522).

the *Alice* books in some way mirrors what polite, adult society must have looked like to a child like Alice: To children, adult society may have appeared as cruel and unpredictable; but it would gradually lose its threatening quality and might even become the object of ridicule.[34] Wordplay thus functions as a metaphor for the challenges the adult talk of the drawing-room must have presented, just as wordplay in *Much Ado About Nothing* might be said to be a correlative to the intricacies of the relationship of Benedick and Beatrice, and, to the outsider, of court life in general. In mastering these challenges Alice becomes an accomplished member of drawing-room society, in other words, an accomplished courtier. Part of her skill will have consisted in making propositions sharp enough to provoke interlocutors to answer back, but not sharp enough to cause offence. As at Renaissance courts, metalinguistic awareness and ludic, or provocative, competence, as displayed by a mastery of words and of wordplay, allow initiates to keep their ground in a community whose internal rules are terrifyingly complex.

6 References

Bauer, Matthias. 2010. Eating Words: Some Notes on a Metaphor and Its Use in *Much Ado About Nothing*. In Marion Gymnich & Norbert Lennartz (eds.), *The Pleasures and Horrors of Eating: The Cultural History of Eating in Anglophone Literature*, 45–58. Göttingen: Bonn University Press.

Berger, Harry, Jr. 2000. *The Absence of Grace: Sprezzatura and Suspicion in Two Renaissance Courtesy Books*. Stanford, CA: Stanford University Press.

Brown, Penelope & Stephen C. Levinson. [1978] 1987. *Politeness: Some Universals in Language Usage*. Cambridge: Cambridge University Press.

Carroll, Lewis. [1954] 1971. *The Diaries of Lewis Carroll*. Roger Lancelyn Green (ed.), 2 vols. Westport, CT: Greenwood Press.

Carroll, Lewis. [1895] 1976. What the Tortoise Said to Achilles. In Alexander Woolcott (ed.), *The Complete Works*, 1225–1230. New York: Vintage.

Carroll, Lewis. 1979. *The Letters of Lewis Carroll*. Morton N. Cohen (ed.), 2 vols. London: Macmillan.

Carroll, Lewis. [1865 / 1871 / 1876] 1992. *Alice in Wonderland*. Donald J. Gray (ed.). New York: Norton.

Castiglione, Count Baldassare. [1561] 1900. *The Courtyer of Count Baldessar Castillio Divided into Foure Bookes: Very Necessary and Profitable for Yonge Gentilmen and Gentilwomen*

---

[34] Morton N. Cohen (1995: 94) suggests that many characters and motifs of *Through the Looking-Glass* refer to Alice's experiences of the royal wedding and other incidents of Oxford social life.

Abiding in Court, Palaice or Place, Done into Englyshe by Thomas Hoby. Walter Raleigh (ed.). London: David Nutt. https://scholarsbank.uoregon.edu/xmlui/bitstream/handle/1794/671/courtier.pdf (17 July 2015).

Castiglione, Conte Baldesar. [1528] 1910. Il cortegiano. Vittorio Cian (ed.). Firenze: Sansoni.

Castiglione, Count Baldassare. [1561] 1966. The Book of the Courtier. Trans. Sir Thomas Hoby. London: Dent.

Clark, Anne. 1981. The Real Alice: Lewis Carroll's Dream Child. London: Michael Joseph.

Cohen, Morton N. 1995. Lewis Carroll: A Biography. London: Macmillan.

Culler, Jonathan. 1988. The Call of the Phoneme. In Jonathan Culler (ed.), On Puns: The Foundation of Letters, 1-16. Oxford: Blackwell.

De Grazia, Margreta. 2001. Shakespeare and the Craft of Language. In Margreta de Grazia & Stanley Wells (eds.), The Cambridge Companion to Shakespeare, 49–64. Cambridge: Cambridge University Press.

Elam, Keir. 1984. Shakespeare's Universe of Discourse: Language Games in the Comedies. Cambridge: Cambridge University Press.

Grice, H. Paul. 1975. Logic and Conversation. In Peter Cole & Jerry L. Morgan (eds.), Speech Acts, 41–58. New York: Academic Press.

Jakobson, Roman. 1981. Linguistics and Poetics. In Selected Writings: Poetry of Grammar and Grammar of Poetry 3. 18–51. The Hague: Mouton.

Jonson, Ben. [1601] 2012. Cynthia's Revels: Quarto Version. In Eric Rasmussen, Matthew Steggle (eds.), The Cambridge Edition of the Works of Ben Jonson 1. 429–547. Cambridge: Cambridge University Press.

Kohl, Norbert. 1966. Das Wortspiel in der Shakespeareschen Komödie: Studien zur Interdependenz von verbalem und aktionalem Spiel in den frühen Komödien und den späten Stücken. Frankfurt a. M.: Goethe University Frankfurt dissertation.

Lecercle, Jean-Jacques. 1994. Philosophy of Nonsense: The Intuitions of Victorian Nonsense Literature. London: Routledge.

Leech, Geoffrey N. 1969. A Linguistic Guide to English Poetry. Harlow: Longmans.

Mahood, Molly. [1957] 1968. Shakespeare's Wordplay. New York: Methuen.

Mahood, Molly. 1996 / 97. "Shakespeare's Wordplay–Some Reappraisals": A Reply, Connotations 6 (2). 135–137.

Maitland, Julia. [1843] 2004. Letters from Madras: During the Years 1836–1839. Alyson Price (ed.). New Delhi: Oxford University Press.

Müller, F. Max. 1901. My Autobiography: A Fragment. London: Longmans, Green, and Co.

Müller, Wolfgang G. 1996. Drei Formen des Wortspiels bei Shakespeare: Paronomasie, Paronymie, Polyptoton. In Clausdirk Pollner, Helmut Rohlfing & Frank-Rutger Hausmann (eds.), Bright is the Ring of Words: Festschrift für Horst Weinstock zum 65. Geburtstag, 205–224. Bonn: Romanistischer Verlag.

Oxford English Dictionary, 2nd edn. 2014. http://www.oed.com (17 July 2015).

Schlauch, Margaret. 1987. The Social Background of Shakespeare's Malapropisms. In Vivian Salmon & Edwina Burness (eds.), A Reader in the Language of Shakespearean Drama, 71–99. Amsterdam: John Benjamins.

Shakespeare, William. [c. 1599] 2001. King Henry V. T. W. Craik (ed.). London: Thomson Learning.

Shakespeare, William. [1600] 2007. Much Ado About Nothing. Claire McEachern (ed.). London: Methuen.

Sidney, Sir Philip. [1580 / 1912] 1999. *The Countess of Pembroke's Arcadia (The Old Arcadia)*. Katherine Duncan-Jones (ed.). Oxford: Oxford University Press.

Spenser, Edmund. [1590, 1596] 1978. *The Faerie Queene*. Thomas P. Roche & C. Patrick O'Donnell (eds.). Harmondsworth: Penguin.

Zirker, Angelika. 2010. *Der Pilger als Kind: Spiel, Sprache und Erlösung in Lewis Carrolls Alice-Büchern*. Münster: LIT.

Maik Goth
Double Entendre in Restoration and Early Eighteenth-Century Comedy

Abstract: This article reassesses the notion of *double entendre* by placing it at the intersection of dramatic text, theatrical performance and contemporary criticism in the seventeenth and eighteenth centuries. The first part discusses the theory of *double entendre*, providing a definition that elaborates on the structural properties of *double entendre* and its dependence on speaker-hearer interaction in the theatre. Identifying *double entendre* as a play on the two related senses of a word or phrase, this section proposes a taxonomy that distinguishes four basic types: the first correlates two lexicalised meanings of a phrase with one another; the second adds a metaphorical to a literal meaning; the third literalises a metaphor; the fourth supplements a phrase with a further metonymic sense. The theory section then assesses theatrical *double entendre* in terms of speaker-hearer interaction as speaker-induced and hearer-induced wordplay, and places it at the intersection of the internal communication between the characters on stage, and the external communication between the playwrights and their audiences. The second part elaborates on the interplay between these structural and interactional categories by providing functional analyses of *double entendres* in Wycherley's *The Country Wife* (1675) and in Steele's *The Funeral* (1701 / 1702). Both plays point to a significant interactional feature of *double entendre*: they deploy innocuous terms to discuss social taboos. In *The Country Wife*, the taboo is illicit sex; in *The Funeral*, the taboo is the cynical attitude to death and money. These examples illustrate that *double entendre*, constantly reappropriated after the *Interregnum*, joins different comic modes with one another.

Keywords: double entendre, Jeremy Collier, pun, Richard Steele, speaker-hearer interaction, Thomas Durfey, Thomas Shadwell, William Congreve, William Wycherley, wordplay in drama

1 Introduction*

Eighteenth-century collections of conundrums relied on funny and irreverent wordplay, as this cheeky question demonstrates: "Why is a Fart like a double Entendre?" The answer has more than a whiff of truth about it: "Because it is taken in two Senses."[1] This mephitic jape about *double entendre* plays with the double meaning of the word *sense*. On one level, the noun refers to the two types of sense perception involved by the release of gastric gases, namely hearing and smelling. On another, the expression *two senses* explains that this particular *double entendre* consists in a word or phrase that comprises two meanings.[2] The riddle is hence not only in itself a *double entendre* but also a reflection on the nature of this particular kind of wordplay.

Although *double entendre* was popular in post-Renaissance comedy, it remains an underspecified phenomenon in literary criticism, often confused with other types of wordplay and predominantly seen as obscene.[3] In order to correct these entrenched views, I aim to reassess *double entendre* in the seventeenth and the eighteenth centuries by placing it at the intersection of dramatic text, theatrical performance, and contemporary criticism.[4] My article serves a dual purpose, combining (1) a definition and typology of *double entendre* that elaborates on its structural properties and its dependence on speaker-hearer interaction with (2) a functional analysis of bawdy *double entendre* in William Wycherley's *The Country Wife* (1675) and of satirical *double entendre* in Sir Richard Steele's *The Funeral: or, Grief a-la-Mode* (1701 / 1702). These readings demonstrate that such wordplay is not necessarily bawdy or restricted to the generic conventions of late-seventeenth century comedy and farce, but can also be adapted to non-bawdy and satirical contexts.

---

* I would like to thank Burkhard Niederhoff, Lena Linne and the anonymous reviewers of the article for their insightful critical comments, and Michelle Lecolle for the French translation of my English abstract. This article is for my parents, whose infectious humour inspired my interest in wordplay.
1 The conundrum and its solution were published separately in *The Puzzle* (1745: 3) and in *The Nutt's Crack'd* (1745: 3).
2 See *Oxford English Dictionary* (2014): "sense" n. I. and III.
3 For unspecific usage and the reduction of *double entendre* to the sexual, see e.g. Fujimura (1952: 35); Cecil (1966); as well as Hughes and Hammond (1978).
4 Kabatek's article in this volume also treats wordplay and discourse traditions in a specific social, cultural and historical context.

2 Definition and Typology

2.1 Playing with Sound vs. Playing with Sense

As the conundrum explains, *double entendre* is a word or phrase with two meanings. This double meaning does not consist in the phonetic identity or similarity between words, as in homophonic or homoeophonic wordplay and paranomasia, but in polysemy or in the combination of a literal with a figurative meaning.[5] I will demonstrate this distinction by providing brief examples of the phonetic pun and the *double entendre*.

A famous instance of the phonetic pun features in Shakespeare's comedy *As You Like It* ([1623] 1975) when Jacques recounts his first meeting with the jester Touchstone in the Forest of Arden. Drawing a watch from his pocket, Touchstone seemingly expounds at great and boring length on the passage of time in human lives:

> "It is ten o'clock.
> Thus we may see," quoth he, "how the world wags:
> 'Tis but an hour ago since it was nine,
> And after one hour more 'twill be eleven;
> And so from hour to hour we ripe, and ripe,
> And then from hour to hour we rot, and rot,
> And thereby hangs a tale."
>
> ([1623] 1975: 2.7.22–28)

Despite its apparent triteness, Jacques finds the passage nothing short of hilarious: "I did laugh, sans intermission, / An hour by his dial" (2.7.32–33). Touchstone's jest lies in his playing with sound, because, in Elizabethan pronunciation, the words *hour*, *rot* and *tale* sounded similar to *whore*, *rut*, and *tail*.[6] Hence, what appears to be a dull statement on the transitory nature of human life is in fact also a narrative about prostitutes, sexual excitement, and male genitalia. The relation between both meanings is purely coincidental, as it lies in the fortuitous phonetic similarity of unconnected words.

---

5 On the distinction between puns, polysemous wordplay and equivoce, see Niederhoff (2001: 99–101). Plett (2010: 175–179) differentiates between polysemic, homonymic, homophonic, and homoeophonic types of wordplay. The distinction between playing with sense ("Sprachspiel") and playing with sound ("Klangspiel") is put forward by Grassegger (1985); see also Delabastita (1997: 5). Winter-Froemel (2009) offers an exhaustive typology of wordplay.
6 See Kökeritz (1953: 57–59), and Delabastita (2011: 155).

Double entendre plays with the different senses of words and phrases. In Wycherley's *The Country Wife* ([1675] 1979), Mr Pinchwife visits London with his young and inexperienced wife Margery, the country wife of the title. Seeking to conceal her from the corrupting influence of the young rakes Horner, Harcourt and Dorilant, he pretends she is not with him: "She's too auker'd, ill favour'd, and silly to bring to town." Harcourt uses Pinchwife's suspiciously evasive remarks against him, replying that "you should bring her, to be taught / breeding" (1.1.360–362). The wittiness of this reply lies in Harcourt's playing with different senses of the word *breeding*. On one level, it refers to the refined manners of polite London society: as Mrs Pinchwife lacks such refinement, she can learn it in the city. On another level, Harcourt's response carries a sexual meaning: as breeding is another word for conceiving a child, Harcourt hints at the wife's possibilities of engaging in the adulterous liaisons of London society. Both senses of the word *breeding* are here connected through different lexicalised meanings.[7]

Phonetic wordplay and *double entendre* were judged very differently in Restoration and eighteenth-century comedy. The sound-based pun, although a favourite in Renaissance drama, met with universal criticism.[8] In Thomas Shadwell's *Bury Fair* (1689), e.g., the punster Mr. Oldwit is ridiculed as "a paltry Old-fashion'd Wit, and Punner of the last Age" (Shadwell 1927, vol. 4: 300). The *double entendre*, however, remained a token of wit and hence a part of comic writing, because its two meanings are closely related.[9] Accordingly, seventeenth- and eighteenth-century criticism distinguished acutely between playing with sound and playing with sense. A trenchant contemporary definition of *double entendre* features in *The Centinel* (1758, vol. 1: 210), a periodical of literary essays and journalistic articles. One anonymous contributor praises *double entendre* as a French specialty, and criticises his fellow Englishmen for their inability to create proper *double entendres*: "we degenerate double entendre into pun." While the former "never infringes upon grammar or spelling," the latter "always [infringes] upon one, sometimes both."[10] The author, echoing contemporary sentiments, here expresses his admiration for wordplay involving

---

7 See *OED* (2014): "breeding" *n.* 4 and 1.
8 For a comprehensive survey, see Niederhoff (2001: 95–97), especially his list of contemporary remarks against such puns (97n25).
9 See Niederhoff (2001: 101).
10 *The Centinel* was a journal that ran at 140 issues throughout 1757; the essay discussed here was first published on August 30th, 1757, in No. 45 (1758, vol. 1: 208–212). The author's critique prefigures Leech's notion of the asyntactic pun (1969: 211). On the latter see also Bross, this volume.

polysemous and figurative expressions that keep the syntax of a statement intact, while at the same time scolding puns, often dubbed jingles, as vacuous and puerile.[11] This definition also elicits significant questions about the exact workings of *double entendre*: what connects the two levels of meaning with one another? And how does *double entendre* work in the speaker-hearer interaction of a theatrical performance?

2.2 A Typology of *Double Entendre*

An examination of the structural properties of *double entendre* helps specify the different rhetorical relations between the two meanings.[12] *Double entendre* can (1) be polysemous and consist in correlating two lexicalised meanings of a word or phrase with one another. Additionally, *double entendre* can be figurative,[13] and (2) add a metaphorical to a literal meaning, (3) literalise a metaphor, or (4) supplement a phrase with a further metonymic significance. In type (1), the additional sense already exists in the lexicon, whereas in types (2) and (4), the second, figurative sense only arises in the context of an utterance. Type (3) is a special case, because literalisation often depends on reactivating a dead and hence lexicalised metaphor in a specific situation.

POLYSEMIC *DOUBLE ENTENDRE*

The first type of *double entendre* plays with related lexicalised meanings of the same word. Such wordplay occurs when Valentine, Tattle and Scandal discuss women in the first act of William Congreve's *Love for Love*:

> TATTLE. Upon my Soul, *Angelica's* a fine Woman—
> and so is Mrs. *Foresight*, and her Sister Mrs. *Frail*.
> SCANDEL [sic!]. Yes, Mrs. *Frail* is a very fine Woman; we all know her.
>
> ([1695] 1982: 1.1.490–493)

---

11 Cecil (1966) demonstrates the distinction between both kinds of wordplay. Cf., among others, John Dryden's devaluation of "the gingle of a [...] poor *Paranomasia*" (in a letter prefaced to the poem *Annus Mirabilis: The Year of Wonders, 1666*; see Dryden 1956: 53). Samuel Butler called puns "Tricks with words of the Same Sound, but different Senses" (cited in Niederhoff 2001: 98). Other derogatory terms for puns were *clench* and *quibble* (for examples, see Niederhoff 2001: 97n25).
12 My typology is an elaboration of Niederhoff (2001: 99–101).
13 In the late seventeenth century, French critic François de Callières described *double entendre* as the witty combination between the literal and the figurative sense of a word (*Des bon mots et des bons contes* [1692], cited in Cecil 1966: 575).

What begins as a praise of the play's female characters quickly turns into bawdy wordplay revolving around the different meanings of the verb *to know*. The first is the standard meaning of the verb, 'to be acquainted with'; the second is the biblical sense, 'to have sex with.'[14] Scandal thus effectively identifies Mrs. Frail as a woman of loose sexual morals. Playwrights had at their disposal an arsenal of such well-established semantic *double entendres*. For instance, the noun *will* can refer to preference or wish, as well as to sexual lust[15]; the word *breeding* has a social sense ('the manners appropriate for polite society') as well as a sexual one ('conceiving a child')[16]; and the adjective *frank* means 'sincere' or 'unreserved,' and 'generously trusting' (hence: gullible).[17]

Figurative *Double Entendre*: Metaphor

The second type of *double entendre* combines the literal with the metaphorical sense of a word or phrase. An effective example of metaphorical *double entendre* features in Thomas Durfey's *A Fond Husband; or, The Plotting Sisters* (1677). Peregrine Bubble, the credulous husband of the title, tells the libertine Rashley that his wife Emilia is angry because "you promised to give her a squirrel that night, and never / kept your word, and she loves squirrels passionately" (2.2.81–82).[18] What the gullible husband understands as a reprimand for Rashley's forgetting to present his wife with a fashionable gift is in fact bawdy wordplay: Emilia employed the squirrel as a metaphor of the phallus, and hence of sexual intercourse.[19] Unlike Bubble, Rashley disambiguates the phrase correctly as Emilia's censure for an unsuccessful sexual encounter.[20] *Double entendre* is here employed as a secret code about whose true meaning the messenger himself

---

14 See *OED* (2014): "know" v. II.6. and II.8. Words describing acquaintance, familiarity, and knowing are often used as material for bawdy *double entendre*.
15 See William Congreve, *The Way of the World* ([1700] 1982: 4.1.180–184), and Niederhoff (2001: 99).
16 See the example from *The Country Wife* (1.1.360–362), discussed above.
17 See Wycherley, *The Country Wife* (3.2.327–330), and Dixon's commentary *ad loc.* in Wycherley (1996), where the passage covers 3.2.328–330.
18 For the text see Fisk (2005) and her commentary *ad loc.*
19 The relation between phallus and sexual intercourse depends on contiguity, and is hence metonymic.
20 See also Rashley's reply: "I was disappointed utterly of my squirrel that night myself, / for I got very drunk, and from thence sprung this fatal consequence" (2.2.84–85).

remains oblivious. Other instances of metaphorical *double entendre* feature in Congreve's *Love for Love*, where Mr. Foresight's obsession with astrology elicits bawdy wordplay. In the third act, the rake Scandal makes sly advances to Mrs. Foresight in the presence of her husband, while ostentatiously discussing astrological phenomena with Mr. Foresight: "and I / hope *Mars* and *Venus* will be in Conjunction—while / your Wife and I are together" (3.1.709–711). Scandal's utterance comprises three meanings: the astrological, the allegorical (Mars and Venus as gods), and the contextual (Mars and Venus as the speaker and his wife). That Mr. Foresight does not detect Scandal's blatantly obvious sexual innuendo makes the hapless husband the butt of the joke.

FIGURATIVE *DOUBLE ENTENDRE*: LITERALISATION

Type three of the *double entendre* reduces the figural use of a term to the literal. In an early scene from George Farquhar's *The Recruiting Officer* ([1706] 1976), Melinda, a Shropshire Lady of Fortune, and her maid Lucy bicker about Silvia, who is infatuated with Captain Plume, right after she has left the stage:

> MELINDA. Did you not see the proud nothing, how she swells upon
> the arrival of her fellow?
> LUCY. Her fellow has not been long enough arrived to occasion any
> great swelling, madam. I don't believe she has seen him yet.
>
> (1976: 1.2.95–98)

Melinda first uses the verb *to swell* as part of the collocation *to swell with pride* in order to reprimand Silvia for her display of excessive arrogance. Acting with the cheek and garrulousness of the typical maid, Lucy instantaneously picks up the idea of swelling and converts it into bawdy wordplay, which consists in remotivating a dead metaphor[21]: Silvia would literally swell by becoming pregnant after sleeping with Captain Plume.[22] Lucy's snide remark not only adds further insult through the use of wordplay; it also serves a social purpose: by using *double entendre* she supports Melinda's misgivings, and thus strengthens her bond with her superior.

---

[21] On remotivation see Käge (1980: 93).
[22] There is an additional metonymic quality to this *double entendre*, because Lucy alters the reason for Silvia's swelling: not pride but sexual intercourse would make Silvia's body tumescent.

FIGURATIVE *DOUBLE ENTENDRE*: METONYMY

The fourth type is the metonymic *double entendre*, in which both meanings are linked by contiguity, e.g. by cause and effect. Niederhoff (2001: 100) identifies a trenchant example of metonymic wordplay in Act 3, Scene 1 of Congreve's *Love for Love*. In a passage rife with sexual innuendo, Scandal tries to talk Mr. Foresight into believing that he suffers from ill health, while making advances to his wife. In order to communicate her sexual readiness, and to arrange an assignation with Scandal without her husband taking notice, Mrs. Foresight uses a seemingly innocuous statement: "I cannot say that he [Mr. Foresight] has once broken / my Rest, since we have been Married" (3.1.674–675). Mr. Foresight understands his wife's remark literally, i.e. as a comment about his deep and sound sleep. Scandal, however, disambiguates the phrase "broken my rest" as an invitation to sexual intercourse: as Mr. Foresight sleeps all the time and thus does not satisfy his wife's sexual needs, Scandal can have a clandestine affair with the oversexed Mrs. Foresight without her husband's awareness. As Niederhoff conclusively explains, this second sense is connected to the first by way of metonymy: adultery is here the effect elicited by Mr. Foresight's sound sleep. Metonymic wordplay does not only lie in changing the consequence, but also the cause of a statement or action. In Steele's *The Lying Lover* (1705), Young Bookwit seeks to circumvent his father's marriage designs by pretending to join the army, and claims that "Honour calls me to the Field, / where I may perpetuate your Name by some brave Exploit!" Old Bookwit, intent on having an heir to continue his lineage, picks up the idea of continuing one's name and changes the reason from battlefield glory to fathering a child: "You may do it much better, *Tom*, at home by a brave / Boy" (Steele 1971: 2.2.49–52).

2.3 Theatrical *Double Entendre* in Speaker-Hearer Interaction

While the typology of *double entendre* helps clarify its structural properties, it does not account for its exact workings in theatrical communication. As *double entendre* is intricately linked to what is going on between groups of speakers and hearers, it is imperative to analyse such wordplay in terms of speaker-hearer interaction, an approach that has been used by Winter-Froemel and Zirker in an insightful article on ambiguity (2010). Taking my cue from their work, I seek to clarify how *double entendre* works in the context of theatrical interaction, which involves playwright, play text, actors, and audience in a complex communicative process.

In general terms, every *double entendre* consists in an ambiguous utterance made in the context of speaker-hearer interaction.[23] This circumstance suggests various possible relations between the speaker and the hearer of this message, which depend on the different constellations of ambiguity and deliberation:

(1) The speaker creates a *double entendre* which the hearer deciphers.
(2) The speaker creates a *double entendre* which the hearer does not decipher.
(3) The speaker does not utter a *double entendre*, but the hearer unwittingly understands it as such.
(4) The speaker does not utter a *double entendre*, but the hearer deliberately reinterprets it as such.

Items (1) and (2) constitute speaker-induced *double entendre*, whereas items (3) and (4) exemplify hearer-induced *double entendre*. Linked to this is the question of the intentionality of wordplay. In items (1) and (2), the speaker intends to utter a *double entendre*, in items (3) and (4) he does not. An utterance leading to hearer-induced wordplay (types 3 and 4) can either be completely innocuous or unintentionally ambiguous.[24]

The constellations of speaker-hearer interaction sketched here are rendered more complicated in the theatre, because *double entendre* is placed at the intersection of the internal communication between the characters on stage, and the external communication between the playwright and his audience.[25] On the internal level, successful speaker-induced wordplay forefronts the speaker's intellectual supremacy, because he delivers an encoded message requiring interpretation by the hearer (as in Scandal's sly use of the verb *to know* as a reference to sexual intercourse). Similarly, hearer-induced wordplay underscores the hearer's verbal dexterity, when the *double entendre* depends on his creative ability to generate unexpected and surprising disambiguations for an

---

23 See also the research programme of the *Graduiertenkolleg Ambiguität: Produktion und Rezeption*, Tübingen University.
24 The distinction between speaker-induced and hearer-induced *double entendre* can also be explained by resorting to the terminology of structural linguistics: as Hausmann (1974: 16–19) and Delabastita (1996: 128) explain, wordplay can function either on the vertical axis (paradigmatic) or on the horizontal axis (syntagmatic). Accordingly, in a vertical *double entendre*, one word or phrase contains two or more meanings simultaneously, whereas in a horizontal *double entendre*, an innocuous phrase is repeated, and a second level of meaning added to the first.
25 On performative aspects of *double entendre* see Styan (1986: 201–203).

unequivocal speech act (cf. Lucy's cheeky repartee on *swelling*). It can also stress a hearer's narrow-mindedness when he sees a *double entendre* where there is none. Matters are complicated in instances where different hearers in the character configuration of a particular scene react (or are supposed to react) differently to an ambiguous utterance (as in Mrs. Foresight's metonymic *double entendre*). On the external level, the playwright uses *double entendre* deliberately as an ambiguous phrase that has to be recognised and solved by the playgoers or readers in the process of interpretation. In this respect, wordplay serves to characterise the *dramatis personae* and their relations, and allows for value judgements about the characters' verbal and intellectual abilities. It is hence on the external level of communication that comedy is created.

An effective example of how *double entendre* exploits the various possibilities of theatrical communication features in Thomas Durfey's *The Modern Prophets: or, New Wit for a Husband* (1709). At the beginning of the second act, Zekiel Magus, a fake prophet, praises his daughter Fidelia's good character to Lord Noble's steward Solid.

> MAGUS. Yet, tho' I have [...] withdrawn my self from the World and its Vanities, my Daughter's Youth may a while divert with it; she has not yet had a Call—from the World: She's my Cashire Friend, apply thy Master's Occasions to her, she's ready always; she has wherewith to satisfy him.
> SOLID. O Lord! I don't doubt it in the least, Sir, and most incomparably too. Madam, *voulez vous plaire*—
> FIDELIA. He understands *French* too, and laughs at my Father's last Speech by way of *double Entendre*.
>
> (1709: 16–17)

The sequence revolves around Magus's ambiguous recommendation of his daughter's qualities, "she's ready always; she has wherewith to satisfy him," which Solid seems to endorse as well. However, Solid's reply is not as innocuous as it seems. In an aside, Magus's quick-witted daughter Fidelia identifies it correctly as a covert *double entendre*. This demonstrates that hearer-induced wordplay was well established as one variety of *double entendre* during the Restoration: the steward has disambiguated Magus's praise of Fidelia as a reference to her sexual readiness, and reinterpreted the verb *to satisfy* as the gratification of carnal appetite. Fidelia also reveals Solid's conversational aim: he attempted to ridicule her father without his noticing ("laughs at my Father's last Speech"). In the internal communicative situation, Solid thus forefronts *double entendre* in order to establish his superiority over Magus, while Fidelia's metadiscursive aside demonstrates her ability to detect Solid's insult. On the external level of communication, her comment creates an alliance between her and the audience, while the audience laughs at Magus, whose choice of words leads to hearer-induced wordplay. That Magus is an impostor playing the part of an unworldly prophet adds a further ironic level to the use of *double entendre*: using what appears to be unintentional wordplay is here part of role-playing and make-believe.

In the following sections, I will demonstrate in detail how exactly the structural and interactional properties outlined above work in Restoration and eighteenth-century comedy. I will first analyse the china scene in William Wycherley's *The Country Wife* as perhaps the most famous example of bawdy *double entendre*, and will then examine the thematic use of satirical *double entendre* in Richard Steele's *The Funeral* in order to demonstrate that *double entendre* is not always bawdy.

3 Bawdy *Double Entendre*: William Wycherley's *The Country Wife* (1675)

The Country Wife (1675) is in many ways the quintessential Restoration comedy. Staged fifteen years after the Restoration of the monarchy and the reopening of the theatres in 1660 (they were closed by the Puritans in 1642), the comedy deals with amorous and sexual relations such as courtship, marriage and adultery, as well as with social and moral issues such as affectation.[26] Due to its blend of wit, humour and libertinism so characteristic of Restoration comedy, *The Country Wife* also offers a rich and diverse array of *double entendres*. The play revolves around the rake Horner, a libertine who resorts to elaborate and preposterous trickery to engage in sexual liaisons with the married "ladies of quality": he disseminates the rumour that the medical treatment of a venereal disease has rendered him impotent. As the ladies' husbands now deem him incapable of performing sexual intercourse, they will not see him as a risk for their wives' marital fidelity – and thus give him free entrance to their spouses. I will examine the notorious china scene (*The Country Wife*; Wycherley 1979: 4.3) in order to illustrate the complex interplay between speaker- and hearer-induced *double entendre*, paying particular attention to *double entendre* as a significant part of theatrical conversation and as a means to battle for social power.

---

[26] See Corman (2000) on Restoration comedy; and Novak (2001) on libertinism.

In the raunchy and farcical china scene, Lady Fidget, who is married to the dunce Sir Jaspar, has a clandestine meeting with the rake Horner, whose telling name refers to his putting horns on the heads of husbands. Just when she is about to commit adultery with him, Sir Jaspar turns up at Horner's lodging, asking his wife why she is not at the china house buying porcelain.[27] Making a virtue of necessity, Lady Fidget resorts to verbal trickery. Horner, she explains to her husband, "knows China very well, and / has himself very good, but will not let me see it, lest I should beg / some" (4.3.102–104). What sounds uncompromising to Sir Jaspar is in fact an example of improvised, hearer-induced *double entendre*: Lady Fidget quick-wittedly converts the term china into a metaphor of sex (and, particularly, the phallus) in order to communicate her desires to Horner and to lead him to the adjacent room where they can consummate sex. *Double entendre* here works on different levels of theatrical communication. In the internal communication system of the play, Lady Fidget creates ambiguity by assigning *china* a second meaning, which her lover understands correctly as a covert invitation to sexual intercourse.[28] The discontinuity between china and sex elicits comic responses: whereas china epitomises clean artificiality and cultural vogues, sexual intercourse evokes associations of the primal and dirty.[29] As a representative of the witless or fool, Sir Jaspar understands the word in its literal sense, and is excluded from the alliance between Lady Fidget and Horner, who rises to the occasion. The success of wordplay on the level of internal communication hence depends on a combination of interactional constellations (1) and (2): whereas the hearer understanding the *double entendre* (type 1) enters into a bond with the speaker, the hearer who does not decipher the wordplay (type 2) is excluded from this group. In the external communication system of the play, Wycherley uses this *double entendre* to make the audience fraternise with the adulterers against the cuckolded husband.[30] The audience thus sides with the wits and the author against the witless characters.[31]

---

27 On the role of china in this famous scene, see Jenkins (2013: 81–83).
28 On the deliberate use of ambiguity in speaker-hearer interaction, see Winter-Froemel and Zirker (2010: 84–86).
29 Alexander Leggatt underscores that "[t]he wit of such passages depends on claiming similarity where there is really difference" (1998: 22). Elizabeth Kowaleski Wallace (1997: 56) notes that the hardness of china "makes it an appropriate phallic image."
30 On Sir Jaspar's relation to language, see Thompson (1984: 83).
31 For a similar communicative situation see George Farquhar, *The Beaux' Stratagem*, 4.1.68–101 (Farquhar 1988, vol. 2). When the rogue Aimwell pretends to swoon, Archer, who poses as his servant, uses a series of metaphorical *double entendres* based on the word *fit* (4.1.81–83) in

This remains so when Sir Jaspar is left alone onstage, and addresses his wife offstage. Indeed, so witless is Sir Jaspar that he unintentionally adds insult to his own injury when warning her laughingly that the rake "is coming into you the / back way" to "catch you, and use you roughly" (4.3.125–128): entirely unaware of the true goings-on, Sir Jaspar uses phrases that in the physical context of adulterous intercourse become *double entendres* the playwright directs at the audience at the expense of the cuckolded husband.[32] The first, the warning that Horner "is coming into you the back way," is a metaphorical *double entendre*.[33] On the literal level, it refers to entering a room through the backdoor. The audience, knowing Horner's intentions only too well, will understand it metaphorically as a reference to sexual intercourse *a tergo*.[34] The second, the exclamation "catch you, and use you roughly," works similarly. While Sir Jaspar here warns his wife about Horner's violent attempts at retrieving his precious china, the audience will relate this to Horner's lustful behaviour during sexual intercourse. That Lady Fidget answers "Let him come, and welcome, which way he will" (4.3.127) shows that she disambiguates her husband's unwitting *double entendre* according to her own physical context, and exposes her husband to further ridicule.[35] One can thus argue that Wycherley combines two interactional situations in one wordplay: on the internal level, the *double entendre* is hearer-induced, because Lady Fidget adds a sexual meaning to her husband's utterance (type 4); on the external level, Wycherley deliberately creates a *double entendre* and uses Sir Jaspar as a mouthpiece to communicate it to his audience (type 1).

The play on double senses in the china scene becomes progressively farcical when Mrs. Squeamish, one of Horner's other mistresses, enters the scene,[36] and likewise desires intercourse with him. When the adulterers return, with Lady Fidget carrying a piece of china as a trophy and visual representation of consummated sex, the women combat over Horner[37]:

---

order to communicate his master's sexual availability to Mrs Sullen past Lady Bountiful. See Styan (1986: 203, 234); Niederhoff (2001: 100).
32 *Physical context* is a term used in pragmatics to describe the physical environment in which an utterance is made (see Cummings 2012: 306; Robinson 2006: 115).
33 Other editions favour "is coming in to you the back way" (e.g. Dixon in Wycherley 1996).
34 See Adamson (2000: 612).
35 Adamson (2000: 612) discusses this passage with reference to Locke, who claimed that if there "is no natural connection between word and referent, then a word's meaning may vary according to context and user."
36 Mrs Squeamish's name means "prudish" (*OED* 2014: "squeamish" *adj.* II.7.a.).
37 Chernaik (1995: 5–6) reads the scene in Hobbesian terms as a struggle for dominance.

> MRS. SQUEAMISH. O Lord I'le have some China too, good Mr. *Horner*, don't think to give other people China, and me none, come in with me too.
> HORNER. Upon my honour I have none left now.
> MRS. SQUEAMISH. Nay, nay I have known you deny your China before now, but you shan't put me off so, come—
> HORNER. This Lady had the last there.
> LADY FIDGET. Yes indeed Madam, to my certain knowledge he has no more left.
> MRS. SQUEAMISH. O but it may be he may have some you could not find.
> LADY FIDGET. What, d'y think if he had had any left, I would not have had it too, for we women of quality never think we have China enough.
>
> (1979: 4.3.180–192)

The farcical altercation between Horner and his two mistresses extends the *double entendre* almost *ad infinitum*, thus entirely substituting the literal meaning with the figurative. As the lack of china evokes dwindling masculine potency as well as Horner's diminished supply of semen, the audience's attention is now directed away from the horned husband towards the adulterer, whose sexual exertion has rendered him unable to perform. Thus, the rake has temporarily become what he pretended to be at the outset of the play: a eunuch.

It is here that the social implications of *double entendre* become fully apparent. While fending off Mrs. Squeamish's advances, Horner seeks to establish a truce between the two contestants by adapting the potent *double entendre* on china to a new character configuration. Promising Mrs. Squeamish that "I will have a Rol-waggon for you too, another time" (4.3.194), he deliberately chooses a hyponym of china, namely a cylindrically shaped vase, for its associative connection to the phallus. By employing a piece of china for bawdy, metaphorical *double entendre* he in effect guarantees Mrs. Squeamish sexual intercourse as soon as his virility has been restored. At the same time, he reassures Lady Fidget that Mrs. Squeamish "has an innocent, literal under- / standing" (4.3.197–98) and will not grasp the metaphorical meaning of the *double entendre*. Horner here not only extends the bawdy metaphor, but also seeks to exclude Lady Fidget from the discourse she has originated, and thus effectively attempts to deceive his first alliance to create a second one by using interactional types (1) and (2) to his own advantage.[38]

---

[38] See Thompson (1984: 84–85): "The exchange implies that figurative language must be mastered in order to intrigue."

Wycherley's histrionic use of obscene wordplay calls to mind Jeremy Collier's late seventeenth-century criticism of the state of Restoration comedy in the treatise *A Short View of the Immorality, and Profaneness of the English Stage* (1698). Collier took umbrage at "the poor refuge of a Double Meaning," because in bawdy puns and *double entendres* the second, obscene meaning takes precedence over the innocuous one: "when the Sentence has two Handles, the worst is generally turn'd to the Audience. The Matter is so contrived that the Smut and Scum of the Thought now rises uppermost; And like a Picture drawn to *Sight* looks always upon the Company" (1698: 12). Collier explicitly censures *double entendre* for its manipulative quality: in the external communication system, the dramatist forces the playgoers to understand only the reprehensible meaning of a statement, and thus turns the theatres into schools of vice. Collier is right inasmuch *double entendre* indeed foregrounds the second, illicit meaning on the external communicative level. Biased by his moral predilections and by the demand for an unequivocal language, he however fails to appreciate *double entendres* as significant ingredients to the comedies of his age.[39]

The china scene illustrates the multi-levelled communication in *double entendre* particularly well. As a complex theatrical event, *double entendre* is exploited as a means to heighten the histrionics of libertine comedy and farce[40]; it is subject to ever-shifting character configurations and onstage blocking[41]; and it particularly exemplifies the processes by which dramatic characters connive to exclude third-party hearers.[42] Moreover, the scene illustrates the dynamic relation between the two meanings of a *double entendre* in the course of the scene. First used unambiguously by Sir Jaspar, china is developed into a metaphor of sex by Lady Fidget, while retaining its literal meaning. The latter is fi-

---

39 Contemporary playwrights countered Collier's attack by condemning his undifferentiated view and instead called for a measured response taking into account the context of the speech act (see Dawson 2005: 209–211).
40 Richard Flecknoe defines farce as "a *merry Play*, [which] affords / You *Mimick Gesture*, to your *Comick words*" (cited in Holland 2000: 108). Farces are often short plays, which are characterised by exaggerated plot and characterisation, like interludes.
41 Bowman and Ball (1961: 32) define the term thus: "Block out, to work out the principal business, positions and movements of actors, including their entrances and exits, during rehearsals."
42 "The whole point of the 'china scene' in *The Country Wife* is to display the skill with which a brilliant rake and a few obliging 'right' women can conduct *un discours licentieux* without disconcerting one another or discovering themselves to a suspicious intruder" (Cecil 1966: 576).

nally as good as obliterated when the ladies of quality fight over Horner.⁴³ It is this last stage that renders the *double entendre* and the scene in which it appears downright farcical. That "the Smut and Scum of the Thought [...] rises uppermost" at the end, is thus significant for the success of the passage. The china scene is a master class that demonstrates how an "epic *double entendre*"⁴⁴ can be used histrionically to orchestrate an entire scene, and bring it to its comic climax.

Pre-empting Collier's criticism, Wycherley provided a satirical commentary on the reactions the china scene elicited from audience and critics in his satirical comedy *The Plain Dealer* (1676), which premiered one year after *The Country Wife*. When Olivia, the mistress of the play's protagonist Manly, discusses the china scene with her cousin Eliza she cannot hold back her criticism:

> I say, the lewdest, filthiest thing, is
> his *China*; nay, I will never forgive the beastly Author his *China*:
> he has quite taken away the reputation of poor *China* it self, and
> sully'd the most innocent and pretty Furniture of a Ladies Chamber;
> insomuch, that I was fain to break all my defil'd Vessels.
>
> ([1676] 1996: 2.1.433–438)

Like Collier in his critique of bawdy wordplay, Olivia holds Wycherley accountable for ridding the word *china* of its literal meaning: it no longer signifies a refined collector's item, but lecherous and illicit sex,⁴⁵ and has thus become a taboo word. Olivia's preoccupation with sex is underscored by her unwitting use of phrases that extend the *double entendre* of *The Country Wife*: her attacking the author for "sully[ing] the most innocent and pretty Furniture of a Ladies Chamber" harks back to the spatial and carnal particulars of the china scene itself.⁴⁶ It is this obsession that ultimately makes Olivia the object of Wycherley's ridicule: her taking umbrage at sexual innuendo, and her ensuing flights of erotic fancy about satyrs, goats and bulls mark her as a sexual hypocrite.⁴⁷

---

43 This imbalance is underlined by incongruous phrases such as Horner's "I cannot make China for you all" (*The Country Wife* 4.3.193).
44 The happy phrase is Chadwick's, who defines "epic *double entendre*" as a scene "in which some key word is repeated so insistently that it becomes invested with an extra-literal significance" (1975: 45).
45 Cf. Holland (1979: 194–195).
46 "The more Olivia insists on the play's being obscene, the more the obscenity adheres to her" (Jenkins 2013: 86).
47 "[F]or when you have those filthy creatures in your / head once, the next thing you think, is what they do" (*The Plain Dealer* 2.1.421–422).

While testifying to the notoriety of the china scene, Wycherley's playful reflection on the power of *double entendre* thus launches criticism at prudish critics who cannot tell farce from reality.

4 Satirical *Double Entendre*: Sir Richard Steele's *The Funeral* (1701 / 1702)

Although *double entendre* is often seen as a type of bawdy wordplay, this is by no means exclusively the case, for Restoration and eighteenth-century comedies also illustrate the poignancy with which *double entendre* can be used in non-sexual, satirical contexts. Richard Steele, the progenitor of sentimental drama, ties *double entendre* to the main themes of his early plays. His first comedy, *The Funeral: or, Grief a-la-Mode* (first acted in December 1701, first printed in 1702) revolves around the apparent death of Lord Brumpton, and features morally dubious undertakers, false widows, and devious lawyers. Lord Brumpton's presumed death becomes the exciting force that sets the plots in motion and gives the characters ample opportunities to reveal themselves and their true motivations: Steele here tears down the mask of bigotry from the funeral culture of the early eighteenth century. In order to do so, he uses *double entendre* with regard to characters who want to profit from Lord Brumpton's death: the widow Lady Brumpton, the lawyer Puzzle, and the undertaker Sable.

Lord Brumpton fakes his death to see if his wife is only interested in his money. That his suspicions are indeed justified becomes clear to the audience during her first appearance in the play, when she discusses marital matters with her maid and confidante Mrs. Tattleaid. Indeed, the maid is just as corrupt as her mistress:

> TATTLEAID. [...] Fie, Fie, Madam you a Widow these Three hours, and not look'd on a Parchment Yet—Oh Impious to neglect the Will of the Dead!
> WIDOW. As you say indeed there is no Will of an Husbands so willingly Obey'd as his Last.
>
> (1971: 1.2.143–146)

The wittiness of Lady Brumpton's reply lies in her play with the polysemous noun *will*, which conforms to conversational type 4 (hearer-induced wordplay). Whereas Tattleaid uses *will* unambiguously in the sense of 'testament,' Lady

Brumpton deliberately reinterprets it in the sense of 'wish' or 'desire.'[48] By thus joking about her husband's last will, the widow reveals her cynical attitude to marital love and her greediness for her husband's inheritance. To the playwright, *double entendre* here becomes an essential tool of satirical comedy on the external level of theatrical communication, because it exposes corrupt characters.

Other characters disclose their true intentions in similar ways. One of these is the lawyer Puzzle, whose name (literally, 'to confound') hints at his exploiting legal jargon for his own ends.[49] In the second scene of the first act, Puzzle, who manages the deceased's financial affairs, explains to his nephew Tom how he dealt with Lord Brumpton's estate and finances:

> PUZZLE. [...] Know then
> Child that the Lord of this House was one of your Men of Honour, and Sense, who lose the latter in the former, and are apt to take all men to be like themselves; Now this Gentleman intirely [sic] trusted me, and I made the only use a man of Business can of a Trust, I cheated him; for I, imperceptibly, before his Face made his whole Estate liable to an Hundred *per Annum* for my self, for good Services etc.
> [...] a True Lawyer never
> makes any man's Will but his own[.]
>
> (1971: 1.2.163–170)

Puzzle employs a polysemous *double entendre*, because he plays with the two meanings of the word *trust*. The first meaning is *trust* in the sense of the "[c]onfidence in or reliance on some quality or attribute of a person or thing, or the truth of a statement" (*OED* 2014: "trust" n. 1.a.). As such, the word relates to character quality, to the very core of human relations or dealings, and to society's dependence on the adherence to moral values. Puzzle openly confesses that he abused Lord Brumpton's trust in his reliability and integrity as the family lawyer. The second meaning of *trust* is a legal one and closely tied to the administration of Lord Brumpton's property. According to this definition, a trust is "[t]he confidence reposed in a person in whom the legal ownership of property is vested to hold or use for the benefit of another; hence, an estate committed to the charge of trustees" (*OED* 2014: "trust" n. 6.). The second meaning is hence a

---

[48] See *OED* (2014): "will" $n.^1$ I.1., I.3. and IV.23. For another example of *will* in the dual sense of 'wish' and 'pleasure,' see William Congreve, *The Way of the World* ([1700] 1982: 4.1.180–184). The passage is discussed in Niederhoff (2001: 99).
[49] On the *double entendre* used in the language of lawyers, see Holland (1979: 195–196).

formalisation of the first: from the performance of trust to the object invested with such trust. Elaborating on his role as trustee, Puzzle admits that he has feathered his own nest at the expense of Lord Brumpton by making himself the beneficiary of interest derived from the deceased's property.

The use of wordplay is determined by the social context in which it is uttered. The internal communicative situation of Puzzle's morally puzzling speech is noteworthy in that it is a confidential conversation between an uncle with decades of business experience and his nephew, who is still a novice in the trade of law. Puzzle here gives his nephew avuncular advice: he initiates Tom into the secrets of his trade, using *double entendre* almost as a mnemonic device,[50] and thus creates a professional alliance between them. Puzzle establishes a causal link between trust and financial interest: only a person that gains somebody's confidence in his reliability can redeploy that person's money for his own benefit. Hence, the lawyers' use of jargon creates two groups of speakers and hearers: lawyers use *trust* as a *double entendre* which they can decipher (type 1), but their clients cannot (type 2). Near the end of his speech, Puzzle hammers home his message once more through the use of a *double entendre* that is by now already familiar to the audience: "A True Lawyer never / makes any man's Will but his own." These instances of *double entendre* have a significant impact on the external communicative situation: Steele employs a morally outrageous wordplay to satirise and hence brand lawyers for their dubious methods – and teaches his audience how to decipher their jargon by effectively converting them, in terms of speaker-hearer interaction, from type 2 to type 1 hearers so they can exact caution in similar business transactions.[51]

Steele uses *double entendre* for satire of this kind throughout the play. Sable, the undertaker, whose name means 'black' and 'gloomy,' unwittingly uses a self-defeating *double entendre* that reveals his mercantile attitude. Upon finding out that Lord Brumpton has not died, he is immediately concerned with the loss of money this entails. When he charges Lord Brumpton "Ten Pounds for / watching you all your Long fit of Sickness last Winter," Lord Brumpton cannot help but wonder:

LORD BRUMPTON. Watching me? Why I had none but my own
Servants by Turns—
SABLE. I mean attending to give notice of your Death, I had all
your long fit of Sickness last Winter, at Half a Crown a day, a Fellow

---

50 Wordplay is used thus in advertising. See Winter-Froemel (2009: 1439), with reference to, e.g., Tanaka (1992: 101).
51 On law satire, see especially William Wycherley's *The Plain Dealer* (first performed in 1676).

waiting at your Gate, to bring me Intelligence, but you Unfortunately recover'd and I lost all my Obliging pains for your Service.

(1971: 2.2.8–15)

As the *double entendre* on *to watch somebody* is unintentional on the level of the internal communication, Sable has to interpret the second meaning of the phrase for Lord Brumpton (interactional type 2). The misunderstanding occurs because both characters infer the meaning of the verb from different physical contexts[52]: Sable does not talk about taking care of the sick (with its possible associations of preserving life and upholding social values), as Lord Brumpton thinks, but about death as a business transaction, represented by the vulture-like attitude of the mortician. The rift between the two meanings demonstrates that, in a corrupt society, even words do not remain innocent.

The use of wordplay in *The Funeral* suggests that the play of two senses can be adapted to satirical contexts. Lady Brumpton, Puzzle, and Sable as well as other morally corrupt characters thus expose their true motivations in self-defeating *double entendres*. For corrupt characters, *will* has degenerated to testament, *trust* to illicit business transactions, and *watching somebody* to one's anticipation of a long-awaited death knell: thus, all three terms relate to the illicit or cynical acquisition of money from the deceased. Wordplay in *The Funeral* is used as part of Steele's satirical programme, because it encapsulates the tension at the heart of the play's main themes – money, death, and humanity. These issues also suggest a link between sexual and satirical *double entendre*: both use innocuous terms to discuss social taboos. In *The Country Wife*, the taboo is illicit sex; in *The Funeral*, the taboo is the cynical attitude to death and money. Steele's debut comedy hence uses *double entendre* as a didactic tool to address society's main shortcomings: unmasking the characters' standpoints to the audience in the external communicative situation, it lays bare the all-pervasive moral depravity dominating a world in which words lose their primary, neutral meaning and are subsumed by a secondary, subverted meaning.

5 Concluding Remarks

The effectiveness of *double entendre*, which the eighteenth-century conundrum on farts and wordplay has established as a phrase with two meanings, consists in the complex interplay between structural and interactional properties, theat-

---

[52] On misunderstanding see Winter-Froemel and Zirker (2010: 81–84).

rical communication and comic themes. Unlike the phonetic pun, which plays with the identical or similar sounds of words, *double entendre* plays with the different lexicalised and figurative senses of words and phrases: (1) a polysemic *double entendre* consists in joining different lexicalised meanings of a word or phrase; a figurative *double entendre* can (2) combine a literal with a metaphorical meaning, (3) remotivate a dead metaphor by harking back to its literal sense, or (4) relate two meanings by metonymy. From the perspective of speaker-hearer interaction, *double entendre* can be induced by the speaker and by the hearer: speaker-induced *double entendre* is an ambiguous utterance that is either (1) deciphered or (2) not deciphered by the hearer; hearer-induced *double entendre* consists in (3) the unintentional or (4) the intentional activation of a second meaning to an utterance. These constellations are variously realised on the stage on the level of internal communication between the characters to establish their intellectual superiority and to create alliances with one group of hearers while excluding another. On the level of external communication, all four constellations of *double entendre* are deliberate, fashioned by the dramatist to elicit the audience's laughter, and also to establish different relations between the spectators and the onstage characters. Characters with the ability to create and interpret *double entendre* properly are often portrayed as superior to others and thus preferred; however, if the use of *double entendre* foregrounds moral corruption (as in *The Funeral*), these characters are stigmatised. Characters lacking the skill to make or decipher such wordplay, or who even choose their words so unfortunately that they insinuate a second meaning, are exposed to comic ridicule.

Double entendre hence offers manifold possibilities for the comic playwright. The same holds true for the themes it addresses. Although the entrenched view associates *double entendre* with bawdiness, it also can also occur when characters discuss other taboo subjects, such as death, money and social *mores*. Thus, *double entendres* have thematic relevance for the plays in which they appear. As the rake comedies of the Restoration are predominantly about sex, bawdy *double entendre* prevails, to wit wordplay becomes part of a power play over intellectual, sexual, as well as financial prowess. In plays dealing with other themes, like Steele's *The Funeral*, *double entendre* can be used as a tool for satire and social commentary, in this case in censuring the hypocrisy rampant in the funeral culture of the early eighteenth century.

Eighteenth-century comedy inherited the dramatic traditions and theatrical conventions from the seventeenth century, and with them the taste for *double entendre*. Despite criticism about the raunchiness of Restoration comedy, and despite the rise of a sentimental aesthetics in England's cultural landscape, playwrights continued to use bawdy and non-bawdy *double entendre*, as comedies from Susanna Centlivre's *The Stolen Heiress* (1702 / 1703) to Steele's *The Lying Lover; or, The Ladies Friendship* (1703), John Gay's *The Beggar's Opera* (1728), Henry Fielding's *Tom Thumb* (1730), Benjamin Hoadley's *The Suspicious Husband* (1747), Edward Moore's *The Foundling* (1748), and George Coleman's *The Clandestine Marriage* (1766) illustrate. That such a plethora of *double entendre* figures in Restoration and in eighteenth-century comedy demonstrates that it is a particularly popular kind of wordplay, constantly re-appropriated after the *Interregnum*, and joining different comic modes with one another.

6 References

Adamson, Sylvia. 2000. Literary Language. In Roger Lass (ed.), *The Cambridge History of the English Language: Volume 3, 1476–1776*, 539–653. Cambridge: Cambridge University Press.
Bowman, Walter P. & Robert H. Ball. 1961. *Theatre Language: A Dictionary of Terms in English of the Drama and Stage from Medieval to Modern Times*. New York: Theatre Arts Books.
Cecil, C. D. 1966. Delicate and Indelicate Puns in Restoration Comedy. *The Modern Language Review* 61. 572–578.
The Centinel. 1758. 2 vols. Dublin: James Hoey.
Chadwick, William R. 1975. *The Four Plays of William Wycherley: A Study in the Development of a Dramatist*. The Hague: Mouton.
Chernaik, Warren L. 1995. *Sexual Freedom in Restoration Literature*. Cambridge: Cambridge University Press.
Collier, Jeremy. 1698. *A Short View of the Immorality, and Profaneness of the English Stage, Together with the Sense of Antiquity upon this Argument*. London: Printed for S. Keble.
Congreve, William. [1693, 1694, 1695, 1700] 1982. *The Comedies of William Congreve*. Anthony G. Henderson (ed.). Cambridge: Cambridge University Press.
Corman, Brian. 2000. Comedy. In Deborah Payne Fisk (ed.), *The Cambridge Companion to English Restoration Theatre*, 52–69. Cambridge: Cambridge University Press.
Cummings, Louise. 2012. Pragmatic Disorders. In Hans-Jörg Schmid (ed.), *Cognitive Pragmatics*, 291–316. Berlin: de Gruyter.
Dawson, Mark S. 2005. *Gentility and the Comic Theatre of Late Stuart London*. Cambridge: Cambridge University Press.
Delabastita, Dirk. 1996. Introduction. *The Translator, Special Volume on Wordplay and Translation: Essays on Punning and Translation* 2(2). 127–139.
Delabastita, Dirk. 1997. Introduction. In Dirk Delabastita (ed.), *Traductio: Essays on Punning and Translation*, 1–22. Namur: Presses Universitaires de Namur.
Delabastita, Dirk. 2011. Wholes and Holes in the Study of Shakespeare's Wordplay. In Mireille Ravassat & Jonathan Culpeper (eds.), *Stylistics and Shakespeare's Language: Transdisciplinary Approaches*, 139–164. New York: Continuum.
Dryden, John. 1956. *The Works of John Dryden. Vol. 1: Poems 1649–1680*. Edward N. Hooker & Hugh T. Swedenberg (eds.). Berkeley: University of California Press.

Durfey, Thomas. 1709. *The Modern Prophets; Or, New Wit for a Husband: A Comedy*. London: Bernard Lintott.
Farquhar, George. [1706] 1976. *The Recruiting Officer*. Michael Cordner (ed.). London: Benn.
Farquhar, George. 1988. *The Works of George Farquhar*. Shirley Strum Kenny (ed.). 2 vols. Oxford: Clarendon.
Fisk, Deborah Payne (ed.). [1676, 1676, 1676, 1678] 2005. *Four Restoration Libertine Plays*. Oxford: Oxford University Press.
Forschungsprogramm. *Graduiertenkolleg Ambiguität – Produktion und Rezeption*. Tübingen University. http://www.uni-tuebingen.de/forschung/forschungsschwerpunkte/graduiertenkollegs/grk-ambiguitaet-produktion-und-rezeption/forschung/forschungsprogramm.html (17 July 2015).
Fujimura, Thomas H. 1952. *The Restoration Comedy of Wit*. New York: Barnes & Noble.
Grassegger, Hans. 1985. *Sprachspiel und Übersetzung: Eine Studie anhand der Comic-Serie Asterix*. Tübingen: Stauffenburg.
Hausmann, Franz Josef. 1974. *Studien zu einer Linguistik des Wortspiels: Das Wortspiel im Canard enchaîné*. Tübingen: Niemeyer.
Holland, Peter. 1979. *The Ornament of Action: Text and Performance in Restoration Comedy*. Cambridge: Cambridge University Press.
Holland, Peter. 2000. Farce. In Deborah Payne Fisk (ed.), *The Cambridge Companion to Restoration Theatre*, 107–126. Cambridge: Cambridge University Press.
Hughes, Patrick & Paul Hammond. 1978. *Upon the Pun: Dual Meaning in Words and Pictures*. London: Allen.
Jenkins, Eugenia Zuroski. 2013. *A Taste for China: English Subjectivity and the Prehistory of Orientalism*. Oxford: Oxford University Press.
Käge, Otmar. 1980. *Motivation: Probleme des persuasiven Sprachgebrauchs, der Metapher und des Wortspiels*. Göppingen: Kümmerle.
Kökeritz, Helge. 1953. *Shakespeare's Pronunciation*. New Haven, CT: Yale University Press.
Leech, Geoffrey. 1969. *A Linguistic Guide to English Poetry*. London: Longman.
Leggatt, Alexander. 1998. *English Stage Comedy, 1490–1990: Five Centuries of a Genre*. London: Routledge.
Niederhoff, Burkhard. 2001. *"The Rule of Contrary": Das Paradox in der englischen Komödie der Restaurationszeit und des frühen 18. Jahrhunderts*. Trier: Wissenschaftlicher Verlag Trier.
Novak, Maximilian E. 2001. Libertinism and Sexuality. In Susan J. Owen (ed.), *A Companion to Restoration Drama*, 53–68. Oxford: Blackwell.
The Nutt's Crack'd: Being an Answer to the Puzzle: or A Choice Collection of Conundrums. 1745. London: M. Cooper.
Oxford English Dictionary .2014.2nd edn.. http://www.oed.com (17 July 2015).
Plett, Heinrich F. 2010. *Literary Rhetoric: Concepts – Structures – Analyses*. Leiden: Brill.
The Puzzle: Being a Choice Collection of Conundrums. 1745. London: M. Cooper.
Robinson, Douglas. 2006. *Introducing Performative Pragmatics*. London: Routledge.
Shadwell, Thomas. 1927. *The Complete Works of Thomas Shadwell*. Montague Summers (ed.), 5 vols. London: Fortune Press.
Shakespeare, William. [1623] 1975. *As You Like It*. Agnes Latham (ed.). London: Methuen.
Steele, Richard. 1971. *The Plays of Richard Steele*. Shirley Strum Kenny (ed.). Oxford: Clarendon.
Styan, J. L. 1986. *Restoration Comedy in Performance*. Cambridge: Cambridge University Press.

Tanaka, Keiko. 1992. The Pun in Advertising: A Pragmatic Approach. *Lingua* 87. 91–102.
Thompson, James. 1984. *Language in Wycherley's Plays: Seventeenth-Century Language Theory and Drama*. Tuscaloosa: University of Alabama Press.
Wallace, Elizabeth Kowaleski. 1997. *Consuming Subjects: Women, Shopping and Business in the Eighteenth Century*. New York: Columbia University Press.
Winter-Froemel, Esme. 2009. Wortspiel. In Gert Ueding (ed.), *Historisches Wörterbuch der Rhetorik*. Vol. 9: 1429–1443. Tübingen: Niemeyer.
Winter-Froemel, Esme & Angelika Zirker. 2010. Ambiguität in der Sprecher-Hörer-Interaktion. Linguistische und Literaturwissenschaftliche Perspektiven. *Zeitschrift für Linguistik und Literaturwissenschaft* 158. 76–97.
Wycherley, William. 1979. *The Plays of William Wycherley*. Arthur Friedman (ed). Oxford: Clarendon.
Wycherley, William. [1671, 1673, 1675, 1676] 1996. *Love in a Wood; The Gentleman Dancing-Master; The Country Wife; The Plain Dealer*. Peter Dixon (ed.). Oxford: Oxford University Press.

Sheelagh Russell-Brown
The Serious Work of Play: Wordplay in the "Dark Sonnets" of Gerard Manley Hopkins

Abstract: As a student at Oxford University, the young Gerard Manley Hopkins used his notes on Greek philosophy to explore what was to become part of his philosophy of words. In February 1868, he wrote that "the word is the expression, *uttering* of the idea in the mind," and this notion underlay his struggle to "utter" the energy of the word and the Word, or thought and Being, throughout his poetic life. Much has been written about Hopkins's elaborate wordplay, in which punning, neologism, and convoluted and contracted syntax, frequently based in his interest in Anglo-Saxon purism, among other techniques, distill the "scape" of the word and the Word. Joseph Feeney, for example, has provided a detailed examination of Hopkins's poetry in terms of what he calls Hopkins's linguistic playfulness. It is more difficult, however, to trace such "play-as-fun" in what have been called the "Dark Sonnets," those six untitled poems most likely composed in 1885 and 1886 in which Hopkins expresses his sense of isolation from both his poetic gift and the Church. This paper proposes that in the sonnets "To seem the stranger," "I wake and feel," "No worst, there is none," "Carrion comfort," "Patience, hard thing," and "My own heart," Hopkins employs his unique wordplay to "utter" the landscape of the mind and that his distancing of his words from those of "normal" speech echoes the distance that he himself was experiencing.

Keywords: Dark Sonnets, dialect, Gerard Manley Hopkins, inscape, instress, linguistics, ludic function (of language), neologisms, puns, sound effects, sprung rhythm, syntax, wordplay in poetry

1 Introduction

In 1873, in a birthday letter to his mother, Gerard Manley Hopkins voiced his appreciation for the wordplay of the nonsense poet Edward Lear (as well as that of Lewis Carroll): "You must by all means see Edward Lear's new Book of Nonsense. It is something like Alice but much better. It contains nonsense cookery (How to Make Gosky Patties) and nonsense botany, which is illustrated: especially look at the Manypeeplia Upsidownia" (1956b: 121). Hopkins's delight in Lear's and Carroll's exploitation of language would later bear fruit in his own poetry.[1] When, two years later, Hopkins began writing *The Wreck of the Deutschland*, he said, in a letter to his friend Canon Dixon, that he "had long had haunting [his] ear the echo of a new rhythm which [he] now realised on paper." This was, of course, "sprung rhythm," a rhythm that he considered to be "a better and more natural principle than the ordinary system, much more flexible, and capable of much greater effects" (1956a: 14). Hopkins also mentions the use of sprung rhythm in musical refrains, nursery rhymes, weather saws, and popular jingles as having inspired his development of it in serious poetry (cf. 1956a: 14, 1935: 45). Such "informal" verse as Hopkins mentions, of course, also contains instances of wordplay. It was in *The Wreck of the Deutschland* that Hopkins first began to practice what has become known as his distinctive wordplay, a technique that later influenced such poets as Dylan Thomas, W. H. Auden, and Elizabeth Bishop.

Hopkins's wordplay, particularly as it is displayed in *The Wreck of the Deutschland* and in the more celebratory "nature" poetry that followed, has been the subject of much scholarship (see Boyle 1961; Feeney 2008; Milroy 1977, 1984; Sonstroem 1967; Wimsatt 1998). However, the notion of such "playful" use of language in what became known as Hopkins's "Dark Sonnets" may create difficulties if one equates "playfulness" with "play," especially in the sense that Hopkins has used the latter term. Creativity in the application of wordplay, along with contestation with both the limits of language and the limits of his craft, can certainly be perceived in all of Hopkins's extant works. In both the early and late poetry, in the poems that send praise from the soul to God for the beauties of the natural landscape and in the sonnets that call out to God from the darkness of the soul's interior landscape, Hopkins plays with language to capture the inscape of creation and of the poet's soul that cannot be otherwise caught.

Only recently has attention been given to the spare, wrenching, yet equally effective, wordplay techniques in Hopkins's later poetry, particularly in his "Dark Sonnets." Here, Hopkins employs techniques of inversion and interruption, of omission and repetition, to express his sense of the soul's alienation and its aborted progress toward self-actualization. Rachel Salmon has pointed out how these sonnets differ from Hopkins's previous work: "In the nature sonnets, the inscape of another is discovered; in the terrible sonnets [the unfortunate term "Terrible Sonnets" has been in the past attached to these poems], the inscape of the self is in the making" (1984: 392). We can see this "self in the mak-

---

[1] On the wordplay of Lewis Carroll, see the contributions by Kullmann and Schmitz-Emans, this volume.

ing" through examining some of the wordplay techniques in the six poems. Through his wordplay, Hopkins expands the meaning and the potential of the "perfect sonnet," just as he expands the potential of spoken language itself.

2 Hopkins, Wordplay, and the "Dark Sonnets"

Among the most recent and the most complete treatments of the quality of "play" in the poetry of Gerard Manley Hopkins is Joseph J. Feeney's 2008 volume, *The Playfulness of Gerard Manley Hopkins*, in which he employs Johan Huizinga's ludic theory, with its division of playfulness into the qualities of "fun," "creativity," "contest," and "style," to trace Hopkins's sense of play throughout his poetic canon. Although Fr. Feeney singles out "fun" as the salient quality of Hopkins's verse, including in it "such pleasures as whimsy, wit, puns, humor, comedy, parody, irony, satire, incongruity, understatement, exaggeration, jokes, even silliness" (xviii-xix), a narrower focus on Hopkins's "Dark Sonnets," even those like "Patience, hard thing" and "My own heart" that end on a more hopeful note, requires a straining of the definition of "fun" beyond even its most creative limits. Strain and stress are, indeed, among the most significant aspects of Hopkins's world as depicted in these sonnets as he writes of the "pangs" that "will, schooled at forepangs, wilder wring" ("No worst, there is none," 1990: 182) and of the "wretch[ed]" "I" who "lay wrestling with (my God!) my God" ("Carrion comfort," 1990: 183).

It has generally been assumed that a group of six poems written in 1885 and 1886 represent Hopkins's response to the "dark night of the soul" he had experienced after his posting to Ireland in 1884 (see Harris 1982; Hopkins 2009: 372n). Whether one sees these sonnets as more benignly Ignatian in their inspiration or as Hopkins's more "terrible" and "desolate" lament for his loss of faith and of poetic power, they stand apart from Hopkins's other verse both in their darker subject matter and in their exploitation of the imagery of touch, of taste, and of smell, almost to the exclusion of the visual celebrations of the earlier poems. Instead, it is predominantly the auditory potential of language, its ability to both conflate and expand sound and meaning, that Hopkins exploits in the "Dark Sonnets." Hopkins himself seems to have seen these poems as arising from a form of unwilling inspiration apart from his usual more self-willed composition practice. In September 1885, he wrote to his friend Robert Bridges:

> I shall shortly have some sonnets to send you, five or more. Four of these came like inspirations unbidden and against my will. And in the life I lead now, which is one of a contin-

ually jaded and harassed mind, if in any leisure I try to do anything I make no way—nor with my work, alas! but so it must be.

(1935: 221)

Despite Hopkins's disclaimer that these "came like inspirations unbidden," in their wordplay they show signs of consummate craftsmanship. Earlier, in May of the same year, he had told Bridges, "I have after long silence written two sonnets, which I am touching: if ever anything was written in blood one of these was" (1935: 219). Although the order of their composition is not definitive, it is assumed that these poems were the six that came to be known as the "Dark Sonnets" or the "Sonnets of Desolation": "To seem the stranger," "I wake and feel," "No worst, there is none," "Carrion comfort," "Patience, hard thing," and "My own heart."

A satisfactory definition of "wordplay" as practiced by Hopkins in his entire canon is difficult to locate. Johan Huizinga, whose theories set Feeney on his course of tracing Hopkins's playfulness, connects the sense of play in poetry to the setting of enigmas and riddles, in fact employing as examples the very technique that Hopkins was to exploit in his poetry, the Anglo-Saxon (or in Huizinga's case Old Norse) *kenning* or *kenningar*: "When the poet says 'speech-thorn' for 'tongue,' 'floor of the hill of winds' for 'earth,' 'tree-wolf' for 'wind,' etc., he is setting his readers poetic riddles which are tacitly solved" (Huizinga [1938] 1980: 134). According to Huizinga, the knowledge of such wordplay would be assumed by both the poet and his listeners and this very "cult" of knowledge transmits a sense of shared delight. On the other hand, Hopkinsian *kennings* or compounds rest on no such shared knowledge, and the delight that arises comes from the very fact that, rather than having a fixed and single meaning, they refuse to be definitively pinned down. More applicable perhaps to Hopkins's wordplay practice is David Crystal's definition in his book *Language Play* (2001), where he states that language play is in its most basic form manipulation of language: "[W]e take some linguistic feature – such as a word, a phrase, a sentence, a part of a word, a group of sounds, a series of letters – and make it do things it does not normally do" (1; see also Renner, this volume). He adds to this definition that, in the hands of sophisticated writers such as Joyce (and we might add Hopkins here), "several linguistic levels can be successfully manipulated at the same time" (Crystal 2001: 11). Crystal speaks of the "bending and breaking" of the constraints of poetic structure, commenting that "it is usual for several things to be broken at once" (Crystal 2001: 138). As useful as this definition is, however, we must place the emphasis on "bending" rather than "breaking" in the case of Hopkins's verse.

First, Hopkins's wordplay, far from "breaking" the rules of grammar, "bends" the rules of written rhetorical English in favour of capitalizing on the rich possibilities of spoken utterance, especially speech as it is uttered under excitement or stress. This pattern is described by James Milroy, who uses the analogy of game playing to show how Hopkins works from within the formal rules of poetry, while at the same time "heightening" his language through "exploit[ing] the very great freedoms that were still available to him just as a talented player in any game can excel without breaking its rules" (1977: 108). The game for Hopkins is the game of wordplay. From his letters and journals, it is clear that Hopkins believed that the test of the success of poetic wordplay was in its performance: "poetry [is] the darling child of speech, of lips and spoken utterance: it must be spoken: *till it is spoken it is not performed*, it does not perform, it is not itself" (From an unpublished letter, cited in Feeney 2008: 28). The metrical marks over some of the syllables in his poetry "are," he writes, "for the performer and such marks are proper in every art. Though indeed one might say syntactical marks are for the performer too" (1935: 265). Metrical marks or accents show the reader where the stress is strongest, necessary for Hopkins's sprung rhythm that does not follow the regular metronymic of metered feet, nor the counting of syllables. Meredith Martin, in fact, connects Hopkins's insistence on retention of his metrical marking in his poems with the burgeoning interest in philology that was current during Hopkins's lifetime and in which he himself took part (cf. Martin 2008: 245), contributing an estimated eighty-nine usages to Joseph Wright's *English Dialect* Dictionary, mainly from his observations of Irishisms (see White 1987: 326). Martin argues that Hopkins had support for his metrical markings in the standardizing of visual signs for sounds that accompanied the creation of the *New English Dictionary* (Martin 2008: 245). We can assume that by "syntactical marks" Hopkins means the colons, parentheses, dashes, exclamation and question marks, and other punctuation marks that interrupt the straightforward syntax of his verse sentences. Hopkins, in fact, would have found support for his techniques in the words of Richard Trench, one of the most noted philologists with whose work Hopkins would have been familiar. James Milroy, in his volume on Hopkins's poetic language, quotes Trench's comparison of the resonances in a word to that of a poem: "Many a single word also is itself a concentrated poem, having stores of poetical thought and imagery laid up in it" (cited in Milroy 1977: 61). In his poetry, Hopkins opens up such words so that their storehouse of poetical thought and imagery can be exploited to their fullest.

Hopkins's wordplay techniques are intended to carry the inscape of the word and the world. As early as 1868, he had written in his "notebook on the history of Greek philosophy etc." of "three terms belonging to" a word: "its prepossession of feeling; its definition, abstraction, vocal expression or other utterance; and its application, 'extension,' the concrete things coming under it" (1959a: 127). Immediately following, in an essay on Parmenides, he writes: "Being and thought are the same. The truth in thought is Being, stress, and each word is one way of acknowledging Being and each sentence by its copula *is* (or its equivalent) the utterance and assertion of it" (1959a: 129). Hence, through "playing" with the word, Hopkins is assisting the expression of its Being: "[T]wo kinds of clearness one shd. [sic] have—either the meaning to be felt without effort as fast as one reads or else, if dark at first reading, when once made out *to explode*" (1935: 90). Attention to his manipulation of language is rewarded with just such *explosions* of meaning, and like the results of an explosion, the effects are far-reaching and often limitless.

Hopkins's wordplay is his method of capturing the inscape of each "being" and each "doing." In his notes on "Poetry and Verse," Hopkins writes that "design, pattern or what I am in the habit of calling 'inscape' is what I above all aim at in poetry" (1959a: 289). Throughout his life, Hopkins was to add to his definition of "inscape," whose clearest definition is perhaps that it is that in each object of creation which contains its *haecceitas* or "thisness," a term that Hopkins borrowed from Duns Scotus to refer to uniqueness of being. "Instress" is that which conveys "inscape" to the sight and to the mind. Hopkins was to write of inscape as the sign of God within each part of creation. In a statement remarkably close to the words of the philologist Max Müller that "there is a law which runs through nearly the whole of nature, that everything that is struck rings. Each substance has its peculiar ring" (cited in Plotkin 1989: 38), and to his own words in the sonnet "As kingfishers catch fire" ("Each hung bell's / Bow swung finds tongue to fling out broad its name"), Hopkins asserts that "All things [...] are charged with love, are charged with God and if we know how to touch them give off sparks and take fire, yield drops and flow, ring and tell of him" (1959b: 195). Interestingly, in the sestet of "As kingfishers catch fire," Hopkins also employs the word "play" to signify the instressing of Christ within the entirety of creation: "Christ plays in ten thousand places" (1990: 141). Words, then, share in the instressing of inscape, revealing the presence of God in their phonological and semantic connections. They do this, says Hopkins, through their repetition of sound and of sense. Using his own idiosyncratic coinages, he writes that "*oftening, over-and-overing, aftering* of the inscape must take place in order to detach it to the mind and in this light poetry is speech which afters and oftens its inscape, speech couched in a repeating figure" (1959a: 289). Such "aftering" and "oftening" of inscape is accomplished through repetition and ideally reveals the presence of God within the world. In the "Dark Sonnets," however, Hopkins depicts his search for signs of God in the inscapes of his world as unrewarding, as "cries like dead letters sent / To dearest him that lives alas! away," his wordplay aptly instressing the "cries countless" of the seemingly abandoned soul. Nevertheless, in the "Dark Sonnets," as in Hopkins's more celebratory nature poems, close attention to wordplay rewards the reader with concussive force, an outcome that Hopkins recognized in his journal notes:

> The further in anything, as a work of art, the organization is carried out, the deeper the form penetrates, the prepossession flushes the matter, the more effort will be required in apprehension, the more power of comparison, the more capacity for receiving that synthesis of (either successive or spatially distinct) impressions which gives us the unity with the prepossession conveyed by it.
>
> (1959a: 126)

Hopkins's wordplay, then, whereby one word, one phrase may carry the weight of several patterns of meaning, rewards the frequently strenuous effort of comprehension with a seemingly infinite deepening of inscape.

Hopkins's interest in the spoken word, an interest that he was to exploit in his poetry, is evident in his journals and diaries as well as in other of his papers. In 1868, he captured examples of his cousin Mildred's "baby-talk" which sound strikingly close to his own practice in verse: "*Did be to go* = was going to—*Baby cuts* = little scissors—*Church-pockie* = alms box" (1959a: 160). Dialect is another form of spoken speech that fascinates Hopkins and that finds its way into his poetry and that he records in his journals: "Br. Wells calls a grindstone a *grindlestone*"; "To *lead* north-country for to *carry* (a field of hay etc.). *Geet* north-country preterite of *get*: 'he geet agate agoing'" (1959a: 191).

3 Wordplay as Sound and Sense

The alliteration in the final example above is a reminder that, even early on in Hopkins's journals, he connected meanings and sounds, speculating on the connections between words that he thought to be derived from the same root. Hopkins's poetry frequently proceeds through a series of metaphor chains, lists or catalogues of words and expressions, and a sort of "leaping" from one word and idea to the next, frequently relying on the connection between sound and sense that Hopkins had intuited early on and that had been reinforced by his later readings in the Victorian philologists: "Soul, self; come, poor Jackself, I do advise / You, jaded, lét be" ("My own heart," 1990: 186); "My cries heave, herds-long; huddle in a main, a chief- / Woe, wórld-sorrow" ("No worst, there is none," 1990: 182). Hopkins's earliest diary entry, from September 1863, in fact, is a fragment in which he tentatively explores just such a relationship:

> [...] growth, anything growing vigorously, blooming it may be, but yet producing fruit. Hence *mead* in the sense of meadow, or *meadow*, mean a field of fresh vegetation. *Mead* the drink and *meat*, (active forms from the same root,) are so called from *strengthening*, nourishing. For *maid* compare the parallel resemblance between *virgo* and *virga*. Cf. 'our sons shall grow up as *young* [...].
>
> (1959a: 4)

In his next entry, he comments that "The various lights under which a horn may be looked at have given rise to a vast number of words in a language," proceeding to link "horn" to "grain," to "crown," and to "heron," among other words. Such speculations arise from Hopkins's familiarity with and exploitation of the onomatopoeic theory, the notion that language had its roots in imitating sounds in nature and transferred this linkage to poetic language, which had found favour in Frederic Farrar's *Essay on the Origin of Language* as well as in Trench's *On the Study of Words* and *English Past and Present*, all works which it appears Hopkins had read. In stating (following the above etymological lists) that "[i]n fact I think the onomatopoetic theory has not had a fair chance" (1959a: 5), Hopkins counters Müller's denigration of this theory as the "bow-wow" theory of the origins of language with his own theory – that indwelling in the similarity of sounds between words exists a sort of linguistic DNA, the genetic substance of the root words carried forward into the offshoots, each word sharing somewhat in the inscape of the other: "Wisest my heart breeds dark heaven's baffling ban / Bars or hell's spell thwarts" ("To seem the stranger," 1990: 181). Both alliteration and internal rhyming (identified by Hopkins as Norse *skothending*) reinforce the claustrophobic sense of the speaker's being frustrated at every turn (1959: 283-287).

4 Punning and Metaphor

In his wordplay, Hopkins may also link otherwise incongruent terms in particularly striking or amusing ways. In his study of Hopkins's "playfulness," Feeney expands Huizinga's ludic theory with borrowings from Koestler's *The Act of Creation* (1964), in particular his description of the creative moment as "bisociation," a linking of two usually incompatible "matrices" of thought and behaviour (Feeney 2008: 48–49). The notion of incongruity, a quality in fact of much comic playfulness, also informs Hopkins's "Dark Sonnets," where both the subject matter and its treatment forcefully yoke otherwise incompatible modes of being, sometimes through punning, through linguistic pairing, and through metaphorical links, both direct and implied.

In Hopkins's poetry, punning combines with other of Hopkins's techniques to strengthen and expand the inscape of the words and of the world of the verse. Stefan Kjerkegaard describes punning as "involv[ing] an interaction between a semiotic deficit and a semantic surplus" (2011: 1); in other words, one sign (one word) extends itself into two or more meanings or significances. Hopkins's use of puns goes beyond a display of cleverness to become a means of expanding the significance of the word so that it "explodes," the fragments of its meaning propelling the poetic line itself. As David Sonstroem puts it: "Hopkins progresses by double meanings, entering a word through one, departing through another" (1967: 197). Hopkins's punning is not mere exploitation of coincidental sounds – "[l]ittle wonder that his progress is more painful and tortuous than that of Lear, for he is playing a more demanding game" (Sonstroem 1967: 200). In Hopkinsian punning, two possible meanings may expand or explode into a seemingly infinite number of significations, often returning on themselves, making the sonnet space even more crowded. For example, the sonnet "I wake and feel" rests upon a form of punning (as well as "chiming," explained below): "I wake and feel the fell of dark, not day" (1990: 181). "Feel" and "fell," according to Hopkins's theories, may derive from the same root; hence their meanings "bleed" into each other. Furthermore, the word "fell" (a common word in Hopkins's lexicon) has at least a triple, and perhaps a quadruple, meaning: the past form of "fall" (here Hopkins again disrupts the order of parts of speech), the pelt of an animal (the darkness surrounds the poet like a smothering animal skin), the adjective meaning "dark" or "evil," and the noun that designates in northern England an area of high land (most commonly "fells"). While punning and chiming are common in all of Hopkins's poetry after his youthful verse, here it has a darker effect whereby Hopkins exploits the dangerous and desolate connotations of many of his word choices. The word "fall" or "fell" is also found in the sonnet "No worst, there is none," where the Fury shrieks "Let me be fell," and where the speaker describes the mountains of the mind as "cliffs of fall / Frightful, sheer, no-man-fathomed," a usage which would seem to support the fourth meaning of Hopkins's semantic chain (1990: 182). In "I wake and feel" and "No worst, there is none," the words "fell" and "fall" are richly evocative with connotations of smothering darkness, of the threat of evil, and of perilous heights. In the latter sonnet, its use as an adjective carries these resonances and more, especially when paired with the next line. Fury's "fell" is transmuted to the "cliffs of fall" that characterize the landscape of the mind.

For Hopkins, punning is more than a language game, for he believes that sound similarity is not accidental and that expressing the inexpressible, the inscape of the world and of the soul, is the function of his poetry. As he writes in his journals, "[a]ll the world is full of inscape and chance left free to act falls into an order as well as a purpose: looking out of my window I caught it in the random clods and broken heaps of snow made by the cast of a broom" (1959a: 230). In fact, he says that his poetry "[n]o doubt [...] errs on the side of oddness," but that "as air, melody, is what strikes me most of all in music and design in painting, so design, pattern or what I am in the habit of calling 'inscape' is what I above all aim at in poetry" (1935: 66). Deciphering Hopkinsian punning can amount to what John Shoptaw calls "lyric cryptography," which, he states, is "productive reading" of wordplay that may be either phonemic or graphemic. Graphemic "crypts" are those in which "the marker may add, subtract, scramble, change, or scatter the cryptograph's letters and signs" (225). Shoptaw's description is particularly apt in terms of Hopkins's poetic practice in punning and in other forms of "chiming."

The third quatrain of "I wake and feel" employs punning and wordplay to exploit the senses of taste and smell, beginning with the first line, where "I am gall, I am heartburn" (1990: 181) plays upon the meaning of "gall" as bile, as the more figurative bitterness of spirit, as brazenness (how does he have the "gall" to cry out to heaven?), and perhaps also as it is used in the earlier sonnet "The Windhover," in which the "blue-bleak embers [...] / Fall, gáll themsélves, and gásh góld-vermílion" (1990: 144). In "The Windhover," the verb "gall" seems to be associated through chiming with the verb "gash," and may be derived from the noun *gall* designating an injury or wound. All four meanings are appropriate for the tone and tenor of the poem and are sealed by the "dead" metaphor "heartburn." In fact, Kjerkegaard suggests that "dead metaphors" and clichéd expressions "have a tendency to generate wordplay" (2011: 4), a phenomenon that is certainly evident in Hopkins's renovation of the patterns of common and regional speech discussed below. In "I wake and feel," the placement of the word "Bitter" at the beginning of a line and before instead of after the verb adds emphasis to the words "gall" and "heartburn" of the previous line, and the chiasmus / chiming "me taste: my taste was me," with its repetition of "me" / "my" and of "taste" as first a verb and then a noun, bound by alliteration has the effect of compressing meaning as an echo of the hellish compression of spirit within the "bone-house" of the body: "Bones built in me, flesh filled, blood brimmed the curse." The bitter taste of the spirit, reiterated in the repetition of "b" in "bones," "blood" and "brimmed," carries over into the final stanza's coining "Selfyeast of spirit." The generative power of the spirit, when tainted by self, "sours" the potentially nutritive manna.

5 Chiming and "vowelling off"

Closely related to Hopkins's punning is a technique that he called "vowelling" or "vowelling off," reinforced by his discovery, during his time in Wales and in his reading of Welsh poetry, of *cynghanedd*, or "consonant-chime" (1935: 38). In "vowelling off" and *cynghanedd*, consonants in a series of words remain constant while their vowels change. We can see examples of this practice in the "Dark Sonnets"; for example, "This to hoard unheard, / Heard unheeded" ("To seem the stranger," 1990: 181). Here, again, Hopkins's attachment to the potentialities of the onomatopoeic theory means that "hoard," "(un)heard," and "unheeded" share more than sound, and their combination in a line or lines of poetry provides a resonance that derives from more than the sum of the parts. Sometimes Hopkins combines *cynghanedd* with assonance to create a complete rhyme, often within rather than at the ends of poetic lines ("hell's spell"; "This night! what sights"), and, as discussed previously, for Hopkins the phonological links in a chain of words often reflect semantic links.[2] Yet Hopkins's serious wordplay here also has one foot at least in the world of less serious play. Sonstroem points out that Hopkins's "vowelling off" is similar to the word-game in which the player must move through a series of steps, changing one letter at a time, from "black" to "white" for example (1967: 200–201). However, in Hopkins's "chiming," breaks or implied links may be hidden between the words, gaps whose very existence set the reader on a search for the connections. This is one form of a rhetorical device that Shoptaw identifies as "transumption or metalepsis (a figurative chain of three or more associations, the middle links being obscured or 'transumed')" (2000: 237). In terms of the "Dark Sonnets," however, the movement is frequently not from "black" to "white," but from "gray" to "black" or from "black" to "blacker."

An example may be seen in what is taken to be the first of the "Dark Sonnets," "To seem the stranger," where Hopkins laments the sense of separation

---

[2] This is described by Michael Sprinker as "the auditory repetition of the poet's experience of the world"; Hopkins "sees things anew in each succeeding moment" (1980: 61). Milroy describes this technique as "gradience" (1977: 142).

arising from his decision to convert to Catholicism and to become a Jesuit, made two decades before, along with his recent posting to Ireland:

> To seem the stranger lies my lot, my life
> Among strangers. Father and mother dear,
> Brothers and sisters are in Christ not near
> And he my peace / my parting, sword and strife.

(1990: 181)

This poem is rife with alliteration, evident in this first stanza, particularly double alliteration (a variation on vowelling off), in which alliterating words are paired, often in apposition: "my lot, my life"; "my peace / my parting"; "sword and strife." The slash between "peace" and "parting" acts as an "either-or" conjunction. *Cynghanned* is evident in the juxtaposition of such words as "Father and mother," as well as combined with assonance in "hell's spell" later in the sonnet.

In the later "No worst, there is none," the gentler (by comparison) alliterating of the previous sonnets here takes on a connotation of frenzy (1990: 182). The biting "p" of "pitched," "past," "pitch," "pangs," and "forepangs," combined with the wail of "w" in "worst," "will," "wilder," and "wring," in the first two lines alone, establishes the flavour of the rest of the poem: "No worst, there is none. Pitched past pitch of grief, / More pangs will, schooled at forepangs, wilder wring." Feeney points to Hopkins's playfulness in the phrase "My cries heave, herd-long," "comparing his moans to the mooing of cows" (2008: 28). This rather homely image, however, is overshadowed by Hopkins's alliterating of "h": "My cries heave, herds-long; huddle in a main." As we have seen, Hopkins's alliterations are rarely mere sound effects; more frequently, they are also meant to be linked semantically, a distinct possibility with "herds" and "huddle," heightened by the implied image of cows huddling in a field under the threat of a storm – perhaps the "whirlwind" of the end of the sonnet. The natural compound "whirlwind" is joined by Hopkins's own coinings, "forepangs" or previous pains, and "wórld-sorrow," perhaps a translation of the German "Weltschmerz." Hopkins was intrigued by the practice of Germanic compounding when in search of the *mot exact* to express his ideas. This practice often results in Hopkins's own interpretation of compounding through using a number of pre-modifying constructions such as "no-man-fathomed," although here the epithet follows the noun in a string of adjectives: "Frightful, sheer, no-man-fathomed." Another compound precedes "world-sorrow," the expression "chief- / Woe," and here we have another run-over rhyme with the effect of foregrounding the "Woe" of the speaker's sense of estrangement.

In what appears to be Hopkins's final "Dark Sonnet," "My own heart," the absence of homely "comfort" is again evident, strengthened through the alliteration of "c" and "g" in the first two lines of the second stanza (1990: 186). The noun "comfort" is suffixed to become "comfortless," an adjective, yet used as a noun, a more striking and hence affecting substantive than the "comfortlessness" or the "comfortless heart" that the syntax would seem to demand. "Comfortless" is linked analogically with "blind" and "thirst," again through the elliptical expression "than blind / Eyes in their dark can [get] day," and thirst's analogue to "day" is found in the homely compound "all-in-all" (as in "she was all-in-all to him").

6 Rhyme and Enjambement

Wordplay may also operate in the area of rhyme. Sonstroem, among others, has commented on Hopkins's practice of "forced rhyme," the most famous of which is his rhyming of "boon he on" with "Communion" in "The Bugler's First Communion." Hopkins also splits words at line ends – a sort of morphological enjambement, expanding the possibilities of conventional enjambement through his use of hyphens, that sometimes has the dual effect of foregrounding the first syllable, frequently exploiting its semantic potential, and then adding to its possible meanings with the addition of the suffix that begins the following line. This seems to be a particularly Hopkinsian wordplay, as Hopkins calls it "my rhyming system, using the first letter of the next line to complete the rhyme in the line before it" (1935: 48). Not only does the split put emphasis on the root word at the end of the line, it also may lead the reader into changing the part of speech or even add ambiguity or double meanings to the word. The run-over rhyme of "wear- / Y" in "To seem the stranger" plays on the sense of "wear" as verb meaning both "tire" and "don clothing," as well as the word "weary" as both verb and adjective: "I weár- / Y of idle a being but by where wars are rife" (1990: 181). In another run-over, this time in "No worst there is none," the Fury's shriek of "No ling- / Ering!" forces the reader (and the speaker) to linger over the pain of the poem, although, in the next line, Fury admonishes, "Let me be fell: force I must be brief" (1990: 182).

7 Word Coining and Neologism

When dialect, "chiming" or punning do not satisfy the needs for a heightened poetic diction, Hopkins resorts to coinages and neologisms sometimes formed on the basis of Germanic compounding or Anglo-Saxon *kennings* (see Sablayrolles, in *The Dynamics of Wordplay* 2). In Hopkins's "Dark Sonnets," these are frequently epithets: "no-man-fathomed," "wring-earth." They may also be compounds such as "lionlimb" and "betweenpie." The use of such compounds in the "Dark Sonnets" represents both an attempt to find in English words for the feelings he wishes to convey, and an attempt to express through this form of wordplay his sense of the connectedness of words themselves – the words connect, while he cannot.

Hopkins also "plays" on words in the sense of using a known word or phrase to echo a more common usage. In the second stanza of "Patience, hard thing," Hopkins's "these away" is an echo of the common usage "these absent" (that is, in the absence of these), "away" being a homelier, Germanic form more suitable for the homely imagery of the poem, which equates Patience with a plant that roots in the weary, war-ravaged, and wounded heart ("Patience, hard thing," 1990: 185). Patience, "Natural heart's-ivy," may also derive from the popular designation of the flowering plant "impatiens," popularly known as "Patience plant," symbolic of motherly love, whose "purple eyes and seas of liquid leaves" may describe the common colouring of its prolific flowers and the silvery sheen of its leaves.

Hopkins sometimes also "plays" on the semantic extensions that can be made from a common word. In a later poem, "That Nature is a Heraclitean Fire," Hopkins, after both regretting and celebrating the constant changefulness of the natural world, ends with "the comfort of the Resurrection," that with the "flash" and "trumpet crash" of death, he becomes "What Christ is" and "This Jack, joke, poor potsherd, patch, matchwood, immortal diamond, / Is immortal diamond" (1990: 197-198). Is Hopkins in the "Dark Sonnet" "My own heart" anticipating this chiming wordplay in his use of the more tentative "Soul, self; come, poor Jackself" of the third stanza? Addressing the soul as "self," he cements an identification between the two – here, the self and soul are not separate as they may have appeared in the earlier of the "Dark Sonnets," and the tender "poor Jackself" underlines the lowliness of the tormented human creature. The speaker advises his "jaded" self to "let be," the adjective "jaded" as enclosed in commas following the noun could apply to either "I" or "you," yet both are the same as the speaker addresses his own soul, and "let be" is an informal expression for "let it be" or "leave it alone." The self is advised to "leave comfort root-room," the compound reminiscent of the organic imagery of "Patience" (1990: 186).

At the end of the third stanza of "My own heart," Hopkins employs the noun "size" as verb and carries a run-over rhyme to the next stanza. "Size," like such verbs as "heighten" from "height" or "widen" from "wide," carries the implication of "grow" that follows from "root-room," while the absence of the "en" or a similar suffix gives a physical substance and strength to the term that the verb might lack. The informal use of "Jack" to refer to man is underlined by the poem's "God knows when to God knows what," as well as by the contraction "'s": a more traditional written form might be "Whose smile's [smile is] not wrung." The interjection "see you" appears to be a reminiscence of Hopkins's time in Wales and his study of Welsh dialect, as "see you" is commonly recognized as the equivalent of such expressions as "you know" or "listen." Rather than being "wrung" or forced, God's smile, writes Hopkins, appears "unforeseentimes," the compound built on "sometimes" and the verb omitted, and is compared to the sight of "skies / Betweenpie mountains." In her notes on the poem, Catherine Phillips suggests that "betweenpie" is most likely a verb, playing on the notion of "pied" or "variegated" found in Hopkins's "Pied Beauty" (Hopkins 2009: 377n). However, it may also be seen as a variation of "between," the shape of the piece of sky when suddenly viewed between mountain peaks resembling the shape of a piece of pie. Both meanings share in the homely rural flavour that Hopkins sought to give to his poetry.

Hopkins seems to have seen neologisms and nonce words as arising from a natural tendency of language, as he writes to his friend A. W. M. Baillie in 1886: "Even words [...] are sometimes two words rolled into one, approximated until they blend meanings" (1956b: 119). In an earlier letter to Baillie, he uses the term "underthought" to characterize the thought frequently contained in metaphors "often only half realised by the poet himself, not necessarily having any connection with the subject in hand but usually having a connection," while the overthought is "that which everybody, editors, see." It is overthought that can be "abridged or paraphrased" (1956b: 105). Underthought, too, may be subsumed under Shoptaw's "lyric cryptography," for the reader must exercise perseverance and perception in deciphering it.

8 Wrenched Syntax

Not only does Hopkins extend the meanings of words beyond their boundaries so that they "bleed" into the words to which they are linked phonologically and perhaps semantically (see the contributions by Renner and Knospe, this volume); he also wrenches English syntax into unfamiliar and sometimes uncomfortable shapes, engaging in what Michael Sprinker calls his "strenuous linguistic somersaults" (1980: 14). Similar gymnastic feats are also required of the reader of Hopkins. Such convoluted syntax, however, Hopkins thought not untypical of spoken (particularly regional and dialectical), if not of written, speech, a fact which Hopkins is quick to point out in his "cribs" that he sends with a combination of amusement and frustration to Bridges, Dixon, and Patmore. In fact, as he wrote to Bridges, he planned to attach "short prose arguments" to some of his poems, since "[p]lainly if it is possible to express a subtle and recondite thought on a subtle and recondite subject in a subtle and recondite way and with great felicity and perfection, in the end, something must be sacrificed, with so trying a task, in the process, and this may be the being at once, nay perhaps even the being without explanation at all, intelligible" (1935: 265–266).[3] Hopkins at times foregrounds the object ("My own heart let me have more pity on") in periodic sentence structure. He interrupts subject and verb or verb and object with interjections, either framed in dashes or in parentheses. The patterns of spoken (that is, broken) speech are present in "I wake and feel" in such interjections as "O" and "alas!" and the repetitions with added words: "What hours, O what black hours we have spent / This night!" (1990: 181). The multiple commas in the third and fourth lines of the first quatrain, which add a staccato rhythm to the broken speech, also lend the flavour of the stress arising from putting thoughts into speech. Hopkins again employs repetition in "cries countless, cries like dead letters," each addition mimicking the speaker's efforts to put words to his cries, and the unusual placement of the adjective "countless" after the noun manages to emphasize both noun and negative epithet. Another unusual epithet usage is "dear" (a favourite of Hopkins) whose position before the pronoun "him" accentuates the homely comfort of love for Christ or God before the comfort is undercut by the relative clause "that lives alas! away."

Hopkins also omits opening words and relative pronouns; he violates "poetic decorum" by moving parts of speech to what seem to be "unnatural positions." For example, in "To seem the stranger," Hopkins manipulates syntax and word placement in the second line, where "Father and mother dear" may signify 'Dear mother and father' or 'Father and mother, although (or 'are') dear' (1990: 181). In both cases, compression and skewed word order place an added stress on the word "dear," and, by extension, on its rhyme in the next line,

---

[3] Sprinker comments that "[f]or Hopkins, poetry is speech, and speech is, paradoxically, a kind of writing" (1980: 69).

"Brothers and sisters are in Christ not near," where the placement of "not near" at the end of the line, rather than after "are" again foregrounds the sense of distance. Syntax-play, in this case based on a more common idiom, is also evident in the phrase "idle a being," which may be an implied play on such more conventional expressions as "How beautiful a day it is" or (in the context of Hopkins's sonnet) "How idle a being I am," as well as more directly reversing "I weary of being idle."

The dual participial and substantive forms of "being" suggested in the line, combined with the adjective / noun dualities of 'weary" and "idle" emphasize the speaker's ennui. In addition, the technique of chiasmus, in which one word, or a form of a word, is used in adjacent phrases, but in inverted syntax, reflects both a deceptive sense of closeness combined with a wrenching dislocation; Hopkins writes that he is "in Ireland now; now I am a third / Remove," and later, that England "would neither hear / Me, were I pleading, pleading nor do I." With the foregrounding of the distancing "Remove," combined with the repeated negatives, these chiasmi create a chasm in the poem itself that is reiterated in the final two lines: "This to hoard unheard, / Heard unheeded, leaves me a lonely began." "Heard" also plays on the word "hoard," and we know from Hopkins's word notes in his journals that he most likely assumed a semantic association between such phonologically similar words. The conversion of the past tense verb "began" to end the poem to a noun denoting someone who has begun but who has never fulfilled his promise, through dislocating the rules of grammar dislocates the speaker himself.

Hopkins employs a similar technique in "Patience, hard thing," where he begins with employing a sort of chiasmus combined with zeugma, as Patience is called a "hard thing" ("hard" implying not only difficult but also stony, strict or rigid), and then the hardness is qualified with "the hard thing but to pray, / But bid for, patience is!" The statement "Patience who asks / Wants war, wants wounds," with its absence of punctuation after "asks," implies that this virtue is developed not through simple asking for, but through the necessity of adversity and pain. Like the wretch wrestling with his God, the sinner "wants war" so that his patience, "Natural heart's-ivy," may grow (1990: 185).

As Charles Kreszewski has pointed out, Hopkins may have found precedence for such devices in dialect English, particularly in the poetry of the Dorset poet William Barnes (1995: 14; see also Russell-Brown 1986). Hopkins had, in fact, written of Barnes's work in dialect: "Its lawful charm and use I take to be this, that it sort of guarantees the spontaneousness of the thought and puts you in the position to appraise it on its merits as coming from nature and not books and education" (1935: 87–88). Hopkins's use of the epithet "lawful" here is significant, for it demonstrates that, rather than violating the "laws" of poetic English, Hopkins's intention is to follow what he considers to be a "higher" law – that of boosting "natural" speech to the level of poetry: "the poetical language of an age shd. [sic] be the current language heightened, to any degree heightened and unlike itself, but not [...] an obsolete one" (1935: 89). In this heightening of language, Hopkins was very much aware of the possibilities of spoken language that allowed more flexibility to instress the inscapes of the exterior and interior world. As Peter Dixon reminds us, "Hopkins was not lax in matters of grammar" (1989: 35): Hopkins's grammar, at least as he justifies it, comprises both written and spoken speech.

The sense of disorientation in the "Dark Sonnets" is created in part by the techniques of interruption and omission. In his letters and journals, Hopkins frequently defended his word and syntax choices by making reference to the cadences of speech. He wrote to Coventry Patmore: "Such verse as I do compose is oral, made away from paper, and I put it down with repugnance" (1956b: 380). He also noted any unusual forms of syntax that he had picked up in his travels. In the poem "Carrion comfort," the broken thoughts of a fractured mind are echoed both in the many repetitions of negative forms and in the interruptions signalled by the frequent interjections as well as the omission of pronouns:

> Not, I'll not, carrion comfort, Despair, not feast on thee;
> Not untwist—slack they may be—these last strands of man
> In me ór, most weary, cry *I can no more*. I can;
> Can something, hope, wish day come, not choose not to be.
>
> But ah, but O thou terrible, why wouldst thou rude on me
> Thy wring-earth right foot rock? lay a lionlimb against me? Scan
> With darksome devouring eyes my bruisèd bones? And fan,
> O in turns of tempest, me heaped there; me frantic to avoid thee and flee?
>
> Why? That my chaff might fly; my grain lie, sheer and clear.
> Nay in all that toil, that coil, since (seems) I kissed the rod,
> Hand rather, my heart lo! lapped strength, stole joy, would laugh, cheer.
>
> Cheer whóm, though? The heró whose héaven-handling flúng me, fóot tród
> Me? Or mé that fóught him? O whích one? is it eách one? That níght, that year
> Of now done darkness I wretch lay wrestling with (my God!) my God.

(1990: 183)

Sprinker notes of this sonnet that it "protests, it refuses, it resists, but all this in the negative mode" (1980: 130). And the negative mode begins with the first word, "Not," reiterated throughout the first stanza, along with the modal "can"; the speaker will not "cry *I can no more.* I can; / Can something, hope, wish day come, not choose not to be." The first "I can" that closes with the semicolon seems is an assertion of will, each successive verb moving from the vague "can something" through the hopeful "wish day come," to the convolutions of the double negative "not choose not to be." In other words, the speaker cannot choose the "comfort [that] serves in whirlwind," the carrion comfort of death. The "comfort" of the final lines of "No worst, there is none" is now "carrion comfort, Despair," the alliterating and consonantal expression followed by "not feast" picking up the notion of deadly comfort from the previous poem.

9 Conclusion

It is possible to see Hopkins's wordplay in the "Dark Sonnets" as a function of the disciplined compression of the sonnet form itself. Feeney describes the "Dark Sonnets" in terms of competition, another of Huizinga's ludic criteria; the Sonnets represent "a private, poignant contest between expressing self-dissolution and obeying the formal rules of a sonnet," a contest which '[t]he perfect sonnet always wins" (2008: 49). Critics such as Jennifer Ann Wagner, however, disagree that in this contest the "perfect sonnet" has won, for Wagner sees Hopkins as one of a few poets since Wordsworth who have, in a sense, experimented with and redesigned the sonnet to accommodate their own private visions: Sometimes this experimentation "produces sonnets that trope their own thematic mortification" (1996: 19). Such is the case with Hopkins's "Dark Sonnets." Hopkins, indeed, makes serious work of play in the "Dark Sonnets," in which the sonnet framework serves as a visible container for the claustrophobia experienced by the self.

As I have begun with reference to the theories of Joseph Feeney, so will I use them to make an end. Feeney characterizes the "moments of play" in the "Dark Sonnets" as "a counterpoint to the pain they express" (2008: 123). I would argue, however, that such "playing with words" to be found here should not be regarded as counterpoint, but rather as a complement to and extension of their very pain. Hopkins's "Dark Sonnets," frequently disregarded or given short shrift in any study of the poet's wordplay, themselves share in both the motivation and the implementation of the techniques that he had so fruitfully exploited in his earlier celebratory nature poetry. I have used Hopkins's own words explaining his poetic craft to trace the intricate patterns of language play in these six poems, with their "cliffs of fall" on the surface so starkly different from the "azurous hung hills" of Hopkins's harvest scenes. I have also had, at times, to engage in just as complex a dance of words as Hopkins himself would have given, but without his sureness of foot. Stefan Kjerkegaard comments in his study of puns in literature that "[t]here is something cross-eyed [...] about every explanatory poetics" (2011: 241), and I apologize for any critical strabismus that my analyses may have engendered. As I continue to work more extensively and systematically with the variety of wordplay in these poems, tracing connections between "The Dark Sonnets" and the full body of Hopkins verse, I hope to show more clearly how Hopkins's sense of play was not confined to his nature and earlier religious poetry, but also to those poems written from a sense of exile.

10 References

Boyle, Robert. 1961. *Metaphor in Hopkins*. Chapel Hill, NC: University of North Carolina Press.
Crystal, David. 2001. *Language Play*. Chicago: University of Chicago Press.
Dixon, Peter. 1989. Hopkins's "No worst, there is none." *Explicator* 47(2). 35–36.
Feeney, Joseph J. 2008. *The Playfulness of Gerard Manley Hopkins*. Aldershot: Ashgate.
Harris, Daniel A. 1982. *Inspirations Unbidden: The "Terrible Sonnets" of Gerard Manley Hopkins*. Berkeley: University of California Press.
Hopkins, Gerard Manley. 1935. *The Letters of Gerard Manley Hopkins to Robert Bridges*. Claude Colleer Abbott (ed.). London: Oxford University Press.
Hopkins, Gerard Manley. 1956a. *The Correspondence of Gerard Manley Hopkins and Richard Watson Dixon*. Claude Colleer Abbott (ed.). London: Oxford University Press.
Hopkins, Gerard Manley. 1956b. *Further Letters of Gerard Manley Hopkins, Including His Correspondence with Coventry Patmore*. Claude Colleer Abbott (ed.). London: Oxford University Press.
Hopkins, Gerard Manley. 1959a. *The Journals and Papers of Gerard Manley Hopkins*. Humphry House & Graham Storey (eds.). London: Oxford University Press.
Hopkins, Gerard Manley. 1959b. *The Sermons and Devotional Writings of Gerard Manley Hopkins*. Christopher Devlin (ed.). London: Oxford University Press.
Hopkins, Gerard Manley. 1990. *The Poetical Works of Gerard Manley Hopkins*. Norman H. MacKenzie (ed.). Oxford: Clarendon.
Hopkins, Gerard Manley. 2009. *The Major Works*. Catherine Phillips (ed.). London: Oxford World's Classics.
Huizinga, Johan. [1938] 1980. *Homo ludens: Proeve eener bepaling van het spel-element der cultuur* [Homo Ludens: A Study of the Play-Element in Culture]. London: Routledge and Kegan Paul.
Kjerkegaard, Stefan. 2011. Seven Days without a Pun Makes One Weak: Two Functions of Wordplay in Literature and Literary Theory. *Journal of Literature, Language and Linguistics* 3(1). 1–9.
Kreszewski, Charles S. 1995. Hopkins's "My own heart let me have more pity on" and Barnes's Poems in the Dorset Dialect. *Explicator* 54(1).14–17.

Martin, Meredith. 2008. Gerard Manley Hopkins and the Stigma of Meter. *Victorian Studies* 50(2). 243–253.

Milroy, James. 1977. *The Language of Gerard Manley Hopkins*. London: Andre Deutsch.

Milroy, James. 1984. Hopkins the Purist (?): Some Comments on the Sources and Applications of Hopkins's Principles of Poetic Diction. In John S. North & Michael D. Moore (eds.), *Vital Candle: Victorian and Modern Bearings in Gerard Manley Hopkins*, 143–155. Waterloo: University of Waterloo Press.

Plotkin, Cary Howard. 1989. *The Tenth Muse: Victorian Philology and the Genesis of the Poetic Language of Gerard Manley Hopkins*. Carbondale: Southern Illinois University Press.

Russell–Brown, Sheelagh. 1986. *Hopkins, Barnes, and the "Teutonizers": The Role of William Barnes and the Anglo-Saxon Purists in the Formation of Gerard Manley Hopkins' Poetic Language*. Fredericton: University of New Brunswick dissertation.

Salmon, Rachel. 1984. Prayers of Praise and Prayers of Petition: Simultaneity in the Sonnet World of Gerard Manley Hopkins. *Victorian Poetry* 22(4). 383–406.

Shoptaw, John. 2000. Lyric Cryptography. *Poetics Today* 21 (1). 221–262.

Sonstroem, David. 1967. Making Earnest of Game: G. M. Hopkins and Nonsense Poetry. *Modern Language Quarterly* 28(2). 192–206.

Sprinker, Michael. 1980. *"A Counterpoint of Dissonance": The Aesthetics and Poetry of Gerard Manley Hopkins*. Baltimore: Johns Hopkins University Press.

Wagner, Jennifer Ann. 1996. *A Moment's Monument: Revisionary Poetics and the Nineteenth-Century English Sonnet*. Madison: Fairleigh Dickinson University Press.

White, Norman. 1987. G. M. Hopkins's Contributions to the *English Dialect Dictionary*. *English Studies* 68(4). 325–335.

Wimsatt, James I. 1998. Alliteration and Hopkins's Sprung Rhythm. *Poetics Today* 19(4). 531–564.

II Linguistic Techniques of Wordplay

Vincent Renner
Lexical Blending as Wordplay

Abstract: This article deals with wordplay in word-formation and centers on lexical blending. It claims that, because of their very formation process, lexical blends are instances of wordplay. Drawing on examples from a variety of languages, it offers a categorization of the different features which may be argued to increase wordplayfulness into five classes: formal complexity, structural transgression, graphic play on words, semantic play on words, and functional ludicity.

Keywords: backronymy, Basque, clipping, compounding, English, French, German, Hungarian, Italian, Korean, Latvian, lexical blending, ludic function (of language), Malay, Mandarin Chinese, Modern Greek, Modern Hebrew, naming function, Polish, Serbian, Spanish, word-formation

1 Introduction: Wordplay in Word-Formation

> We play with language when we manipulate it as a source of enjoyment [...]. I mean "manipulate" literally: we take some linguistic feature [...] and make it do things it does not normally do.
> David Crystal (2001: 1)

The aim of this article is to apply the concept of wordplay to the linguistic domain of word-formation. The definition of wordplay adopted for this research is the following: an intentional and formally ingenious way of associating the semantics of two or more words in a new morphological object. It only partially overlaps with the definition of word-creation as described by Ronneberger-Sibold (2010). Word-creation is centered on the concept of formal creativity and it encompasses all intentional extra-grammatical morphological processes, i.e. operations in which the output form is not fully predictable from an input and a given rule and is impervious to (un)grammaticality judgments. If lexical blending can be said to be a technique which is both creative and playful, clipping is creative but is not playful (wordplay as defined above crucially involves two inputs) while compounding can be playful – as in the case of metaphtonymic echo compounds (see below) – but is not creative in the sense of Ronneberger-Sibold as it is a concatenative process.

Several types of outputs can illustrate wordplay in word-formation, for instance metaphtonymic echo compounds, backronyms and lexical blends.[1] Metaphtonymic echo compounding consists in concatenating words which are formally quasi-identical into a metonymy- and / or metaphor-based compound. Formal variation may appear at the onset (1)–(5) – the compounding elements have the same rime or superrime – or word-internally in case of medial vocalic alternation (6):

(1) *Aga saga* 'middle-class novel'[2]
(2) *brain drain* 'loss of skilled labor'
(3) *kick flick* 'martial arts movie'
(4) *sin bin* 'penalty box'
(5) *trout pout* 'collagen-enhanced lips'
(6) *shit sheet* 'negative campaign flyer'

Backronymy is a playful process in which the operation of initialization leads to an already existing word, as in (7)–(11):

(7) ALICE < *all-purpose lightweight individual carrying equipment*
(8) MACHO < *massive compact halo object*
(9) SQUID < *superconducting quantum interference device*
(10) WASP < *White Anglo-Saxon Protestant*
(11) WIMP < *weakly interacting massive particle*

Playfulness is increased when the meaning of the earlier word is associated with that of the new backronym, as in (12)–(16):

(12) BASIC < *beginners' all-purpose symbolic instruction code* 'easy-to-learn programming language designed to provide computer access to non-science students'
(13) GIFT < *gamete intra-fallopian transfer* 'assisted reproductive technique against infertility'
(14) RIDE < *reduce impaired driving in Etobicoke*[3] 'campaign against drink-driving'
(15) START < *strategic arms reduction treaty* 'treaty intended to stop the nuclear arms race between the US and the Soviet Union'

---

[1] For a discussion of more types, see Sablayrolles in The Dynamics of Wordplay 2.
[2] The metonymy alludes to the "popularity of Aga cookers among the English middle classes" (*Collins English Dictionary*).
[3] Etobicoke is a district of the city of Toronto, Ontario.

(16) USA PATRIOT < uniting (and) strengthening America (by) providing appropriate tools required (to) intercept (and) obstruct terrorism 'Act of the US Congress signed into law in October 2011, in the wake of 9 / 11'

Lexical blending refers to the act of coalescing several words into one after an act of clipping (17), of overlapping (18), or of both clipping and overlapping (19)[4]:

(17) caplet < capsule + tablet
(18) sexpert < sex + expert
(19) positron < positive + electron

Because of the wide variety of attested patterns, blending can be claimed to be the most complex form of wordplay in word-formation, and this article aims to lay bare these formal intricacies. In the following section, the salient formal and semantic features of lexical blends are introduced, and in Section 3 a detailed taxonomy of playful techniques is then proposed.

2 A Brief Description of Lexical Blends

Lexical blends crop up in a variety of domains, from slang (20) to technoscientific terminology (21), from popular media culture (22) to the corporate world (23)–(24):

(20) chillax < chill + relax
(21) disulfiram < disulfide + tetraethylthiuram
(22) Merkozy < (Angela) Merkel + (Nicolas) Sarkozy
(23) Gemalto < Gemplus + Axalto
(24) ABB < ASEA (< Allmänna Svenska Elektriska Aktiebolaget) + BBC (< Brown, Boveri and Cie)

Blending is a cross-linguistically widespread process. Brdar-Szabo and Brdar (2008) hypothesize that it can appear in any language in which compounding and clipping are both attested morphological operations. The phenomenon is mainly documented in Indo-European languages, but it is also observed in languages as typologically diverse as Korean (Kang 2013), Malay (Dobrovolsky

---

[4] Segment overlapping is marked through underlining.

2001), Mandarin Chinese (Ronneberger-Sibold 2012) and Modern Hebrew (Bat-El 2013).

The precise definition of lexical blending is not beyond debate. Some morphologists consider that a lexical item qualifies as a member of the category if at least one source word has been clipped in the blending process (e.g. Mattiello 2013; Miller 2014), but others exclude several types of complex words on various grounds:

- for Ralli and Xydopoulos (2012) and Villoing (2012), a complex word is to be categorized as a blend only if no source word has remained intact, which leads to the exclusion of items such as *contrail* (< *condensation* + *trail*) and *tenoroon* (< *tenor* + *bassoon*);
- for Bat-El (2006), a complex word is unequivocally a blend only if clipping occurs at the "inner edges," i.e. if the left source word has been back-clipped and the right one fore-clipped, which leads to the exclusion of items such as *modem* (< *modulator* + *demodulator*) and *frohawk* (< *afro* + *mohawk*);
- for Dressler (2000), complex words whose source words are not semantically coordinate (i.e. are in a modifier-head relation), such as *rockumentary* (< *rock* + *documentary*) and *wallyball* (< *wall* + *volleyball*), are to be removed from the category of blends; similarly, for Plag (2003: 123), "proper blends" are those items which semantically "resemble copulative compounds," i.e. are in a coordinate relation;
- for Arcodia and Montermini (2012), complex words which do not manifest overlapping of their source words are not part of the category, which leads to the exclusion of items such as *ginormous* (< *gigantic* + *enormous*) and *humiture* (< *humidity* + *temperature*).

In order to reconcile these conflicting views, one may opt for a prototype approach to categorization and consider that the most inclusive definition is to be retained and that the above traits are not to be taken as defining features, but as typicality features. A blend like *cafetorium* (< *cafeteria* + *auditorium*) is a central member of the category as it displays clipping of both source words at the inner edges, medial overlapping (one shared segment at the graphic level, two at the phonic level) and coordinate semantics.

Various semantic classifications of lexical blends have been suggested in the literature. Fradin, Montermini and Plénat (2009: 39–41), for instance, list five main types of semantic interpretations: coordinate, intersective, argumental, equative, causal. Gries (2012: 154–155) does the same, but with wholly different categories: synonymic, co-hyponymic, contractive, frame relation, other. One can also unproblematically extend the existing typologies of the compounding literature to blends.[5] Table 1 illustrates the transcategorial dichotomy between coordinative and subordinative items,[6] which is primordial, even more so for blends than for compounds in view of the significant proportion of items for which the two source words are on an equal semantic footing. In English, only a tiny minority of compounds (about 2%) have a coordinative interpretation (Berg 2009: 134) while this is the case of a sizeable minority (about one out of four) of blends (Renner 2014).

Tab. 1: A dual semantic classification of lexical blends

	coordinative	subordinative
nominal	*zonkey* (< *zebra* + *donkey*)	*rockoon* (< *rocket* + *balloon*)
adjectival	*solunar* (< *solar* + *lunar*)	*fugly* (< *fucking* + *ugly*)
verbal	*meld* (< *melt* + *weld*)	*gazunder* (< *gazump* + *under*)

In the case of the largest category – that of noun-noun nominal blends –, the classification can be refined as follows: one may distinguish between subordinative items with a relational (25) or an attributive (26) interpretation,[7] and coordinative items with hybrid (27), multifunctional (28), additional (29) or tautological (30) semantics[8]:

(25) *netiquette* 'etiquette practiced on the net'
(26) *advertorial* 'advert that looks like an editorial'
(27) *siabon* 'hybrid offspring of a siamang and a gibbon'

---

5 See Scalise and Bisetto (2009); and Arnaud and Renner (2014) for an overview.
6 Subordinative units are characterized by the presence of a semantic nonhead-to-head relation between the source words (e.g. a rockoon is a rocket that is launched from a balloon) while coordinative units are characterized by the absence of such a relation.
7 The semantic relation of modification in the subclass of attributive subordinatives consists in the attribution of features of the non-head to the head. The subordinatives which do not exhibit analogy in their nonhead-to-head relation are grouped together in the subclass of relational subordinatives.
8 A hybrid interpretation corresponds to an A+B unit defined as a hybrid of A and B, a multifunctional interpretation to a unit defined as an A which is also a B, an additional interpretation to a unit defined as an A plus a B, a tautological interpretation to a unit composed of two near-synonyms (see Renner 2008).

(28) *Spork* 'utensil that can be used both as a spoon and a fork'
(29) *Quechumaran* 'group of languages composed of the Quechuan and Aymaran families'
(30) *doohickey* 'doodad; hickey'

3 A Typology of Wordplayfulness in Lexical Blending

Any process of lexical blending – e.g. *breakfast* + *lunch* > *brunch* – can be considered as involving some form of wordplay as it is an operation which plays with a variety of potential output forms to name a new conceptual combination. In some cases, this potential is actualized, and different outputs generated from the same two source words are co-institutionalized,[9] with identical (31) or different (32)–(34) meanings:

(31) Engl. *tigon / tiglon* 'hybrid offspring of a male tiger and a female lion'
(32) Engl. *apriplum / plumcot* '50-50 plum-apricot hybrid'
(33) Engl. *aprium* 'apricot-heavy hybrid'
(34) Engl. *pluot* 'plum-heavy hybrid'

Various features can be claimed to increase the wordplayfulness of a blend. They will be detailed and illustrated in the subsections to follow, and have been grouped under five general headings: formal complexity, structural transgression, graphic play on words, semantic play on words, and functional ludicity.

3.1 Formal Complexity

Segment overlapping at the inner edges is a frequent feature of lexical blending. The overlapping segments are underlined in examples (35)–(39)[10]:

(35) Mod. Hebr. *pomelit* 'pomelo-grapefruit hybrid' < *poméla* 'pomelo' + *ʔeškolit* 'grapefruit'

---

9 A unit is said to be institutionalized when its meaning has been established in a particular domain within a community (see Bauer 2004: 56).
10 (35) is taken from Bat-El (1996: 320); (36) from Borgwaldt and Benczes (2011: 233): (37) from Thornton (1993: 151); (38) from Artiagoitia, Hualde and de Urbina (forthcoming); and (39) from Veisbergs (2013: 49).

(36) Hung. *citrancs* 'grapefruit' < *citrom* 'lemon' + *narancs* 'orange'
(37) Ital. *mandarancio* 'mandarin-orange hybrid' < *mandarino* 'mandarin' + *arancio* 'orange'
(38) Bsq. *sagardo* 'cider' < *sagar* 'apple' + *ardo* 'wine'
(39) Latv. *mēstule* 'spam' < *mēslu* 'excrement' + *vēstule* 'letter'

It is maximized in a phenomenon which Piñeros (2011: 75) describes as "extensive overlapping," in which all but a few segments of both source words have been kept in a so-called "contour blend" (Ronneberger-Sibold 2006: 170), that is a blend which retains the prosodic structure (i.e. the syllabic length and stress pattern) of the longer source word:

(40) Engl. *ambisextrous* 'bisexual' < *ambidextrous* + *sex*
(41) Span. *dedocracia* 'arbitrary exercise of power' < *a dedo* 'through string-pulling' + *democracia* 'democracy'[11]

Formal complexity also occurs in case of sandwich blending, when a blend has more alternating fragments than it has source words:

(42) Engl. *chortle* < *ch* + *ort* + *le* < *chuckle* + *snort*
(43) Engl. *humongous* < *hu* + *mon* + *g* + *ous* < *huge* + *monstrous*
(44) Pol. *KoPuNa* 'KPN as a communist party' < *K* + *o* + *P* + *u* + *N* + *a* < *KPN* 'Confederation of Independent Poland' + *komuna* 'communists'[12]

The recovery of the source words is in a similar way made less easy – and thus more playful – in case of cryptoblending, when the output is formally identical to a part of one of the source words:

(45) Germ. *Ostalgie* 'nostalgia for East Germany' < *Osten* 'East' + *Nostalgie* 'nostalgia'[13]
(46) Engl. *avigation* 'aerial navigation' < *avi-* + *navigation*
(47) Engl. *tween* 'child between middle childhood and adolescence' < *teen* + *between*

Formal complexity may also correspond to cases of multiple blending, i.e. the process of simultaneously coalescing more than two source words into one:

---

[11] (41) is taken from Piñeros (2011: 96).
[12] (44) is taken from Konieczna (2012: 61).
[13] (45) is taken from Friedrich (2008: 424).

(48) Engl. *turducken* 'turkey stuffed with a duck which is stuffed with a small chicken' < *turkey + duck + chicken*

(49) Fr. *camfranglais* 'mixture of Cameroonian Creole, French and English'< *camerounais* 'Cameroonian Creole' + *français* 'French' + *anglais* 'English'

(50) Engl. *Cablinasian* (a term coined by US professional golfer Tiger Woods to refer to his mixed ethnic ancestry) < *Caucasian + Black + Indian + Asian*[14]

(51) Engl. *Christmahanukkwanzadandiwalstice* (an inclusive term used to refer to the December holidays) < *Christmas + Hanukkah + Kwanzaa + Ramadan + Diwali + (Winter) Solstice*[15]

Blends composed of more than three source words (50)–(51) are exceptionally rare and therefore highly marked.

3.2 Structural Transgression

The violation of structural well-formedness rules may occur in the phonology, as in (52), with an output form that contains a syllable onset cluster which is phonotactically illicit in Modern Greek, or (53), which goes against the English syllable constraint which dictates that "if a nasal occurs in the second slot of an onset no nasal occurs in the coda" (Davis 1985: 25):

(52) Mod. Grk. *mbatáta* 'rubbish thing' < *malakía* 'junk' + *patáta* 'crap'[16]

(53) Engl. *smang* 'have sex' < *smash + bang*[17]

More commonly, violations are attested in the grammar of the language. Lexical blending may allow combinations of lexical categories which are illicit in compounding, as the following verb-verb verbal units (54)–(55) and noun-verb verbal units (56)–(57) illustrate[18]:

(54) Fr. *pleurire* 'cry and laugh' < *pleurer* 'cry' + *rire* 'laugh'

(55) Fr. *somnobavait* 'was drowsing and drooling' < *somnoler* 'be half-asleep' + *baver* [drool]

(56) Fr. *cadonner* 'give as a present' < *cadeau* 'present' + *donner* 'give'

(57) Fr. *valdorloter* 'pamper in the Aosta Valley' < *val d'Aoste* 'Aosta Valley' + *dorloter* 'pamper'

---

14 See *Word Spy* (2008: "Cablinasian" *n.*).
15 See *Urban Dictionary* (2007: "Christmahanukkwandiwalstice" *n.*).
16 (52) is taken from Ralli and Xydopoulos (2012: 43).
17 See *Urban Dictionary* (2011: "smang" *v.*).
18 (54)–(55) are taken from Doppagne (1973: 97); (57) is from Bonhomme (1998: 95).

Another case of transgression is the violation of the linear ordering rules which are applicable in compounding (58)–(59) and in syntax (60)–(61):

(58) Fr. *gazinière* 'gas stove' < *gaz* 'gas' + *cuisinière* 'stove'
(59) Engl. *Terylene* (a proprietary name for polyethylene terephthalate) < *terephthalate* + *polyethylene*
(60) Fr. *imméprévision* 'nowcast' < *immédiate* 'immediate' + *prévision* 'forecast'
(61) Engl. *planetesimal* 'miniature planet' < *planet* + *infinitesimal*

Left-headedness is the norm in French compounding, and so is right-headedness in English. Right-headed compounding is attested in French (e.g. *photojournalisme, véloroute*[19]), and so is left-headed compounding in English (e.g. *clams casino, endgame*[20]), but such cases are exceedingly rare. Likewise, attributive adjectival modification is prenominal in English whereas postnominal modification is the unmarked case in French.

Finally, it should be noted that a lexical blend may denote a group of individuals even though such a thing is impossible in the grammar of compounding of the language in question:

(62) Engl. *Billary* < *Bill (Clinton)* + *Hillary (Clinton)*
(62') "*it really just reinforced this idea that it is Billary* [*Bill-Hillary] *that is the candidate*" (Corpus of Contemporary American English / COCA 2008: "Billary" n.)
(63) Engl. *Brangelina* < *Brad (Pitt)* + *Angelina (Jolie)*
(63') "*sometimes I just want to read People magazine and check in with how Brangelina* [*Brad-Angelina] *are doing*" (COCA 2010: "Brangelina" n.)

3.3 Graphic Play on Words

Graphic play on words groups together the techniques of wordplayfulness which are formally perceptible only in writing. Graphic blending corresponds *sensu stricto* to cases in which the output is homophonous with one of the source words:

---

19 *Photojournalisme* [photojournalism] refers to a type of journalism in which news stories are presented primarily through photographs and *véloroute* [bicycle route] to an uninterrupted and signposted cycling itinerary using public roads and / or independent bikeways.
20 *Clams casino* refers to a clam dish which was reportedly first served in a casino restaurant (see Olver 2009) and *endgame* to the closing stage of a game of chess.

(64) Engl. *pharming* 'production of pharmaceuticals from genetically altered plants or animals' < *pharmaceutical* + *farming*

(65) Engl. *Jewbilee* < *Jew* + *jubilee*

Other cases of graphic play on words involve the alternation of capital and lower-case letters (66)–(67) and the use of parentheses (68)–(70) or symbols (71)[21]:

(66) Serb. *nagRADIO* ('an ad slogan of a radio station which gives out prizes to its listeners' < *nagradio* 'gave out a prize' + *radio*)
(67) Pol. *ROPucha* 'ROP as a disgusting political party' < *ROP* 'Movement for the Reconstruction of Poland' + *ropucha* 'toad'
(68) Pol. *ban(knoty)* 'banknotes which were a flop' < *banknoty* 'banknotes' + *knoty* 'flops'
(69) Pol. *(za)piski* 'squealing noise' < *zapiski* 'notes' + piski '*squeal*'
(70) Germ. S(CH)EISS 'shitty Switzerland' < *Scheiß(e)* 'shit' + *CH* 'country code for Switzerland'
(71) Germ. *ANL€GER* (the title of a bank's personal finance magazine) < *Anleger* 'investor' + € 'euro'

The upper-case / lower-case contrast (66)–(67) and the parentheses (68)–(70) are used to mark the internal boundaries of the shorter source word in case of full overlapping. The use of a symbol in example (71) is a special case with limited applicability – it is only possible if the symbol in question corresponds to a quasi-alphabetic character.

3.4 Semantic Play on Words

Wordplayfulness does not necessarily only involve the formal manipulation of the source words. In a remarkable number of instances, the association of source words is guided by a salient semantic relation. Examples (72)–(77) are all to be interpreted in the same way – a meaningful segmental string of the longer source word is identified and replaced by its antonym:

(72) Engl. *underwhelm* < *under* + *overwhelm* [under / over]
(73) Engl. / Fr. *sousveillance* 'countersurveillance' < *sous* 'under' + *surveillance* [sous / sur][22]

---

[21] (66) is taken from Halupka-Rešetar and Lalić-Krstin (2009: 118); (67)–(69) are from Konieczna (2012: 61, 62); and (70)–(71) from Friedrich (2008: 281, 448).
[22] The blend was reportedly coined in English – but with French source words – by Steve Mann, a Canadian academic. See *Word Spy* (2005: "sousveillance" n.).

(74) Fr. *tapuscrit* 'typed manuscript' < *tapé* 'typed' + *manuscrit* 'manuscript' [Fr. *tap(é)* / Lat. *manu*]
(75) Fr. *embrouillamaxi* 'giant muddle' < *embrouillamini* [muddle] + *maxi(mum)* [*maxi / mini*]
(76) Fr. *pantacourt* 'capri pants' < *pantalon* 'pants' + *court* 'short' [*court / long*]
(77) Span. *dictablanda* 'soft dictatorship' < *dictadura* 'dictatorship' + *blanda* 'soft' [*blanda / dura*][23]

3.5 Functional Ludicity

To gauge the playfulness of a blend, one may also take into consideration the relative foregrounding / backgrounding of two antagonistic (albeit coexisting) functions of word-formation: its naming function, and the corollary information condensation function in the specific case of complex words, and its ludic (i.e. playful) function. Playfulness is backgrounded when the act of word-formation primarily has a naming and an information condensation function, as is the case for blends belonging to a technical terminology in the widest sense (78)–(81), for opaque blends with metaphtonymic semantics (82) and for items which combine these two features (83)–(84):

(78) Fr. *carburéacteur* 'jet fuel' < *carburant* 'fuel' + *réacteur* 'jet engine'
(79) Fr. *pénaltouche* 'penalty kicked into touch' < *pénalité* 'penalty kick' + *touche* 'touch'
(80) Engl. *bit* < *binary* + *digit*
(81) Engl. *praziquantel* 'type of drug against parasitic worms' < *pyrazine* + *quinoline* + *anthelmintic*
(82) Fr. *midinette* 'dressmaker's apprentice' < *midi* 'noon' + *dînette* 'light meal'
(83) Engl. *nicad* 'battery with a nickel anode and a cadmium cathode' < *nickel* + *cadmium*
(84) Engl. *splake* 'type of hybrid trout' < *speckled (trout)* + *lake (trout)*

Relative positions on a cline can be assigned, and it might be argued that blends which have retained minimal material from their source words – like example (80) – are closer to the naming end of the cline, i.e. are less playful, than complete blends – like example (82) –, which contain their source words in full.

Conversely, playfulness is foregrounded when the act of word-formation primarily fulfills a ludic function. This is for instance the case when the opera-

---

23 (77) is taken from Pharies (1987: 273).

tion of blending is chiefly motivated by the possibility of maximizing overlapping[24]:

(85) Mod. Grk. *krévome* 'burp while having a haircut' < *kurévome* 'have a haircut' + *révome* 'burp'
(86) Fr. *babarbiturique* 'tranquillizer strong enough to sedate an elephant' < *Babar* (the name of a well-known fictional elephant) + *barbiturique* 'barbiturate'
(87) Fr. *discourbette* 'flattering words uttered to be seen in a favorable light by one's boss' < *discours* 'speech' + *courbette* 'low bow'

Examples (86)–(87) fall at the extreme ludic end of the cline and could be termed *semasiological blends*[25] as they are not attested in discourse and have been coined on purely formal grounds, a humorous definition being forged only subsequently to the formation of the blend. Dictionary-like books containing long lists of such coinages and their definitions have become popular in France since the 1980s (see Léturgie 2012).

4 Conclusion

Coining a new lexical blend is an act of wordplay. Even the simple clipping and fusing of *breakfast* and *lunch* into *brunch* is, as the following excerpt – which is the earliest attestation of the blend recorded in the *Oxford English Dictionary* (2014: "brunch" *n*.) – illustrates:

> The combination-meal, when nearer the usual breakfast hour, is "brunch," and when nearer luncheon, is "blunch."
>
> *Punch* (1896, vol. 111: 58)

The new form may be rendered more playful if the coiner does not simply aim at clipping a source word, but is also eager to repeat the act (sandwich blending, multiple blending), to play with phonemes (overlapping, cryptoblending) and characters (graphic play on words), with morphemic segmentation and sense relations (antonymic play on words), to break combinatorial rules (phonological

---

24 (85) is taken from Ralli and Xydopoulos (2012: 43); (86)–(87) are from Finkielkraut (1981).
25 Galisson (1987) (cited in Léturgie 2012: 204) speaks of semasiological neology as the neological process moves from form to meaning: a new complex word is coined before a matching definition is sought.

and grammatical violations). These different features of wordplay can be combined and thus lead to a prototype-based typology of wordplayfulness in lexical blending. Some blends may be considered to be more playful than others as they associate several features of playfulness. *Planetesimal* (61) and *Billary* (62) for instance involve both segment overlapping (i.e. formal complexity) and grammatical transgression.

Processing a novel blend is, in a similar way, akin to a language game, in which the hearer / reader is expected to identify the source words which have been condensed in the output form and to compute a semantic relation which is contextually plausible. Lexical blends can thus be seen as the building blocks of a singular form of interpersonal rapport between the speaker / writer and hearer / reader which is founded on the ludic exploration of the limits of verbal inventiveness and recognizability. Linguistic ingenuity is required in both the encoding and decoding of a novel blend, establishing a common ground which leads to phatic bonding between the speaker / writer and hearer / reader.

5 References

Arcodia, Giorgio Francesco & Fabio Montermini. 2012. Are Reduced Compounds Compounds? Morphological and Prosodic Properties of Reduced Compounds in Russian and Mandarin Chinese. In Vincent Renner, François Maniez & Pierre J. L. Arnaud (eds.), *Cross-Disciplinary Perspectives on Lexical Blending*, 93–113. Berlin: De Gruyter Mouton.
Arnaud, Pierre J. L. & Vincent Renner. 2014. English and French [NN]$_N$ Lexical Units: A Categorial, Morphological and Semantic Comparison. *Word Structure* 7(1). 1–28.
Artiagoitia, Xavier, José Ignacio Hualde & Jon Ortiz de Urbina. Forthcoming. Basque. In Peter O. Müller, Ingeborg Ohnheiser, Susan Olsen & Franz Rainer (eds.), *Word-Formation: An International Handbook of the Languages of Europe*. Berlin: De Gruyter Mouton.
Bat-El, Outi. 1996. Selecting the Best of the Worst: The Grammar of Hebrew Blends. *Phonology* 13(3). 283–328.
Bat-El, Outi. 2006. Blend. In Keith Brown (ed.), *Encyclopedia of Language and Linguistics*, 2nd edn, vol. 2, 66–70. Amsterdam: Elsevier.
Bat-El, Outi. 2013. Blends. In Geoffrey Khan (ed.), *Encyclopedia of Hebrew Language and Linguistics*, 371–373. Leiden: Brill.
Bauer, Laurie. 2004. *A Glossary of Morphology*. Edinburgh: Edinburgh University Press.
Berg, Thomas. 2009. *Structure in Language: A Dynamic Perspective*. New York: Routledge.
Bonhomme, Marc. 1998. La néologie par télescopage en français contemporain : Le cas de la publicité. In Giovanni Ruffino (ed.), *Atti del XXI congresso internazionale di linguistica e filologia romanza*, vol. 3, 89–98. Tübingen: Niemeyer.
Borgwaldt, Susanne & Réka Benczes. 2011. Word-Formation Patterns in a Cross-Linguistic Perspective. In Doris Schönefeld (ed.), *Converging Evidence: Methodological and Theoretical Issues in Linguistic Research*, 221–245. Amsterdam: Benjamins.

Brdar-Szabo, Rita & Mario Brdar. 2008. On the Marginality of Lexical Blending. *Jezikoslovlje* 9(1–2). 171–194.
Collins English Dictionary. http://www.collinsdictionary.com/dictionary/english (17 July 2015).
Corpus of Contemporary American English. http://corpus.byu.edu/coca (17 July 2015).
Crystal, David. 2001. *Language Play*. Chicago: University of Chicago Press.
Davis, Stuart Michael. 1985. *Topics in Syllable Geometry*. Tucson, AZ: University of Arizona dissertation. http://arizona.openrepository.com/arizona/handle/10150/187997 (17 July 2015).
Dobrovolsky, Michael. 2001. Malay Blends – CV or Syllable Template? *Calgary Working Papers in Linguistics* 23. 14–29.
Doppagne, Albert. 1973. Le néologisme chez Raymond Queneau. *Cahiers de l'Association Internationale des Études Françaises* 25. 91–107.
Dressler, Wolfgang U. 2000. Extragrammatical vs. Marginal Morphology. In Ursula Doleschal & Anna M. Thornton (eds.), *Extragrammatical and Marginal Morphology*, 1–10. Munich: LINCOM Europa.
Finkielkraut, Alain. 1981. *Petit fictionnaire illustré*. Paris: Éditions du Seuil.
Fradin, Bernard, Fabio Montermini & Marc Plénat. 2009. Morphologie grammaticale et extragrammaticale. In Bernard Fradin, Françoise Kerleroux & Marc Plénat (eds.), *Aperçus de morphologie du français*, 21–45. Saint-Denis: Presses Universitaires de Vincennes.
Friedrich, Cornelia. 2008. *Kontamination: Zur Form und Funktion eines Wortbildungstyps im Deutschen*. Erlangen and Nürnberg: Friedrich-Alexander-Universität Erlangen-Nürnberg dissertation. http://opus4.kobv.de/opus4-fau/frontdoor/index/index/docId/745 (17 July 2015).
Galisson, Robert. 1987. Les dictionnaires de parodie comme moyens de perfectionnement en langue française. *Études de linguistique appliquée* 67. 57–118.
Gries, Stefan Th. 2012. Quantitative Corpus Data on Blend Formation: Psycho- and Cognitive-Linguistic Perspectives. In Vincent Renner, François Maniez & Pierre J. L. Arnaud (eds.), *Cross-Disciplinary Perspectives on Lexical Blending*, 145–167. Berlin: De Gruyter Mouton.
Halupka-Rešetar, Sabina & Gordana Lalić-Krstin. 2009. New Blends in Serbian: Typological and Headedness-Related Issues. *Annual Review of the Faculty of Philosophy (Novi Sad)* 34(1). 115–124.
Kang, Eungyeong. 2013. An Optimality-Theoretic Analysis of Lexical Blends in Korean. *The Journal of Studies in Language* 28(4). 653–672.
Konieczna, Ewa. 2012. Lexical Blending in Polish: A Result of the Internationalisation of Slavic Languages. In Vincent Renner, François Maniez & Pierre J. L. Arnaud (eds.), *Cross-Disciplinary Perspectives on Lexical Blending*, 51–73. Berlin: De Gruyter Mouton.
Léturgie, Arnaud. 2012. *L'amalgamation lexicale en français: Approches lexicologique et morphologique. Vers une grammaire de l'amalgamation lexicale en français*. Cergy-Pontoise: Université de Cergy-Pontoise dissertation.
Mattiello, Elisa. 2013. *Extra-Grammatical Morphology in English: Abbreviations, Blends, Reduplicatives, and Related Phenomena*. Berlin: De Gruyter Mouton.
Miller, Gary. 2014. *English Lexicogenesis*. Oxford: Oxford University Press.
Olver, Lynne M. 2009. The Truth about Clams Casino. *Gastronomica* 9(1). 88–90.
Oxford English Dictionary, 2nd edn 2014. http://www.oed.com (17 July 2015).
Pharies, David A. 1987. Blending in Spanish Word-Formation. *Romanistisches Jahrbuch* 38. 271–289.

Piñeros, Carlos-Eduardo. 2011. ¿Es el entrecruzamiento léxico realmente un proceso sustractivo? *Lingüística Española Actual* 33(1). 75–100.
Plag, Ingo. 2003. *Word-Formation in English*. Cambridge: Cambridge University Press.
Punch. 1896. Brunch v. Blunch! Vol. 111, 58. London: Punch Publications. http://archive.org/stream/punchvol110a111lemouoft#page/58/mode/2up (17 July 2015).
Ralli, Angela & George J. Xydopoulos. 2012. Blend Formation in Modern Greek. In Vincent Renner, François Maniez & Pierre J. L. Arnaud (eds.), *Cross-Disciplinary Perspectives on Lexical Blending*, 35–50. Berlin: De Gruyter Mouton.
Renner, Vincent. 2008. On the Semantics of English Coordinate Compounds. *English Studies* 89(5). 606–613.
Renner, Vincent. 2014. *French and English Blends in Contrast*, unpublished manuscript, Université Paris Diderot.
Ronneberger-Sibold, Elke. 2006. Lexical Blends: Functionally Tuning the Transparency of Complex Words. *Folia Linguistica* 40(1–2). 155–181.
Ronneberger-Sibold, Elke. 2010. Word Creation: Definition – Function – Typology. In Franz Rainer, Wolfgang U. Dressler, Dieter Kastovsky & Hans Christian Luschützky (eds.), *Variation and Change in Morphology*, 201–216. Amsterdam: Benjamins.
Ronneberger-Sibold, Elke. 2012. Blending between Grammar and Universal Cognitive Principles: Evidence from German, Farsi, and Chinese. In Vincent Renner, François Maniez Pierre J. L. Arnaud (eds.), *Cross-Disciplinary Perspectives on Lexical Blending*, 115–143. Berlin: De Gruyter Mouton.
Scalise, Sergio & Antonietta Bisetto. 2009. The Classification of Compounds. In Rochelle Lieber & Pavol Štekauer (eds.), *The Oxford Handbook of Compounding*, 34–53. Oxford: Oxford University Press.
Thornton, Anna M. 1993. Italian blends. In Livio Tonella & Wolfgang U. Dressler (eds.), *Natural Morphology: Perspectives for the Nineties*, 143–155. Padova: Unipress.
Urban Dictionary. http://www.urbandictionary.com (17 July 2015).
Veisbergs, Andrejs. 2013. *English and Latvian Word Formation Compared*. Riga: The University of Latvia Press.
Villoing, Florence. 2012. French Compounds. *Probus* 24(1). 29–60.
Word Spy. http://wordspy.com (17 July 2015).

Pierre J. L. Arnaud, François Maniez and Vincent Renner
Non-Canonical Proverbial Occurrences and Wordplay: A Corpus Investigation and an Enquiry Into Readers' Perception of Humour and Cleverness

Abstract: This article is an investigation of wordplay – defined as the clever and humorous formal manipulation of language strings – in the use of proverbs in written discourse. A set of 303 occurrences of six English proverbs was collected in the Corpus of Contemporary American English and the non-canonical occurrences were analysed and classified. It appears that most of these manipulations are simple contextual adaptations including noun-phrase substitutions, and only very few occurrences could qualify as instances of wordplay. To verify this, a questionnaire with 32 of the non-canonical occurrences was administered to a group of 12 native speakers who rated them for humour and cleverness. A comparison of the five occurrences with the highest ratings and the five with the lowest ones confirmed that the simple contextual adaptation of proverbs does not create wordplay, which requires semantic complexity combined with humour.

Keywords: cleverness, English, humour, phraseologism, proverb, semantic complexity

1 Introduction*

The research presented here deals with wordplay in proverbs. Langlotz (2006: 195) notes that in general, "*wordplay* is a fairly vague term for which no clear-cut definition exists," and our first task is therefore to reach an operationalizable definition of the term. A useful starting point is Guiraud's (1979: 97) distinction between witticisms (Fr. *mots d'esprit*), which only concern ideas (e.g. *Youth would be an ideal state if it came a little later in life*; Herbert Henry Asquith), and wordplay (Fr. *jeux de mots*). Wordplay must involve word manipulation, but, that said, different positions are to be found in the literature. According to the

---

* We are grateful to our anonymous reviewers for their useful comments and suggestions.

broad definition given by Nilsen and Nilsen (1978; cited in Lippman and Dunn 2000: 185–186), wordplay refers to any use of language that has a purpose beyond the direct communication of ideas. Most definitions, however, explicitly include humour, like McArthur (1992: 787), who defines wordplay as "[a]ny adaptation or use of words to achieve a humorous, satirical, dramatic, critical, or other effect." We will retain this component and add to it the component of cleverness, following Attardo (1994: 324), who claims that, since humour requires extra processing, it is linked with cleverness, and also Lippmann and Dunn (2000), who investigate the perception of these two variables in manipulated jokes. We therefore define wordplay as the clever manipulation of the form of a language string or the use of polysemy resulting in an amusing effect. The term *language string* covers manipulations on segments, words and phraseological units.

We define proverbs as exhibiting the following characteristics (see Arnaud 1991: 8–11):
a) they are lexicalized (they are phraseological units of the lexicon);
b) they are syntactically autonomous (they constitute sentence-level phraseologisms);
c) they are endowed with textual autonomy (they do not depend on a conversational turn or include exophoricity);
d) they express general truths (contrary to "sayings"; Moon 1998: 62);
e) they have no known author (vs. aphorisms and slogans).

These conditions are necessary and sufficient, i.e. we do not consider that other criteria should restrict the category of proverbial units further, like tradition (Norrick 1985: 69), metaphoricity (Greimas 1960; Rodegem 1972), or rhythmic characteristics (Anscombre 2003). This is not incompatible with a prototypical view and, within the category, a unit like *Great oaks from little acorns grow* is obviously a more prototypical proverb than *Enough is enough*. A notable fact is that there is considerable variation in the knowledge of proverbs by individuals (see Arnaud 1992 and Ettinger 2012 on French; Cox 1999 on German).

The study of phraseologisms is notoriously difficult, not only because their taxonomy is complex, but also because in many cases their occurrences tend to differ from the form that is recorded by lexicographers (the canonical form). Longer phraseologisms have more potential for modification, and since proverbs are usually sentence-level phraseologisms, they tend to be long units. Moon (1998: 115, 172) has found that some proverbial variants, in particular truncated forms or VPs, may be institutionalized,[1] as is the case with "is in the eyes of the beholder," which never occurs with its canonical subject (*beauty*) in Moon's corpus. To Langlotz (2006: 54), a model of idiom representation and variation should account for the distinction between systematic variability and wordplay. Which modified occurrences of proverbs contain wordplay?[2] The principal aim of the present research is to answer this question.

2 Corpus Study

2.1 Methodology

A corpus search was preferred to day-to-day collection for its coverage and rapidity of execution. Examples of earlier work on corpora in the field of phraseology are Lennon's (2004: 17) apparently manual investigation of allusions in newspapers, and electronic corpora were used by Moon (1998) on idioms and fixed expressions as well as by Partington (2009) on wordplay.

The search was undertaken on the 1990-2011 section of the *Corpus of Contemporary American English* (henceforth *COCA*), which was created by Mark Davies at Brigham Young University[3] (Davies 2009). It was decided to concentrate on an exhaustive search on a restricted number of well-known proverbs selected for their imagery and potential for manipulation as estimated from the number of possible substitutions. The proverbs were drawn from an unpublished pedagogical selection; they all feature in the *Concise Oxford Dictionary of Proverbs* (Simpson and Speake 1992) and the *Dictionary of American Proverbs* (Mieder 1992).

(a) A drowning man will clutch at a straw.
(b) A leopard does not change his / its spots.
(c) Actions speak louder than words.
(d) Hell hath no fury like a woman scorned.[4]
(e) The pen is mightier than the sword.
(f) Variety is the spice of life.

---

[1] A unit is said to be institutionalized when its meaning has been established in a particular domain within a community (Bauer 2004: 56).
[2] We are well aware that some proverbs include wordplay in their canonical forms (e.g. *Haste makes waste*; *Might is right*), but no such proverbs are included in this study.
[3] All the following examples have been taken from *COCA*.
[4] This is originally an aphorism by William Congreve, but it fits our definition of the proverb as it has become anonymous for most users.

Appropriate queries were formulated to extract as many occurrences as possible. For instance, in the case of (a), the following requests were used:
- clutch / ing / es / ed at
- drowning man / woman
- drowning [...] straw(s)
- at (a) straw(s)

As expected, this method returned a lot of noise and redundant hits, which were eliminated manually. We were well aware of the fact that 100% detection of modified proverbs in a corpus of the size of *COCA* is not possible.[5] For instance, Rosamund Moon mentions a serendipitous occurrence of the proverb *He who sups with the Devil must have a long spoon* in the sentence *I do not have a straw that is long enough to take a drink with him*, in which the only two surviving words are *have* and *long*, but the proverb is still recognizable in the context (Arnaud and Moon 1993: 325). An example from our own day-to-day collection – "For the United States and Iran the 1979 Iranian revolution [...] has proved to be the geopolitical divorce from hell" (Sadjadpour 2012), an occurrence of *Some marriages were made in heaven* where none of the original words is to be found – has led to the introduction of antonyms and co-hyponyms in some of the queries, and this increased the recall to a large extent.

Another problem arose from strings in which the presence of the proverb was uncertain. For instance, in the case of *Actions speak louder than words*, which of the following hits should be retained?
  (a) "silence speaks louder than a thousand words"[6]
  (b) "the tale of the tape spoke louder than a husband's plea"
  (c) "a picture that spoke louder than the politicians' words"
  (d) "in him the convert spoke louder than the ecumenist."

It appears that when the only substring that corresponds to the proverb is *speak(s) / spoke louder than*, the proverb is not evoked by informants in an informal oral query, so (b) and (d) can be rejected.

---

5 See also Lennon (2004: 16) on allusions in the press.
6 This modification is probably the result of a blend with *A picture's worth a thousand words*.

2.2 Data

Like all lexical units, proverbs have different frequencies of occurrence. Table 1 shows the total number of occurrences of each of the six proverbs under investigation. *Actions speak louder than words* is by far the most frequent of the units. Note, incidentally, that Arnaud and Moon (1993) have found that the relative frequency of proverbs does not necessarily correspond to their ranking by degree of knowledge by a sample of speakers as measured on a questionnaire.

Tab. 1: Number of occurrences and percentage of canonical forms for each proverb

	number of occurrences	number of canonical forms	percentage of canonical forms
A drowning man will clutch at a straw.	20	2	(10.0%)
A leopard does not change its / his spots.	34	2	(5.9%)
Actions speak louder than words.	154	34	(22.1%)
Hell hath no fury like a woman scorned.	26	11	(42.3%)
The pen is mightier than the sword.	45	5	(11.1%)
Variety is the spice of life.	24	13	(54.2%)
All	303	67	(22.1%)

In the following, we examine and categorize the occurrences. Many publications include taxonomies of phraseological modifications, which have been refined and expanded with the development of this field of research, and Barta's (2005, 2006) is a good basis. This author distinguishes three main categories: metaplasms, metasemes, and metalogisms. Metaplasms involve segments and include deletions, additions, substitutions and permutations (examples will be found further on in our analyses of occurrences). Metasemes are semantic modifications, like demetaphorizations, uses of antonymy, inversions of polarity, and questions. Metalogisms include tautologies, but have apparently more to do with "anti-proverbs," i.e. playfully fabricated proverbs, which are marginal in our data. Please note that a given occurrence may exhibit several modifications and thus belong to multiple categories, like the following, *My thoughts spoke louder than the words we exchanged*, where the main verb is in the past tense, the first NP results from a substitution, and the second NP is made definite and expanded by a relative clause.[7] As a result, some of the categories are not mutually exclusive, so that the totals may exceed 100%. The number of categories was limited in order to prevent a combinatory explosion, which might have led to placing many occurrences in categories of their own.

Table 1 also indicates the numbers and percentages of occurrences where the canonical form is reproduced in its entirety, whether it constitutes an independent sentence, a declarative clause, or is interrupted by an incidental clause. Taken together, the six proverbs appear in their full form 67 times, that is in 22.1% of their occurrences only, which confirms that proverbs are no exception to the variability of phraseologisms. The number of canonical occurrences relative to their overall frequency is significantly different from one proverb to another (χ^2 = 17.85, p < .01, 5 d.f., Yates's correction), which shows that proverbs have different contextual behaviours: *Variety is the spice of life* is the most resistant unit, while *A leopard does not change its / his spots* has only 5.9% of its occurrences in canonical form. An explanation can be suggested: a metaphorical proverb may invite manipulation through its images (see Moon 1998: 170), while a more literal one may be less open to modifications.

Other occurrences have undergone minor syntactic modifications. For instance, in some cases, the main verb is in the past tense or the -ING form, or one of the NPs is pluralized, as in *Leopards don't change their spots*, which may be considered a simple variant. In other cases, a canonically singular closed-class occurrence like a possessive is in the plural due to agreement with a plural substitute NP as in the preceding example. It is worth noting that these syntactically modified occurrences may exhibit other modifications as well. Table 2 shows the numbers and percentages of such occurrences and, here again, large differences appear. These syntactic modifications *per se* are simple adaptations of the canonical form, which may either remain otherwise unmodified or have additionally undergone changes involving lexical words.

Like Wozniak (2009: 186), who calls such occurrences *proverbes modifiés* and more basic changes *proverbes détournés*, we will call those occurrences that are only syntactically modified *adapted proverbs* and refer to other types (like those involving lexical substitutions) as *manipulated proverbs*. Again, note that the numbers and percentages in Table 1, col. 3 did not include occurrences that

---

[7] This, incidentally, implies losing the generic reading that was originally suggested by the use of the bare NP. In fact, many of the modifications result in the proverb losing some or all of its genericity.

have only been syntactically adapted. While three of the proverbs are left syntactically unaltered, "A drowning man [...]" has 80% of its occurrences adapted.

Clearly, Barta's (2005, 2006) taxonomy is more concerned with manipulated occurrences. The next type of modification in our data is semantic and therefore manipulative, since it involves a modification of the modal contents of the proverbs or their polarity, or else their transformation into an interrogative sentence, with possible combinations:

(1) [...] the pen may be mightier than the sword [...]
(2) A leopard does not necessarily change his spots.
(3) Can a leopard change his spots?

Numbers and percentages of this type of modification are presented in Table 2, col. 3.

Tab. 2: Minor modifications

	syntactic modifications	modal and polarity modifications
A drowning man will clutch at a straw.	16 (80%)	0
A leopard does not change its / his spots.	15 (44.1%)	9 (26.5%)
Actions speak louder than words.	32 (20.8%)	22 (14.3%)
Hell hath no fury like a woman scorned.	0	5 (19.2%)
The pen is mightier than the sword.	0	9 (20%)
Variety is the spice of life.	0	2 (8.3%)
All	63 (20.8%)	47 (15.5%)

Substitutions (Table 3), in which one or several NPs or other substrings of the canonical form are replaced by other substrings, constitute the most distinctive type of manipulation in the data.[8] Single substitutions with adaptation to the context are common manipulations, in which one substring related to the context is substituted for a substring of the canonical form, and the meaning of the proverb consequently applies to the context:

---

8 For a discussion of substitution and wordplay, see also Jaki, in *The Dynamics of Wordplay* 2.

(4) [About a famous football coach who felt victimized] Hell has no fury like a genius scorned.
(5) Even in a democracy, where money speaks louder than words.
(6) [About the fact that credit card and mail order purchases are scanned by business interests] Our actions speak louder than the surveys.

Tab. 3: Substitutions

	single substitutions	multiple substitutions	all substitutions	single or multiple substitutions with simple adaptation to context
A drowning man will clutch at a straw.	2 (10%)	1 (5%)	3 (15%)	0
A leopard does not change its / his spots.	0	0	0	0
Actions speak louder than words.	23 (14.9%)	19 (12.3%)	42 (27.2%)	21 (13.6%)
Hell hath no fury like a woman scorned.	5 (19.2%)	8 (30.8%)	13 (50%)	5 (19.2%)
The pen is mightier than the sword.	12 (26.7%)	8 (17.8%)	20 (44.4%)	10 (22.2%)
Variety is the spice of life.	6 (25%)	1 (4.2%)	7 (29.2%)	5 (20.8%)
All	48 (15.8%)	37 (12.2%)	85 (28%)	41 (13.5%)

This kind of occurrences clearly corresponds to Lennon's (2004) "allusions." Half the occurrences of "Hell hath no fury [...]" include substitutions. This unit has the added characteristic that it includes more multiple substitutions than substitutions on a single substring. This is a case of a substring, "– hath / has no fury like –", becoming predominant and probably lexicalized in its own right (see above).

All of the substitutions analysed serve a purpose and fit the context (with one exception, see (16) below), but there are differences between them. Five cases are simple substitutions by a synonym, which do not change the meaning of the proverb and produce a mere variant, as in:

(7) [...] I hung on to it like they say a drowning man holds on to a straw.

Such instances can hardly be considered as manipulations and presumably result from the presence of an approximate form in the writer's lexicon. Four substitutions result in a formal effect, as in the following complex occurrence:

(8) Sometimes words speak louder than swords.

In (8), the graphic sequence <words> is repeated. We return to such occurrences in the Discussion (see below, 2.3).

Tab. 4: Deletions and additions

	deletions	additions
A drowning man will clutch at a straw.	14 (70%)	3 (15%)
A leopard does not change its / his spots.	14 (41.2%)	6 (17.6%)
Actions speak louder than words.	7 (4.6%)	53 (34.4%)
Hell hath no fury like a woman scorned.	0	0
The pen is mightier than the sword.	14 (31.1%)	3 (6.7%)
Variety is the spice of life.	0	8 (33.3%)
All	49 (16.2%)	73 (24.1%)

The numbers and percentages of deletions are presented in Table 4.[9] Two of the proverbs, "A drowning man [...]" and "A leopard [...]" show a very high number of deletions and as many as 70% of the occurrences of the former are in a truncated form. Examples are:

---

[9] Again, some of the categories of manipulation are not mutually exclusive, so that the totals may exceed 100%.

(9) I know it's silly, not much more than a gussied-up version of computer dating, but *I'm clutching at straws.*[10]

(10) Barannikov's replacement, Nikolai Golushko, while vastly more able than Yerin, also embodied a talent for *changing his spots.*

Such cases were classified as deletions rather than substitutions, because, while they still evoke the canonical proverb and thus constitute allusions, they are far removed from the metaphor present in the whole proverb and are so numerous that the preserved segments acquire a lexical existence of their own (see Section 2.1). The NPs are also frequently substituted by personal pronouns or proper names, i.e. by NPs that do not denote classes of entities. A different example of anterior deletion is:

(11) [*song title*] Louder than Words.

No final deletions were observed, but there are some cases of central deletion, allowing the heads of the two NPs to survive, as in the following:

(12) Pen and Sword Books.

Additions constitute the third main category of formal manipulation. About one quarter of the occurrences are somehow expanded (Table 4). Various subtypes can here again be distinguished. The proverb may receive an appendix that adds a participant connecting it to the context, as in:

(13) Leopards don't change their spots and neither do men.
(14) Variety is the spice of life – and the bane of dieters.

Close to this type are occurrences where an extra participant is coordinated with one of the canonical NPs:

(15) Leopards and old dons don't usually change their spots.
(16) [...] unless Aristide has changed his spots or his stripes [...].

---

10 The relevant segments of examples longer than one line are in bold type for better visibility.

Example (15) connects the proverb with the context, but (16) does not seem to fulfil any textual function beyond expansion of the proverb itself. In other cases, one of the NPs is modified, thus providing contextual relevance:

(17) America's actions speak louder than words.
(18) Plus variety is the spice of Angelina Jolie's red carpet life.

The last type of metaplasm, permutation, is marginal:

(19) Both Democrats and Republicans have demonstrated that "words speak louder than action."

Another set of 34 occurrences were found to include such complex and heterogeneous modifications that they were placed in a "various" category, whose comprehensive description is beyond the scope of this article. An example of this is (20):

(20) "From the sword to the pen" [...].

This involves central deletion, permutation of the NPs, and transformation into a verbless sentence consisting of two prepositional phrases.

Finally, we found 17 cases of "signalling" (Moon 1998: 305), in which the writer metalinguistically mentions the presence of a proverbial occurrence. The devices are varied:

(21) The pen, it is said, is mightier than the sword.
(22) [...] so it proves the old adage, "The pen is mightier than the sword."
(23) As we all know, actions speak louder than words.

2.3 Discussion

The data produced by the present corpus search are consistent with earlier research (see Arnaud and Moon 1993; Moon 1998; Lennon 2004), although with minor differences: for instance, Lennon (2004: 171) found only 4 out of 44 proverbial occurrences that were verbatim (9.1% vs. our 22.1%). Such differences are certainly attributable to the different corpora used, as Lennon's was made up of newspaper text only, and Moon (1998: 170) notes that in her corpus "exploitation," i.e. manipulation, is strongly associated with journalism.

Why do speakers (and in the present study, writers) insert proverbs into their discourse? Proverbs in context have a triple meaning (see Arnaud 1991): a propositional content or denotation (a piece of general truth about man or the world); a referential meaning or reference, in that they connect an occurrence (a situation) to a type; and a functional meaning, as they constitute an irrefutable argument by their appeal to an impersonal authority and – as intertextual elements – establish common ground on the basis of shared cultural knowledge between speaker / writer and hearer / reader.

Why do speakers / writers manipulate phraseologisms? First of all, because it is possible to do so without disrupting communication. Lennon (2004: 180) has found evidence of "highly structured correspondences of a lexico-grammatical nature" between canonical phraseologisms and their manipulated occurrences, which must be part of the reader's competence. He suggests that the newspaper reader must first identify phraseologisms in the text and establish their literal or allusive nature. Lennon further presents a taxonomy of the functions of allusions, among which the following seem particularly relevant here:

- to attract reader attention;
- to achieve physical economy of expression;
- to evaluate new information against existing cultural values and vice versa;
- to achieve ironic effects of ridicule or criticism;
- to achieve humorously grotesque effects;
- to convince by appeal to cultural values shared with the reader;
- to cognitively challenge the reader and encourage him to read on;
- to establish common ground with the reader;
- to impart aesthetic pleasure to the reader. (Lennon 2004: 235–243)

The reasons why writers manipulate proverbs and not simply phraseologisms in general can therefore be seen as a combination of the two sets of reasons above, with a reinforcement of the cultural and intertextual aspects. In addition, differences between a memorized canonical form and a modified occurrence result in defeated expectations, a frequent component of the humour in jokes (Chiaro 1992: 15).

We can now return to our goal and look at "the fragile and gradual distinction between systematic idiom-variation and idiom-based wordplay" (Langlotz 2006: 195). Applying our definition and combining humour and cleverness as a result of formal manipulation, it appears that many metaplasms like the following examples do not qualify as wordplay:

(24) Some of the most interesting people I've met are sixty and still don't know what they want to do with their lives. Chasing dreams is the spice of life.
(25) Now, because of him and his party, married couples will continue to be punished through higher taxes by the federal government for being married, and people who get divorces will be rewarded. The actions of Democrats speak louder than their words about families.
(26) [...] Mr. Roeper is a writer. His pen, or typewriter, is mightier than any gun or badge around.

These passages appear as routine, perfunctory allusions. Some of the functions of Lennon's list, like the achievement of economy of expression may be fulfilled, but the components of our definition of wordplay (manipulation of a language string, clever and amusing effect) are apparently absent. Examples cannot be multiplied for reasons of space, but most of the manipulated proverbial occurrences in the data are equally unremarkable in this respect.

Some occurrences, however, fulfil the criteria for wordplay to a greater extent. The following example rests on repetition:

(27) Well, I trust you're a critic, young man, a budding one at least. But has no one told you that *the pen is mightier than the ... pen knife*?

Pen knife is a loose co-hyponym of *sword* for which it is substituted ("objects with a blade"), it repeats the occurrence *pen*, and it presumably adapts the proverb to the notion of a beginner in journalistic criticism, so it is much more than a simple substitution. The next example combines two effects:

(28) Powerful computers and high-tech scanners now enable marketers to closely monitor how, where and when you spend your money. *These electronic transactions speak much louder than words* because they reflect actual behavior.

The more salient one is a pun by addition of a segment (*actions > transactions*), and in the less conspicuous one *speak* takes on a less metaphorical meaning than in the canonical proverb, as electronic data are *read* by the computers and scanners.

Reduced to its NPs, *The pen is mightier than the sword* becomes "the pen / the sword," and we have already seen an instance of this type of central deletion in example (12). In (29), the two terms are inverted, which provides a salient formal effect, and they refer metonymically to a former weapon site turned into a school. This is a pun by permutation:

(29) Few schools are able to say that their campus once harbored missiles. Talcott Mountain Science Center, perched upon a ridge overlooking Hartford, Connecticut sits on a former Nike antiaircraft missile site. "*From the sword to the pen,*" says Donald La Salle, Talcott's director.

We reach marginal areas of wordplay with the last two occurrences:

(30) "You can't change the spots on a leper." Or a leopard, for that matter.

This is an anti-proverb based on a paronymic pun with a one-segment phonetic deletion. It is a direct-speech quotation, so it is self-contained, and the substitute for *leopard* does not have to produce meaning within the context. Independently from the context, it may be efficient, however, because of the formal proximity between *leopard* and *leper* and because, encyclopaedically, both leopards and lepers have spots (and, *terribile dictu*, leper jokes are attested). Other examples are presented in the questionnaire below (see Section 3).

Between these few identifiable cases of wordplay and the many routine substitutions, a few occurrences may fit our definition, like the following:

(31) [About the role of the Internet in toppling dictators] The key pad is mightier than the sword.

In this case, where *the sword* still metonymically represents violence, *the keypad* is a loosely co-hyponymous substitute ("writing implements") and still functions metonymically, but with less distance between source and target.

3 An Investigation of Readers' Perceptions of Proverbial Occurrences

To summarize the data collected in the *COCA* corpus, 77.9% of the occurrences of the six proverbs investigated are non-canonical. Based on a definition of wordplay with, on the one hand, formal manipulation and, on the other hand, the perception of humour and cleverness, most of the non-canonical occurrences do not seem to constitute wordplay, because only the formal condition is satisfied. They are routine manipulations of a rather mechanical nature. Only nine occurrences (3%) can be seen as cases of wordplay. Some of these were already discussed in the preceding section (8), (19), (27)–(29), (30), (31); the other occurrences are:

(32) The penis is mightier than the sword.
(33) No, everything doesn't have to be spicy. Variety (remember?) is the spice of life. And that means a variety of flavors, textures, aromas, colors, serving styles.
(34) His expression was that of a man who had clutched at the last straw and caught the whole bale.

Wordplay depends on the intention of the speaker / writer (which in the case of a corpus study can only be inferred, as we did), but it also depends on the hearer / reader's reaction: intended wordplay may well fall flat or pass unnoticed and thus fail as such. To observe how wordplay is perceived and thus confirm our analyses, we administered a paper questionnaire to native speakers of English. The questionnaires were filled out on a volunteer basis and in their own free time by 12 respondents, 6 of whom were British and 6 American, 10 female and 2 male, aged 21 to 70, who were present in Lyon at the time.

The questionnaire consisted of a sample of 32 of the occurrences in the corpus with the necessary context, selected in order to include the six proverbs of the investigation represented in a variety of non-canonical occurrences. In particular, those occurrences we had identified as wordplay were included to confirm our definition of cleverness and humour as essential ingredients of wordplay. The participants were asked to circle a number corresponding to one of four categories:

    0 - I do not even recognize the allusion.
    1 - I do not find this example particularly clever and amusing.
    2 - I find this example moderately clever and amusing.
    3 - I find this example clearly clever and amusing.

The presence of four options precluded attraction by a central option. Two versions in different random orders were used so as to counter the effects of questionnaire fatigue. One of the versions is reproduced in the appendix. The responses were converted into 0 to 4 scores, which were standardized, and the mean standard score of each item was computed. The items were then classified in decreasing order of mean z-scores.

We now examine the five occurrences with the lowest mean scores and then the five with the highest scores. The scores appear in Table 5. The occurrence that was perceived as the least clever and amusing (rank 32) was:

(35) I mean, this is information that's been available for at least – in their records for 30 years. I don't know what has transpired over the last year that allows them now to make this, I think, PR move. I think *in many respects the leopard really hasn't changed its spots*. I mean, if you carefully look at the language that they've used, they agree with a consensus. I mean, nicotine is addictive and smoking causes various diseases.

Tab. 5: Perception of humour and cleverness in occurrences

rank	occurrence	mean z-score
1	If it helps, [...]	0.7099
2	Tyasan [...]	0.5790
3	Shane had never [...]	0.5319
4	Is it possible [...]	0.5063
5	Both Republicans [...]	0.4929
[...]		
28	Elsewhere Farhan [...]	0.4197
29	We don't think [...]	0.4329
30	Governor [...]	0.5637
31	She reaches for [...]	0.7818
32	I mean, this [...]	0.8118

The verb form shows that (35) is an adapted proverb, and it exhibits modalization. Connection with the context is provided by the substitution of the definite article for the indefinite. These simple adaptive modifications of the canonical form obviously are not sufficient to evoke cleverness or humour. In addition, the modalizing effect of the three occurrences of *I mean* and the two occurrences of *I think* may have cumulatively weakened the perception of the speaker's possible humorous intent by the informants.

(36) She reaches for Walt's hand and, as he feels her grope for him, he grabs her. Takes hold of her before she can take hold of him. It is a reflex between them. *He clutches at her like a drowning man*, but it doesn't bother her as it does at home.

In (36), the main verb of the canonical form appears in the main clause and its canonical subject appears in a comparative prepositional phrase. A pronoun is substituted for the indirect object of the canonical sentence, thus connecting the occurrence with the context. This is an obvious allusion, but its effect is simply to intensify and dramatize the scene, without apparently attracting attention to the form itself.

(37) GOVERNOR: "*Actions speak louder than words.* And the President's *actions* are killing jobs in this country." REPRESENTATIVE: "He has failed all Americans when it comes to job creation."

Example (37) is an item with a canonical form which was placed in the questionnaires as a control. Although the connection appears in the second occurrence of *actions*, this is a simple case of appeal to shared knowledge.

(38) "We don't think that it is the license threat that is going to get the broadcasters to move, but public activity," she said. "Once the Parents and Teachers Associations rouse the community, once ratings start to drop, then the stations will begin to care. *The networks aren't going to change their spots,*" Miss Charren says.

Example (38) results from the separate lexicalization of *change one's spots* (see Section 2.2), and since nothing in the context has anything to do with literal leopards or spots, what we have here is the simple use of an idiomatic phraseologism.

(39) Elsewhere Farhan states that the [Muslim] Brotherhood "will not spill one drop of blood or vandalize any public or private property." This derives from a belief that "*Sometimes words speak louder than swords.*"

We stated earlier that a simple occurrence of *speak louder than* should not be taken as an instance of the proverb *Actions speak louder than words*. However, in (39), we have a substitution of the prepositional complement of the canonical form (i.e. *words*) for the subject (*actions*), i.e. a partial inversion. Furthermore, as already mentioned, a visual pun may have been intended as the graphic segment <words> is repeated in <swords>. If this was the case, the low rating by our subjects shows that a spelling-based pun is less efficient than a pronunciation-based pun.

The next five occurrences received the highest ratings for humour and cleverness ((40) is repeated from (19)).

(40) Both Republicans and Democrats have demonstrated that "*Words speak louder than action.*"

Contrary to the preceding occurrence, this manipulation of *Actions speak louder than words* is efficient. It is a simple case of metaplasm by noun-phrase inversion, which defeats expectations and negates the received wisdom in connection with a cliché about politicians.

(41) Is it possible that a group of expedient men in Washington could have deliberately withheld critical intelligence data from the officers at Pearl Harbor? And why would they do such a terrible thing? Simple: They needed an excuse to rouse and unite the country to war. Because *Hell would have no fury like a nation broadsided from its sleep on Sunday morning*.

In (41), the occurrence is grammatically adapted by the verb form, but more conspicuously, the final NP, *a woman scorned*, has been substituted by a much longer one, which defeats expectations as to sentence length. The concept *fury* is activated by *rouse* and *nation* by *country*, and *hell* is an echo of *Pearl Harbor* and *war*. In contrast, the notion of sleep on a Sunday morning may appear trivial, but it also underlines the attention given to the news of the attack. This is clearly a semantically complex case.

(42) Shane had never been one for *words*, he'd always believed *actions spoke louder than explanations*. But sometimes the truth needed to be spoken – not just implied or assumed.

In addition to the adaptation manifested by the verb form, example (42) involves substitution (by the name of a contiguous concept) of the final NP, which is however activated by an occurrence of *words* earlier in the sentence, thus producing another case of defeated expectations.

(43) Tyasan looked up. His expression was that of a man who had clutched at the last straw and caught the whole bale.

This is another complex case in which the *last straw*, a separately lexicalized segment of *It is the last straw that breaks the camel's back*, is fused into an occurrence of *A drowning man clutches at a straw*. *Straw* is thus very much in focus, and the second feature is an addition by coordination which includes a hyperbolic increase (*bale*) within the field of associates of *straw*, hyperbole being a source of humour.

(44) If it helps you to start a dish with supermarket roast chicken or pre-chopped salad greens or already-layered puff pastry, just grab it and get cooking. No, everything doesn't have to

be *spicy. Variety (remember?) is the spice of life*. And that means a *variety* of flavors, textures, aromas, colors, serving styles.

In (44), the most highly rated occurrence, which is metadiscursively signalled (see Section 2.2), the topical connection is provided by the pre-occurrence of *spicy* and the post-occurrence of *variety*. In the proverb, *spice* is metaphorical, but in a context referring to cooking and tastes, it takes on its non-figurative meaning: this is an example of demetaphorization, therefore of a metaseme. The passage superimposes two meanings for one form: the metaphorical one of the proverb alluded to (with the addition of *remember?* to drive the point home), and the literal one in the context. The presence of two meanings for one form means that we have a homonymic pun, which is also metasemic, and we are here well beyond simple allusion.

If we compare the two groups of occurrences – those judged most humorous and clever and those judged least so – in the light of our initial definition of wordplay, this confirms that simple uses of proverbs or lexicalized proverbial segments and / or simple adaptations to the context (whether syntactic or involving lexical substitution) do not constitute wordplay. Impressions of humour and cleverness require both defeated expectations and semantic complexity.

4 Conclusion

In this study, we extracted from the 1990-2011 *COCA* corpus the 303 occurrences of six English proverbs and examined their modifications in the 77.9% of occurrences that were not canonical. Based on a definition that includes formal manipulation, humour and cleverness, very few – nine, i.e. 3% – of these modified occurrences seemed to constitute wordplay. Native speakers rated a sample of 32 occurrences for humour and cleverness, and a comparison of the items with the highest and lowest ratings confirmed that simple adaptations to the context without an additional semantic motivation are not perceived as wordplay and that some semantic complexity is necessary in addition to the formal manipulation. As some of the possible examples of wordplay were not particularly highly rated, it appears that only a tiny minority of manipulated proverbial occurrences are actually perceived as wordplay.

5 References

Anscombre, Jean-Claude. 2003. Les proverbes sont-ils des expressions figées? *Cahiers de lexicologie* 82(1). 159–173.
Arnaud, Pierre J. L. 1991. Réflexions sur le proverbe. *Cahiers de lexicologie* 59(2). 5–27.
Arnaud, Pierre J. L. 1992. La connaissance des proverbes français par les locuteurs natifs et leur sélection didactique. *Cahiers de lexicologie* 60(1). 195–238.
Arnaud, Pierre J. L. & Rosamund Moon. 1993. Fréquence et emploi des proverbes anglais et français. In Christian Plantin (ed.), *Lieux communs, topoï, stéréotypes, clichés*, 323–341. Paris: Kimé.
Attardo, Salvatore. 1994. *Linguistic Theories of Humor*. Berlin: Mouton de Gruyter.
Barta, Péter. 2005. Au pays des proverbes, les détournements sont rois : Contribution à l'étude des proverbes détournés du français (I). *Paremia* 14. 61–70.
Barta, Péter. 2006. Au pays des proverbes, les détournements sont rois. Contribution à l'étude des proverbes détournés du français (II). *Paremia* 15. 57–71.
Bauer, Laurie. 2004. *A Glossary of Morphology*. Edinburgh: Edinburgh University Press.
Chiaro, Delia. 1992. The Language of Jokes: Analyzing Verbal Play. London: Routledge.
The Corpus of Contemporary American English. http://corpus.byu.edu/coca (30 March 2013).
Cox, Heinrich L. 1999. Morgenstund hat Gold im Mund. Sprichwörter mit einer Zeit-Komponente im Sprichwortschatz Bonner Student(inn)en: Ein Versuch zur begrifflichen Kategorisierung der Signifikate. *Rheinisches Jahrbuch für Volkskunde* 33. 81–95.
Davies, Mark. 2009. The 385+ Million Word Corpus of Contemporary American English (1990-2008+): Design, Architecture, and Linguistic Insights. *International Journal of Corpus Linguistics* 14(2). 159–190.
Ettinger, Stefan. 2012. Einige phraseodidaktische Überlegungen zur Frequenz, zur Disponibilität und zur Bekanntheit französischer Idiome und Sprichwörter. In Dávid Szabó (ed.), *Szavak, frazémák, szótárak = Mots, phrasèmes, dictionnaires: Írások Bárdosi Vilmos 60. születésnapjára = Mélanges offerts à Vilmos Bárdosi pour ses 60 ans*, Revue d'études françaises, numéro spécial, Budapest, 85–104.
Greimas, Algirdas Julien. 1960. Idiotismes, proverbes, dictons. *Cahiers de lexicologie* 2. 41–61.
Guiraud, Pierre.1979. *Les Jeux de Mots,* 2nd edn. Paris: Presses Universitaires de France.
Langlotz, Andreas. 2006. Idiomatic Creativity: A Cognitive-Linguistic Model of Idiom Representation and Idiom Variation in English. Amsterdam: Benjamins.
Lennon, Paul. 2004. Allusions in the Press: An Applied Linguistic Study. Berlin: Mouton de Gruyter.
Lippmann, Louis G. & Mara L. Dunn. 2000. Contextual Connections within Puns: Effects on Perceived Humor and Memory. *The Journal of General Psychology* 127(2). 185–197.
McArthur, Tom (ed.). 1992. *The Oxford Companion to the English Language*. Oxford: Oxford University Press.
Mieder, Wolfgang (ed.). 1992. *A Dictionary of American Proverbs*. New York: Oxford University Press.
Moon, Rosamund. 1998. *Fixed Expressions and Idioms in English*. Oxford: Clarendon Press.
Nilsen, Don Lee Fred & Alleen Pace Nilsen. 1978. *Language Play: An Introduction to Linguistics*. Rowley, MA: Newbury House.
Norrick, Neal R. 1985. How Proverbs Mean: Semantic Studies in English Proverbs. Berlin: Mouton.

Partington, Alan Scott. 2009. A Linguistic Account of Wordplay: The Lexical Grammar of Punning. *Journal of Pragmatics* 41(9). 1794–1809.
Rodegem, Francis. 1972. Un problème de terminologie: Les locutions sentencieuses. *Cahiers de l'Institut de Linguistique de Louvain* 1(5). 678–703.
Sadjadpour, Karim. 2012. Three Decades of Mistakes and Mistrusts: *The Twilight War* by David Crist. *The New York Times*. http://www.nytimes.com/2012/07/31/books/the-twilight-war-by-david-crist.html (17 July 2015).
Simpson, John A. & Jennifer Speake. 1992. *The Concise Oxford Dictionary of Proverbs*, 2nd edn. Oxford: Oxford University Press.
Wozniak, Audrey. 2009. Le proverbe détourné: Étude théorique appliquée à un corpus bilingue franco-espagnol. *Paremia* 18. 185–196.

6 Appendix

An Enquiry about Wordplay

We are investigating the nature of wordplay, and for this purpose we have assembled a collection of examples of 6 proverbs used in texts (articles, books, screenplays, etc). The proverbs are:
– A drowning man will clutch at a straw.
– A leopard does not change his / its spots.
– Actions speak louder than words.
– Hell hath no fury like a woman scorned.
– The pen is mightier than the sword.
– Variety is the spice of life.

Please circle the number corresponding to your reaction to each of the examples below:

0   I do not even recognize the allusion
1   I do not find this example particularly clever and amusing.
2   I find this example moderately clever and amusing.
3   I find this example clearly clever and amusing.
(if you are doing the task on your computer, please use other means like highlighting the relevant number, substituting an "X" for it, etc.). Please do the questionnaire in your own time. It is anonymous, but we need the following information:

your age?   your sex?   M / F

Thank you very much for your participation.

[In the film "It Happened one Night" (1934), Clark Gable and Claudette Colbert need a lift. He repeatedly fails at thumbing a car. She then stops the first passing car by displaying one of her

legs.] Claudette Colbert, an escaped heiress, teaches the hero that the "limb is mightier than the thumb" when it comes to hitchhiking.
0 1 2 3

Powerful computers and high-tech scanners now enable marketers to closely monitor how, where and when you spend your money. These electronic transactions speak much louder than words because they reflect actual behavior.
0 1 2 3

"Did you see his expression?" M. Lousteau asked, smiling conspiratorially. "You thwarted his efforts to protect you from... well, from me, I guess. Hell hath no fury like a man prevented from inflicting his good intentions on others."
0 1 2 3

"We don't think that it is the license threat that is going to get the broadcasters to move, but public activity," she said. "Once the Parents and Teachers Associations rouse the community, once ratings start to drop, then the stations will begin to care. The networks aren't going to change their spots," Miss Charren says.
0 1 2 3

Elsewhere Farhan states that the [Muslim] Brotherhood "will not spill one drop of blood or vandalize any public or private property." This derives from a belief that "Sometimes words speak louder than swords."
0 1 2 3

"If we were competitors in business, would you expect me to suppress my own best interests simply by virtue of the fact that we were friends, or whatever?" She laughed. "Dalmar, you don't know me very well. Competition is the spice of life. I thrive on it. You can try to best me at my own game, but I give you fair warning, in business, I always go for the jugular."
0 1 2 3

V told me Roger has been so sweet and charming lately, bringing her flowers, cooking dinner, blah blah blah. Ever since he moved back in, he's been the model husband. "Do you think a leopard can change his spots?" she asked me.
0 1 2 3

If it helps you to start a dish with supermarket roast chicken or pre-chopped salad greens or already-layered puff pastry, just grab it and get cooking. No, everything doesn't have to be spicy. Variety (remember?) is the spice of life. And that means a variety of flavors, textures, aromas, colors, serving styles.
0 1 2 3

"Well, I trust you're a critic, young man, a budding one at least. But has no one told you that the pen is mightier than the... pen knife?"
0 1 2 3

Still, rock stars and social matrons alike seem willing to risk the leaks and blots of indelible misfortune for the dash and flair of a fountain pen. You buy them because you people like to show them off when you use them. I mean, it's a little bit of a throwback. It's moving away from the laptop. And while not even a collector would suggest the fountain pen is mightier than the laptop, you'll never have to replace a pen with the next latest model.
0 1 2 3

Shane had never been one for words, he'd always believed actions spoke louder than explanations. But sometimes the truth needed to be spoken – not just implied or assumed.
0 1 2 3

"Did – did you think the president took the easy way out on your question, Walter?" "No. I think it's a good point. I'm glad that he answered it that way because his actions will speak louder than his words."
0 1 2 3

Hell hath no fury like Al Pacino scorned. The descent into fire and brimstone territory happens within the first five minutes of this interview. Question: "As the devil in your new movie, you say that vanity is the best sin. Do you have any personal favorites?" Pacino gets that don't-mess-with-me Godfather face. His eyes go a little wild. "This is why I didn't want to come here today," he snaps.
0 1 2 3

I mean, this is information that's been available for at least – in their records for 30 years. I don't know what has transpired over the last year that allows them now to make this, I think, PR move. I think in many respects the leopard really hasn't changed its spots. I mean, if you carefully look at the language that they've used, they agree with a consensus. I mean, nicotine is addictive and smoking causes various diseases.
0 1 2 3

As a result of the political and social changes of recent decades, cultural pluralism is now generally recognized as an organizing principle of this society. In contrast to the idea of the melting pot, which promised to erase ethnic and group differences, children now learn that variety is the spice of life....
0 1 2 3

Few schools are able to say that their campus once harbored missiles. Talcott Mountain Science Center, perched upon a ridge overlooking Hartford, Connecticut sits on a former Nike antiaircraft missile site. "From the sword to the pen," says Donald La Salle, Talcott's director. "Where once stood instruments of destruction now only stand instruments of discovery."
0 1 2 3

"One way in which the U.S. can help bloggers and Twitter users trapped in repressive regimes is to spend money. And that we are doing, 25 million this year, according to an announcement today by Secretary of State Clinton to shield these users, Shannon, from jamming uncensor-

ship." – "Technology has certainly changed the way these protests develop and how they play out as well." – "The key pad is mightier than the sword."
0 1 2 3

JOHN QUINONES: But why would she make a list of Congressmen and their seating charts? RHODA BERENSON: It could be a list of people she was planning to interview. I have no idea. JOHN QUINONES: Might she have been involved in terrorism and you didn't know? MARK BERENSON: My daughter has been a totally non-violent person who, again, lives by the pen and not the sword. She said to me she has never touched, fired or held a weapon.
0 1 2 3

Both Republicans and Democrats have demonstrated that "Words speak louder than action."
0 1 2 3

SAM: "Are you in love with Charlotte? You're always together." WILL: "No, I'm just helping with the band." SAM: "She used to be a cheerleader and prom queen and all that. She was the kind of girl who'd never talk to..." WILL: "People like us?" SAM: "Leopards and cheerleaders don't change their spots. Let's get together soon to finish our project."
0 1 2 3

Is it possible that a group of expedient men in Washington could have deliberately withheld critical intelligence data from the officers at Pearl Harbor? And why would they do such a terrible thing? Simple: They needed an excuse to rouse and unite the country to war. Because Hell would have no fury like a nation broadsided from its sleep on Sunday morning.
0 1 2 3

"If I'm ordered to go into the army, I have to go. I'll go whether I like it or not." Steve raised scornful eyes to his father. "You're pretty safe. They're hardly going to reach your age bracket." "Oh," he said almost gleefully, "there's a saying I came across last week. Somebody named Charles Edward Montague, I don't know who he was, but he wrote, War hath no fury like a noncombatant. That sums it up pretty well."
0 1 2 3

So, as he discusses his joy, he has no choice. Standing up, he looks around his nondescript hotel suite with a devilish grin. Then he jumps on the couch. Hands raised triumphantly above his head, he bounces up and down for a moment before taking his seat again. Of course, it's not the first time that Cruise's actions have spoken louder than his words.
0 1 2 3

GOVERNOR: "Actions speak louder than words. And the President's actions are killing jobs in this country." REPRESENTATIVE: "He has failed all Americans when it comes to job creation."
0 1 2 3

[script of a scene from the film *Austin Powers*] AUSTIN (singing) "Hey, watch out, squares... You make us bored! The penis is mightier than the sword." Austin does various groovy dance moves like the Rock'em sock'em robot and the Heavyweight.
0 1 2 3

Most of the typists, young women who worshipped at the shrine of the shopping mall, had long broken off for lunch. Only a few stragglers who were victims of tyrannical superiors were still at it, tapping at their keyboards and brusquely responding to telephone enquiries. Hell hath no fury like a woman done out of her lunch hour.
0 1 2 3

To Yogi Berra, 90 percent of baseball was 10 percent mental. To DeBerry, 99 times out of 10, the team that makes fewer mistakes is going to win. At 58, DeBerry isn't about to change his ways or his sayings. Because, as he likes to tell people, "You can't change the spots on a leper." Or a leopard, for that matter.
0 1 2 3

Will he do what he says? The best way to find out, says Joan Moody, public affairs director of Defenders of Wildlife, is to check his record. "Actions speak louder than words," she says. "If you look at the records, you'll be able to see through the rhetoric."
0 1 2 3

Tantalize him with a touch. Body language speaks louder than words, says Sharyn Wolf, author of *Guerrilla Dating Tactics* (Plume, 1998), so to pique his interest, brush a guy you're sweating subtly on the forearm while making a point or asking a question.
0 1 2 3

Tyasan looked up. His expression was that of a man who had clutched at the last straw and caught the whole bale.
0 1 2 3

She reaches for Walt's hand and, as he feels her grope for him, he grabs her. Takes hold of her before she can take hold of him. It is a reflex between them. He clutches at her like a drowning man, but it doesn't bother her as it does at home.
0 1 2 3

Sebastian Knospe
A Cognitive Model for Bilingual Puns

Abstract: Puns form a highly creative type of wordplay which can be encountered in both oral and written discourse, e.g. in literary works and the press, but also in everyday language. Although they are traditionally less esteemed in Germany than in France, Britain and the US, Görlach (2003: 30) observes a growing inclination to use them in a German context if they have a bilingual shape, i.e. amalgamate German and English material. This notwithstanding, the number of studies devoted to this phenomenon is rather limited so far. Building on press examples of German / English puns, this paper seeks to show that their particular communicative attractiveness can be accounted for by considering their linguistic make-up and the way in which they are cognitively processed in light of the contexts in which they are used. It is argued that they are special in that they result from a structural blending of material from two linguistic codes (here: German and English), while also representing blends from a cognitive and conceptual point of view like many other linguistic phenomena such as metaphors and metonymies. Acknowledging the present status of English in Germany, it is shown what cognitive investments readers have to make to get behind the meaning of bilingual puns and what discursive effects may unfold when they are implemented in journalistic texts.

Keywords: Anglicism, blended space bilingual pun, code blending, code blend, conceptual blending, conceptual blend, diamorph, English, generic space, German, homonymy, input space, polysemy

1 Introduction*

Although puns represent a ludic device documented in different linguistic cultures, as is shown by Attardo (1994), it is especially in examples from English and French that this type of wordplay stands out (see Redfern 1984: 160). Not only is it found in the literature of different periods, for instance in the works of Geoffrey Chaucer, William Shakespeare (Delabastita 1993), Lewis Carroll (see, e.g., Zirker 2010; Kullmann, this volume), and Vladimir Nabokov, to present a

---

* I would like to thank the editors of this volume and the anonymous reviewers for their very useful comments.

brief selection of writers, but also in the diction of newspapers (cf., e.g., Alexander 1997: 93–99), including printed ads (see Tanaka 1992, 1999). Moreover, puns may appear in everyday life humor, e.g. in jocular verbal combats known as "ping-pong punning," in which the participants try to outplay each other by initiating clever linguistic moves (cf., e.g., Chiaro 1992: 17; Alexander 1997: 73–92; Crystal 1998: 1-5; Blake 2007: 68–80). Distributed across different domains of oral and written use and harboring humorous potential (Alexander 1997: 128), puns, without having been made a central topic of research (see Attardo 1994: 108, 141–142), have thus caught the attention of scholars from various disciplines. These include the fields of stylistics, humor and translation studies, as well as social psychology and philosophy (see Attardo 1994: 14–59).

Research typically focuses on puns that operate within one language. Witness the following monolingual examples that are similar to each other in that they share a comic function, but differ in terms of the punning mechanisms used (see also Section 3):

(1) What is grey, has four legs, a long tail and a trunk? – A mouse going on holiday. (Alexander 1997: 52)
(2) Only kings worry about a receding heir line.

In example (1), the joke-teller confronts the hearer with a seemingly straightforward question. While the first three traits adduced in the opening line (*grey color, long tail, four legs*) all seem to point towards a mouse or rat, the fourth feature named, i.e. the word *trunk*, leads the hearer towards a different interpretation, creating the assumption that an elephant is described here. However, this impression is cancelled again by the resolution, which creates an amusing effect because it turns out that the initial interpretation was indeed the correct one. To create this effect, the narrator exploits the different meanings of English *trunk* that may refer to different entities: amongst other things, an elephant's nose or a solid piece of luggage.

In (2), the joke-teller deploys a different punning mechanism by playing with the English nouns *heir* [ɛə(r)] and *hair* [hɛə(r)]. Importantly, only one of the two nouns is materialized in the written code; yet, the second unit is cognitively activated by competent recipients as well. Its evocation is supported by three factors: firstly, *hair* and *heir* are almost identically pronounced, at least in rapid speech, secondly, the compounds *hair line* and *heir line* (or *lineage*) can both be considered as institutionalized English items. Thirdly, the adjective *receding* creates a particular semantic context that lets one expect *hair* rather than *heir*. As a result, most hearers or readers are likely to establish a connection between the word *heir*, which appears on the level of linguistic expression in the written version, and the word *hair*. All this serves as the structural anchor for a joke which addresses thoughts that are said to occupy only a king's mind.

In fact, the statement made in (2) is ambiguous in that it can be read in two ways: On one level, we may take it as indicative of the monarch's fear to gradually lose his hair – a fate a person of this social status might be more concerned with than other men who stand much less in the limelight. On another level, however, the one-liner alludes to the consequences that a ruler may be afraid of when he remains without offspring. This implies a complex connection between alopecia, infertility, and the end of his dynasty.

In this interpretation, *heir* is treated as an English element, although, unlike the noun *hair*, the word has no Germanic origin (*OED* 2014: "hair" *n.*), but was borrowed from French *(h)eir* in Middle English (*OED* 2014: "heir" *n.*), similar to *trunk* which goes back to French *tronc* (*OED* 2014: "trunk" *n.*). What is decisive in this respect is not the etymology of the words, but the fact that both *heir* and *trunk* have been completely anglicized, i.e. adopted an English form. From this point of view, the wordplay initiated in examples (1) and (2) is monolingual in nature because the loanword status of one of the two elements at play is not transparent any longer. In contrast to that, there are cases in which puns are based on an "interlinguistic" (Crystal 2008: 135) or bilingual play (Stefanowitsch 2002) with material that can be synchronically attributed to two different languages in contact with each other (see Bauer, this volume, who studies secret wordplay, which partly includes bilingual punning). It is this category of puns that will be at the heart of this article. As already suggested, the interpretation of these puns as "bilingual" is grounded in a synchronic, formally based criterion, i.e. even loanwords well-established in use are treated as foreign as long as their pronunciation, spelling and / or morphology have not or only partly been nativized (see Görlach 2003: 1; Onysko 2007: 62–94; Knospe 2014: 51–81). Accordingly, in contrast to example (2), the wording in (3) can be classified as bilingual:

(3) Cool-tur (Stefanowitsch 2002: 69)

Morphologically, this expression blends the German noun *Kultur* [kʊl'tuɐ] 'culture' and the formally unintegrated Anglicism *cool* [kuːl], which appears in the first syllable of the coinage, but, unlike the German noun, contains a long [uː]. In line with the structural amalgamation accomplished, the form blends two meanings, showing the attempt of the coiners to work against the prejudice that culture means boredom. Instead, they promise "cool" cultural attractions that are also interesting for young people. The configuration in example (3) was used in an advertising campaign run in several German cities.

While there is a persuasive component contained in (3), the main function of (4) seems to be ludic (cf. examples (1) and (2)). In the joke unfolding, the narrator, a German radio announcer, wonders why there is rarely snow in London in the winter:

(4) Warum haben die in London eigentlich keinen Schnee?
 Weil sie den Tower haben.
 [Why do they actually have no snow in London?
 Because they have the [taʊɐ].] (Koll-Stobbe 2000: 116)

The punchline in (4) wittily takes advantage of the homophony of the nativized form of the English proper name *Tower* [taʊə(r)], which is likely to be realized as [taʊɐ] by most German speakers similar to the pronunciation found in British English, and the German ad hoc creation *Tauer* [taʊɐ]. In the given situation, the latter term can be interpreted as a nonce equivalent to the more complex technical term *Taugerät* 'thawing system, defroster,' since it is analyzable as a derivation which consists of the morphological root *tau* 'to melt' and the agentive suffix *-er*. Hence, the phonic realization of the element *Tower* is reinterpreted in a different sense denoting an object that is capable of melting away ice and snow (see Koll-Stobbe 2000: 35). Structurally, it is the well-known unit *Tower* which is activated first, but via homonymic links, i.e. due to the identical pronunciation of the forms, recipients, in light of the context provided, are able to identify the German ad hoc form, viz. *Tauer*.

According to Stefanowitsch (2002: 67–68), puns like (3) and (4) which juggle with German material and items adopted from the English language have become ubiquitous, especially in written German discourse. By looking at examples from German press texts, this contribution aims to show that they are a product of consciously implemented discursive choices whose deciphering requires specific processing skills from its readers and thus causes additional cognitive efforts leading towards recognition which is seen as rewarding. To present the challenges bilingual puns pose in the interaction between producers and recipients, I seek to depict their linguistic 'ingredients' and the dynamic cognitive mechanisms they are connected with. It is argued here that bilingual puns are special in that they spring from the combination of two mechanisms of blending: a structural and a cognitive-conceptual one. Structurally, bilingual puns are code blends (Sebba 2011), manipulating German and English material which converge in form, often also as a result of phonetic adaptation processes

Anglicisms are submitted to, as in the case of *Tower* and *Tauer* (also see Winter-Froemel 2008, 2011). However, it is assumed that the two structurally merged input forms, once they have been identified, are also conceptually blended, a process which, e.g., can be observed as well with metaphors and metonymies (see Fauconnier 1994; Fauconnier and Turner 2002).

Before illustrating in greater detail the complex cognitive processes involved in bilingual punning, this article will explain the general premises on which this investigation is built, pointing out why a study of German-English language contact may offer crucial insights into the topic at hand. This issue is linked to the sociolinguistic status of English in Germany today. It is claimed here that a gradual bilingualism with English has been established among younger German speakers and that this, along with the structural similarities between the two languages, promotes various forms of playful use of the English language, including the phenomenon under scrutiny (also see Knospe 2014: 25–49). Section 3 moves on to a closer study of the basic structural principles of bilingual puns in written use, considering their status as code blends and their functions in press texts. Taking up these examples, which mainly stem from the German news magazine *Der Spiegel,* and assuming a gradual bilingual competence, the final section then sketches a cognitive approach centered on an interpretation of bilingual puns as conceptual *cum* code blends.

2 The Status of English in Germany

2.1 The Presence of English in Different Domains

According to Stefanowitsch (2002: 73), German-English language contact "provides [...] ideal conditions for the emergence of a widespread practice of bilingual punning." One factor supporting this statement lies in the high degree of structural overlaps between the systems of English and German, since they are both part of the West Germanic branch of the Indo-European language family. This genetic affiliation is reflected in a set of similar phonological patterns, especially in the consonant system, and a great deal of shared vocabulary items (cf. König and Gast 2012). Yet, for bilingual puns to emerge, this pool of interlingually shared features is not sufficient. Rather, what is required as well are creative language users who are able to make use of the options ensuing from the overlaps between the two systems. Recently, a group of gradual bilinguals with English as their L2 has emerged in Germany, related to a change of the sociolinguistic status of English in Germany from that of a foreign language towards that of a lingua franca (for a diachronic perspective see Hilgendorf 2001; Stefanowitsch 2002).

Notable evidence for this development can be found when looking at the institutional embedding of English in Germany. Since the 1960s, it has been the non-native language taught first in German schools, not least due to the role which British and American Allies played after the end of the Second World War. These days, English is often even taught from kindergarten age on, so that, on average, every German pupil has the chance to study it for at least nine years. In the hierarchy of languages chosen as subjects in German schools, French has managed to defend the second rank, although it is less popular than in previous decades. What follows next in the ranking is Latin or, leaving apart this classical language, which can only be opted for from grade 5 on, Spanish (see Table 1).

Tab. 1: Ranking of languages apart from German taught at German schools of general education (school year 2012 / 13)

School language	Number and proportion of pupils learning this language (grade 1–4)		Number and proportion of pupils learning this language (grade 5–12 / 13)	
English	1,861,744	(64.40%)	5,581,941	(99.00%)
French	114,789	(3.97%)	1,484,284	(26.32%)
Latin	...		740,302	(13.13%)
Spanish	1,753	(0.06%)	383,028	(6.79%)
Russian	8,570	(0.30%)	99,821	(1.77%)
Italian	420	(0.01%)	58,385	(1.04%)

Furthermore, English plays a crucial role in adult education, e.g. in German community colleges (*Volkshochschulen*) (cf. Stefanowitsch 2002: 74). In addition to that, the growing impact of English in Germany is based on the increasing internationalization of its system of tertiary education, going back to the much debated Bologna Reform. Initiated at the end of the 1990s, it has been accompanied by the implementation of Bachelor's and Master's programs in all EU countries and by the introduction of a European Credit Transfer System (ECTS) which is to facilitate the acknowledgement of study accomplishments during semesters abroad.[1]

However, owing to the economic predominance of the USA and the existence of globally intertwining markets, the presence of English is most manifest in business and commerce, and can be regarded as a prominent characteristics of globally operating enterprises (cf. Vollstedt 2002: 106; Meckel and Schmied 2008: 256). Further economic impulses for the use of English spring from the growing prevalence of service industries in which large firms keep customer contact around the globe (Hilgendorf 2001: 104–125; Heller 2003). Additionally, people working in the tourism sector need to have at least some command of English (Graddol 2006: 29).

Taking all this together, one can thus state that, on the one hand, English fulfills intra- and international functions across various professional registers, without calling into question the primary role of German in most communicative domains. This is a development often discussed under the rubric of *English for Special Purposes* (ESP, cf. Robinson 1980; Dudley-Evans and Saint John 2001; Kim 2008). On the other hand, English has also gained foothold as a language of popular culture. For instance, Jenkins (2003: 38) makes out a growing importance of English "as a language of socialisation," which is roughly equivalent to what Preisler (1999: 241) names an informal, non-standard "English from below." Coining the designation *English for Cultural Purposes* (ECP) to describe this phenomenon, Koll-Stobbe (2000: 81) sees considerable advances in the average English competence that result from an interplay of institutional instruction and unconscious learning processes which are largely driven by the media. In this context, she refers to the functions of English in different communicative fields such as advertising, soft news and edutainment, but also films and literature, music, sports, and youth culture. The following passages approach these sectors in a more detailed manner, assuming that the use of English also enforces creative linguistic practices:
– This trend is, for instance, quite evident in German advertising. Since the 1980s, it has seen a constant increase of brand names and slogans which ei-

---

[1] According to the most recent account on the realization of the Bologna aims, available from the Federal Ministry of Education and Research (BMBF 2009: 32, 34), German universities and technical colleges run about 100 joint degree programs, in which at least one foreign university takes part so that English is among the educational languages. Additionally, based on these statistics, there are 460 Bachelor's and Master's programs offered in English, the majority of which is found in business sciences and in technical subjects. The quota of programs held in English amounts to 5 % of all study programs – with an increasing tendency.

ther appear fully in English or play with both languages, especially in campaigns designed for cigarettes, clothes, and for products of youth culture or information technology (cf. Hilgendorf 2001: 104–106; Piller 2001, 2003; Androutsopoulos, Bozkurt, Breninck, Kreyer, Tornow and Tschann 2004: 15; Kelly-Holmes 2005). For Schütte (1996: 270–302) and Piller (2003), this illustrates that, in advertising, English acts as a linguistic resource which conveys symbolic connotations such as modernity, a cosmopolitan attitude, and an openness towards innovation (see also Onysko and Winter-Froemel 2011).
- Similarly, current statistics attest an overwhelming presence of English in the media. Departing from the data collected by media control (2011) for the years between 2005 and 2010, an average of 70 out of the 100 top German music titles had English lyrics. Clip and album charts exhibit comparable trends.
- Moreover, the findings from Insidekino (2011) bring to light that out of the 20 top films broadcast in Germany in the same period three quarters were either entirely produced or at least co-produced by American movie production companies. Although they are usually dubbed, cinemas in big German cities, as in the Netherlands and the Scandinavian countries, sometimes also show the original film versions and do often not translate the English titles. This may contribute to rendering certain linguistic elements chunks of knowledge, even to speakers who only have a low English competence (Blommaert 2010: 102–106).
- Finally, a glimpse at the book market reveals that, from the years 2005 to 2010, 40 % of the Top 100 publications among the hardcover and pocket fiction books came from Anglophone authors (Buchreport 2011). While English is used in most of the scientific publications today (Ammon 1999; Ammon and McConnell 2002; Sano 2002), popular books are usually translated, but may hold on to English words, too. Through the media, these may make their way into the German language where they are then available for fresh combinations.

2.2 Attitudes towards English in Germany

The figures cited above confirm that, today, English is conspicuously used additionally to German, both in professional domains and in popular culture. Undeniably, however, its present position has a socio-psychological or attitudinal base as well. Coulmas (2005: 165) makes out a special prestige or "lure of English" which is rooted in its globally valid functional utility in the professional domains mentioned above and the symbolic values different groups of speakers ascribe to it, regarding it as a medium of communication that gives them the opportunity to succeed in higher education and to participate in various spheres of life. Numerous studies, e.g. the Eurobarometer published by the European Commission (2005) as well as the investigations by Mollin (2006: 173–178) and Berns, de Bot and Hasebrink (2007: 5), indicate that these views are also held by the majority of German speakers of English.

Yet, the public discourse on the role of English is a dual one. Critical voices regarding the impact of English basically emanate from private individuals[2] or NGOs, such as the *Verein Deutsche Sprache* (VDS), whose positions are often echoed in the media. Thus, McArthur (2003: 160) refers to Germany as a "moot nation," while also emphasizing that the positive attitudes towards the English language prevail. Further evidence for this can be seen in the German state, despite some ongoing debates on the pros and cons of fixing German as the national language in the Constitutional Law (*Grundgesetz*), having as yet refrained from passing any regulating language laws.

2.3   Emergence of a Gradual "bilingualism with English"

In light of this, English can be said to work as a lingua franca in Germany today (cf. Modiano 1999: 8–9; Seidlhofer 2001, 2004; Jenkins 2007). This point of view is also supported by the growing English competence of many Germans. It is true that it is surpassed by the command of English generally found in the Scandinavian countries and the Netherlands, where English has even become a second language. Still, Germans hold an advanced middle position in this regard, as is pointed out unanimously by the studies of Viereck (1996: 16), Cenoz (2000: 5–12), and Mollin (2006: 173–178). Looking at the whole of Europe, Hoffmann assumes a regionally differentiated "bilingualism with English" (1996: 48). She notes that

> this bilingualism is of a particular kind: it is "achieved bilingualism," i.e. it is not naturally acquired bilingualism; it is neither popular bilingualism (found among vast numbers of the population) nor can it be labelled as elite bilingualism. (Hoffmann 1996: 48)

---

2 For discussions on the potential promotion of a hybrid form of language use named "Germlish" or "Denglish" through a continuing spread of English in Germany see Hensel (2000) and Paulwitz (2000). Spitzmüller (2005) contrasts such popular or laymen positions with those of the linguistic discourse about the consequences of contact between different languages, an issue also taken up by Onysko (2009).

Arguing in a similar vein, Koll-Stobbe (2000: 62) speaks of a "gradual bilingualism" with English. This concept does not start from ideal conceptions of bilingualism as the "native-like control of two languages" (Bloomfield 1933: 65). Instead, it allows for a range of competences on an individual scale depending on the domains entered and the language modalities chosen. Partly, speakers may rely on a "truncated" knowledge only (Blommaert 2010: 102–106).

2.4 Language Mixing with English in *Journalese*: Anglicisms, Codeswitching, and Bilingual Puns

These considerations lead us back to the central topic of this study. In a nutshell, the claim made here is that the present status of English and the gradual bilingual competences it ties in with entail a higher susceptibility to practices of language mixing. There are two aspects at stake: firstly, borrowing leading to new items that often become conventionalized in the German lexicon and that are known as Anglicisms; secondly, occasional language mixing or situative "switches in and out of English" (Swann 1996: 3) promoting nonce forms. Traces of these practices can be found in oral and written communication (cf., e.g., Piller 2001, 2003; Onysko 2007; Knospe 2014). Stefanowitsch (2002), Görlach (2003: 30), and Vaid (2006: 158) also list bilingual puns as an outcome to be expected from the intensification of contact with English, although puns, despite certain traditions in German literature and in comedy, represent a pattern somewhat disesteemed in German (cf. Görlach 2003: 30; for a short comparison of German and English humor also see Alexander 1997: 159–174). Still, it seems to Görlach that the reservations against this type of wordplay are neutralized if it "involves English word-building material" (Görlach 2003: 30). Against the background of this statement, this article seeks to show that the attractiveness of bilingual puns resides in two aspects, namely in the prestige of English, which is bound to a gradual bilingualism, as well as in the specificity of bilingual puns that, as code *cum* conceptual blends, require an additional cognitive effort, which leads to a particular sense of achievement if the addressee succeeds in understanding the pun.

Methodologically, the approach taken in the present context is not intended as an empirical one in the narrow sense, but rather pursues a case-study format. This paper focuses on press data, since it covers a broad spectrum of topics and text types and is directed at a wider audience. In addition to press language (cf. Stefanowitsch 2002; Görlach 2003: 2–4, 30; Onysko 2007: 311–312; Knospe 2010, 2014), bilingual puns are also popular in German advertising (cf. Koll-Stobbe

2000: 15–19, 88–90; Stefanowitsch 2002; Piller 2003). Furthermore, they show up in brand names in the Linguistic Landscapes of bigger German commercial cities (cf. Fuller 2012: 109; Koll-Stobbe 2015). Even though an approach comparing the fruitfulness of different domains for punning would exceed the length of this article, some of the examples to ensue, because of intertextual references, also include creative patterns which have been absorbed from advertising discourse or were coined by speakers quoted in the article. At the same time, the puns used for illustration exhibit a range of structural and discursive options and are linked to different press sections. Most of the examples are taken from Knospe (2014), who investigates practices of language mixing with English in the news magazine *Der Spiegel,* covering the years 2006 / 2007. This choice conforms to Clyne's (1995: 129) observation that punning in Germany is mainly "the province of creative writers (including journalists who write for such periodicals as *Der Spiegel*)."[3]

3 Structural Make-up and Discursive Functions of Bilingual Puns

The context of mono- and bilingual representatives of *puns* demands at least a working definition of the term. According to Alexander (1997), a "'genuine' pun" can be characterized as a linguistic instantiation in which

> either the polysemy of a single word (ie one form with multiple meanings) or the uses of homonyms or near-homonyms (ie lexical items having identical or, less often, similar phonetic or graphic form but different meanings) are involved. (Alexander 1997: 18–19)

Checked against the instances which were discussed above (see Section 1), the first constellation – namely the exploitation of polysemy – can be attributed to example (1), where the two meanings of *trunk* are historically related.[4] Given

---

3 Moreover, what speaks in favor of *Der Spiegel,* which covers a range of articles on politics, economy, but also on technology and lifestyle, is that the magazine has the reputation of being one of the medial entry gates for English words (cf. Carstensen 1965: 22). For this reason, it has been investigated for traces of English lexical influence more systematically than any other German paper (cf. Carstensen 1963, 1965; Schelper 1988; Yang 1990; Zürn 2001; Onysko 2007; Knospe 2014).
4 On the one hand, the elongated nose is a central feature of an elephant as is the trunk (= main stem) of a tree, which amounts to a metaphorical similarity. On the other hand, *trunk* in

that the concept of polysemy, as explicated by Alexander, refers to "one word with multiple meanings," this notion must be seen as intrinsically monolingual. Indeed, multiple meanings result from an extension of a core meaning, a process which may also affect borrowed material (see Busse and Görlach 2002: 26–28; Fischer 2008: 3; Winter-Froemel 2011: 21–23).[5] By contrast, homonymy is a relation which holds between several linguistic units that have a different etymology and show no semantic relation, but have accidentally developed into the same form. Judged from a formal-synchronic point of view (see Section 1), the two items concerned may belong to either one language (like example (2)) or to several languages. If the forms (irrespective of whether they come from the same or two distinct languages) differ in at least one phoneme, they are labeled *paronyms* by Hausmann (1974). Thus, both relations of homonymy (see example (4) *Weil sie den Tower haben*) and paronymy (see example (3) *Cool-tour*) may serve as a basis for bilingual puns. This requirement imposes a considerable structural constraint on bilingual puns (see Attardo 1994: 121–126; Stefanowitsch 2002: 81). In short, it presupposes the availability of nearly or fully identical elements of different language indexing which Haugen (1950: 220) names *diamorphs*.[6] Only rarely are diamorphs full homonyms, i.e. both interlingual homophones and homographs. Rather, partial German / English homonyms, which either constitute (near-)homophones or homographs, predominate. As a consequence, most bilingual puns which appear in written texts also

---

the meaning of 'box or case for putting clothes in,' (*Oxford English Dictionary* 2014: "trunk" *n.* II.7.a.) can be accounted for by the fact that such boxes were originally made of wood (see *OED* 2014: "trunk" *n.* II. on this metonymic extension). However, these links between the two meanings are probably not seen by the average speaker. Thus, the example is a case of diachronic polysemy which may be considered an instance of synchronic (or secondary) homonymy. On the distinction between diachronic and synchronic definitions of homonymy and polysemy see Blank (2001: 112); Winter-Froemel and Zirker (2010: 81n8).

5 Another process in which a word turns polysemous in situations of language contact is that of semantic borrowing (cf. Betz 1949: 24; Haugen 1950: 220). This is, however, not relevant in the present context since in this case the semantic scope of a native word is broadened. Moreover, representations of *overlapping polysemy*, i.e. the option that "a word in one language is polysemous, and [that] there exists an equivalent in the other language that, by and large, exhibits the same polysemy" (Alsina and DeCesaris 2002: 221) has no significance here as this constellation implies a close semantic proximity, while all the bilingual puns discussed in this article use semantically different elements from two linguistic codes. However, this may not necessarily hold for all cases of bilingual wordplay (see the examples studied by Bauer, this volume).

6 Puns based on near-homophones (see example (3) above) are also named paronomasic or impure puns (Sobkowiak 1991).

involve the level of orthography (also cf. Cook, Bassetti and Vaid 2012: 120). This feature can be observed for examples (3) and (4). Sometimes, the diamorphs also make part of different word classes, which are rendered meaningful in the linguistic cotext and the extra-linguistic context they appear in. This, in turn, is the case with example (3) *Cool-tur,* where the adjectival Anglicism *cool* breaks up the integrity of the German noun *Kultur,* but not with (4), since both *Tower* and *Tauer* are nouns.

Bearing this in mind, let us now take a look at two more examples of bilingual puns, first from a functional and then from a structural point of view. Both configurations are taken from an interview between the *Spiegel* journalists and the German linguist Nina Janich who discusses the question whether English poses a threat to German. From a functional point of view, the two puns, which Janich spotted in German advertising campaigns, are thus made the target of metalinguistic reflection:

(5) fun-tastisch
(6) We kehr for you (*Spiegel Online* 20 October 2000)[7]

From a structural perspective, pun (5) *fun-tastisch* [fanˈtastɪʃ], similar to the configuration (3), *Cool-tur,* touches the sub-lexical level because *fun* ([fʌn], the integrated pronunciation found in German is [fan]), modifies the German adjective *fantastisch* [fanˈtastɪʃ] 'fantastic.' By contrast, (6) is based on an interlingual paronymy manifest on the lexical level. Judged from the data in *Der Spiegel* and similar to Stefanowitsch's (2002: 69–70) findings, bilingual puns hinging on morphemes or other segments of words tend to be generally more frequent as these elements are shorter and thus more likely to be homophonous or paronymous across languages.

The nonce formation (5) *fun-tastisch* advertises a mobile phone with buttons that offers special functions so as to meet the needs of *Generation Fun*. For this, similar to the practice in the monolingual pun (2), a morphological blend is realized; this time, however, with homonymous German and English material. In fact, the first syllable of formation (5) foregrounds the prominent Anglicism *fun* and separates it from the rest of the unit by a hyphen. As the noun *fun* and the initial element *fan-* are homophonous diamorphs in German, this leaves the conventionalized German adjective *fantastisch* 'fantastic' almost intact. Another important aspect to be stressed is that *fantastisch* is spelled with an initial <f>

---

[7] Grimm (2000); also cited in Onysko (2007: 311).

here. This follows the new German orthography, while the former spelling, in line with the Greek origin of the adjective, was marked by the initial consonant cluster <ph> *(phantastisch)*, similar to the older English spelling *phantastic*. Consciously opting for the spelling with an initial <f>, the coiners thus only change one grapheme, namely the vowel letter, substituting <u> for <a> to add another layer of meaning. Due to the blending of the two codes achieved in this part of the configuration, both the fabulous qualities of the gadget and the fun factor are highlighted. Furthermore, in this example, the root element *-tast-* can be reinterpreted as if it were related to the German noun *Taste* 'key, button' with which it is identical in pronunciation and spelling except for the final *e*. As a result, the signification of the whole formation gets even more complex, emphasizing three main qualities of the product, i.e. the fact that (1) it can be used for fun purposes, (2) has a fantastic design, and (3) offers additional functions accessible via a special button (*Taste*).

While the wordplay in example (5) *fun-tastisch* touches the sub-lexical (morphological) level, the pun in (6), *We kehr for you*, operates on the supra-lexical level. In this case, the verb, framed into a larger phrasal structure,[8] is rendered semantically ambiguous. This slogan, incorporating a salient bilingual pun, was placarded by the city waste management company of Berlin for some time and is discussed as an example of linguistic creativity in the *Spiegel* article. On the one hand, because of the semantics of the German verb *kehren* 'to sweep,' the catch phrase exposes the daily services of the company, which manages waste and cleans the streets in the German capital. What is hidden below the surface and adds another layer of meaning is the formulaic expression *We care for you*, which is retrievable because the verb form *kehr* [keːɐ̯] is phonetically close to a potential Germanized pronunciation of the English verb *care* [kɛə(r)] (cf. Mair 1995: 15–16; Busse and Görlach 2002: 22). The wordplay engendered constructs the image of a service provider which fulfils its prescribed duty by tidying up all public places, and, at the same time, also taking care of the city in an all-encompassing way. The broader mission implied is to make both visitors and permanent city-dwellers feel comfortable. Again, this semantic upgrading is achieved through a formal modification. In this case, however, it does not only alter the spelling, resulting in the form *kehr* instead of the habitual form *care*, but also touches the level of inflectional morphology, since the typical German infinitival suffix *-en* ('Wir kehren') gets elided so as to phonetically match the English verb form.

---

[8] For creative modifications of fixed expressions, which are used as constructional frames as in (6), also see Rasulic (2010).

All the examples discussed so far have in common that they play with content words or parts of the latter. Besides these, one also finds bilingual puns that are built around proper names, which form indeed the basis for most of the bilingual puns in *Der Spiegel*. Strictly speaking, proper names are not necessarily part of one language only, but the referents labeled through them usually belong to one particular culture. Hence, in the present context, cases involving proper names are accounted for, albeit as bilingual puns with a special status. Consider, for example, the paronymous pun

(7)   Alles im Wunderland (*Spiegel* 17 February 2007: 150)

which has an intertextual dimension because it alludes to the famous novel *Alice im Wunderland* (English title: *Alice's Adventures in Wonderland*) by Lewis Carroll. The wordplay builds on the proximity in pronunciation of a partly Germanized form of the first name *Alice* – an initial [a] instead of [æ] is realized by some German speakers (see *Duden* Online) so that the usual English pronunciation ['ælɪs] is changed into [a'liːs]– and the indefinite pronoun *alles* [aləs] 'all, everything.'[9] In the *Spiegel* corpus, the formula occurs as the catchy headline of an article plunging into the miraculous world of the Internet in which virtually everything appears to be possible.

Moving beyond the fields of entertainment and consumer culture, the next example shifts our attention to the domain of politics:

(8)   Roll Beck (*Spiegel* 2007: 23)

Like (7), this wordplay is based on incomplete homophony, although the preposition *back* [bæk] is liable to be rendered like the proper name *Beck* [bɛk] by many Germans. The pun succinctly tries to characterize the attempts of Kurt Beck, then the leader of the German Social Democrats, to calm down his somewhat rebellious party by proposing some changes to incisive reforms that had been realized on the job market and in the social welfare system by the former German center-left federal government. As Beck had supported these measures beforehand, the *Spiegel* presents his altered attitude as a political roll back. Similarly negative undertones are at work in the comment:

(9)   Da ist mehr im Bush (*Spiegel* 10 July 2006: 76)

---

9 Alternatively, if one assumes a pun on the dialectal variant *älles* [ɛləs] found in Swabian, the phonic similarity is still increased.

It exploits the full homonymy that exists between the German noun *Busch* [bʊʃ] and the proper name *Bush* [bʊʃ], and is used as a journalistic peg for shedding light on the politics of the former US president. Like (6), this configuration is based on a quotation, mirroring the pointed diction of the Bush critic Elsässer, who questions the official explanations regarding the background of the terrorist attacks on the World Trade Center on September 11, 2001. From the point of view of the author, who is described as a "conspiracy theorist" in a later paragraph of the article, there could be still more to discover about the antecedents of this assault and the role of George W. Bush. The modified spelling suggests a new interpretation of the German idiom *Da ist mehr im Busch* ('There is more to it'), yielding the construction *Da ist mehr im Bush* (literally 'There is hidden more in the bush / in, i.e. by, [President] Bush').

Apart from incorporating proper names, bilingual puns, according to the *Spiegel* corpus, may also be used as proper or brand names themselves (on this also see Lillo 2007; Koll-Stobbe 2015). This option is reflected in example

(10) fair-liebt (*Spiegel* 11 June 2007: 147)

Originally, this pun was coined for advertising purposes and serves referential functions in the *Spiegel* article. In this case, the interlingual homophony, which is situated on the sub-lexical level, resides in the similarity in the pronunciation of the German prefix *ver-* [fɛɐ̯] and that of the Anglicism *fair* [fɛː, fɛ(ə)r], which stands out through its separation by a hyphen from the second element *liebt*, i.e. the past participle form of *lieben* 'to love, to adore.' The formation *fair-liebt* thus plays on German *verliebt* 'to be in love with' and seeks to entice potential customers by promising a range of attractive products of fair trade origin.

This set of examples should suffice to give a first impression of the typical make-up of bilingual puns. Summing up the major insights gained, one can say that they are usually wielded with the help of prominent lexical items – German ones and Anglicisms or chunks of well-established imported English words, including proper names. From a discursive angle, the *Spiegel* data reveals that bilingual puns may sometimes serve as ironic comments (see examples (7) *Alles im Wunderland* and (8) *Roll-Beck*). In other cases, they are also used as intertextual units which echo the opinion of others or become the object of metalinguistic reflection (see examples (5) *fun-tastisch*, (6) *We kehr for you*, (9) *Da ist mehr im Bush*, (10) *fair-liebt*). This suggests a variety of discursive options, but, due to the limited amount of examples, should not be regarded as a closed list by any means. Structurally, as has become apparent from the case study above, bilingual puns presuppose homophones or paronyms, i.e. same- or similar-sounding elements in the two languages or diamorphs that are words in language A and sub-lexical units (or chunks) in language B. Another point to be remembered is the use of orthographic deformations in the written code, since interlingual (near-)homophones which do not share the same spelling predominate. Full interlingual homonymies, i.e. instances in which the two forms are homophones and homographs at the same time, are, however, not excluded. This possibility, which did not show up in the *Spiegel* examples, can be illustrated by the pun

(11) MISS-Stimmung (Stefanowitsch 2002: 68)

Example (11) is taken from a journal article on conflicts between the female participants during a Miss World contest. It puns on the German noun *Missstimmung* '(atmosphere full of) discord,' which contains the negative prefix *miss-* [mɪs] (spelt *miß-* before the German orthographic reform), and the Anglicism *Miss* [mɪs].[10] Yet, even this example underlines that the authors often use additional means such as hyphens or capitalization to signal that a double meaning is intended. To put it differently: bilingual puns in written language use typically involve a combination of a play with sounds *and* spelling plus additional typographic means in order to indicate the pun (cf. also Alexander 1997: 21; Renner, this volume). These manipulations represent problem spots which, on reflection, open structural access points leading to the deciphering of the code blend and the double meaning of the pun behind this surface form.

With this statement, we have left the realm of a primarily structurally oriented description which considers the resulting form only. A structural approach, after all, is rather static, since it eclipses the complex processing at play in bilingual punning. In fact, to arrive at a sensible interpretation, the recipients have to follow specific paths and are, at least partly, directed in this by punsters anticipating the addressees' interpretative needs.

---

10 The classification of this pun as bilingual is legitimated by the fact that the honorific *Miss* borrowed from English reveals formal features of foreignness at least in its plural form, *Misses*, which deviates from the *-e* plural that we find in German nouns such as *Biss* [bite] or *Riss* [rip; fissure; crack].

4 A Cognitive Model: Bilingual Puns as Conceptual *cum* Code Blends

4.1 Scope of the Model

To capture the complexity and the dynamics involved in the production and comprehension of bilingual puns, a cognitive linguistic framework seems to be promising.[11] It offers a holistic perspective because it not only integrates the linguistic structures involved and the concepts they are linked to, but also studies their entrenchment as well as the communicators' linguistic competence (see Section 2.3), their language awareness, and their cognitive activities such as thinking, imagining, comparing, and integrating or shifting attention (see, e.g., Croft and Cruse 2004: 1–6; Evans and Green 2006: 27–53). This section provides a draft of what such a cognitive model for bilingual puns could look like. Following the directions of this article, the model has been specified for wordplay in the written code that merges material from two closely related languages. Thus, it cannot be projected one-to-one onto bilingual puns which arise in different linguistic constellations and / or other medial realizations (see Section 5).

4.2 Setting the Stage: Conceptual Blending Theory

The backbone of the model proposed here is formed by the theory of conceptual blending, which has become central in cognitive linguistics because of the influential work of Fauconnier (1994) and Fauconnier and Turner (2002). Within this field of linguistics, this theory is used as an explanation for different phenomena such as linguistic categorization, analogy, counterfactual reasoning, metaphor, and metonymy. The question is whether it may also be fruitful for bilingual puns which could be classified as both conceptual and code blends.

In the following, the general framework devised by Fauconnier (1994) and Fauconnier and Turner (2002) will be briefly presented. One of its central tenets is that communicators are knowledgeable social agents who, while cognitively

---

[11] For a cognitive model also see Lundmark (2003), who focuses on polysemy-based monolingual puns. Some cognitive notions (e.g. entrenchment, frame) are also entailed in Stefanowitsch's (2002) article on bilingual puns and in Koll-Stobbe's (2000: 15–19, 162–186) broader psycholinguistic work on the encoding and decoding of ad hoc wordings in which she also discusses the question how concepts are mapped onto words.

and communicatively active, construct mental spaces which form "small conceptual packets" (Fauconnier and Turner 2002: 40). This happens in language production, whenever concepts are verbalized, e.g. in oral speech and in written (journalistic) texts, as well as in language comprehension, where the recipients (i.e. hearers or readers) have to cope with available linguistic forms and their meanings. Either way, the communicators involved are believed to fill mental spaces with concepts that may be pointed to and identified through specific phenomena such as metaphors, metonymies (Fauconnier 1994: 2), and, as is argued here, bilingual puns.

According to the theory of conceptual blending, mental constructions come about in larger cognitive domains that are, *inter alia*, shaped by the situational context and the surrounding discourse (Langacker 2008: 45). In the process of blending, several mental spaces are activated (Fauconnier and Turner 2002: 40–50; Croft and Cruse 2004: 32–39):

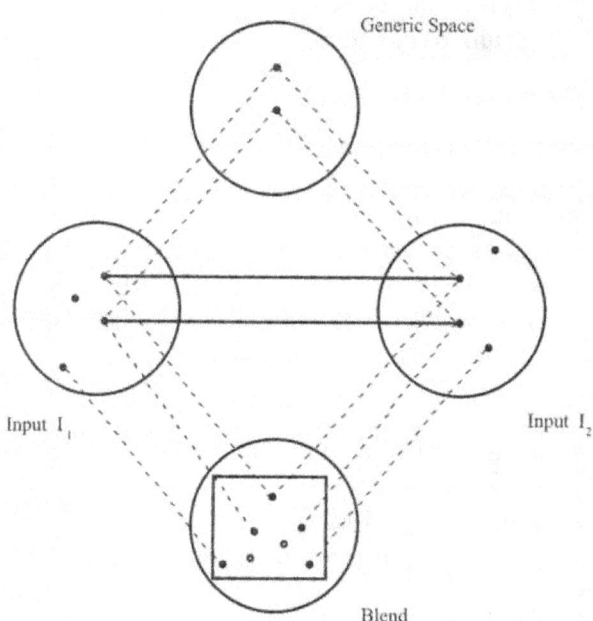

Fig. 1: "Basic diagram" for conceptual blending (following Fauconnier and Turner 2002: 46)

– As a starting point, for a conceptual blend to happen, speakers need to draw on at least two input spaces. These encapsulate different concepts selected by the communicators, i.e. they evoke available linguistic units asso-

ciated with particular semantic features and specific pieces of background knowledge (cf. Fauconnier and Turner 2002: 48) or encyclopedic knowledge (see Langacker 2008: 48–53).
- Although the content in the different input spaces is usually largely distinct, even concepts which are entirely different often share some highly abstract, meaning-relevant components. These enter the generic space when the speakers identify deeper, but highly abstract relations like identity, time, space, cause and effect, role, property, part / whole, (dis)similarity, or intentionality (cf. Fauconnier and Turner 2002: 93–102).
- Finally, through selective projection, some of the elements supplied by the input spaces are merged. This is achieved in the blended space, often only referred to as the blend. At the moment of its initiation, the blend creates a novel, often surprising discursive effect because it "develops emergent structure that is not in the inputs" (Fauconnier and Turner 2002: 42). It "is delivered to consciousness" while we, as speakers, go through many of the other processes unconsciously or "at the moment of solution [...] have already lost most of the structure of the preceding steps" (Fauconnier and Turner 2002: 57).

As a rule, cognitive linguistics visualizes the mental spaces and the links between them by means of diagrams that take the form of networks, emphasizing that they represent "essential aspects of blending" (Fauconnier and Turner 2002: 57). In Figure 1, the circles display the mental spaces with their conceptual units appearing as dots. The solid lines indicate the connections between the input spaces and the dotted lines the links to the other spaces. Finally, the box in which the blend appears in Figure 1 encloses the emergent meaning.

4.3 Conceptual Blending in Bilingual Puns

As already indicated and as the designation "basic diagram" suggests, cognitive linguistics assumes that this model may help to elucidate a number of linguistic phenomena. Many creative instances may thus be traced back to similar processes of conceptual blending. However, every group of blends and every single case of blending is specific in its own way.

So what is particular about bilingual puns then? To answer this question, one has to recall one important issue, namely the material or structural side of bilingual puns, which are in fact code blends (Sebba 2011), connected through interlingual homonymy or paronymy. Indeed, getting behind this connection is the point where the conceptual blend starts. According to Koll-Stobbe (2000:

116), a successful interpretation presupposes that the communicators have realized the potential of a coincidence of form for creating a double meaning, i.e. the option that a linguistic component, taken from language A, evokes a homonymous or paronymous element in language B. In the cognitive reality of (gradual) bilingual speakers, the ability to mentally cross language boundaries builds on associative links which, as has been verified by some recent psycholinguistic studies, e.g. by Broersma and de Bot (2006), are particularly active in the case of diamorphs. In light of the context information provided, the connection of the two formally quasi-congruent forms triggers the activation of the different concepts they are coupled with, and drives on the processing from the input spaces over the generic space to the blend (Fauconnier and Turner 2002: 48). On the whole, this template of blending is easier to achieve with highly entrenched units so that well-known native words and Anglicisms or parts of those are preferred in bilingual punning (see Section 3).

To figure out how the conceptual blending works *in concreto* – "the creative part comes in running the blend for the specific case" (Fauconnier and Turner 2002: 72) –, I will study some of the examples already discussed in sections 1 and 3 based on this model, followed by a detailed analysis of the processing tasks for the producers and recipients of bilingual puns. In doing so, I postulate that the form which enters the first input space opens a cognitive window onto the second one; this happens due to homonymy or paronymy networks in the bilingual speakers' minds which are activated in light of the concrete utterance and particular contextual cues (e.g. on the orthographic level).

Looking again at example (4) *Weil sie den Tower haben,* it can be claimed that the first input space contains the unit *Tower,* which denotes one of the most famous historical sites in London. The blend maps this concept onto a technical one, namely a defroster (German: *Tauer*), sharing with it its abstract form as an object in the external world and suggesting a comic explanation for the mild winter days in the British capital. The blending is summarized in Figure 2. For reasons of typesetting, the circles representing the different spaces were replaced by boxes. Moreover, the associative links between the diamorphs and the discourse context were added to the diagram because readers, to be successful in their search for meaning, must also include the surrounding information:

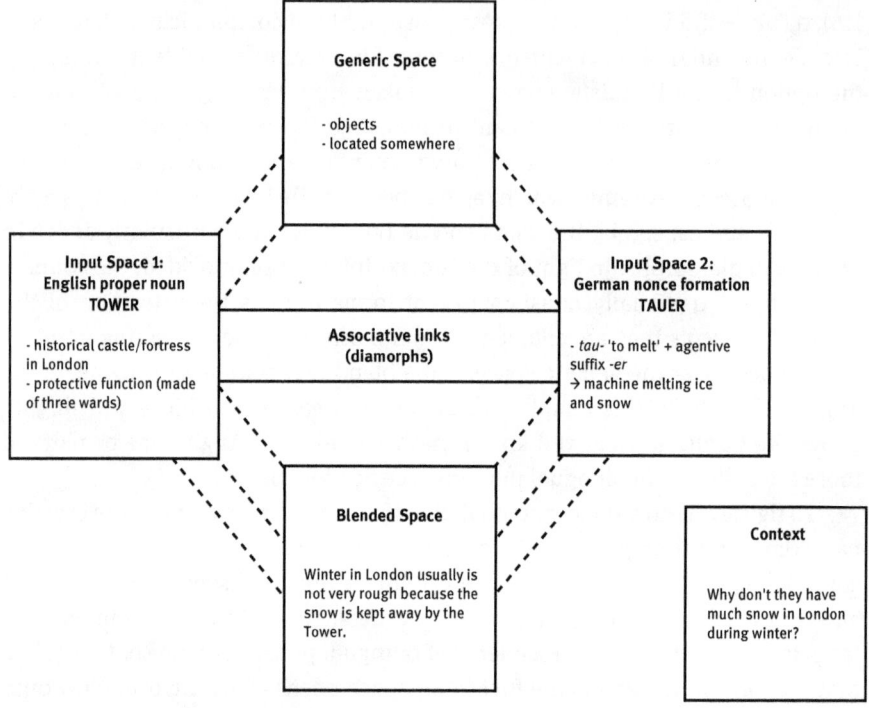

Fig. 2: Processes of blending involved in example (4)

Let us also reconsider example (9) in view of the blending model. Here, the two input spaces are filled with concepts evoked by the homophonous elements *Bush* and *Busch*. The blend suggests hidden political truths and, via the shared abstract features in the generic space that conceptualizes Bush and a bush as containers, constructs a relation between the former US president and what he may know, and a place in which (political) secrets can be concealed. The idea of concealing certain pieces of information from the public is then projected onto Bush's mind which is believed to hide a bush of facts,[12] i.e. a maze of political secrets:

---

12 On the expression *bush of facts* see Prickett (2002: 27).

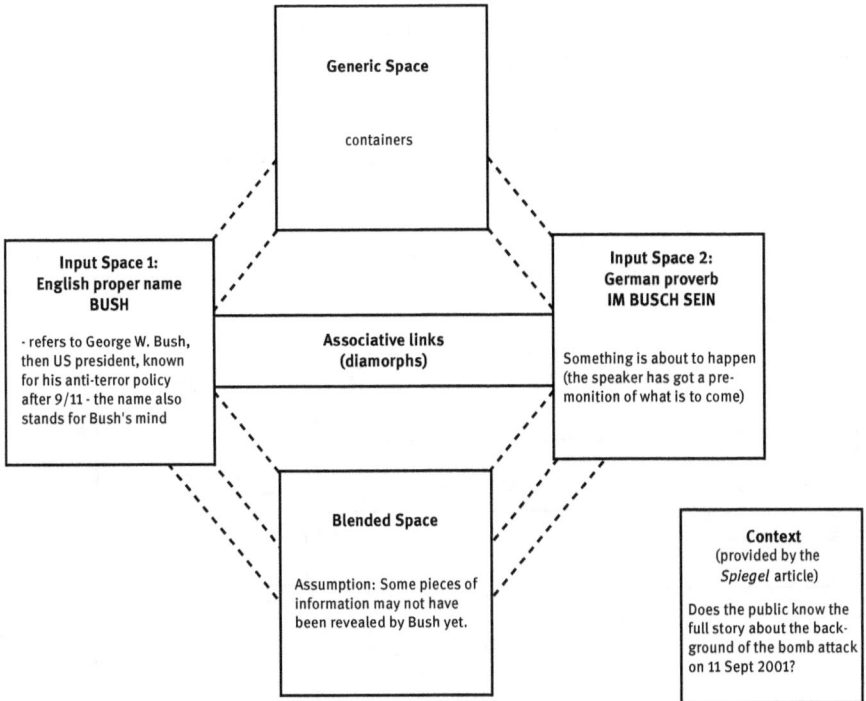

Fig. 3: Processes of blending involved in example (9)

As has been shown, the operation of conceptual blending can be specified in a straightforward manner for the puns at the lexical level discussed above. Slightly more challenging are, by contrast, those puns which affect the sub-lexical level. It is, however, assumed here that such units are themselves a bound part of more complex units and that the latter enter the blending process. For instance, in (8) *Roll Beck*, due to the foregrounding of the form *Beck*, the first input space can be said to be linked to the politician Kurt Beck. As *Beck* and *back* are quasi-diamorphs, the proper name evokes the preposition *back* in gradually bilingual speakers, which then activates the political Anglicism *roll back*. As a consequence, the second input space is connected to a movement leading back to a position something or someone once had. More precisely, the metaphorical image of a human being performing a backward motion in the political sphere is at stake here, which is the result of another blend. Since motions, like all activities, are situated in the time and space in which human beings move, these elements enter the generic space. As already presented in section 3, the blend profiles the contortions performed by a party leader who had to give up on his former positions so as to ensure that his followers continue to accept his political course. This is illustrated in Figure 4:

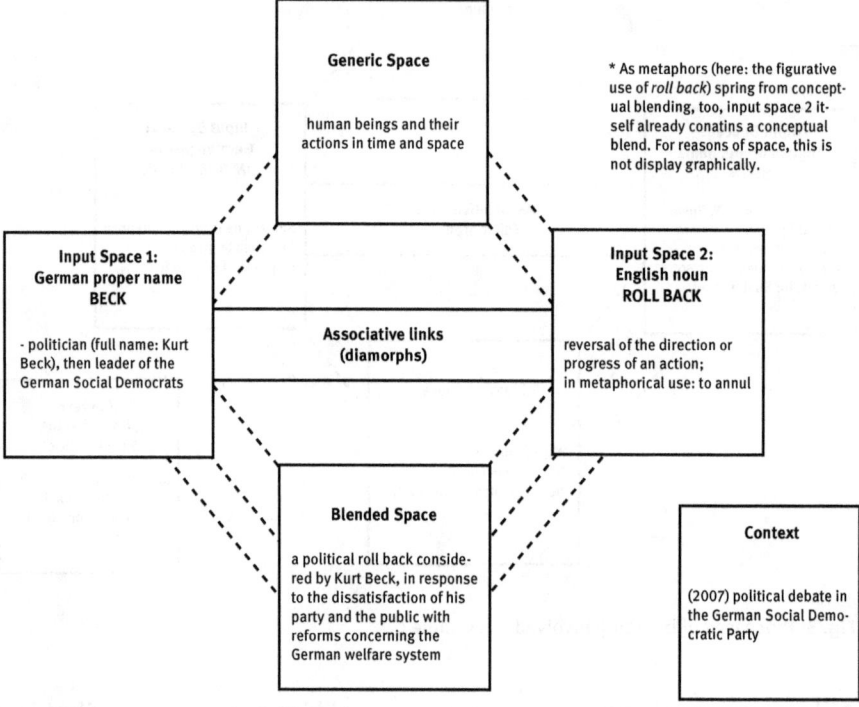

Fig. 4: Processes of blending involved in example (8)

Let us now study example (10) *fair-liebt* again, with a focus on the punsters' lines of thinking. Here, the idea of fairness and that of delectable products on offer in a shop are blended, which is possible due to the fact that the generic space is linked to human beings and their actions as well as to the properties the sold goods may have:

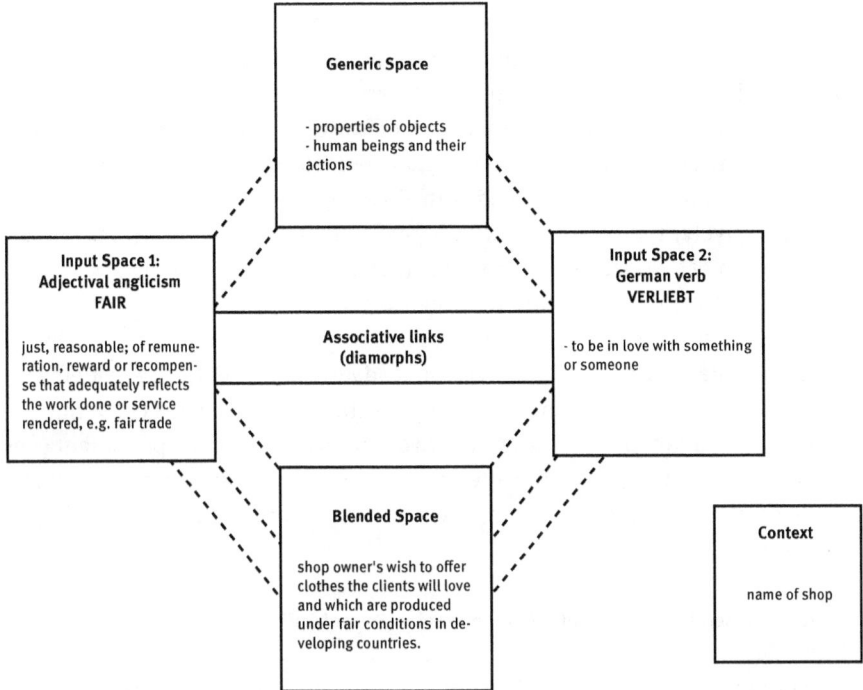

Fig. 5: Processes of blending involved in example (10)

As has been illustrated by the diagrams above, the context is important for the interpretation in all these cases of blending since it channels the recipients' attention towards certain features and filters the elements entering the individual mental spaces.

4.4 Bilingual Puns – Punsters and Recipients

The examples suggest that bilingual punning requires considerable communicative and cognitive work, although the multidimensionality of these processes could only be hinted at by the dotted lines of the "basic diagram" in Figure 1. Therefore, this section aims to specify some of the demands speakers and audiences face in the joint activity of punning:

- In the first place, punsters must be able to think across language boundaries so as to be in a position to grasp specific structural parallels, in this case phonetic congruencies between German and English elements, which are the structural basis of this type of wordplay. Therefore, the creators have to show at least gradual bilingual competences, which enable them to compare and link the two codes in their repertoire (see Sobkowiak 1991). Discursively, the producers of bilingual puns must also be willing to take communicative risks since in some cases readers might not be able to find out what meaning is to be indicated by the spelling manipulations. This may, for instance, hold for (3) *Cool-tur*, an example showing a feature of high-context communication typical of advertising which some readers may not be able to fill with meaning, despite the fact that *cool* is conventionalized in German. In other cases, the two senses of a bilingual pun might even go totally unnoticed, for the altered spelling of such configurations, without any further cues, might be dismissed as a typographical error. Consider, for example:

(12) Massen-Demo: Die große Schill-out-Feier (*Spiegel Online* 20 August 2003)

where the letter <s> in *Schill-out* might be misinterpreted as a mere spelling mistake. However, the coinage is intended as a pun playing with the Anglicism *chill-out* and the German proper name *Schill* which is associated with a former German right-wing politician. Schill had become Senator in Hamburg in 2001 after an electoral campaign during which he, as a judge known for his strict verdicts, had pleaded for law-and-order politics. However, after various scandals, the First Mayor of Hamburg dismissed him in 2003, which, according to the headline of the article, was celebrated by Schill's opponents as a "Schill-out-Party," suggesting their satisfaction and relief about his dismissal. To guide the readers in their interpretation and to avoid the potential impression that the use of the grapheme <s> in *Schill-out-Feier* might be a mistake by the authors, the sub-headline clarifies the context: "Nach der Entlassung von Hamburgs Innensenator Ronald Schill jubeln in Hamburg die Schill-Gegner. Am Dienstagabend kam es zu spontanen Demonstrationen und Partys." [After the dismissal of Hamburg's Senator of the Interior, Schill's opponents in Hamburg are in a state of exuberance. On Tuesday night, there were spontaneous demonstrations and parties.] At the same time, the article contains a photograph showing demonstrators with posters which reflect their excitement through comments like "Freu, Freu, Freu" [joy, joy, joy] and "Haha! Tschüss" [Haha, Bye!]. As seen in the exam-

ples above, other devices may involve the use of hyphens (e.g. (3) *Cool-tur*; (5) *fun-tastisch*) and / or capitalization (e.g. (11) *MISS-Stimmung*).
– Apart from the punsters, it is, of course, also the recipients who have to do particular interpretative work so as to be part of the game. For Crystal (1998: 11), this reciprocity is inherent to wordplay: "all features of ludic language [...] require that the participants should be aware of the rules of the game [...]." Ideally, the readers should be on a par with the punsters in their competence profiles. However, mass media address a diverse audience, which explains why authors utilize additional attention-channeling cues in the surrounding text. As stated before, these, are used to prompt readers "to perform conceptual integrations" (cf. Fauconnier and Turner 2002: xvii). Above all, the recipients must seize the orthographically altered form of the sign as a cipher and be ready to engage in an "effort after meaning" (Bartlett [1932] 1997: 44), i.e. in activities of problem-solving, since the appearance of puns with their typical "homonymic or homophonic clash" (Alexander 1997: 25) does not match with routine forms of language use that can be more easily processed because they follow a linear mode (see Koll-Stobbe 2000: 162–185). To decode bilingual puns, for which this is not true, interlocutors need to go through different meaning hypotheses. In the course of their search for a coherent interpretation, they have to retrieve known linguistic units from their mental lexicon, compare them to the linguistic form they are confronted with, and mentally reorganize the material. For this, they need to integrate their linguistic, communicative and encyclopedic competences, as well as the context information and potential graphic or metalinguistic cues provided (see Koll-Stobbe 2000: 162–185). Still, the jocular moment may not be perceived by the recipient. Thinking of polysemy-based monolingual puns, Lundmark (2003: 7–8) mentions a possible "inability to access the second input" or the potential non-availability of the generic space, which makes the necessary cognitive connections fail. Accordingly, the "successful" decoding costs considerable cognitive energy, but is gratifying to all those who enjoy wordplay as linguistic food for thought.

5 Conclusions and Outlook

Bilingual puns are complex configurations, the encoding and decoding of which is connected to specific cognitive and communicative demands. To describe those, this paper has developed a cognitive framework that complements the necessary structural description by a dynamic procedural perspective. To that end, I have used the theory of conceptual blending and shown that, in the case of bilingual puns, the process of blending ties in with a structural blending of material from two codes (Sebba 2011), which is mediated through the use of homophonous diamorphs or paronyms. Because interlingual (quasi-)homonyms are limited in number, despite the close typological relatedness of English and German, bilingual puns are *per se* structurally constrained. Another constraint already pointed out by Stefanowitsch (2002) and confirmed by the *Spiegel* examples is that the English (sub-)lexical units used must be sufficiently known to be successfully recognized in the process of decoding.

The typical strategy of bilingual punning is to foreground one element, in most cases the English one which co-activates the same- or similar-sounding German one. Thus, the formal side of the sign is usually orthographically modified. To make the readers aware of the homonymous or paronymous link of the two elements, journalists may additionally provide interpretative cues such as hyphens or metalinguistic / metadiscursive comments.

Despite the attempt to offer a comprehensive explanation, the purview of the model sketched is limited in several respects. Firstly, I have not discussed to what extent this model can be combined with larger theories of en- and decoding, a question Koll-Stobbe (2000: 162–168) addresses more profoundly. Secondly, I have attempted no comparison with other forms of creative language use which are also explained by the theory of conceptual blending in the literature (see, e.g., Stockwell 2002; Benczes 2006; Langlotz 2006; Rasulic 2010). Above all, this concerns metaphors and metonymies (although puns, as became clear by examples (8) *Roll Beck* and (9) *Da ist mehr im Bush*, may also involve metaphorical or metonymical meanings). Thirdly, all the examples studied here only refer to bilingual puns in written discourse where no direct, on-line interaction between different communicative agents is involved and where orthography and other graphematic elements are intended as guiding elements. Another limitation results from the focus on press texts. What is more, concepts and conceptual blends are also culture-dependent (cf., e.g., Kövecses 2006: 292), an aspect that had to be neglected as well, because the present article exclusively focuses on German-English data. Thus, there is plenty of room for further investigation on practices of bilingual punning.

6 References

Alexander, Richard. 1997. *Aspects of Verbal Humour in English*. Tübingen: Narr.
Alsina, Victòria & Janet DeCesaris. 2002. Bilingual Lexicography, Overlapping Polysemy, and Corpus Use. In Bengt Altenberg & Sylviane Granger (eds.), *Lexis in Contrast: Corpus-Based Approaches*, 215–230. Amsterdam: Benjamins.
Ammon, Ulrich. 1999. *Deutsche Sprache international*. Heidelberg: Groos.
Ammon, Ulrich & Grant D. McConnell. 2002. *English as an Academic Language in Europe: A Survey of its Use in Teaching*. Frankfurt a. M.: de Gruyter.
Androutsopoulos, Jannis K., Nevin Bozkurt, Simone Breninck, Catrin Kreyer, Markus Tornow & Verena Tschann. 2004. Sprachwahl im Werbeslogan: Zeitliche Entwicklung und branchenspezifische Verteilung englischer Slogans in der Datenbank von slogans.de. *Networx – Online-Publikationen zum Thema Mediensprache* 41.
http://www.mediensprache.net/de/networx/docs/networx-41.asp (17 July 2015).
Attardo, Salvatore. 1994. *Linguistic Theories of Humor*. Berlin: de Gruyter.
Bartlett, Frederic Charles. [1932] 1997. *Remembering: A study in Experimental and Social Psychology*. Cambridge: Cambridge University Press.
Benczes, Réka. 2006. *Creative Compounding in English: The Semantics of Metaphorical and Metonymical Noun-Noun Combinations*. Amsterdam: Benjamins.
Berns, Margie, Kees de Bot & Uwe Hasebrink. 2007. *In the Presence of English: Media and European Youth*. New York: Springer.
Betz, Werner. 1949. *Deutsch und Lateinisch: Die Lehnbildungen der althochdeutschen Benediktinerregel*. Bonn: Bouvier.
Blake, Barry. 2007. *Playing with Words: Humour in the English Language*. London: Equinox.
Blank, Andreas. 2001. *Einführung in die lexikalische Semantik für Romanisten*. Tübingen: Niemeyer.
Blommaert, Jan. 2010. *The Sociolinguistics of Globalization*. Cambridge: Cambridge University Press.
Bloomfield, Leonard. 1933. *Language*. New York: Holt.
BMBF (Federal Ministry of Education and Research). 2009. *Bericht zur Umsetzung des Bologna Prozesses in Deutschland*. BMBF.de. (17 July 2015).
Broersma, Mirjam & Kees de Bot. 2006. Triggered Codeswitching: A Corpus-Based Evaluation of the Original Triggering Hypothesis and a New Alternative. *Bilingualism: Language and Cognition* 9(1). 1–13.
Buchreport. 2011. *Bestseller Belletristik und Sachbücher, 2005–2010*.
http://www.buchreport.de (17 July 2015).
Busse, Ulrich & Manfred Görlach. 2002. German. In Manfred Görlach (ed.), *English in Europe*, 13–36. Oxford: Oxford University Press.
Carstensen, Broder. 1963. *Amerikanismen der deutschen Gegenwartssprache: Entlehnungsvorgänge und ihre stilistischen Aspekte*. Heidelberg: Winter.
Carstensen, Broder. 1965. *Englische Einflüsse auf die deutsche Sprache nach 1945*. Heidelberg: Winter.
Cenoz, Jasone. 2000. *English in Europe: The Acquisition of a Third Language*. Clevedon: Multilingual Matters.
Chiaro, Delia. 1992. *The Language of Jokes: Analyzing Verbal Play*. London & New York: Routledge.

Clyne, Michael. 1995. *The German Language in a Changing Europe.* Cambridge: Cambridge University Press.
Cook, Vivian, Benedetta Bassetti & Jyotsna Vaid. 2012. The Writing System at Play. *Writing Systems Research* 4(2). 120–121.
Coulmas, Florian. 2005. *Sociolinguistics: The Study of Speakers' Choices.* Cambridge: Cambridge University Press.
Croft, William & Alan Cruse. 2004. *Cognitive Linguistics.* Cambridge: Cambridge University Press.
Crystal, David. 1998. *Language Play.* London: Penguin.
Crystal, David. 2008. *Dictionary of Linguistics and Phonetics,* 6th edn. Malden, MA: Blackwell.
Delabastita, Dirk. 1993. *There's a Double Tongue: An Investigation into the Translation of Shakespeare's Wordplay with Special Reference to* Hamlet. Amsterdam: Rodopi.
Duden. http://www.duden.de (17 July 2015).
Dudley-Evans, Tony & Maggie-Jo Saint John. 2001. *Developments in ESP: A Multi-Disciplinary Approach.* Cambridge: Cambridge University Press.
European Commission. 2005. Europeans and Languages. *Europa.eu.* http://ec.europa.eu/public_opinion/archives/ebs/ebs_237.en.pdf (17 July 2015).
Evans, Vyvyan & Melanie Green. 2006. *Cognitive Linguistics: An Introduction.* Edinburgh: Edinburgh University Press.
Fauconnier, Gilles. 1994. *Mental Spaces: Aspects of Meaning Construction in Natural Language.* Cambridge: Cambridge University Press.
Fauconnier, Gilles & Mark Turner. 2002. *The Way We Think: Conceptual Blending and the Mind's Hidden Complexities.* New York: Basic Books.
Fischer, Roswitha. 2008. Introduction: Studying Anglicisms. In Roswitha Fischer & Hanna Pułaczewska (eds.), *Anglicisms in Europe: Linguistic Diversity in a Global Context,* 1–14. Newcastle upon Tyne: Cambridge Scholars Publishing.
Fuller, Janet M. 2012. *Bilingual Pre-Teens: Competing Ideologies and Multiple Identities in the U.S. and Germany.* London: Routledge.
Görlach, Manfred. 2003. *English Words Abroad.* Amsterdam: Benjamins.
Graddol, David. 2006. *English Next: Why Global English May Mean the End of "English as a Foreign Language."* London: British Council.
Grimm, Rudolf. 2000. Anglizismen: "We kehr for you." *Spiegel Online.* http://www.spiegel.de/wissenschaft/mensch/anglizismen-we-kehr-for-you-a-98974.html (17 July 2015).
Haugen, Einar I. 1950. The Analysis of Linguistic Borrowing. *Language* 26(2). 210–231.
Hausmann, Franz Josef. 1974. *Studien zu einer Linguistik des Wortspiels: Das Wortspiel im Canard enchaîné.* Tübingen: Niemeyer.
Heller, Monica 2003. Globalization, the New Economy, and the Commodification of Language and Identity. *Journal of Sociolinguistics* 7(4). 473–492.
Hensel, Horst. 2000. Muttersprache Denglish? Über die Anglisierung der Muttersprache durch die Werbung. *Sprachspiegel* 56. 167–174.
Hilgendorf, Suzanne K. 2001. *Language Contact, Convergence, and Attitudes: The Case of English in Germany.* Ann Arbor: University of Urbana-Champaign dissertation.
Hoffmann, Charlotte. 1996. Societal and Individual Bilingualism with English in Europe. In Reinhard R. K. Hartmann (ed.), *The English Language in Europe,* 47–60. Oxford: Intellect.
Insidekino. 2011. Top 100 Deutschland. *Insidekino.com.* http://www.insidekino.com (30 July 2012).

Jenkins, Jennifer. 2003. *World Englishes: A Resource Book for Students*. London: Routledge.
Jenkins, Jennifer. 2007. *English as a Lingua Franca: Attitude and Identity*. Oxford: Oxford University Press.
Kelly-Holmes, Helen. 2005. *Advertising as Multilingual Communication*. Basingstoke: Palgrave Macmillan.
Kim, Dan. 2008. *English for Occupational Purposes: One Language?* London: Continuum.
Knospe, Sebastian. 2010. Ambiguisierende Nonce-Bildungen im deutsch-englischen Sprachkontakt – ein Ausdruck interlingualer Kreativität? *TRANS* 17. http://www.inst.at/trans/17Nr/5-6/5-6_knospe17.htm (17 July 2015).
Knospe, Sebastian. 2014. *Entlehnung oder Codeswitching? Sprachmischungen mit dem Englischen im deutschen Printjournalismus*. Frankfurt a. M.: Lang.
Koll-Stobbe, Amei. 2000. *Konkrete Lexikologie des Englischen: Entwurf einer Theorie des Sprachkönnens*. Tübingen: Niemeyer.
Koll-Stobbe, Amei. 2015. Ideofiers in the commercial city. A Discursive Linguistic Landscape Analysis of Hairdressers' Shop Names. In Anastassia Zabrodskaja & Mikko Laitinen (eds.), *Dimensions of Linguistic Landscapes in Europe: Materials and Methodological Solutions*, 53–76. Frankfurt a. M.: Lang.
König, Ekkehard & Volker Gast. 2012. *Understanding German-English Contrasts*, 3rd edn. Berlin: Schmidt.
Kövecses, Zoltán. 2006. *Language, Mind, and Culture: A Practical Introduction*. Oxford: Oxford University Press.
Langacker, Ronald. 2008. *Cognitive Grammar: A Basic Introduction*. Stanford: Stanford University Press.
Langlotz, Andreas. 2006. *Idiomatic Creativity: A Cognitive-Linguistic Model of Idiom-Representation and Idiom-Variation in English*. Amsterdam: Benjamins.
Lillo, Antonio. 2007. Turning Puns into Names and Vice Versa. *SKY Journal of Linguistics* 20. 429–440.
Lundmark, Carita. 2003. Puns and Blending: The Case of Print Advertisements. Paper presented at the 8th International Cognitive Linguistics Conference, Theme Session on Cognitive-Linguistic Approaches to Humour. Logroño, Spain, 20–25 September. http://wwwling.arts.kuleuven.ac.be/iclc/Papers/Lundmark.pdf (17 July 2015).
Mair, Christian. 1995. *Englisch für Anglisten: Eine Einführung in die englische Sprache*. Tübingen: Stauffenburg.
McArthur, Tom. 2003. *Oxford Guide to World English*. Oxford: Oxford University Press.
Meckel, Miriam & Beat F. Schmied. 2008. *Unternehmenskommunikation: Kommunikationsmanagement aus Sicht der Unternehmensführung*, 2nd edn. Wiesbaden: Gabler.
media control. 2011. Charts.de: Offizielle Deutsche Top 100 Single Charts. *Charts.de*. http://www.charts.de/year.asp?cat=s&country=de (30 July 2012).
Modiano, Marko. 1999. International English in the Global Village. *English Today* 15(2). 22–28.
Mollin, Sandra. 2006. *Euro-English: Assessing Variety Status*. Tübingen: Narr.
Oxford English Dictionary, 2nd edn. 2014. http://www.oed.com (17 July 2015).
Onysko, Alexander. 2007. *Anglicisms in German: Borrowing, Lexical Productivity, and Written Codeswitching*. Berlin: de Gruyter.
Onysko, Alexander. 2009. Exploring Discourse on Globalizing English: A Case Study of Discourse on Anglicisms in German. *English Today* 25(1). 25–36.
Onysko, Alexander & Esme Winter-Froemel. 2011. Necessary Loans – Luxury Loans? Exploring the Pragmatic Dimension of Borrowing. *Journal of Pragmatics* 43(6). 1550–1567.

Paulwitz, Thomas (ed.). 2000. *Engleutsch? Nein Danke! Wie sag ich's auf deutsch? Ein Volks-Wörterbuch*. Erlangen: Verein für Sprachpflege.

Piller, Ingrid. 2001. Identity Constructions in Multilingual Advertising. *Language in Society* 30(2). 153–186.

Piller, Ingrid. 2003. Advertising as a Site of Language Contact. *Annual Review of Applied Linguistics* 23. 170–183.

Preisler, Bent. 1999. Functions and Forms of English in a European EFL Country. In Tony Bex & Richard J. Watts (eds.), *Standard English: The Widening Debate*, 239–267. London: Routledge.

Prickett, Stephen. 2002. *Narrative, Religion and Science: Fundamentalism versus Irony 1700-1999*. Cambridge: Cambridge University Press.

Rasulic, Katarina. 2010. *Long Time, No Buzz*: Fixed Expressions as Constructional Frames. *CogniTextes*. Vol. 5: *Grammaires en Construction(s)*. http://cognitextes.revues.org/356 (17 July 2015).

Redfern, Walter. 1984. *Puns*. Oxford: Blackwell.

Robinson, Pauline. 1980. *ESP (English for Specific Purposes): The Present Situation*. Oxford: Pergamon.

Sano, Hikomaro. 2002. The World's Lingua Franca of Science. *English Today* 18(4). 45–49.

Schelper, Dunja. 1988. *Die Anglizismen in der Zeitschrift Der Spiegel, 1974 bis 1987*. Québec: Université Laval MA thesis.

Schütte, Dagmar. 1996. *Das schöne Fremde: Anglo-amerikanische Einflüsse auf die Sprache der deutschen Zeitschriftenwerbung*. Opladen: Westdeutscher Verlag.

Sebba, Mark. 2011. Unimagined communities: Print Languages, Prescription and Multilingual Writing. Plenary Talk Presented at the Third Conference on Language Contact in Times of Globalization, University of Greifswald, 30 June – 2 July.

Seidlhofer, Barbara. 2001. Closing a Conceptual Gap: The Case for a Description of English as a Lingua Franca. *International Journal of Applied Linguistics* 11(2). 133–158.

Seidlhofer, Barbara. 2004. Research Perspectives on Teaching English as a Lingua Franca. *Annual Review of Applied Linguistics* 24. 209–239.

Sobkowiak, Włodzimierz. 1991. *Metaphonology of English Paronomasic Puns*. Frankfurt a. M.: Lang.

Spiegel Online. 2003. Massen-Demo: Die große Schill-Out-Feier. *Spiegel Online*. http://www.spiegel.de/politik/deutschland/massen-demo-die-grosse-schill-out-feier-a-261955.html (17 July 2015).

Spitzmüller, Jürgen. 2005. *Metasprachdiskurse: Einstellungen zu Anglizismen und ihre wissenschaftliche Rezeption*. Berlin & New York: de Gruyter.

Statistische Bundesamt. 2013. Bildung und Kultur: Allgemeinbildende Schulen. *Destatis.de*. https://www.destatis.de/DE/Publikationen/Thematisch/BildungForschungKultur/Schulen/AllgemeinbildendeSchulen21101100137004.pdf?_blob=publicationFile (17 July 2015).

Stefanowitsch, Anatol. 2002. Nice to *Miet* You: Bilingual Puns and the Status of English in Germany. *Intercultural Communication Studies* 11(4). 67–84.

Stockwell, Peter. 2002. *Cognitive Poetics: An Introduction*. London & New York: Routledge.

Swann, Joanne. 1996. Style shifting, Codeswitching. In David Graddol, Dick Leith & Joanne Swann (eds.), *English: History, Diversity and Change*, 301–324. London: Routledge.

Tanaka, Keiko. 1992. The Pun in Advertising: A Pragmatic Approach. *Lingua* 87(1-2). 91–102.

Tanaka, Keiko. 1999. *Advertising Language: A Pragmatic Approach to Advertisements in Britain and Japan*. London: Routledge.

Vaid, Jyotsna. 2006. Joking across Languages: Perspectives on Humor, Emotion, and Bilingualism. In Aneta Pavlenko (ed.), *Bilingual Minds. Emotional Experience, Expression and Representation*, 152–182. Clevedon: Multilingual Matters.

Viereck, Wolfgang. 1996. English in Europe: Its Nativisation and Use as a Lingua Franca, with Special Reference to German-speaking Countries. In Reinhard R. K. Hartmann (ed.), *The English Language in Europe*, 16–23. Oxford: Intellect.

Vollstedt, Marina. 2002. *Sprachenplanung in der internen Kommunikation internationaler Unternehmen: Studien zur Umstellung der Unternehmenssprache auf das Englische*. Hildesheim: Olms.

Winter-Froemel, Esme. 2008. Unpleasant, Unnecessary, Unintelligible? Cognitive and Communicative Criteria for Judging Borrowings and Alternative Strategies. In Roswitha Fischer & Hanna Pułaczewska (eds.), *Anglicims in Europe: Linguistic Diversity in a Global Context*, 16-41. Cambridge: Cambridge Scholars Publishing.

Winter-Froemel, Esme. 2011. *Entlehnung in der Kommunikation und im Sprachwandel: Theorie und Analysen zum Französischen*. Berlin: de Gruyter.

Winter-Froemel, Esme & Angelika Zirker. 2010. Ambiguität in der Sprecher-Hörer-Interaktion: Linguistische und literaturwissenschaftliche Perspektiven. *Zeitschrift für Linguistik und Literaturwissenschaft* 158. 76–97.

Yang, Wenliang. 1990. *Anglizismen im Deutschen: Am Beispiel des Nachrichtenmagazins* DER SPIEGEL. Tübingen: Niemeyer.

Zirker, Angelika. 2010. *Der Pilger als Kind: Spiel, Sprache und Erlösung in Lewis Carrolls Alice-Büchern*. Münster: LIT.

Zürn, Alexandra. 2001. *Anglizismen im Deutschen: Eine Untersuchung zur Häufigkeit von Anglizismen und deren Inkorporiertheit im Deutschen am Beispiel dreier deutschsprachiger Nachrichtenmagazine; mit einem historischen Abriß und einer Typologie der Entlehnungsarten*. Karlsruhe: Universität Karlsruhe Dissertation.

Ian Duhig
Interview: A Perspective from Practical and Professional Experience – Wordplay in Poetry

Abstract: In the following interview conducted by Angelika Zirker, the poet Ian Duhig, as a practitioner of literary wordplay, discusses the possibility of poetry to express more in few(er) words, all the while self-consciously stressing poetry's own formation in language. He considers wordplay, comic and serious, to be one of the most important ways to intensify literary language. Phenomena he specifically focuses on in this interview are the temporal dimension of wordplay in the flow of reading (or performance), the effects achieved through paronomasia as "a condensation of language," and the integration of context in the ambiguity introduced by wordplay.

Keywords: allusion, ambiguity, audience, comic wordplay, Laurence Sterne, naming, polyphony, serious wordplay, *Tristram Shandy*, wordplay in poetry

1 About the Author

After working with homeless people for fifteen years in England and Northern Ireland, Ian Duhig was made redundant, then became a full-time writer. Since then he has held several university fellowships, including servings as International Writer Fellow at Trinity College Dublin. He has written six collections of poetry, most recently *Pandorama* (2010), and won a Forward Prize, the National Poetry Competition twice and was three times shortlisted for the T. S. Eliot Prize. A Cholmondeley Award recipient and Fellow of the Royal Society of Literature, Duhig writes across genres, and his most recent short story was published in Comma's *The New Uncanny* (2008) anthology, which won a Shirley Jackson Award in 2008. He works extensively with musicians from medieval performers to avant-garde composers, contributing texts recently to the Clerks' recent CD "Don't Talk: Just Listen" (2009) and Christopher Fox's "Natural Science" (2009–2010). In September, he will be teaching the relationship between lyrics and traditional music for Maddy Prior at her Stone Barn Project. Duhig is currently putting together his next book of poetry, *The Blind Roadmaker*, due 2016.

2 Interview

Angelika Zirker: *Is there such a thing as 'bad' wordplay? Or particularly 'good' or successful wordplay?*

Ian Duhig: One of my favourite books is *Tristram Shandy* ([1759–1767] 1996), which is full of 'good' and 'bad' wordplay, and there the distinction does not matter as the purpose is to constantly draw the reader's attention to the duplicitous nature of language, undermining its users' intentions at every turn. This chimes well with some modern approaches to poetry, for example with the so-called Cambridge School or the work of Geoffrey Hill, not to mention Language and Conceptual poetry in the US. But poetry has always drawn attention to the medium it employs because it is so concentrated. I am thinking of such as the self-reflexive metaphor in "Upon Appleton House," where Marvell writes: "The River in it self is drown'd" ([1651] 1971: 77, l. 471). Shakespeare, of course, employs brilliant and protean wordplay constantly; for playwrights as for poets its power to control the passage of time is vital, much as in football a forward speeds up and slows down his runs, hypnotising defenders with his movement. Plays cannot stop in performance, so there it allows some character an extended moment of meaning or light relief by virtue of our noticing, enjoying and dwelling on this linguistic trick. In poetry, the opposite applies to more extreme effect: Celan's wordplay, if you can call it anything as trivial as that, stops time altogether while we let the semantic implications of his texts ripple outwards in our minds. Rhyme does the same thing in terms of slowing up poetry to the extent that in the thirteenth century *dérimeurs* were employed to remove the rhymes from older verse tales as readers were beginning to turn to prose for quicker delivery of narratives.

For technical reasons, then, there is often no real difference between 'good' and 'bad' wordplay because they are both doing the same job. Someone pointed out that the reason bad jokes are so popular is that they unify the audience: those who normally like jokes groan because this type of joke requires that as the appropriate response, while those who do not like jokes normally groan because that would be their response anyway.

Could you give examples of 'bad' and 'good' wordplay?

Duhig: Keith Douglas's choice of the word "spreadeagled" ([1941] 1951: 48, l. 2) to describe the swordfish in "The Marvel" always struck me as uncomfortable. It has the appropriate connotations of power and majesty, but these dissipate in the bathetic visual comparison of wings and fins, to my understanding, limited though that may be. Good wordplay, because it is so dense (two monosyllables) and rich in suggestiveness, Heaney's "Ground gives" ("Anything Can Happen," 2006: l. 14) in his version of Horace's Ode I, 34 on Fortune ("A Joyful Return," [1914] 1964: 97), moving from its meaning of agricultural bounty to the sudden collapse beneath our feet of what we had thought was safe. This is like Shandean language, but instead of giving way to humour, in Heaney it gives way to wonder.

Do you have a favourite wordplay from other authors or from your own work?

Duhig: When Uncle Toby offers to show the Widow Wadman where he was wounded in the war, after some wrestling with her sense of decorum, thinking she would get to inspect how maritally disabling his 'upper thigh' injury really was, after a series of digressions such as I am making now, said, yes she would like to see where Toby was hurt, only for Toby to whip out a sheaf of maps and say, more or less, 'Well it was here, at the Siege of Namur...' (cf. [1759–1767] 1996: 9.26.449–450).

How would you define wordplay? What is covered by the term in your view, what is not?

Duhig: A bit like play in the sense that rope has, a sudden looseness enough for the user to tie knots or do tricks, like whipping ripples along it, which was my idea of playing when I was a very young child. I have a very flexible and promiscuous idea of what constitutes wordplay, but I would say it contrasts with that broader use of patterning a writer employs over a longer work, where meanings develop over time and space and the availability of more information. For me, wordplay means it gets you here and now, whatever it may contribute to your overall structure, as Joyce's and Sterne's jokes and digressions do. Poetry is about unpacking the consequences of language and a self-conscious way of doing that is what I mean by wordplay. At the moment anyway.

A while ago, a British Council literary anthology had a section called 'Short Texts' which covered poetry and very short prose, if not exactly prose poems. There is so much overlap here that I also do not think dwelling on distinctions serves any practically useful purpose to the manufacturer of texts. If a prose writer develops an effective verbal device a poet can use, the poet will steal it and vice versa.

How often do you use wordplay in your poetry? Has the frequency increased or decreased in the course of your writing career? Has it stayed the same?

Duhig: Well, it is a connection between the Irish attitude to literature that I inherited (as in James Joyce's comment that the most Holy Roman and Apostolic Catholic Church was founded on a pun (cf. Ellmann [1959] 1982: 546), to the almost-obsessive punning of Sterne (an Irishman in Yorkshire) and the contemporary Leeds poet Tony Harrison, I feel both humorous and deadly serious wordplay has formed a consistent part of my immediate intellectual class environment. It is a way of answering back to those who have power over you, even at school.

Perhaps because of my very wide definition of wordplay it is in my mind constantly as I write. When I was putting "The Badly-Loved" (1991: 30–31; see Appendix) poem about Apollinaire's relationship with Annie Playden together, I noted in my reading that when they first met neither spoke the other's language. A misunderstanding of the sound *we / oui* was one of my ways into the material. The possibility of linguistic confusion and wordplay was also something I used in this short and unsuccessful love poem:

From the Irish

According to Dineen, a Gael unsurpassed
in lexicographical enterprise, the Irish
for moon means 'the white circle in a slice
of half-boiled potato or turnip'. A star
is the mark on the forehead of a beast
and the sun is the bottom of a lake, or well.

Well if I say to you your face
is like a slice of half-boiled turnip,
your hair is the color of a lake's bottom
and at the center of each or your eyes
is the mark of the beast, it is because
I want to love you properly, according to Dineen.

(1991: 9)[1]

Here I am using the speaker's problems with expressing themselves in Irish as an analogy for men's problems in speaking the language of emotions. Language

---

[1] The permission to reprint "From the Irish" in full length was kindly given by Ian Duhig. The copyright rests with the poet.

betrays the speaker's intentions but we can still understand them, the love shaping its incompetent declaration.

What do you think does wordplay add to a poem?

Duhig: Everything really, in the sort of poetry I am particularly interested in, which is about the effects produced by the condensation of language. An extreme example would be the following, from Edwin Morgan's sequence "Nine One-Word Poems" ([c. 1967]):

Homage to Zukovsky

the

Morgan develops Ian Hamilton Finlay's form where the trick is to make the title do most of the work. There are wordless poems like Don Paterson's Zen one (and more since) while jokes attempt the same thing, like the one that goes "What do you get when you cross a joke and a rhetorical question?"[2] In this view of poetry and humour, it is all about getting more into fewer words, charging language with meaning to the utmost, loading every rift with ore. There are other traditions in both: rambling shaggy dog stories and US poetry, from Whitman, through Olson's American space to Conceptual poet Kenny Goldsmith talking about printing off the entire contents of the internet. As Olson implies, European traditions have been about depth and age while US power is expansive and contemporary. I do not believe one superior to the other, or that art makes progress in the way sciences do. Music changed after Bach but it did not necessarily get any better.

What is the relation, in your view, between ambiguity and wordplay? E.g. in "De Senectute" (2007: 41)?

Duhig: I am not sure there is much going on linguistically, a flat contradiction in a kind of strange sentence-long rhyme to suggest an unreliable speaker. The unreliable narrator pressured by language is the sort of thing I tried in "Fundamentals" (1991: 10). This is the bicentenary of David Livingstone, but I was sur-

---

[2] There is no answer to this question: its formal resemblance to a joke makes it sound like it should have one, but its rhetorical nature means the question is put without the expectation of a reply.

prised to read in Tim Jeal's biography that in all his time in Africa, he only made one convert. In Livingstone's notebooks, he blamed translation problems of key words which I have taken as my basis. It is a forced sermon because his single convert, a chief, did so for reasons of military rivalry with neighbouring tribes and lapsed virtually immediately.

Ambiguity, as William Empson explained to us, comes in at least seven types, which we do not have the space to go into here. I would broadly subsume it under wordplay for my circumstances rather than pursue the taxonomical distinctions important to critics. In general terms, ambiguity in simple mathematical terms extends the possibilities of your words' interpretations.

When reading your poems, I noticed that you like to refer to names (e.g. in "Boxeur Nègre" (2010: 2) and "Charivari" (2010: 5–6) but also very much in "Freed Time" (2007: 54–55) and "Mencken Sonnet" (2007: 59)), use allusions to other literary works (e.g. "A Room With a View" (2010: 37)). Would you regard these as wordplay?

Duhig: I come onto "Freed Time" in a later question, but its true in general that I have got a bit of an obsession with names. Partly it is like Walter Shandy, a *nomen est omen* essentialism pausing over one that seems richly apt to the person it is attached to as in a Jonsonian comedy of humours. I do not think it started from anything so elevated, though: being able to coin a killer nickname for your enemy was like a magic shield. Names are as random as rhyme and there is an almost Oulipian whimsicality to forms like the clerihew. People can just evaporate into their names, as we all do in the end anyway.

In a different political way I also feel the names of those lost from general awareness can sometimes be worth repeating. My brother was a boxer, middleweight champion of the Navy, who would rave about the Nigerian middleweight we know as Dick Tiger, who was implanted in my mind before it came to Matisse. Dick Tiger ended up as a security guard at the Metropolitan Museum of Arts in New York, but also spoke out against the Nigerian Civil War, returning his CBE in protest over it; an admirable figure in my eyes.

Admirably in a different way, Mencken said the martini was the USA's sole achievement of civilization to match the European sonnet. If that comment does not deserve having one named after him, I do not know what would.

"A Room With a View" grew out of getting shortlisted for the T. S. Eliot Prize and blowing the lot on a massive telly. In fact, we called it "the Telliot" and after this was reported in an interview, some poets were appalled, given Eliot's views on TV. Auden's were pretty snobbish too, so he is in my poem for them. Cultural snobbery still seems to me more virulent in Britain than elsewhere. Class is hard to talk about nowadays but social inequality is worse here than at any time in my life.

On the subject of "Charivari," this was written as part of a specific commission to update a number of songs from the Roman de Fauvel for the Clerks group, a vocal consort specialising in pre-baroque music. It contains the first charivari in European music, the lower orders cavorting with masks and drums to show their displeasure at the behaviour of their social betters.

Do you begin to write with a particular allusion in mind – or do these things develop and evolve in the course of writing?

Duhig: Sometimes: I was struck once on reading "The Waste Land" how his "Weialala leia / Wallala leialala" ([1922] 2004: 69, l. 277–278, 70, l. 290–291) quotation from the Rhine maidens Wagner's *Die Götterdämmerung* (1876) by its similarity to the Irish song "Weile Weile Waile," with its chorus of "Down by the River Saile." Incest from Wagner's work went into the poem about Irish labourers tunnelling under the Thames. When water broke in, they would blow out their lamps because of their belief that water was attracted to light. This ended up as "Babylon" (1991: 55–57), its title an allusion to another ballad, which also supplies my poem's last line, in a *lumpenproletariat* version of the twilight of the gods, which is still overly bound up with Eliot.

Do you expect your audience to recognize these plays and allusions? Or do you think it is possible to "understand" or enjoy your poetry without these recognitions?

Duhig: I know the latter is the case from what people have said to me, while it is unlikely that anybody gets them all. I hope more might be generated by people who hang around with them for a while – or do internet searches, which changed everything to do with the availability of obscure information in my lifetime. I think I would have written differently at the start of my career, when I felt a bit chippy about working-class writers being considered obscure if they write out of their own tradition simply because it was unavailable to academics. Now pretty much everything is available to everybody. Academia, of course, is not simply concerned with knowledge but the structures of knowledge; Bourdieu writes about the disconnected nature of the autodidact's learning, comparing it to beads on a necklace. I am sure this is true of me: I left school at 16, as soon as legally possible over here, and took the exams that qualified me for university entrance some time later at nightschool, by which time I had got into the habit of learning rather than being educated.

Do you use pointers toward wordplay? Meaning: is it embedded in a particular way, or pointed to typographically (again I am thinking, e.g. of "Freed Time")?

Duhig: I play typographical games as the humour takes me, as in "The Badly-Loved" (1991: 30, l. 18):

> At times I left her speechless with my dash –

In "Freed Time" it starts with the title, as DJ Alan Freed is widely credited with coining the term 'Rock and Roll' when it was common in the Afro-American community for decades before. That linguistic appropriation seemed to parallel musical appropriation that has led some people in the US to want to rename Jazz as 'Black American Music.' There is a great resistance among post-WWII baby boomers to consider any part of their 'alternative culture' as built on racist exploitation but the music is haunted, hence the Phil Spector / spectre play that carries though the citing of "'Ghost Town'" (2007: 54, l. 19) to the Rylean ending of "black ghost white machine" [sic] (2007: 55, l. 28). The black and white colour imagery of the poem is another aspect of this political / cultural play.

What audience do you aim at when using wordplay? Do you sometimes have different audiences in mind for different poems?

Duhig: There was an Irish druid of such wit and wisdom that he could be asked nine different questions and give one answer satisfying them all. I know that different elements of my readership, such as it is, respond to different elements in my poetry, although I hope not to the complete exclusion of other readers or at least no more than they already experience from other poets. Reading *Tristram Shandy*, you have a constant feeling of insecurity in his language as it teeters constantly on the edge of obscenity, which actually adds to the pleasure of the text as far as I am concerned. I called my second book *The Mersey Goldfish* (1995) after a Northern slang term for a turd – people know something is going on in the book in relation to that, not least because of poems about Ubu and so on, but few middle class readers will pick up the reference unless they read interviews like this. Similarly, in "Babylon," people who know the ballad the title refers to will understand its allusion to incest, even if they do not get it from Wagner's Siegmund and Sieglinde.

Have your readers ever commented on this?

Duhig: Lots of people have, but the late lamented Dennis O'Driscoll talked to me about it in greatest detail when I was International Writer Fellow at Trinity College Dublin. In his view, "You never quite knew where a Duhig poem was coming at you from," which he at least took to be an interesting experience. I think people should be surprised by poetry and have some of their assumptions challenged. One of the ways I try and do this is by having a lot of voices in my books, seeking a polyphonic effect, which had been specifically required in the Fauvel poems. The nature of the lyric 'I' has come in for much recent scrutiny (although it is there in *Tristram Shandy*: "as sure as I am I – and you are you – And who are you? said he. – Don't puzzle me; said I" ([1759–1767] 1996: 7.33.367), and the unreliable narrator is a commonplace of fiction, but there seems to be a continued expectation of a poem that its contents be 'truer' than those in a novel if it is cast in the first person. I have always felt people trust poets too much: I remember my mother telling me that in her part of Ireland if you met poets you never gave them your real name.

In your own reading: do you prefer authors / poets that use wordplay?

Duhig: They will tend to have that in their locker, as football commentators say. But I can enjoy Dr Johnson's works, who thought *Tristram Shandy* would not last and took a very dim view of certain kinds of wordplay, supposedly saying "He who would make a pun would pick a pocket."[3] In *Rasselas* ([1759] 1965), he makes a very important observation for me in saying that nothing can be useless to the poet: I think of this as giving me something like an *Arte Povera* licence to hunt around in the rag and bone shops of the world as well as the heart. I would read a whole book for a good line, idea or joke and I find them everywhere. A book about fancy rats introduced me to the fact that a term of classification is 'self,' as in 'a dark-eyed self' which was a strange kind of accidental wordplay I like to stumble upon in my rambling, a serendipitous version of Baudelaire's "Trébuchant sur les mots comme sur les pavés" ("Le Soleil," ([1861] 1972: 115, l. 7)) in terms of luck as well as putting the work together.

---

3 Comment by the editors: According to *Brewer's Dictionary of Phrase and Fable*, Dr. Johnson is wrongly credited with this saying, which finds its origin in a remark the critic John Dennis addressed to the 'bad' punning of Henry Purcell: "Any man who would make such an execrable pun would not scruple to pick my pocket" ([1870] 1970: 874).

Is there anything you would like to add or comment on?

Duhig: I discovered on a random walk that the main road from my house into the centre of Leeds was made by a blind man, Jack Metcalfe. He tested stones in Beckettian manner by rolling them around in his mouth "like new words," as my informant put it, and I do the same, with ideas as well as words. I have never felt entirely in control of how I got here in my like, so make something of a creative fetish from getting lost – which is why I have always liked that quotation from the Qur'an: "Only those who are lost in error follow the poets. Do you not see how they rove aimlessly in every valley, how they never follow their words with actions?" (2010: 138, translated by M. A. Abdel Haleem) So getting lost – and poverty: the verbal richness of languages like Irish and Arabic with their huge vocabularies, has something to do I feel with the genius of the people going into the language, particularly with regard to its possibilities for entertaining themselves as they were not rich in alternatives: the song of the nomad as opposed to the prose of the farmer, as Brodsky characterised it; wanderings sometimes finding only blind roads; as Machado wrote, the roads are made by walking but around here, those are exactly the roads Metcalfe bypassed in the name of blind efficiency. Poets are a surplus in society now, and it is impossible to take what they do completely seriously even if their medium was not so ripe in itself for comedy. Wordplay evidences the miscegenating promiscuity of language that mimics in its betrayals of meaning our own betrayals – over here, a slang term for an extra-marital affair is 'playing away' and that is what language does sometimes as well. Poetry has always seemed to me more like sex than marriage, which I imagine tied up with prose. For me, poetry can be about debauching the language of the tribe as well, or at least grappling with that debauch, which cannot help but be comic. I do not entirely go along with Patrick Kavanagh's notion that "Tragedy is underdeveloped Comedy" ([1964] 1972: xiv), not least because of the example of poets like Celan and Geoffrey Hill, but I find my own circumstances and experiences comic more often than not, corrupting what might have been a fuller tragic vision in me, perhaps, but you play the cards you are dealt.

3 References

Baudelaire, Charles-Pierre. [1861] 1972. Le Soleil. In Claude Pichois (ed.), *Les Fleurs du Mal*, 115. Paris: Gallimard.

Brewer, Ebenezer Cobham. [1870] 1970. Pun. He Who Would Make a Pun Would Pick a Pocket. In Ivor H. Evans (ed.), *A Dictionary of Phrase and Fable*, 874. London: Cassell.

The Clerks. 2009. *Don't Talk – Just Listen*. Signum Records.
Douglas, Keith. [1941] 1951. The Marvel. In John Waller and G. S. Fraser (eds.), *The Collected Poems of Keith Douglas*, 48. London: Editions Poetry London.
Duhig, Ian. 1991. *The Bradford Count*. Newcastle upon Tyne: Bloodaxe.
Duhig, Ian. 1995. *The Mersey Gold Fish*. Newcastle upon Tyne: Bloodaxe.
Duhig, Ian. 2007. *The Speed of Dark*. London: Picador.
Duhig, Ian. 2008. The Un(heim)lich(e) Man(oeuvre). In Sarah Eyre & Ra Page (eds.), *The New Uncanny: Tales of Unease*. [no place]: Comma.
Duhig, Ian. 2010. *Pandorama*. London: Picador.
Duhig, Ian. Forthcoming 2016. *The Blind Roadmaker*. London: Picador.
Eliot, T. S. [1922] 2004. The Waste Land. In *T. S. Eliot: The Complete Poems and Plays*, 59–80. London: Faber and Faber.
Ellmann, Richard. [1959] 1982. *James Joyce: New and Revised Edition*. New York & Oxford: Oxford University Press.
Heaney, Seamus. 2006. Anything Can Happen. *Poets.org*. http://www.poets.org/poetsorg/poem/anything-can-happen (17 July 2015).
Horace. [1914] 1964. Ode 33: A Joyful Return. In Horace: *The Odes and Epodes*, 97. London: Heinemann.
Johnson, Samuel. [1759] 1965. Rasselas. In R. T. Davies (ed.), *Samuel Johnson: Selected Writings*, 203–255. London: Faber and Faber.
Kavanagh, Patrick. [1964] 1972. Author's Note. In *Collected Poems*, xiii–xv. London: Martin Brian & O'Keeffe.
Marvell, Andrew. [1651] 1971. Upon Appleton House, To My Lord Fairfax. In H. M. Margoliouth (ed.), *The Poems and Letters of Andrew Marvell*, vol. 1. Poems, 62–86. London: Oxford University Press.
Morgan, Edwin. [c. 1967]. Nine One Word Poems. *Scottish Poetry Library*. http://www.scottishpoetrylibrary.org.uk/poetry/poems/nine-one-word-poems (17 July 2015).
The Qur'an: English Translation and Parallel Arabic Text. 2010. Oxford & New York: Oxford University Press.
Sterne, Laurence. [1759–1767] 1996. *Tristram Shandy*. London: Wordsworth Editions.
Thompson, E. P. [1963] 1965. *The Making of the English Working Class*. London: Victor Gollancz.

4 Appendix: Some Poems Mentioned in the Interview

The permission to reprint the poems "The Badly Loved", "Fundamentals", "Babylon," and "From the Irish" in full length was kindly given by Ian Duhig. The copyright rests with the poet.

The Badly-Loved

Apollinaire

No man was good enough to be my father;
the Registrar of Bastards being up to D
my mother called me Kostrowitzky,
but at Neuglück hard by the Seven Mountains,
downstream from the miraculous head,
I became its namesake, the poet that I am.
Neuglück! The fish-skinned Vicomtesse designed it,
her pumpernickel velvety with ergot, the day
her father's boarhounds ate their dolls-house.
She loved me deeply, as did they all,
but I had chosen the English governess
with her Virgin-of-the-Bean blue eyes,
those eye-pods the colour of Egyptian lentils
and that mouth, a royal barge of Carthage
flaming behind the white cities of her teeth.
Our words poured like honey from a madman's tongue,
pledges of the flesh redeemed by starlight.
At times I left her speechless with my dash –
as on Drachenfels where Siegfried conquered.
She was all *Yes, Yes* on the precipice,
but down among the accordions and Rhenish tenors
barking roundelays for chopping sauerkraut
her nerve failed. My love died like her eyes
and I strode forward, master of my voice.

Annie

I remember the secretary's pear-shaped skull
always in a cloud of shag – smoking a narcisse,
his chest whistled like a pan of shellfish –
but it is the Countess I'll never forget!
She was sporting black then for Count Unicorn,
who'd earned his nickname for one outstanding cyst,
while her daughter knocked some corners off the Greek
lined up to fill his slippers. We pitied Kostro
with his damp hands and flat, beseeching cheekbones:
like my father, his voice seemed to come from his neck.
Men are such dummies. I'd walk him for her
where the wind took his smoke and endless French –
I didn't speak it, which certainly helped.
Once, though, I'm sure he suggested we should marry.
I felt hunted. *We?* I kept repeating, *We?*

So did he, which really got on my nerves,
especially during the harvest concert.
I could have cheerfully cut off his head.
About that time I chose to live abroad,
somewhere far, somewhere beginning with A.
Barring once in the earthquake I've never wavered.
Now you come with talk of Kostro's poetry,
of Beatrice and Laura – my name is Annie,
and I'd like to hear about the Countess' daughter.

Fundamentals

Brethren, I know that many of you have come here today
because your Chief has promised any non-attender
that he will stake him out, drive tent-pegs through his anus
and sell his wives and children to the Portuguese.
As far as possible, I want you to put that from your minds.
Today, I want to talk to you about the Christian God.

In many respects, our Christian God is not like your God.
His name, for example, is not also our word for rain.
Neither does it have for us the connotation 'sexual intercourse'.
And although I call him 'holy' (we call Him 'Him', not 'It',
even though we know He is not a man and certainly not a woman)
I do not mean, as you do, that He is fat like a healthy cow.

Let me make this clear. When I say 'God is good, God is everywhere',
it is not because He is exceptionally fat. 'God loves you'
does not mean what warriors do to spear-carriers on campaign.
It means He feels for you like your mother or your father –
yes I know Chuma loved a son he bought like warriors
love spear-carriers on campaign – that's *Sin* and it comes later.

From today, I want you to remember just three simple things:
our God is different from your God, our God is better than your God
and my wife doesn't like it when you watch her go to the toilet.
Grasp them and you have grasped the fundamentals of salvation.
Baptisms start at sundown but before then, as arranged,
how to strip, clean and re-sight a breech-loading Martini-Henry.

Babylon

The worm went round inside my head
when my brother left me,
his child in my belly;
I drove gold nails in the soft deal board,
brass nails into his bootprints, and the worm
went round the nails instead,
                              down
into masts of Ipswich pine,
Quebec Yellow, Yankee hackmatack;
round anchor-flukes and catheads,
under the crew in ticking jackets
and duck trousers with bloodied knees
from praying to the Star of the Sea,
drilling moonlight through the binnacle,
down through transom and teak ballast,
lipped and peeling garboards
                        and down
into Brunel's imagination,
bursting out a million times its size
four-square on the mud and sewage
of St Mary's Rotherhithe.

              *

'A wrack-survivor showed it me – oak spars
Valencienned by *Teredo navalis* –
I hired him on the spot. And the worm?
The worm modelled for my Patent Tunneller!'
In the violet light of the first banquet
under the Thames, the laughter of sixty angels.

   A cast iron honeycomb seven yards tall
   furred with poling-screws, sixty working cells
   of navvies backed by brickies sealing
   the driving-spasms under a fontanelle
   of crushed gravel scooped like mother-of-pearl.

Brass plumes vaulted the gas candelabrum
from the band of the Coldstream Guards.
The sixty angels of the share certificate
fell among the oysters and champagne;
a toast brought Bandinel of the F.O.
waving that night's Extraordinary Gazette.

The coffer dam scuttled, they shored from below
lacing sacks of blue clay with hazel rods –
still their sky leaked in; beads, brass money, gin-corks,
a child's ivory teething-ring, water.

'Battle at Navarion! Arab Fleet Destroyed!
We will drive back the hordes of Islam
to where that dry creed first drew breath and sword –
so here's to the wine of Melchizedek:
Down with Water and Down With the Prophet!'
Brunel squirmed with the history of it.

    *

Where lingerest thou
my Irish kind,
over the water
under the water?

Wei
  le

      The arches bellied
      in the violet light
      like a knife testing
      a flank for entry.

          wei
            le

'I seed them Hirishers
tumblin' through the harches
screachin' Murther! Murther!
Out with them bloody lights!'

                Waile!
    Down by the river Saile
    I wept for my damned sisters,
    for pleasure-seekers
    when the waters closed;
    for Trimmer Gorman, Cahillane
    and all the nameless exiles,
    Sligo, Semite, Vietnamese.
    My brother's name is Babylon.

III Genre and Meta-Reflection

Johannes Kabatek
Wordplay and Discourse Traditions

Abstract: The aim of this paper is to show that wordplay phenomena are not only determined by the universal ability of humans to play with words and the linguistic possibilities and constraints of particular languages, but also by traditional, culture-specific patterns. The importance of a clear distinction between the different levels of analysis involved in wordplay phenomena (the universal level, the level of the individual language, the level of the concrete utterance and, finally, the level of "discourse tradition") is discussed with reference to different communicative functions and illustrated by means of an example from the comic series *Astérix* and its translation into different languages.

Keywords: *Astérix*, comics, discourse tradition, Eugenio Coseriu, language and humour, metalinguistic function, poetic function, Roman Jakobson, Romance, translation

1 Introduction*

Linguists have an enormous privilege: they are allowed to work on the whole range of aspects associated with human language and languages. They may find pleasure in logical argumentation and the formulae of compositional semantics, enjoy explanations in syntactic theory, work on language contact on Caribbean beaches, or even find themselves analysing wordplay. Human beings have invented science because knowledge is a human necessity; it derives from the two fundamental human characteristics defined by Hegel, the *logos* and the *work*.[1] But we can identify further human necessities that seem to be universal, like metaphysical or religious thought, love, of course, and probably also a ludic side, and thus the need for humour. We assume, like Bergson ([1900] 2012), that laughter is common to all human beings, and by combining humour and language, we soon arrive at wordplay or punning. No doubt, punning is fun, but its obvious attraction for a linguist is also dangerous, since the scientific treatment of the comic frequently involves the danger of neglecting abstrac-

---

* I would like to express my gratitude to Marianne Hundt, the editors of this volume, and the anonymous reviewers for their help and their very useful comments.
1 Cf. Trabant (1996: 20).

tion, clarity and the systematic treatment of the subject matter in the face of a tempting example. What is wordplay? It appears that, in telling a few anecdotes, the mystery might simply disclose itself.

This, however, will not be the purpose of this short paper. It is tempting to stay focussed on the data and to simply keep looking for amusing examples in order to illustrate the many different phenomena at play when we engage in punning. The other extreme would be to construct a purely theoretical model of wordplay, in other words: to establish the categories relevant to an adequate location of the phenomenon in a theory of language. But theory without empirical evidence is void, and it will, as always, be difficult to match both sides, to bring together theory and empirical evidence. A negative delimitation of the phenomenon proves to be even more difficult. Moreover, what we are talking about and what a positive definition of wordplay should look like (cf. Winter-Froemel 2009) seems obvious, and we all have a clear intuition about how some prototypical cases of wordplay work. It is rather difficult, however, if not even impossible to state clearly – and in terms of a semiotic theory – where the limits of wordplay are and what wordplay is *not*. Hence, the aim of this paper will not be to go further into these general theoretical issues but rather to discuss one aspect not typically considered in standard definitions or in specific explanations of wordplay phenomena: The most important notion in what follows will be that of *tradition*, and the starting hypothesis – deriving from a language theory that distinguishes between linguistic, pragmatic, and *traditional* features (adopting the notion of *discourse traditions* from Koch 1987, 1988, 1997) – will claim that here, as in any study of linguistic phenomena, *traditional* phenomena play a crucial role.

It might be important to define more clearly what I mean by tradition, since a particular language itself could be regarded as a tradition.[2] A simple example may serve to explain this: the fact that in Spain, people say *Buenos días* to each other in the morning might be explained by the universal pragmatic need for greeting, or by facts of the Spanish language (which contains the two words, their morphology and syntax). But neither universality nor the Spanish gram-

---

[2] In the sense of Hockett (1963: 11-12), who claims tradition to be one of the universals of human language: "The conventions of a language are passed down by teaching and learning, not through the germ plasm. Genes supply potentiality and a generalized drive since nonhuman animals cannot learn a (human) language and humans can hardly be prevented from acquiring one. Bee-dancing is probably genetic. [...] Every human language has tradition [...]. If we design and build a collection of machines that communicate among themselves with a language, this property will be lacking."

mar explain why they greet each other exactly like that rather than in a different way. One could even point out that it is almost illogical to use the plural form when, generally, the reference is to a particular day only, or discuss why the adjective *buenos* is preposed in a language where the unmarked adjective should find itself in postposition.

The notion of "discourse tradition" refers to these kinds of traditional repetitions, and the greeting formula is just a simple example that allows for the explanation of the more general phenomenon: according to Koch (1997), the creation of utterances is always based on both the knowledge of a particular language (its grammar and lexicon), and the knowledge of discourse traditions; the latter including formulae like *Buenos días* and textual forms like letters, sonnets, newspaper articles or even forms of so-called "informal" everyday communication. Discourse traditions are – as can be seen from the example of the sonnet – not limited to a particular language, and they can be distinguished from universal pragmatic factors and from the grammar of a language, although they interact with both. This interaction is both a direct and an indirect one: on the one hand, discourse traditions are *loci* of preservation and innovation of linguistic features (e.g. preservation of archaic forms in legal formulae or in religious texts; innovation in new textual environments, see Koch 2008); on the other, given their inter-linguistic mobility, the adoption of discourse traditions is a source of interference with other languages (such as the Italian influence in Spain when the sonnet as a form was adopted from Italy).

The basic effect of wordplay derives from an element of surprise: playing on words achieves its expressive effect only when new and unexpected elements are introduced. However, as we will see in what follows, wordplay phenomena can be strongly linked to discourse traditions, and they can spread across languages by translation. The example I will take as my starting point is drawn from the well-known French comic strip series *Astérix* and its translation into several languages, a particular case that will allow me to discuss some general issues and get back to the theoretical discussion about the role of discourse traditions and its relationship to wordplay.

2 The Corsican Map

Obviously, there are textual genres and kinds of linguistic interaction where wordplay is a staple of expression, such as jokes, advertising, humoristic plays, comedy shows etc., and comics. In the French comic series *Astérix* (see also Blancher, in *The Dynamics of Wordplay* 2), wordplay has been one of the chief features from the beginning, and maybe also one of the reasons for the worldwide success of the little Gaul hero who makes the whole Roman empire look ridiculous. A particularly fruitful area of wordplay in *Astérix* are proper names, and one might even argue that, in some way, the proper names are keys to entire stories: Names characterise places, persons and peoples, and the fundamental opposition between Romans and Gauls is underlined by different kinds of names and different suffixes. The Romans have comical names ending in *-us*, the Gauls humorous names ending in *-ix* (derived from the historical Gaul's leader Vercingetorix, defeated by Caesar), and Roman place names mostly end in *-um*. The humoristic effect is produced by a few techniques that are repeated systematically: In some cases, an amusing, transparent word characterizing a person or place is combined with the respective ending. More often, however, a transparent word or a group of words is created that does not bear any semblance to either Latin or any of the other languages (or caricatures of languages) that appear in the stories, by making use of the final sequence of sounds that resemble a familiar ending: as in the case of the toponym *Petitbonum*, which sounds like a French-Latin hybrid easily imaginable as a place name (Fr. *Petit* [small], Lat. *bonum* [good]) but is in fact an allusion to *petit bonhomme* [toddler], and thus simultaneously evokes a completely different meaning. This kind of artificial and arbitrary "folk etymology" is a common technique in punning, and in the case of *Astérix*, the concrete comical imitation of Latin and other locally connoted names has been one of the most frequent procedures for the creation of a humorous effect, as we can see in the names of the protagonists themselves, such as Astérix (<*asterisk*), Obélix (<*obelisk*), Idéfix (<*idée fixe*) etc.

Astérix has been translated into many languages, and the translations have generally tried to adopt the technique employed in the original French text, sometimes not very successfully, as in the case of German *Kleinbonum*, a relatively opaque form that tries to render *Petitbonum* but only achieves the first effect (German-Latin hybrid evoking a Latin toponym) while failing to create the second level of meaning, i.e. the truly humoristic one. In other cases, such as *Babaorum* (an allusion to the French dessert *Baba-au-Rhum*), possibly some francophile German intellectual might have captured the original effect, but surely not the general public. In the English translation, Babaorum is rendered as *Totorum*, an allusion to colloquial English *Tot'o rum*, a shot of rum; so, here the technique was recognised and re-created with a local equivalent that achieves the same effect.

The Corsican map at the beginning of one of the most successful *Astérix*-stories, *Astérix en Corse*, is an example that illustrates the name-based wordplay technique of the comic series particularly well. The map shows the island as a completely Roman-dominated place, with Roman settlements and castles all around the coast (there are 46 invented names and four historic place names). In the French original version, we find authentic Latin words and word groups that are known in the French community without having anything to do with place names (like *Geranium, Tedeum, Postscriptum, Vacuum, Desideratum,* and *Natrium*). Supposedly, not all the names are recognized to the same degree in the community of readers: the map offers easily identifiable cases like *Geranium* but also other, more sophisticated ones, like *Sivispacemparabellum*, a whole sentence that appears as a single word and that requires at least a partial knowledge of Latin.[3]

The translators of *Astérix* have looked for various solutions, with some sticking to the ideal of a close-to-the-source translation, and others giving priority to the technique and the effect produced rather than to fidelity to the original version. The following table shows some examples where the source language is compared to three translations[4]:

Tab. 1: Examples of names of the Corsican map in four versions

French	German	Spanish	Portuguese
Geranium	Geranium	Geranium	Geranium
Postscriptum	Postscriptum	Postscriptum	Postscriptum
Sivispacemparabellum	Hintenrum	Sivispacemparabellum	Sivispacemparabellum
Tedeum	Seisdrum	Tideum	Seraficum

It is interesting to observe that the German translation is the one where the least importance is given to the fidelity criterion. There is even a certain priority to look for names that rather follow the *petit bonhomme* model: German expressions ending in -*um* but without any relationship with Latin, like *Hintenrum* (a

---

3 This Latin proverb (*Si vis pacem para bellum* [If you want peace, prepare war]) was replaced, in the German translation of *Le grand fossé* [Der grosse Graben], by *Si vis pacem evita bellum* [If you want peace, avoid war]. Adolf Kabatek, the German text editor, was then ironically accused of being "subversive" on account of this change.
4 René Goscinny and Albert Uderzo: *Astérix en Corse* (1973a); German version *Asterix auf Korsika* (1975), translated by Gudrun Penndorf, German text edition by Adolf Kabatek; Spanish version *Astérix en Córcega* (1973b), translated by Víctor Mora; Portuguese version: *Astérix na Córsega* (1973c), translated by Cláudio Varga.

colloquial short form of *hinten herum* [from behind] or [round the back]); *Seisdrum* [be it as it were]; *Saudum* – i.e. *saudumm* [very stupid]; *Hauteuchdrum* [fight for it]; or *Toblerorum*, where in the French original we find *Factotum*. The latter form would have had the same effect in a German context, but the translator somehow "exaggerates" the case and prefers to choose a completely different form: The name *Toblerorum* plays with the chocolate flavour and brand name *Tobler-O-Rum*, a combination of the Swiss brand name Tobler, the French contraction of preposition and article *au* pronounced *o* and the word *Rum*. (*Tobler-O-Rum* is milk chocolate with raisins and rum flavour). Thus, the wordplay is based on the imitation of Latin-sounding endings in *–um* in combination with any word or even short phrase with this ending but with no real relationship with Latin (or at least not with toponyms). The comical effect is being created by the dislocation of the word and the aforementioned "pseudo-folk etymology."[5]

Hence, when comparing the different versions, we see that there are two main tendencies: *continuity* (the translation follows the original model, sometimes with partial graphic adaption), or *substitution*, the latter corresponding to a technique derived from other cases and probably due to the necessity in the translation process of introducing additional wordplay in order to counterbalance the obvious loss of humour produced by local allusions in the original version. We could now go into a detailed analysis of all the forms and comment on them, but the examples so far shall suffice to serve as a starting point for a more general discussion of the nature and theoretical classification of wordplay.

3 Different Levels of Analysis

The arbitrarily chosen examples of the previous section allow me to observe some general characteristics of wordplay:
- We can identify a general property of wordplay: not only the content of the message, but the message itself is the focus of attention. Playing on words is

---

[5] Here again, as in *Sivispacemparabellum*, a further effect is added for a really Latinate readership by the fact that *-orum* could be interpreted as a genitive plural ending, as in *Babaorum*. The quality of the wordplay in *Astérix* is characterised by this multi-level interpretation: there is a first level easily recognised by all readers, and there are further, more sophisticated levels which are more challenging. The various levels of understanding make the stories more appealing for multiple and heterogeneous audiences. The technique of audience stratification invites readers to comment metalinguistically on the stories and it creates a difference between "experts" and "laymen."

not simply saying something by means of words but at the same time playing with something, using words to do something ludic with them.
- We can identify a certain technique or principle underlying the Corsican map; this technique or principle is not linked to one particular language (even if, in this case, it is linked to the common reference to Latin; but we could also formulate the principle in a more abstract way, as loanword imitation or, more precisely, imitation of another language within a language). The concrete means that fulfil the function of language imitation are phonological similarities to well-known morphological endings of the imitated language, morphological *shibboleths*, so to speak. The comical effect is produced through the moment of surprise when the reader becomes aware of the play: a combination of two originally unrelated elements (cf. Bauer, this volume).

Once this technique is established, it serves as a pattern for repetition. Each repetition, even if it also has its own and independent semiotic value, evokes previous instances of the same pattern, and in this way the technique becomes a historical, traditional one. It is not part of the grammar of either language involved in the play: no rule of German grammar says that, by choosing words or phrases ending with *-um*, speakers ironically evoke Latin and provoke a comical effect. In other words, we seem to be dealing with a cross-linguistic technique that is located outside the grammar of the languages involved (cf. Knospe, this volume). The universal basis is the possibility of imitation of a language within a language, but the concrete way of evocating Latin by *-um* and *-orum* endings, through repetition, becomes an established (local) tradition.[6]

Even if punning draws on general techniques, the knowledge required for the concrete interpretation of each of the examples is complex. If we look at the examples of the map, we can identify a considerable amount of different kinds of knowledge that must be activated in order to catch the comical effect: knowledge of words, expressions, of at least a little bit of Latin, etc. If we extend this to the almost endless amount of other wordplay examples, we will see that there is not a restricted set of rules to be activated, but rather evocation of unlimited knowledge: there is an interpretative process necessary for the understanding of each of the individual examples. However, individual diversity left

---

6 When McDonald's in Germany introduced the Mexican weeks by calling them "Los Wochos," a similar comic effect was achieved by adding the Spanish plural morpheme *-os* to the German work *Woche* [week] – with the difference that *Wochos* was a new form in German with a common noun meaning, not a parody of a pre-existing form used as a proper name.

aside, there are also some more general underlying principles that can be subsumed under various categories: we can play with form (rhyme, syllable changes, sound play, etc.), with content (comparison, hyperbolic expressions, taxonomic or other semantic relations, etc.), or with combinations of both.[7]

The *Astérix* example and the more general observations allow us to now move on to a discussion of different levels of analysis. It seems to make sense to relate wordplay phenomena to the fundamental distinction established by Eugenio Coseriu (1985) of three levels in the analysis of any linguistic phenomenon: the *universal level* (what is common to human speech in general), the *historical level* (the level of particular languages), and the *individual level* (the level of concrete utterances). Wordplay is a universal phenomenon, but it depends strongly on the possibilities and techniques of a particular language. Moreover, each instance of wordplay has an individual side, and to capture its concrete function in a particular situation is an issue of interpretation. To these three levels we will have to add a further dimension, more or less independent of the grammatical and technical side of the historical language and not limited to the individual utterance: the dimension of *discourse tradition* (cf., e.g., Kullmann, this volume). In the remainder of this paper, I will go through these four different dimensions and comment on some aspects of their relevance for wordplay.

3.1 Wordplay and Communicative Functions

If we begin with the first of Coseriu's levels, the universal one, we have already taken for granted that playing with words, like playing in general, is a universal human activity not limited to any cultural or linguistic space (an assumption valid at least until some anthropologist discovers an Amazonian tribe that does not play with words; cf. Huizinga [1938] 1987). But what is the universal character of wordplay? If we look at Karl Bühler's classic semiotic model, we can state that wordplay highlights the expressive and the conative function: it showcases the expressive creativity and ingenuity of the speaker and attracts the hearer's attention or has a concrete effect on him. The less important function is the referential one.

---

[7] It seems to be contradictory to claim the importance of "unlimited knowledge" on the one hand and to postulate categorisation, on the other hand. Of course, there are useful attempts for classifying the *types* of knowledge involved in the process of understanding of utterances, such as Coseriu's *Umfelder* (1955–1956; see also Aschenberg 1999; Winter-Froemel 2013: 156). But the possibility of grouping together different domains of knowledge into types does not contradict the principal lack of limitation of knowledge itself.

But this does not yet suffice for a localization of wordplay on a universal level. A simple shout such as *stop it!* also highlights both functions without having anything to do with wordplay. Some authors have discussed the relationship between wordplay and metalinguistic reflection, so a consideration of Jakobson's additional communication functions (see 1960) might bring us closer to a fuller understanding of the process involved in wordplay.

Of the three functions Jakobson added to Bühler's model, we may leave aside the phatic function, the assurance of the communication channel, but we should have a closer look at the *metalinguistic* and the *poetic* function. The metalinguistic function in Jakobson's theory (1960) refers to those speech acts where the message itself becomes the centre of attention of the message. The poetic function refers to the essential characteristics of poetry and literature. Several authors – and also several of the contributors to this volume – have claimed that wordplay is in its essence metalinguistic.[8]

But is this really true? In order to find an answer, we will first have to ask how we can define metalanguage. As we know, there are broad and narrow definitions of the concept 'metalanguage.' The narrow definition holds that a metalinguistic statement is just one that says something about language, such as "blue is an adjective" or "house is the subject in *the house is red*." In a broader definition of the concept, also those speech events that suppose a certain level of reflection on utterances are considered metalinguistic, for instance when I say "he said that sadly."[9] Yet others claim that discourse markers and pragmatic particles like "you know," too, are actually metalinguistic. An extreme position is held by Harald Weinrich (1976), who even includes prepositions and conjunctions among the class of metalinguistic elements, on the basis that they do not have any referential value. In such an approach, the whole of grammar and all the synsemantic units (as opposed to autosemantic units)

---

8 One proponent of this view is Yaguello (1998: 3): "There is one significant area where all that metalinguistic activity is brought into full view: wordplay, playing *on* words, playing *with* words, verbal play in all its forms – punning, the rebus, charades, spoonerisms, eye rhymes, nursery rhymes, riddles, portmanteau words, crosswords, anagrams, and so on: everything in our speech which reveals an innate, intuitive linguistics in speakers. Playing, after all, presupposes that one knows the rules and how to bend them, how to exploit the ambiguity which characterises natural languages, as well as the creativity which they allow. For children, language-learning is inseparable from word games, which thereby take on educational value (mainly self-educational as it runs out). Indeed, all wordplay presupposes correct acquisition of the code."

9 For an overview of several traditional – both broad and narrow – definitions, see Ulrich (1997).

would be considered metalinguistic. For the sake of terminological precision, I, personally, would prefer a more restricted definition of what metalanguage is; and I would also adopt Coseriu's criticism of Jakobson's model (2007: 76-92), claiming that there is no need to distinguish a separate "metalinguistic function," since saying something like "blue is an adjective" is a purely referential statement exactly as "Tübingen is a big university with a small town," with the only difference that what we refer to are elements that are part of a language (even if we might accept that these referents are quite special ones). In an approach that restricts metalanguage to the self-referential function (and thus subsumes it under Bühler's referential function), wordplay is not metalinguistic, but something else.[10] But if it is not metalinguistic, what else could it be? Poetic? Jakobson's definition of the poetic function reveals that he uses wordplay to illustrate what is meant by 'poetic': his famous example of the Eisenhower electoral propaganda slogan *I like Ike* plays with a kind of a linguistic Russian doll where *I* is part of *like* and *Ike* and *Ike* is part of *like* (see 1960). Is this wordplay or simply sound play? I would propose that all the elements included in the classical rhetoric notion of *numerus*, the Latin translation for the Greek *rhythmus*, are traditional forms of wordplay. We may no longer consider them to be wordplay in the narrow sense, but this is more due to the commonness of such techniques than to their objective shape. In other words, what Jakobson subsumes under his "poetic function" has at least something to do with wordplay. But, again, I would follow Coseriu in his criticism and suggest that the poetic function is neither poetic nor a communicative function. The mistake of associating formal techniques with poetry is very old, and it was already criticised by Aristotle in his *Poetics*, as Coseriu points out, when he argued that a treatise on natural science does not become a poem only through metre and rhyme:

> people attach the word poet (maker) to the name of the metre and speak of elegiac poets and of others as epic poets. Thus they do not call them poets in virtue of their representation but apply the name indiscriminately in virtue of the metre. For if people publish medical or scientific treatises in metre the custom is to call them poets. But Homer and Empedocles have nothing in common except the metre, so that it would be proper to call the one a poet and the other not a poet but a scientist.
>
> ([1927] 1965: 1447b)

---

10 Cf. also Culioli (1990: 41) who talks about the "jouissance du métalinguistique" and further comments: "on pourrait soutenir qu'il y a du métalinguistique, mais pas de métalangage, au sens d'un langage extérieur à la langue objet."

Obviously, formal definitions are bound to fail in capturing the difference between poetry and other forms of language. The essence of poetry is not form; it is the literary expressivity of the poet, and a simple piece of prose can easily be a poem.[11] Poetry is not a communicative function but another way of speaking, its main aim being the expression of the individual's self rather than communication.

But we started out wanting to define wordplay, not poetry. In the process, we have come to see that there seems to be a formal overlap between some forms of poetry and wordplay. Curiously enough, however, the example Jakobson gives for the poetic function of language is one involving wordplay, not a poem: *I like Ike* is a propaganda slogan, and even if wordplay might be an important element of many instances of poetry, there are also many examples of everyday wordplay without any aim at being poetry. Is wordplay aesthetic? This is another question: apparently, wordplay is aesthetic, but it is not necessarily literary. A kind of common, everyday aesthetic exists, and this is what wordplay frequently is.[12]

Language can be used to simply communicate, but language can also be used to look at the form of the message itself, in the same way we can put on our clothes just to protect our bodies from the weather or, as an added value, a side-effect, we can put on clothes that look nice; as long as clothes fulfil their primary function, their capacity for being ornamental – an *ornatus* – appears to be almost limitless, just as there are no limits to the ornamental element in language, as long as it fulfils its primary function of communication. However, with wordplay we are not on the level of an individual language nor on the universal level: what is universal is the possibility of playing, but the wordplay itself is a matter of the individual level of the concrete text. This means that wordplay is produced through linguistic means, but it is not language in the structural sense, in the sense of *langue* or in the sense of *competence*: wordplay is not part of the grammar of a particular language, as I have pointed out – even in the case of phenomena like the French *verlan* (see Oster, in *The Dynamics of Wordplay* 2) or the Argentine *vesre*, as we will see in the following section. But what exactly are the techniques of wordplay on the individual level? Can we establish rules and norms for wordplay? I do not think that this is feasible; we can only establish an open list of possibilities. Since wordplay is a phenomenon on the level of the concrete utterance, it can involve absolutely everything that is present in

---

11 Cf. also the special issue 23.2 of *Connotations* on "Poetry in Fiction" (Bauer, Leimberg, Niederhoff and Zirker 2013 / 2014).
12 Cf. Stempel's (1983) notion of *Alltagsrhetorik* [everyday rhetoric].

the concrete utterance: we can play with the repetition of syllables, we can omit letters, we can play with the sounds of language, with the shape of letters, with rhythm and with time, with space and with voices, with content and form, with nature and culture, with all the elements that might be in one or another way evoked by a text. One might object that such "techniques" of playing are abstract ones and that they go beyond the individual level. This holds for the technical and possibly traditional aspect of wordplay phenomena, but the concrete function of a concrete instance of wordplay in a concrete text is purely individual.

Since there is almost no limitation to wordplay, we can also play with elements of other languages and – as in Dada poetry, or in Asenso Ferreiras *Trem de Alagoas* – with any kind of sound. What we do might be limited by certain elements of the language we are playing with, or, put differently: we might perceive, in a certain language, specific elements (like compounds, morphology, etc.) that afford us with opportunities to play.[13] But any attempt at providing a closed and limited classification of wordplay is doomed to failure; we can only roughly classify the areas where wordplay is possible: phonic, content-oriented, play with homonyms, play with spelling, etc. And we can analyse the concrete technique that works in one case or another.

However, the question remains whether this kind of analysis is a task for the linguist? Or should we leave it to the field of literary studies? It is not linguistic in a formal linguistic sense, but I would not accept an exclusive language theory that eliminates a large number of phenomena related to language from linguistics, particularly those that are likely to attract the interest of common speakers. Linguistics is not an arrogant discipline that does not care about the layman's opinion: linguistics should consider all possible aspects of language. And the analysis of wordplay is a concrete task of text linguistics, not in the sense of a textual grammar but in the sense of a science of interpreting what happens in a text, in the sense of discovering the phonetic, morphematic, graphemic, semantic etc. techniques that make a text work, and, as a whole, imbue it with its special sense, which – in the case of wordplay – is intellectual exercise. At the same time, wordplay is an aesthetic technique that gives beauty to a text. It always has an aesthetic effect, but there can also be an expressive effect, showing the creativity of a speaker or an artist, or a conative effect on the

---

13 See also the contributions by Knospe and Renner, this volume; as well as Sablayrolles, in *The Dynamics of Wordplay* 2.

hearer who is impressed by a slogan or by the wit and creative abilities of a wordplayer, be it a rapper, a comic author or a comedian.[14]

3.2 Wordplay and Discourse Tradition

Even if the interpretation of a concrete wordplay phenomenon is an individual task, it would be completely wrong to delimit wordplay to the individual level. If this were the case, wordplay could only be analysed as one or the other concrete phenomenon in this or that concrete text, contributing to some concrete sense of that individual text.

There is of course more to wordplay. If we look at the tradition of *numerus*, if we look at odes, at hexameters, at sonnets, at blank verse and at a rapper's techniques of composition, we will obviously identify something else: wordplay is not only actual and individual, but it can build on *tradition*, and to some extent, typically does so. There is a continuum between uniqueness (for instance the omission of the letter *e* in a whole postmodern novel, *La Disparition* by Georges Perec; see Di Blasio in *The Dynamics of Wordplay* 2), and commonness like rhyme; and sometimes more general traditions provide the frame for more 'local' – at times individual – traditions, such as the Petrarcan sonnet and its Shakespearean variant, certain joke patterns and their individual variation, and any other tradition of established wordplay frames with individual variance. The comedian Christian Hirdes mentions an individual tradition when defining what he calls the *Hirdes reduction*, in the sense of a *re-ducere ad sensum*, going back to the original sense, or 'speaking literally.' He claims he has invented this technique of (folk-)etymologizing, but it is of course a well-known and old one, and we might think of Erich Kästner, of Karl Valentin, Franz Hohler, and of Otto Waalkes as exponents of that technique in the German speaking context, and we will surely find others in French, English and elsewhere. The re-motivation of opaque words is a widespread traditional technique, as there are other traditions of wordplay: discourse traditions, as I would call them, traditions that might be local, individual, typical of a certain place or culture like the *limerick* or the *Schüttelreim* (see Rabatel, in *The Dynamics of Wordplay* 2), or even traditional, to a certain degree, within a whole language community. One example would be the technique of syllable inversion in Argentinian Spanish – the so-

---

14 As the German comedian Christian Hirdes (for biographical information, see http://www.christianhirdes.de/seiten/ueber-christian-hirdes.php) somewhat cheekily puts it: the main purpose of his comedy is to make the women in the audience fall in love with him.

called *vesre* – a technique impossible in languages like Chinese, where we do not have real polysyllabic words. While in Spanish, *vesre* is only a local phenomenon, in French, some of the words created by *verlan* like *moeuf* or *beur* have almost become generalised words of the French language (at least in France). Does this mean that *verlan* is part of French grammar? Not at all. It is simply what in other places might be a phenomenon restricted to schoolyard games; in the case of *verlan*, for historical reasons, this game has become a widely accepted element in the French community: a commonly known discourse tradition.

4 Conclusion

To sum up: wordplay is a universal phenomenon that derives from the universal ability of human beings to distinguish between the strictly necessary and what could be considered superfluous. Wordplay is, in some way, a superfluous ornament not necessary for the basic needs of transmitting a message. However, it may serve, as any "superfluous" element, to enhance the effect of the necessary; it may have a purely aesthetic effect or help to give expressivity to the speaker or the message. Moreover, since any aesthetic activity is essential for human beings, wordplay might be superfluous for the message but it can help to fulfil our aesthetic needs, and it can play an important pragmatic role: Wordplay modulates the message, it adds or substracts communicative weight, it alters the relationship between the interlocutors, or it allows a contentless message to be uttered simply for the virtue of its comic effect.

On a historical level, wordplay is (partly) determined by the techniques that a particular language affords, and this is why not all wordplay traditions can be translated into other languages. Sometimes they must be replaced. In our example, the original French *Astérix* is full of wordplay phenomena, but many of them could not be reproduced literally in in the German version. So, facing the fact that many of the original allusions cannot be rendered in the translation and thus get lost, what the team of the German translator and the text editor did was to adopt the general technique of playing with words, sometimes by adoption of the same technique but with different examples, sometimes by creating even new techniques (see Schauffler, this volume).[15]

We also saw that, apart from the universal aspect of wordplay and the historical possibilities and limitations inherent in a particular language, wordplay has traditions. These can be the traditions of an individual (like the particular manner of a comedian or author[16]), they can be traditions of a group or groups (like children's wordplay games or French *verlan*), they can be part of long term or short term literary traditions (like the classical forms of poetry or like rap), and they are common to communities, not necessarily identical with *language* communities. Some of them become traditional in literature, others in popular discourse, yet others in the context of advertising, while some remain individual. They emerge, they are modified, combined, abandoned, but they will always exist, because what is common to all human beings is that they can play with words, and they generally enjoy it.

5 References

Adams, Douglas & John Lloyd. [1983] 1992. *The (Deeper) Meaning of Liff*. London: Pan Books.
Adams, Douglas & John Lloyd. 1992. *The (Deeper) Meaning of Liff* [Der tiefere Sinn des Labenz]. Frankfurt a. M.: Rogner und Bernhard bei Zweitausendeins.
Aristotle. [1927] 1965. *The Poetics*. Cambridge, MA: Heinemann; Harvard University Press.
Aschenberg, Heidi. 1999. *Kontexte in Texten: Umfeldtheorie und literarischer Situationsaufbau*. Tübingen: Niemeyer.
Bauer, Matthias, Inge Leimberg, Burkhard Niederhoff & Angelika Zirker (eds.). 2013/2014. Poetry in Fiction. [Special Issue]. *Connotations* 23(2).
Bergson, Henri. [1900] 2012. *Le rire: Essai sur la signification du comique*. Paris: Payot.
Bühler, Karl. 1934. *Sprachtheorie: Die Darstellungsfunktion der Sprache*. Jena: Fischer.
Coseriu, Eugenio. 1955-1956. Determinación y entorno: Dos problemas de una lingüística del hablar. *Romanistisches Jahrbuch* 7. 24–54.

---

[15] The most famous example is the translation *ils sont fous, ces romains* [they are crazy, these Romans] by Germ. "die spinnen, die Römer," with a rhythmic repetition of the article / pronoun *die*, possible due to a focalising syntactic dislocation. This German pattern became proverbial.

[16] A prime example would be Douglas Adams and John Lloyd's *The (Deeper) Meaning of Liff* ([1983] 1992). This is an interesting case of wordplay, tradition and translation: the idea of remotivating proper names of places as common names with meanings the language supposedly lacks was adopted in a German version (*Der tiefere Sinn des Labenz* (1992)), by the translators Sven Böttcher and with completely different toponyms and completely different meanings – a particularly startling example of quite literally relocating an individual case of wordplay.

Coseriu, Eugenio. 1985. Linguistic Competence: What is it Really? The Presidential Address of the Modern Humanities Research Association, University College, London, 11 January. *The Modern Language Review* 80(4), xxv-xxxv. http://www.coseriu.de (17 July 2015).
Coseriu, Eugenio. 2007. *Textlinguistik: Eine Einführung*, 4th edn. Tübingen: Narr.
Culioli, Antoine. 1990. *Pour une linguistique de l'énonciation: Opérations et representations.* Paris: Ophrys.
Goscinny, René & Albert Uderzo. 1973a. *Astérix en Corse*. Paris: Dargaud.
Goscinny, René & Albert Uderzo. 1973b. *Astérix en Corse*. [Astérix en Córcega]. Barcelona: Bruguera.
Goscinny, René & Albert Uderzo. 1973c. *Astérix en Corse* [Astérix na Córsega]. Rio de Janeiro: Record.
Goscinny, René & Albert Uderzo. 1975. *Astérix en Corse* [Asterix auf Korsika]. Stuttgart: Ehapa.
Hockett, Charles Francis. 1963. The Problem of Universals in Language. In Joseph Greenberg (ed.), *Universals of Language: Report of a Conference Held at Dobbs Ferry, New York, April 13–15, 1961*, 1–22. Cambridge, MA: Massachusetts Institute of Technology Press.
Huizinga, Johan. [1938] 1987. *Homo ludens: Proeve eener bepaling van het spel-element der cultuur* [Homo Ludens: Vom Ursprung der Kultur im Spiel]. Hamburg: Rowohlt.
Jakobson, Roman. 1960. Closing Statement: Linguistics and Poetics. In Thomas Sebeok (ed.), *Style in Language*, 350–377. Boston: Massachusetts Institute of Technology Press; New York: John Wiley.
Koch, Peter. 1987. *Distanz im Dictamen: Zur Schriftlichkeit und Pragmatik mittelalterlicher Brief- und Redemodelle in Italien*. Freiburg im Breisgau: University of Freiburg habilitation thesis.
Koch, Peter. 1988. Norm und Sprache. In Jörn Albrecht, Jens Lüdtke & Harald Thun (eds.), *Energeia und Ergon: Studia in Honorem Eugenio Coseriu*, vol. 2, 327–354. Tübingen: Narr.
Koch, Peter. 1997. Diskurstraditionen: Zu ihrem sprachtheoretischen Status und ihrer Dynamik. In Barbara Frank, Thomas Haye & Doris Tophinke (eds.), *Gattungen mittelalterlicher Schriftlichkeit*, 43–79. Tübingen: Narr.
Koch, Peter. 2008. Tradiciones discursivas y cambio lingüístico: El ejemplo del tratamiento vuestra merced en español. In Johannes Kabatek (ed.), *Sintaxis histórica del español y cambio lingüístico: Nuevas perspectivas desde las Tradiciones Discursivas*, 53–88. Frankfurt a. M. & Madrid: Vervuert-Iberoamericana.
Stempel, Wolf-Dieter. 1983. Fiktion in konversationellen Erzählungen. In Dieter Henrich & Wolfgang Iser, *Funktionen des Fiktiven*, 331–365. München: Fink.
Trabant, Jürgen. 1996. *Elemente der Semiotik*. Tübingen: Francke.
Ulrich, Miorita. 1997. *Die Sprache als Sache: Primärsprache, Metasprache, Übersetzung. Untersuchungen zum Übersetzen und zur Übersetzbarkeit anhand von deutschen, englischen und vor allem romanischen Materialen*. Tübingen: Narr.
Weinrich, Harald. 1976. Von der Alltäglichkeit der Metasprache. In: *Sprache in Texten*, 90–112. Stuttgart: Klett.
Winter-Froemel, Esme. 2009. Wortspiel. In Gerd Ueding (ed.), *Historisches Wörterbuch der Rhetorik*, vol. 9, 1429–1443. Tübingen: Niemeyer.
Winter-Froemel, Esme. 2013. Ambiguität im Sprachgebrauch und im Sprachwandel: Parameter der Analyse diskurs- und systembezogener Fakten. *Zeitschrift für französische Sprache und Literatur* 123(2). 130–170.
Yaguello, Marina. 1998. *Language Through the Looking Glass: Exploring Language and Linguistics*. Oxford: Oxford University Press.

Svea Schauffler
Wordplay in Subtitled Films – An Audience Study

Abstract: The project which this paper addresses represents a rarely undertaken, yet arguably crucial type of research in the field of (audiovisual) Translation Studies. A receptor-oriented, experimental study, it investigates the reception of two different strategies for subtitling English wordplay into German. The short film *Wallace and Gromit* in *A Matter of Loaf and Death* was subtitled into German, creating two different renditions which only differ in terms of the translation of the numerous cases of wordplay. One translation prioritised the transfer of humour, while the other focusses on non-divergence from the original dialogue (the latter being the official translation). Both versions were screened for separate German-speaking audiences, while the original version was tested on an English-speaking control group. The reaction on the part of the audiences was then documented in questionnaires. The study also explores the influence of source language comprehension on the reception of both versions, as it is assumed that a formally different subtitle text could be interpreted as "incorrect" by members of the audience with knowledge of English. Finally, the question of subtitling acceptance in a language community such as the German one, traditionally labelled a "dubbing country," was investigated.

Keywords: animated films, audiovisual translation, dubbing, humour, puns, subtitling, wordplay in film

1 Introduction

If something has a comic effect in one language and associated cultural context, can it be transferred into another language and still have the same effect as in its original form? And if so, is a word-for-word approach the appropriate way of tackling this task of translation? Is there perhaps such a divergence between tastes in humour and the cultural conventions as to what is considered comic in both language communities that even the most skilful translators are unable to accomplish a successful cultural transfer? These questions have remained at the centre of research into humour translation for a long time,[1] even leading to discussions between scholars as to whether or not linguistic humour is translatable at all. One area where such questions require practical solutions on a daily basis is the transfer of wordplay in audiovisual translation (AVT). As wordplay is an integral part of comedy films and series (and likely to remain so), the question arises as to how – not if – it is possible to achieve a successful transfer of wordplay into a target language, in this particular case for subtitling purposes.

Subtitling is characterised by the simultaneous presence of two texts, which means that this mode of language transfer allows the viewer to compare the source and target text and therefore to arrive at an evaluation of the translation of any one utterance. Evidently, this is only possible if the viewer possesses sufficient knowledge of the source language to enable such judgements, as is the case with many German viewers of English films. Therefore, another relevant question to be investigated is whether source language comprehension interferes with the reception of wordplay which has been subtitled using different strategies and how this interference manifests itself.

2 Wordplay Translation

When it comes to the translation of wordplay, the translator faces a dilemma between the maintenance of formal fidelity to the source text (as well as the consequent prioritisation of the transfer of information) on the one hand, and the preservation of comic value by selecting the funniest option – even if this entails moving away from the original – on the other hand (see also Di Blasio, in The Dynamics of Wordplay 2). Subtitled comedy films represent a genre in which these two priorities meet and often clash. If the first approach is chosen, there is a distinct possibility that the humorous quality of a scene is lost or reduced in the process. In the second case, the audience might recognise the formal divergence between source and target text and interpret this as a "wrong" translation. This approach, however, could also be received successfully by viewers if they are able to recognise the creative effort that has gone into the translation in order to retain comic effect, which could add a further positive dimension to the viewing experience. In order to establish a tendency of prefer-

---

[1] Most notably Raphaelson-West (1989); Chiaro (1992, 2007, 2006); Delabastita (1994, 1996, 1997); Schröter (2005); Vandaele (2002, 2011). On approaches for translation of wordplay used for place names see also Kabatek, this volume.

ence towards one or the other, an experiment was conducted which aims to gauge the audience's reaction to each translation approach through the use of two different German translations of the same film dialogue. It was deemed important to investigate exactly which features characterise a good or high-quality translation to the prospective audience, thereby taking into consideration the transparency of subtitling as a translation method (which means that the source text is audible at all times), by conducting an experimental reception study which involves English-speaking as well as German-speaking viewers.

In order to conduct this study, two subtitled versions of the animated short feature *Wallace and Gromit: A Matter of Loaf and Death* (Park 2008a) as well as an un-subtitled version were screened to three different groups of viewers, who then recorded their response in a questionnaire. A control group of English native speakers watched the original, un-translated version of the film, in order to provide a basis on which the evaluation by the two experimental groups could be compared. Two groups of native speakers of German viewed two slightly different subtitled versions respectively, which only differ in the translation of wordplay. One version is based on the existing German translation which was broadcast on television and published on DVD, whilst the alternative translation was developed specifically for this project. Díaz Cintas and Remael argue that "the traditional notion of formal fidelity [...] has now been revised and made all translations more flexible, but this is especially the case of subtitling and other forms of audiovisual translation" (2007: 11). Can we consider, however, that such flexibility extends to wordplay, where, in the majority of cases, formal fidelity and equivalent effect constitute a classic dichotomy?

3 Two Different Approaches

When analysing the existing translation of the film, it becomes evident that the translator seems to have focused on formal similarity (or was simply too pressed for time to employ a more creative approach). Consequently, the alternative translation for the reception study was produced in line with an approach which prioritised the transfer of humorous effect. In a filmic text, the translator dealing with wordplay acts within an exceptionally narrow frame. Many utterances only turn into wordplay based on the interplay with the visual image, for example when idiomatic wordplay emerges due to the image evoking the literal, less salient meaning of an idiom. As the image cannot be altered, a translation which retains the comic value of the original requires great creativity.

Tab. 1: Examples of wordplay based on the visual sign system

Original dialogue	Version A (Existing)[2]	Version B (Alternative)
You can't be everybody's cup of tea, can you? [Wallace and Gromit are clinking their tea cups, disillusioned with their love lives]	Man kann nicht mit jedem gut Kirschen essen. [literal: You can't eat cherries with everyone; figurative: You can't be everybody's cup of tea.]	Naja, erstmal abwarten und Tee trinken. [literal: Well, let's wait and drink tea; figurative: Well, let's wait and see.]
Your buns are as good as toasted! [Villainous Piella to Wallace as he has a bomb stuck in the back of his trousers. He is a baker.]	Du altes Brötchen wirst gleich richtig getoastet! [You old bread roll are about to get a toasting! (no figurative meaning)]	Gleich kriegst du Feuer unterm Hintern! [literal: A fire is about to be lit under you bum!; figurative: You are about to receive a motivational kick in the backside!]

In terms of an appropriate methodological framework, it could be argued that a study involving German participants and subtitled films remains flawed, as dubbing is the more wide-spread method in this language community. The project would not have been feasible using an alternative dubbed version, as it would have been impossible to reproduce an almost identical soundtrack where only wordplay renderings differed from the original (this would have required a recording studio and the same dubbing actors to record the existing version). The question might arise whether presenting a German audience with subtitled material is appropriate seeing as Germany is generally assumed to be a "dubbing country" (where this method is predominantly used and the population is hence unaccustomed to anything else). However, it remains questionable whether the traditional distinction between dubbing and subtitling countries is still appropriate in this day and age.

It should be noted that there has been a remarkable development concerning the influence of the English language in Germany, notably in the incorporation of English expressions into the German vocabulary, as well as a tendency towards earlier and more widespread learning of English in schools. This trend may have an effect on viewers' preference for greater linguistic authenticity, as they are increasingly able to understand the original dialogue of English-language films. Other contemporary phenomena, such as the popularity of fan-subbing, the use of subtitles in mainstream films and the rise of the DVD with its

---

2 See Park (2008b).

choices of viewing modes, might have a similar influence on today's audience. In this study, the level of English amongst the test audiences and its impact upon their reception of a subtitled film as well as their understanding of successful wordplay translation was investigated.

The development described above is not only a potentially influential factor regarding the future of subtitling and its acceptance amongst German speakers, but could, in turn, exacerbate English-language comprehension amongst German viewers. This, then, constitutes a crucial element in the transparency of subtitling as a method of audiovisual translation, and the resulting accountability – the opportunity for viewers to assess the translation by comparing both texts – of the translator (cf. Gottlieb 1994: 268). The overall question remains, therefore, whether the transparency of subtitles as a method – combined with the factor of increasing audience comprehension – is more influential in the reception of a comedy translation than its potential to make viewers laugh.

Although translation can be regarded as a service for the benefit of the user / recipient, research in translation studies is more often than not of a descriptive, rather than experimental, nature (see Fuentes Luque 2003: 293). It is important to assert the significance of a contribution to the (as yet rather underrepresented) receptor-oriented approach to the discipline by conducting a study which focuses on the reception of a translation by the very people for which it is commissioned: the audience. Such projects do not only complement descriptive, text-oriented research but can establish a stronger link between the academic field of translation studies and the translation or audiovisual translation industries, who can then incorporate its findings into contemporary practice.

4 Intersemiotic Interference

As Díaz Cintas and Remael (2007: 45) point out, audiovisual translation is mostly characterised by the semiotic complexity of the text that is translated, where several sign systems co-operate to create a coherent story. It should be pointed out that "the relationship between the different channels in translated film media is first and foremost an issue for the subtitler and the viewers" (Schröter 2005: 39). It is true that the nature of audiovisual texts as polysemiotic entities has implications for the viewer as well as the translator. Due to the additive nature of subtitles, which means that subtitles are added to the existing sign systems without replacing the source text (which is therefore available at all times), there is an ever-present "dual gap" in film subtitling. This gap exists not just between two groups of recipients (the "home" audience and the target audience), but also between the two modes of reception – listening to the source text (SL) dialogue and reading the target text (TL) dialogue (Gottlieb 1997: 211). Depending on the degree to which the target audience can comprehend the source language, this may lead to interference between the two: the so-called *feedback effect*, which can be either an advantage or a problem for the subtitler. As verbal humour "highlights the interplay between the [...] semiotic systems of the medium" – the synchronicity of word and image can be the basis of a joke, as can the interplay between spoken and written language (Linde and Kay 1999: 13). This acts as a restrictive factor for the subtitler faced with the need for a creative solution.

It becomes clear from these theoretical considerations that, based on the unique situation in which the source and target text can be directly compared, subtitles incorporate a type of accountability which is not inherent in any other form of translation. Any translation that differs noticeably from what is said in the original dialogue could be perceived as a "breach of reference" (Pedersen 2009: 35) or indeed an "authenticity problem" (Gottlieb 1994: 269), if the difference is perceived and identified by the viewer. This "intersemiotic feedback" is based on audience comprehension but also refers to the interference of the visual code with the written text (Gottlieb 1997: 219). The nature of subtitled film as a combination of the two could give such a collision between two semiotic channels enough influence to "render a more idiomatic, domesticated rendering counterproductive" (Gottlieb 1997: 268). Therefore, the question was investigated whether this is true for comedy, where a transfer which on the surface looks to be appropriate to a non-expert audience is likely to be unsuccessful from a perspective of humour transfer (as the translator is often required to take advantage of the full comic potential of the target language, which may involve a diversion from the source text surface structure). The likelihood that a translation which prioritises humorous effect and therefore foregoes formal equivalence wherever necessary will achieve a mixed or even negative reception by the target audience is higher in the event that a large part of the audience is able to understand the source language. It was therefore of great interest to see whether or not there is a correlation between a viewer's knowledge of English and their reception of a subtitled comedy film.

5 Methodology

For the purpose of this experiment, the existing translation as used for the dubbed rendition was converted into a subtitled version (**Ex**isting Version). In order to do this, most of the dialogue was retained but condensed in places where this was required due to the space and time constraints associated with subtitling as a method of audiovisual translation. Following this, an alternative translated version was produced and also made into a subtitle file (**Alt**ernative Version).[3] Both sets of subtitles were identical in terms of size, font, timing and segmentation. An un-subtitled version of the film was also used in the experiment as a basis for comparison (**Group CG**). The audience was given a questionnaire to express their reaction. The two subtitled versions were taken to Germany and shown to two separate heterogeneous groups of native German speakers (**Group Alt** and **Group Ex**), whose reaction was also assessed in a questionnaire. Group Alt consisted of 29 people, whilst Group Ex contained a total of 30 participants. A between-group design of the experiment was chosen in order to circumvent the element of comparison – viewers were to assess the film as a stand-alone work rather than one version of several. The process of screening the different versions of the test film to the relevant participants was kept as similar as possible for all three groups.

Both versions of the questionnaire included a general section on age and gender, as well as a set of questions which focused on the reception of the film, specifically in terms of humour. Participants were asked to assign the film to a genre, rate its suitability for specific age groups, specify the elements of the film that most appealed to them and express their opinion on its quality as a humorous film. The German questionnaire additionally included a section focussing on English language proficiency, as well as a question regarding the reception of the subtitles as such and their translation from English.

One of the main methodological challenges of the experiment was assessing the ability of the German audiences to comprehend the original English dialogue. After careful consideration of the options, it was concluded that the method of assessing participants' English to a sufficiently reliable degree would have to be designed specifically to fit the requirements of the experiment. The objective was to gauge their overall language proficiency on the basis of their learning history and habits of language use, as these are variables which can be

---

[3] For a detailed analysis of both versions, too elaborate for a paper of this scope, see Schauffler (2012).

self-assessed relatively objectively and expressed in time duration and frequencies. Within the field of second language acquisition (SLA), much research has gone into the identification of influencing factors which affect its progress.[4] Based on the assumption that an assessment of these factors allows conclusions regarding a person's learning history, with the aim of arriving at an impression regarding their L2 proficiency, a set of five questions was developed which take these influences into consideration: formal tuition, extent of L2 use, length of residency in an English-speaking environment, as well as attitude / confidence. Together these questions made up the second part of the German-language questionnaire; the responses were quantified to form a score between zero and twenty-five which reflects the participants' individual situation regarding English as a second language and therefore the variable *Level of English*.

A similar system was developed for the variable *Humour Reception*. In this case, answers to the question in the relevant section corresponded to points between 0 and 5, in the order they appeared in the questionnaire. In the case of the *Humour Reception* variable, the quantification is slightly more complex. The questions which formed a part of this variable were the ones which dealt with participants' reception of the film, with a particular focus on the reaction to linguistic humour. They include questions regarding genre assignment, targeted age range, specific appeal, and assessment of "funniness." Scores range from a maximum of five points for positive reception, to a score of zero for a response which suggests an indifferent or negative reaction to the humour in the film. Values between zero and five were given to individual answers but also to combinations of answers where it was possible to give more than one response. Together they add up to a score of between zero and twenty.

6 Data Analysis

The independent variables in the experiment are constituted by the three different groups for the test screenings. These were heterogeneous in terms of age, gender, and – in the case of the German-speaking groups – the level of English. Therefore, the variables *Age, Gender* and *Level of English* are extraneous variables, with the variable *Humour Reception* being a dependent (or outcome) variable. Due to the fact that the selection of participants was random, the author's

---

[4] See, e.g., Krashen (1985); Schumann (1986); Flege (1987); Gass and Selinker (1994); Piske, MacKay and Flege (2001); Guichon and McLornan (2007).

hypothesis was that the groups were balanced for all three extraneous variables, which means that there are no significant differences regarding the variables *Age* and *Gender* in all three groups, as well as regarding *Age*, *Gender* and *Level of English* in the two German-speaking groups (see figures and tables).

Tab. 2: Treatment * gender cross tabulation

		Gender		Total
		female	male	
Treatment	Group Alt	12	17	29
	Control Group	14	16	30
	Group Ex	15	15	30
Total		41	48	89

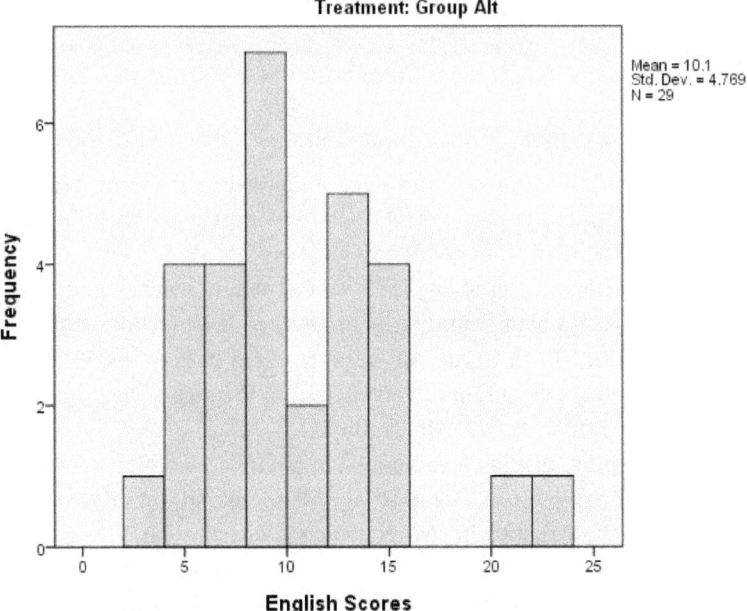

Fig. 1: English scores in Group Alt

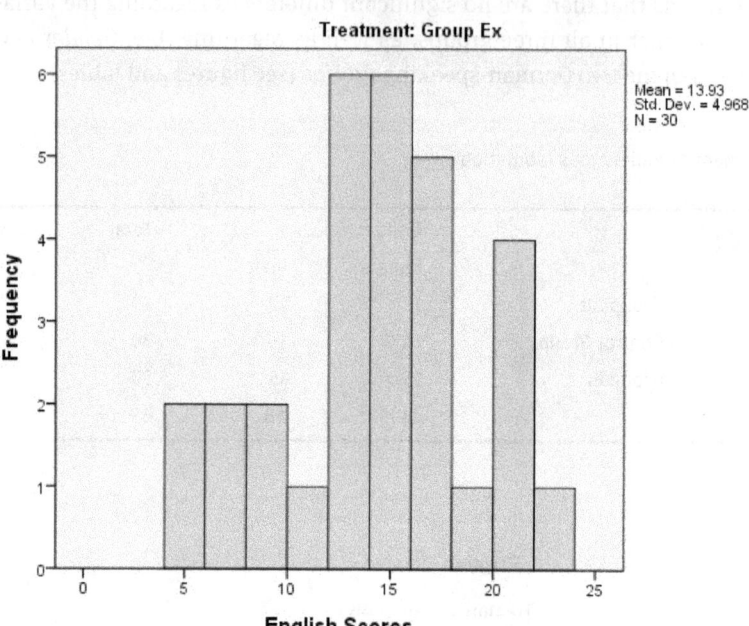

Fig. 2: English scores in Group Ex

For the extraneous variables *Gender* and *Age*, statistical tests (Mann Whitney test (p = 0.547) / chi-square test (p = 0.833)) showed no significant difference between groups, which means that gender and age are not significant variables across the groups. As far as *Level of English* is concerned, however, there was a difference. Group Ex had a significantly higher average level of English (mean score 13.93 compared to 10.1 in Group Alt, t-test resulted in p = 0.0038). Note, however, that the standard deviation (divergence from the mean) was similar in both groups (4.769 in Group Alt, 4.968 in Group Ex).

The histograms below display a difference in average reception scores between the groups (a mean score of 15.9 in Group Alt compared to 13.83 in Group Ex), while at the same time displaying a divergence in distribution. The distribution in Group Alt is relatively homogenous, with a standard deviation of 2.425, while the range of responses in Group Ex is more varied, with a standard deviation of 4.921. The English-speaking control group obtained the highest mean score (16.93) with regards to *Humour Reception*, followed by Group Alt (15.9) and then Group Ex (13.83). The result of a t-test shows a significant difference in humour reception between the two German-speaking groups (p = 0.04624). With regard to the control group there is a significant difference between the average score for the humour reception of this group and that of Group Ex (p = 0.0109) but there is no significant difference between the means of the Control Group and Group Alt (p = 0.2469). Not only was there a significant difference in humour reception between the experimental groups, one of them was similar in response to the control group while the other one was significantly different.

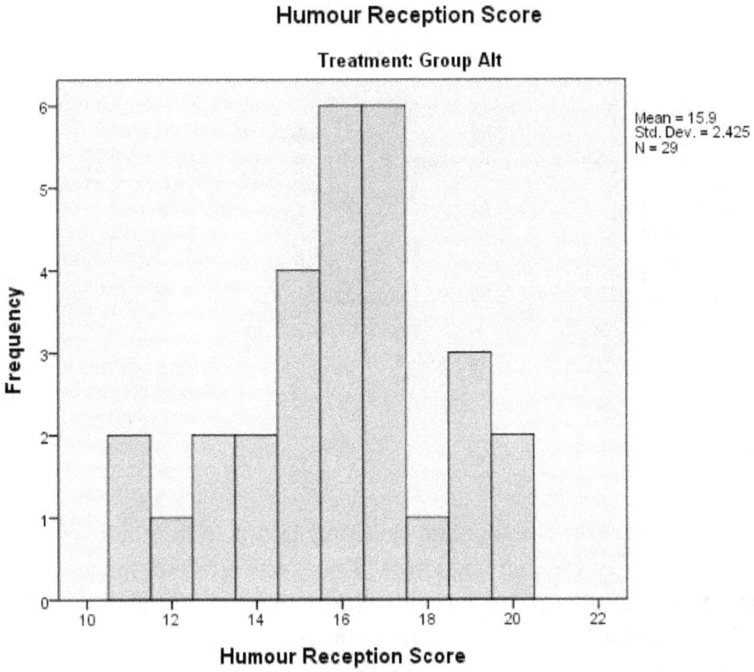

Humour Reception Score
Treatment: Group Alt

Mean = 15.9
Std. Dev. = 2.425
N = 29

Fig. 3: Humour reception in Group Alt

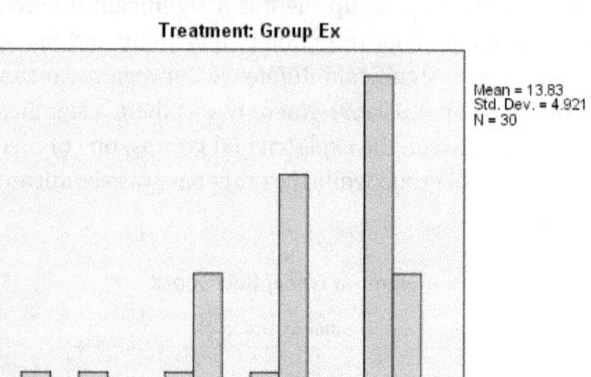

Fig. 4: Humour reception in Group Ex

This means that, comparing the German-speaking groups to the control group, the linguistic humour in the film had virtually the same effect on the audience with one translation approach, but a significantly different effect with the other approach: The humour inherent in the test film received a significantly more positive reaction in Group Alt than in Group Ex. The translation approach based on equivalence of effect evoked a more positive reaction on the whole, in comparison to the approach based on the transfer of information.

Evidently, it was necessary to rule out any interference from the extraneous variables by ruling out correlations, firstly between *Age* and *Humour Reception*. A Spearman's correlation test showed no significant relationship between the variables in two groups (Group Alt: $p = 0.217$, Group CG: $p = 0.225$). In Group Ex the two variables were correlated ($p = 0.000$), meaning that the null hypothesis is rejected. In this group, as age increased, the humour reception score decreased. The fact that this was only the case in one group suggests that this correlation was not due to filmic elements such as the animation technique (which might have been less appealing to older viewers), but rather to group-internal factors.

A Mann-Whitney test for a correlation between *Gender* and *Humour Reception* showed no significant relationship between the two variables *Gender* and *Humour Reception* in any of the groups (Group Alt: p = 0.875, Group Ex: p = 0.061, Control Group: p = 0.702). This means that a participant's gender did not exert any influence on their reception of the film, and any difference between the groups in terms of humour reception is not due to this variable.

A Spearman's correlation for both groups with a correlation coefficient of 0.570 showed that there was a positive correlation between *Level of English* and *Humour Reception* in Group Ex (enjoyment of humour increased while knowledge of English increased), while the p-value of 0.001 proved that this correlation is significant. This was not the case in Group Alt (correlation coefficient 0.089, p = 0.310), which means that in Group Ex, the viewing experience was influenced significantly by the viewers' ability to understand English, while in the case of the alternative translation approach the enjoyment of the film was more independent of source text comprehension. In addition to the non-parametric Spearman's correlation, a parametric test was run in order to support this result. A linear model for the variables *Humour Reception* and *Level of English* obtained the following results: In Group Alt there is no correlation between the two variables (p = 0.669), in Group Ex, however, the linear model produced a significant positive correlation between the level of English of a person and the extent to which they found the film funny (p = 0.008). Consequently, the result from the parametric test confirmed the result from the non-parametric Spearman's correlation: the relationship between the variables *Humour Reception* and *Level of English* is significant only in Group Ex.

The data analysis showed that the function-oriented translation to which Group Alt was exposed was received significantly better than the existing version which prioritised formal equivalence. This is the case regardless of the viewer's age, gender, or level of English. Consequently, the appeal of the translation which aimed to maintain the multi-layered nature of the linguistic humour in the film is broader. Older viewers (including people over the age of 65) were able to appreciate the film to an equal extent as younger members of the audience. This is especially relevant in light of the fact that the official German translation of the feature was broadcast on a children's channel and marketed as appealing to a young audience only. At the same time, source text comprehension was not required for the enjoyment of the humour in this group (Group Alt). Participants who relied on the subtitles found the film no less humorous than those viewers whose English was good enough to follow the original text.

Similarly, there was no significant difference between this group and the control group as far as humour reception was concerned. This result means that humour reception was uninfluenced by source language comprehension in this group, but also and especially that the reception of the subtitled version did not differ significantly from the reception of the original film by a native English-speaking audience.

However, when the translation approach was one of formal equivalence, as in Group Ex, the reception was significantly more negative. There was also a positive correlation between humour reception and level of English in that group, meaning that those viewers who were more proficient in English enjoyed it more than those who had only a basic or poor understanding of the original dialogue. It follows from this result that the appreciation of the linguistic humour required the ability to understand the English text. The results from the statistics suggested that this version of the film was considered funnier by younger members of the audience than by older viewers (the variables *Humour Reception* and *Age* are negatively correlated in Group Ex), suggesting that the more sophisticated, adult-oriented humour is not transferred as well into German as was the case in the alternative version. Furthermore, there was a significant difference between the humour reception in this group and the control group of English speakers.

7 Conclusion

At the beginning of this project, the question was asked whether the approach which is predominantly employed in Europe for the translation of wordplay (Schröter 2005) is indeed received favourably by audiences. It was explored, additionally, whether source language comprehension amongst viewers would stand in the way of a successful transfer, should an alternative approach be pursued in the classic dilemma of form versus effect.

The data analysis showed that the function-oriented translation was received significantly better than the existing version which prioritised formal equivalence. What is more, for the function-oriented translation only, there was no significant difference in reception to the English-speaking audience. When the translation approach was one of formal equivalence, on the other hand, the reception was significantly more negative than in both other groups. Furthermore, there was also a positive correlation between humour reception and level of English in that group, meaning that those viewers who were more proficient at English enjoyed it more than those who had only a basic or poor understanding of the original dialogue.

The main finding, however, to come forth from this project is the difference in audience reception depending on the approach employed by the translator. If we concur that for a translation to be successful the reaction of its receptor should be as similar as possible as that of the original receptor, this means that the approach used for the translation of wordplay in Group Ex is less successful than the translation approach used in Group Alt. Any feedback effect from the source text dialogue, potentially caused by the relative divergence between SL and TL in humour translation, was not strong enough to affect viewers in their enjoyment of the film. The results from the quantitative analysis show that the adult-oriented humour and appeal were acknowledged and appreciated more if the translation approach was one of creative freedom and a focus on humour transfer.

The other highly relevant difference between the reception in both audiences is that the more positive reaction occurred regardless of the knowledge of English, whilst the formally equivalent translation resulted in a reception which was affected by source language comprehension. This suggests that an approach which prioritises equivalence of effect will receive a better reaction from a diverse audience, of which some parts will be highly proficient English speakers, while others concentrate mainly on the German subtitles. Both will appreciate the linguistic humour in a film, meaning that there is no interference from SL comprehension and therefore no valid reason for foregoing this positive reaction by choosing a more conservative approach for the translation of wordplay.

8 References

Chiaro, Delia. 1992. *The Language of Jokes: Analyzing Verbal Play*. London & New York: Routledge.
Chiaro, Delia. 2006. Verbally Expressed Humour on Screen: Reflections on Translation and Reception. In *The Journal of Specialised Translation* 6.
http://www.jostrans.org/issue06/art_chiaro.php (18 February 2015).
Chiaro, Delia. 2007. The Effect of Translation on Humour Response: The Case of Dubbed Comedy in Italy. In Yves Gambier, Miriam Shlesinger & Radegundis Stolze (eds.), *Doubts and Directions in Translation Studies*, 137–151. Amsterdam & Philadelphia: Benjamins.
Delabastita, Dirk. 1994. Focus on the Pun: Wordplay as a Special Problem in Translation Studies. *Target* 6(2). 223–243.
Delabastita, Dirk (ed.). 1996. Wordplay and Translation. *The Translator* 2(2).

Delabastita, Dirk (ed.). 1997. *Traductio: Essays on Punning and Translation*. Manchester: St. Jerome.

Díaz Cintas, Jorge & Aline Remael. 2007. *Audiovisual Translation: Subtitling*. Manchester: Kinderhook; New York: St. Jerome.

Flege, James Emil. 1987. A Critical Period for Learning to Pronounce Foreign Languages? *Applied Linguistics* 8(2). 162–177.

Fuentes Luque, Adrián. 2003. An Empirical Approach to the Reception of AV Translated Humour: A Case Study of the Marx Brothers "Duck Soup." Screen Translation. *The Translator* 9(2). 293–306.

Gass, Susan M. & Larry Selinker. 1994. *Second Language Acquisition: An Introductory Course*. Hillsdale & New York: Erlbaum.

Gottlieb, Henrik. 1994. Subtitling: People Translating People. In Cay Dollerup & Annette Lindegaard (eds.), *Teaching Translation and Interpreting*, vol. 2. Amsterdam & Philadelphia: Benjamins. 264–274.

Gottlieb, Henrik. 1997. You Got the Picture? On the Polysemiotics of Subtitling Wordplay. In Dirk Delabastita (ed.), *Traductio: Essays on Punning and Translation*, 207–232. Manchester: St. Jerome.

Guichon, Nicolas & Sinead McLornan. 2007. The Effects of Multimodality on L2 Learners: Implications for CALL Resource Design. *System* 36. 85–93.

Krashen, Stephen D. 1985. *The Input Hypothesis: Issues and Implications*. London: Longman.

Linde, Zoé de & Neil Kay. 1999. *The Semiotics of Subtitling*. Manchester: St. Jerome.

Park, Nick (dir.). 2008a. *Wallace and Gromit: A Matter of Loath and Death*. Bristol: Aardman Animations.

Park, Nick (dir). 2008b. *Wallace and Gromit: A Matter of Loath and Death* [Wallace & Gromit: Auf Leben und Brot]. Bristol: Aardman Animations.

Pedersen, Jan. 2009. Cultural Interchangeability: The Effects of Substituting Cultural References in Subtitling. *Perspectives 15(1). 30–48*.
http://www.tandfonline.com/doi/abs/10.2167/pst003.0 (17 July 2015).

Piske, Thorsten, Ian R. A. MacKay & James Emil Flege. 2001. Factors Affecting Degree of Foreign Accent in an L2: A Review. *Journal of Phonetics* 29(2). 191–215.

Raphaelson-West, Debra S. 1989. On the Feasibility of Translating Humor. *Meta* 34(1). 128–141.

Schauffler, Svea. 2012. *Investigating Subtitling Strategies for the Translation of Wordplay in Wallace and Gromit – An Audience Reception Study*.
Sheffield: University of Sheffield dissertation.
http://etheses.whiterose.ac.uk/2915/1/Schauffler_Ethesis.pdf (17 July 2015).

Schröter, Thorsten. 2005. Shun the Pun, Rescue the Rhyme? The Dubbing and Subtitling of Language-Play in Film. *New Voices in Translation Studies* 1.
http://www.iatis.org/index.php/publications/new-voices-in-translation-studies/item/382-issue-1-2005 (17 July 2015).

Schumann, John H. 1986. Research on the Acculturation Model for Second Language Acquisition. *Journal of Multilingual and Multicultural Development* 7(5). 379–392.

Vandaele, Jeroen. 2002. (Re)-Constructing Humour: Meanings and Means. *The Translator* 8(2). 149–172.

Vandaele, Jeroen. 2011. Wordplay in Translation. In Yves Gambier & Luc van Doorslaer (eds.), *Handbook of Translation Studies*, vol. 2, 180–183. Amsterdam & Philadelphia: Benjamins.

Monika Schmitz-Emans
Plays around Surfaces and Depths: Transitions between Two- and Three-Dimensionality Reflected by Wordplays and Puns

Abstract: In the following remarks about Lewis Carroll the focus does not lie on concrete strategies of playing with words. There are several important and multi-faceted academic contributions that deal with this topic. My leading interest is dedicated to the preconditions of wordplay in Carroll's texts, specifically in the *Alice* novels. According to my leading thesis, it was not least Dodgson, the mathematician, behind Carroll, the story-teller, who directed the wordplay. Mathematical concepts and ways of thinking can be regarded as an important background of Carroll's linguistic inventions. Metaphorically said: Mathematics provided the stage on which words played their games and roles. Eventually, in my paper I briefly compare Carroll and Lawrence Sterne; this comparison, however, only aims at explaining one thesis: the idea that mathematical concepts as structures – such as line, plane and space – can be of formative influence on literary imagination.

On more than one occasion and in more than one way, Carroll connects his passion for wordplay with mathematical topics. In *Euclid and His Modern Rivals* (1879), for instance, he invents a dialogue between Euclid and Minos, who is most probably chosen as a character for more than one reason: Minos's name sounds like *minus*, and he is associated with the labyrinth as a puzzle as well as with Hades, a world under the earth's surface.

Keywords: *Alice*, depth, geometry, language usage, Lawrence Sterne, Lewis Carroll, mathematics, naming, nominalist philosophy, surface, theatre, three-dimensionality, *Tristram Shandy*, two-dimensionality

1 On Surfaces and Depths

The double concept of *surfaces* and *depths* is linked with several topological models and metaphors that have been of formative influence on the process of interpreting man's relationship with reality as well as with himself. So, for instance, it is often associated with the difference between the visual appearance of human beings – as the respective person's *surface* – and the interior dimension of their selves (the parts situated *deep inside*). As is usually suggested in this context, we should not rely on *superficial* impressions neither with regard to characters nor to other objects that we experience visually. *Deeper meanings* and *deeper qualities* only reveal themselves when surfaces are transgressed or even ignored. In discourses about emotion, *superficial* attitudes are usually opposed to *deeper* inclinations or feelings. All these concepts derived from the opposition of surface and depth are – as might be expressed by an almost inevitable metaphor – *deeply* rooted in the principles of Western thinking.

Evidently, metaphors of surfaces and depths play a major role in the history of Western philosophy, especially in gnoseology, but also in ethics. This has been of crucial importance to the history of human experience, knowledge, and science. Leaving merely *superficial* experiences behind, the subject of experience – according to its own self-interpretation – tries to proceed to the *interior* of the objects of investigation and to achieve *deeper* insights. Many related metaphors refer to a common idea of knowledge and a concept of science that is derived from it: science being defined as a process of questioning the *inner nature* of things, of discovering *fundamental* rules and *basic* reasons, to explore where experience is *rooted*. The distinction between surfaces and depths certainly belongs to the most common and most influential space-metaphorical concepts as far as our self-understanding as subjects of experience and knowledge is concerned. In particular it was of crucial importance within the history of European philosophy and its self-interpretation: Traditional investigation for *reasons* is never satisfied with *superficial* knowledge. Metaphysicians investigate in causes for *foundations* that are situated *beyond the surface* of mere physical appearance and *exterior* signs. Although in modern philosophy the influence of metaphors on philosophical systems and the principles of this thinking has been revealed and discussed, there may be still no self-description of knowledge that can completely abstain from using metaphors connected with distinctions between (metaphorical) spaces *above* and spaces *deep down*, between *superficial* and *profound* concepts or realities.

Beyond the era of metaphysics, the *surface-depth*-distinction at least still serves as a device to explain the difference between traditional thinking and post-metaphysics: the post-metaphysical era reproaches the quest for *foundations* and ostentatiously turns its attentions to surfaces. Postmodernism objects to the suggestive concept of *profound* meanings and abstains from exploring any so-called *deeper reasons*. Post-structuralism does not intend to reveal *deep structures* anymore. The surface thus appears as the only depth. An interesting further perspective on the dichotomy of surfaces and depths emerges, if one regards it as reflected in or at least connected with the tension between two- and three-dimensionality. (In the light of Gilles Deleuze's considerations concerning *Le Pli* (1988), especially moments of transition between two- and three-dimensionality appear as aesthetically delightful and philosophically inspiring.)

The metaphorical notion of surfaces and depths is closely linked with space metaphors referring to geometrical space models, although in a sometimes ambiguous way. At first sight, one might be inclined to identify the dichotomy of *superficial* and *deep* structures with the dichotomy of two-dimensional and three-dimensional objects. Three-dimensional spatial objects, as it seems, have a *dimension of depth*, whereas surfaces are usually imagined as flat, two-dimensional entities, governed by only two coordinates. When the two-dimensional flat surface is extended to the *depth* of space, a world of bodies is constituted by this third coordinate.[1]

But surfaces are not at all necessarily flat, and already in traditional Euclidean geometry there are many different kinds of three-dimensional surfaces. To represent spatial objects visually usually means to represent them on two-dimensional flat planes: on sheets of paper, on painters' canvases. The art of representing spaces by means of perspective is mainly based on strategies of projecting spatial realities on flat surfaces and to create the illusion of three-dimensionality through two-dimensional objects. Different modernist artistic forms and strategies of visualization can be interpreted as examinations of the difference between flat planes and three-dimensional spaces. The works of René Magritte as well as of Maurits Cornelis Escher investigate the conditions and circumstances of creating spatial illusions on flat paper sheets – and, at the same time, they indicate their reflexive interest by creating meta-pictures. Both artists question the principle of illusionism in the visual arts, where imaginary spaces emerge from flat planes; planes that seem to revolt against their flatness. But, provokingly, both Magritte and Escher question and deconstruct the distinction between two- and three-dimensionality by using representation techniques that seem to be derived from this principle. Their images, flat representations of spaces beyond Euclidean geometry, ironically quote traditional concepts of space in order to subvert it: on the flat plane of their paper. I would like to use these notions and apply them to the *Alice* books (1865, 1871) of Lewis Carroll, whose strategy of referring to the world of planes and spaces, as I would

---

[1] In literary imagination, the common distinction between flat planes and spatial bodies has stimulated abundant inventions of worlds different from Euclidean space; Abbott's *Flatland* ([1884] 2006) world is based on distinctions different from the mathematical universe familiar to us.

like to show, may be compared with these works of visual art, as Carroll as well both quotes and deconstructs the difference between two- and three-dimensional realities.[2] It is not too much of a surprise that a mathematician who writes books about invented worlds develops an idea of spaces that appear as altered from a geometrical perspective.

In order to contextualize this kind of geometrical imagination, one has, however, to take into account that even planes in a mathematical sense do not necessarily have to be flat. In non-Euclidean spaces, planes bow and fold, and parallels intersect. The geometry of a sphere's surface as it is conceived of in so-called elliptic geometry illustrates this exemplarily. Here, the Euclidean laws are suspended: the added grades of triangles' corners are more than 180. The surrounding lines of circles are smaller than $2\pi R$, the area of a circle is smaller than π radius squared (πR^2). In general relativity theory, the geometry of cosmic space is modelled in accordance with non-Euclidean concepts. Gravitation fields *bend* the space.

Mathematical figures, structures and spaces can be of crucial importance to literary imagination and the worlds it creates. Lawrence Sterne's *Tristram Shandy* (1759–1767) has been regarded as resulting from a conflict between straight and crooked lines (cf. Müller 2012: 165–166). In the novel, these two types of lines are not only described in different variations, they also serve as rivalling structural models of narration and history. According to my thesis, to the worlds of Lewis Carroll's invention the distinction between two-dimensional planes and bended planes is of analogous importance as the opposition of straight and curved lines are to *Tristram Shandy*'s world. Similar to Sterne, who arranges conflicts between straight linear structures and curved lines, Carroll arranges conflicts and tensions between different types of *planes*, and thus between concepts and imaginations grounded in Euclidean geometry on the one hand, and non-Euclidean geometry on the other.

As a scholar of mathematics, Lewis Carroll – or rather: Charles Lutwidge Dodgson – participated in his contemporaries' discussions about the conflict between those two types of geometry; he even wrote a book dedicated to *Euclid and His Modern Rivals* (1879).[3] His scientific attitude toward Post-Euclidean

---

[2] My focus, accordingly, does not lie on concrete strategies of playing with words. For wordplay in the *Alice* books see, e.g., Spacks (1961); Holquist (1969); Sutherland (1970); Kreutzer (1984); see also Kullmann, this volume.
[3] Carroll wrote treatises about algebra and trigonometry (1860, 1861) as well as an introduction to mathematics for his students. In later years he published comments on Euclid ([1879]

geometry is conservative: he defends traditional mathematics. As a mathematician, Carroll-Dodgson lives – to put it that way – in a space where parallels never meet, because they extend themselves as straight lines in an infinite space, always at the same distance. But in his role as a supporter of Euclid he knows very well that there actually exist other kinds of mathematical theories and thus other imaginary mathematical spaces: spaces where the rules of traditional geometry are not valid anymore, where lines and planes behave differently from those in the old mathematical orbit, spaces where parallels meet and planes extend according to non-Euclidean rules. Dodgson's (that means: the traditionalist mathematician's) geometrical planes are – in a way – still flat. But he is aware of their tendency to bend, as far as other mathematical universes are concerned. And in Carroll's (the narrator's) literary text they properly do this.

As a literary writer, Carroll, by the way, also makes use of the concepts of *flatness* and *superficies* in their quality as rather conventional and familiar metaphors. In his critical-satirical texts he eventually plays with commonplace metaphorical ideas of *superficiality* in order to criticise his opponents or make them appear ridiculous; ironically, he describes their *superficiality* in mathematical terms. So in his satire about theologians, entitled "The New Method of Evaluation, as applied to π" he writes: "Let E=Essays, and R=Reviews; then the Locus of (E+R), referred to multilinear co-ordinates, will be found to be a superficies (i.e. a locus possessing length and breadth, but no depth)" (Taylor 1952: 66).[4] Thus playing with mathematical symbols and formulae, Carroll's satirical text scoffs at empty ceremonies and other kinds of formalism in clerical life, characterizing it as a kind of *superficial* rationalism lacking *deeper* sense.

In two letters to Agnes Hughes, Carroll invents a rather odd example of transforming three-dimensional objects into two-dimensional (flat) ones. The effect here is that these objects can be put into a portfolio, which is a kind of a book, after all. Thus, the reduction process from spatiality to flatness is associatively linked with the process of configuring the contents of books, i.e. of literary writing. The complementary process of transforming *flat* things into *bodies* thus would mean to revitalise literary objects of description by the power of

---

1973) and a two-volumed book entitled *Curiosa Mathematica* (1888 / 1893), followed by a work on *Symbolic Logic* (1896) (cf. Kleinspehn 1997: 36–39).

[4] Taylor's comment highlights the metaphorical sense of this passage: "In other words, the writers of *Essays and Reviews* were superficial. They lived in a world of only two dimensions, a superficies, or surface. This is a more mathematical form of the same idea which he expressed in the trial of the Knave of Hearts, who [...] could not swim, 'being made entirely of cardboard'" (Taylor 1952: 66).

imagination. In his first letter, Carroll tells about three cats sitting at his door and looking "so cross and disagreeable that I took up the first thing I could lay my hand on (which happened to be the rolling-pin) and knocked them all down as flat as pancakes!" (Carroll 1979: 160). In the following letter, we read:

> Of course, I didn't leave them [the cats] lying flat on the ground like dried flowers: [...] I picked them up, and I was as kind as I could be to them. I lent them the portfolio for a bed – they wouldn't have been comfortable in any real bed [...] – they were to thin – but they were *quite* happy between the sheets of blotting-paper – and each of them had a pen-wiper for a pillow. [...] I lent them the three dinner-bells, to ring if they wanted anything in the night.
>
> (Carroll 1979: 161)

2 Two- and Three-Dimensionality in Carroll's Worlds

In how far do flat and curved planes play a role in Carroll's worlds in a way that can be compared to the significance of straight and crooked lines in *Tristram Shandy*? Both in *Alice in Wonderland* and *Through the Looking-Glass* different kinds of planes are of crucial importance. Several times, Carroll depicts situations in which it either seems to be doubtful whether planes are actually only two-dimensional – or in which the idea of flat surfaces is obviously replaced in favour of images of curved and folded planes. Sometimes, superficies are explicitly imagined as body-like entities.

The difference between plane and space (as well as a tendency to level out this difference) is already focussed on by the framing constructions of both the *Wonderland* and the *Looking-Glass* narrative (cf. Carroll [1996] 1998: 9–120, 121–250). So, it already appears to be essential for Alice's way to Wonderland at the beginning of the first *Alice* book: falling down the rabbit-hole, she plunges into an unfamiliar deep space, but, as it seems, she finally arrives at a surface – in the world of the antipodes (as she suspects – but which turn out to be Wonderland). She calls them by a wrong name ("antipathies" ([1996] 1998: 17) instead of *antipodes*) – this pun was, however, only added to the original text (*Alice's Adventures Under Ground* (1863)) when the printed version of Carroll's book was prepared. Obviously, Carroll was interested in situating the story in the antipodes' world, which means: on the other side of the globe's surface, not (as the original version suggested) just somewhere *deep down*. Or rather: the episodes following to Alice's strange journey will take place *deep down, on a sur-*

face – an idea that already confounds commonplace thinking in opposite terms of flatness and spatiality.

Through the Looking-Glass, Carroll's second *Alice* novel, is shaped by ideas that even intensify this confusing effect. The events are situated on a giant chessboard, in a seemingly flat topography. Playing a game of chess has several symbolic meanings that can be related to Carroll's story. With regard to the issue of planes and spaces it should be stressed that chessboard games are based on rules that can be described in terms of distinction between two- and three-dimensionality: Most of the chess pieces are restricted by these rules to move along on the flat chessboard step by step – they are *flatlanders*. Others, however, are characterized by movements that resemble jumps: they can leave the plane and *fly* through the space above the flat playing field, thus reaching their next position more quickly. For the hierarchy between the chess pieces, the destination of *flatlanders* and *space-travellers* is crucial, and thus the flatness of the chessboard is eventually related to all the distinctions the chess game is based on. And, of course, in *Through the Looking-Glass* there is also another plane object which is literally as well as metaphorically essential for the narrative's plot: Alice enters the Looking-Glass world through a mirror. Mirrors as such are a very special species of surface: Reflecting the world in front of their glass surface, they de-stabilize the difference between two-dimensional and three-dimensional realities in an intricate way. Mirrors suggest that there is a space *behind* them, although – or rather: because – they are flat.[5]

As Angelika Zirker (2010: 84) points out, Alice in *Through the Looking-Glass* initially seems to run in a circular movement and to move around a globe.[6] The

---

5 In a way, they produce imaginary spaces, because they are flat. In Alice's case such a space is actually opened up when she passes through the mirror as a threshold. But is it a real space (which is indicated by the subsequent episodes) – or is it an imaginary one? Is the third dimension behind the plane nothing but illusionary? This ambiguity shapes all the following adventures. We might compare the quality of mirrors producing imaginary spaces by the means of flat superficies to the art of writing literary fiction. Here as well imaginary worlds emerge out of flat planes: paper sheets covered with texts take on the part of the mirror.

6 In her book *Der Pilger als Kind*, Zirker argues consequently in the sense of her thesis (presented at the beginning of her study) that Alice's story invites the reader to return into an original world of play and childhood ("in eine ursprüngliche Welt des Spiels und der Kindheit"; 2010: 1). Her investigation in practices of wordplay is subordinated to this concept of revisiting a space of original infancy. My argument, however, follows another trace, supposing that Carroll's attitude toward concepts of childhood is sentimental (*sentimentalisch*) and reflexive to a degree that appears incompatible with the metaphysical notion of "origin." In a world in which time can be reversed, there is no difference between chronological origins and *consequences*; and the idea of *foundation* as such is suspended when *reasons* follow their *conse-*

chessboard, on which the events of *Through the Looking-Glass* take place, is associated with a flat plane, but it turns out to be part of the *global* world in which one can return to the beginning after a circular run. Constructing his imaginary worlds, Carroll seems to keep the difference between flatness and spatiality permanently in mind – not only with regard to the places in which the episodes are situated, but also concerning the characters. In Wonderland, most of the figures involved in the events are playing-cards: flat objects move around like three-dimensional entities. Thus, behaving like spatial bodies, they may, however, still lie down on the flat ground in order to hide; to the Queen they become invisible as soon as they act the way two-dimensional objects usually *behave*. The episodes that take place on the chessboard behind the mirror in Carroll's second *Alice* book are also characterized by permanent cross-overs between two- and three-dimensionality: The characters are distinguished from each other by the mentioned chess rules, according to which some chess pieces are forced to move along on the chessboard plane –, whereas other players (queens and knights) are free to leave their ground temporarily and proceed faster than the others. One might argue that the story itself is based on the distinction between *flatlanders* and more mobile characters. According to Alexander Taylor's comprehensive study about *The White Knight*, the White Knight (who was often interpreted as Carroll's own intradiegetic double) moves around between the flat world of other characters and Alice's spatial world: "He represents a stage half-way between the Queens, who are *flatlanders* pure and simple, and Alice, who is a child or Human Being" (1952: 112). It is evidently this borderline existence that causes his awkwardness, but also his exceptional status: As a chess knight he is allowed to move both horizontally and vertically. (Alice once reminds herself of this rule, when she remembers a chess party played the day before.) As Taylor stresses, the knight's experiments are all con-

---

quences. Originality and authenticity can thus be only subjects of quoting. *Childhood* as such (as it is depicted in the *Alice* books) is an artificial construct derived from Rousseauism, and all plays and games are constitutive of constructed worlds rather than being linked with *origins*, *sources* and *nature*. Playing is the very epitome of following rules and regulations that were set up by the mind in order to create artificial realities. The world of mathematics (of mathematical figures, formula and operations) as well as the world of verbal signs are constitutive of artificial worlds based on rules and intelligible structures. In the strange worlds which Alice experiences, numbers and formula, ideas and concepts (such as *mirroring*, i.e. *reflection*) rule over *nature*; animals are derived from composite words, and verbal expressions determine how *nature* functions. Formula and signs taken from language and from mathematics serve as models for worlds constructed by man and form the basis of human cultural practice and construction beyond *nature*.

nected with new or extraordinary experiences of space (cf. Taylor 1952: 113): All his inventions thus seem to question the difference between two- and three-dimensional objects and realities.[7]

After having crossed the chessboard (which, naturally, is supposed to be flat) Alice arrives at a door which, as it seems, is both front and back door. Has she been moving on a circular path, so that starting point and end are congruent? Has the chessboard plane bended in order to lead Alice back to the beginning of her way? If the chessboard is a *world*, doesn't it have to be a globe? Actually, John Tenniel depicted the chessboard as a plane extending into a vast horizon, covering clearly enough more than eight lines and alluding to perspective representation of the globe (cf. Carroll [1996] 1998: 149). Alexander Taylor describes the world of the chess pieces as a sphere, whose inhabitants probably still believe that their world is flat, because they do not know any better – just like people in the Middle Ages did, ignoring or, rather, being unaware of the fact that they inhabited a globe.[8]

Evidently, Carroll as a story-teller playfully explores different semantic levels of the opposition of surfaces and spatial objects, flat and curved planes – as of a subject that he also alludes to in his mathematical and logical treatises and lesson books.[9] In a way, bodies and surfaces are the main protagonists in his

---

[7] Cf. Taylor (1952: 114–116). The knight's tendency to expand from planes into spaces might, by the way, be compared to the extension of one-dimensional phenomena such as lines into the two-dimensional plane – as it happens, when linear narration turns into a curved line at the occasion of "The Mouse's Tale" (Chapter 3, *Alice's Adventures in Wonderland*).

[8] The looking-glass queens, as Taylor (1952: 107) puts it, live on "a surface which was actually curved": "[T]heir world is no more flat than ours. Like the people of the Middle Ages, they are on a globe and do not know it" (Taylor 1952: 106). Generally, medieval worlds are alluded to ironically by the social structures in Wonderland and the Looking-Glass-Land.

[9] Carroll's book *Game of Logic* (1886) deserves special mention here: "Carroll has no desire to enter into controversy with logicians who operate according to their own quite separate arrangements; that is their prerogative, no matter how little we approve, no matter what the consequences: 'Let us not quarrel with them, dear Reader! There is room enough in the world for both of us. Let us quietly take our broader system: and; if they choose to shut their eyes [...] we can but stand aside, and let them Rush into their Fate!' (*GL*, p. 36). Carroll's own procedure is to present not a series of facts, but a series of agreements for the reader to enter into (*GL*, pp. 5, 37). He proposes certain 'universes.' These encompass all members of a certain class, which may be imagined as occupying each 'cupboard,' or square on the board (which is very like a playing board); a counter is used to signal such occupation (or nonoccupation). So we might have a 'Universe of Cakes,' a 'Universe of Lizards,' a 'Universe of Hornets.' ('Wouldn't *that* be a charming Universe to live in?' *GL*, pp. 6–7). And just because a particular universe is not known on our planet, says Carroll, this does not disqualify it from possible existence on some other. For example, in the case of the 'Universe of Dragons,' he reminds us: 'Remember, I

Alice stories, and the female protagonist's adventures illustrate the difficulties connected with the attempt to distinguish between two- and three-dimensional worlds. Especially surfaces that are not simply *flat* cause severe irritations – as for instance the mushroom's hat in the caterpillar episode, because it does not allow to distinguish "one side" and "the other side" (cf. Carroll [1996] 1998: 53–54). There are other dazzling spatial structures, too, for example spiral shaped paths, and the White Knight's armament.

In a similar manner, Alice's physical metamorphosis after eating the cake can be described as a metamorphosis of her surface: Her feet become distant objects, when she is getting longer like a telescope. There is a direct correspondence between the transformation of Alice's surface and the genesis of portmanteau words: in one case there is a modification of shape by extension, in the other case a modification by *shortening* the original object; extension and shortening are complementary processes of surface manipulation, and it may depend on perspective (on the *telescope*!) how a metamorphosis is interpreted.

The problem of identifying characters is connected with the experience of surfaces on different levels: how can we distinguish between two beings whose surfaces are alike? And how *identical* is somebody whose surface is submitted to metamorphorical change? Alice's extension and contraction can be described as the transformation of her surface. It therefore eventually appears at least sometimes doubtful whether there is something that defines an identity *deep inside*, a true Alice beyond the superficial body shape.

Put generally, the plays performed in Carroll's *Alice* books symbolize life as such – and in this respect both narratives are associated with plane objects: with playing cards on the one hand, and with a chessboard on the other. In the Wonderland world, whose inhabitants are *flat* characters, individuals can hide themselves by lying on the flat ground (they disappear from sight as a consequence of their lack of a third dimension), and identities can be manipulated by changing the colour of surfaces. The world generated by a looking-glass is evidently a *flat* world, consisting of nothing but reflections on a flat surface. But even when Alice enters a (spatial) world *behind* the looking-glass, Carroll links her adventures with a flat plane again: with the chessboard that determines all episodes.

---

don't guarantee the Premisses to be *facts*. In the first place, I never even saw a Dragon: and, in the second place, it isn't of the slightest consequence to us, as *Logicians*, whether our Premisses are true or false: all *we* have to make out is whether they *lead logically to the Conclusion*, so that, if *they* were true, *it* would be true also' (*GL*, p. 25)" (Blake 1974: 69–70; cf. also Carroll [1895] 1958: 1–19, 25, 36, 37–39).

There is especially one kind of *plane* which Carroll's episodes in both narratives often indirectly refer to: the theatre stage as a specific playing ground. The concept of the world as a stage has been of formative influence on Carroll's world view, and his *Alice* stories can be read as narratives about different kinds of *world theatre performances* – different kinds also in the sense of different categories of performing –, as narratives about *playing roles*, about *acting as*, about defining oneself via disguises and masks. Not only in the English-speaking world, Shakespeare's works can be regarded as the dominant reference for the world-as-as-stage concept.[10] And it was characteristic of Shakespearean theatre that for the performing actors there was barely more than a flat stage to play on – a plane from which they created a *space* in more than one sense – a *globe*, as Shakespeare's theatre was called programmatically. As Shakespeare specialists have pointed out, the transformation of the stage into a 'space' mainly depended on words; it was language that compensated the absence of spatial objects and markers.[11]

Another interesting concept that is related to one-, two- and three-dimensional structures is the "knot," which is serving as a model in *A Tangled*

---

10 See also Kullmann, this volume.
11 "Es wird unentwegt geredet, und das Wort übernimmt Funktionen, die im modernen Theater durch das Spiel des Schauspielers wahrgenommen oder durch außersprachliche theatralische Codes – beispielsweise durch die Beleuchtungsregie – zum Ausdruck gebracht werden. Das Wort malt nicht nur Räume aus, sondern es unterstützt und ergänzt auch sonst die sinnliche Wahrnehmung. [...] der Dialogtext [beschreibt] oft nicht nur Dinge, die auf der Bühne gar nicht vorhanden sind und daher durch die Imagination vermittelt werden müssen, sondern auch solche, die Teil des realen Bühnenvorgangs sind: das Aussehen von Personen, ihren Gesichtsausdruck und ihre Gemütsverfassung, ihre Verhaltensweise und sogar ihre Handlungen." [There is constant talking, and the word takes up a position, which is recognized by the actor's play or expressed by extralinguistic theatric codes in Modern Theatre – such as lighting technique. The word does not only fill in the room, but supports and increases sensual perception. [...] Often, the dialog does not only [describe] things, which are not presented on stage and therefore must be imparted through imagination, but also such which are part of the stage acting: the characters' appearance, their facial expression and state of mind, their behaviour and even their actions.] (Suerbaum 1996: 60). – "Die Notwendigkeit, vieles mit Hilfe der Sprache zu machen, was unter anderen Bühnenverhältnissen mit außersprachlichen Mitteln vom Mienenspiel bis zum Scheinwerfer bewerkstelligt wird, führt [...] bei Shakespeare zu der Neigung, den gesamten dramatischen Vorgang dem Text einzuverleiben und dessen Funktionen über das bühnentechnisch erforderliche Maß auszudehnen." The necessity of creating many things with the help of language, which is done with extralinguistic devices from facial expression to lightning under different circumstances, leads [...] Shakespeare to the point of incorporating the whole dramatic action in the text and enlarging its functions beyond the required proportion of stage technology.] (Suerbaum 1996: 61–62).

Tale (Carroll [1996] 1998: 833–969). The expression "knot" not only refers to puzzles, but also to *knots* of files (which are, mathematically spoken, *lines*, i.e. one-dimensional structures, but can form figures situated on planes (for instance, mathematical figures like triangles). A file forming a knot is actually a spatial object.[12] "A Mouse's Tale" (cf. Carroll [1996] 1998: 35) is equally linked with a passage through different dimensions: Firstly, as a *tail* as well as a *tale*, it can be regarded as a line, i.e. as a two-dimensional object. Extending itself on the printed page, it, secondly, becomes a part of a flat surface, a surface however, that can be bent by turning the page. And moreover, the poem's shape may be associated with a way *down* into the depths of space, into an abyss, into death even – corresponding to its content.[13]

3 Language 'surfaces': The Nominalist Concept of Words as Labels or Tags

Since antiquity, metaphors derived from the concept of surfaces and depths have been used to characterize language and the relation between verbal signs and their denotation. According to a suggestive metaphorical image, verbal expressions are surfaces of meanings that are located *behind* them. As part of knowledge theories, traditional language philosophy asks for the *profound* reasons, the *foundations* to naming things. Plato's dialogue *Cratylus* is the most prominent example – and it stimulated many followers. In Platonism, words in their quality as sensually perceived signs were regarded as indicators referring to ideas, but not ontologically linked with their meanings.[14] Ancient rhetoric and philosophy both are characterized by a fundamental suspicion concerning what was regarded as *verbal surfaces*; words and verbal constructions are dis-

---

12 Zirker refers to Carroll's comment on Knot VI, in which he characterizes the first problem as "a mere *jeu de mots*" (cf. Carroll [1996] 1998: 953; Zirker 2010: 137n85).
13 Cf. Zirker 2010: 321: "die Form des Gedichts bildet einen Gang in die Tiefe und damit ins Totenreich ab." ["The poem's shape illustrates a way into the depths and therefore to the realm of the dead"].
14 Plato ([1926] 1996: 428d), cf. Gill (1993: 52); Genette (1976). – Carroll scholar Peter Heath refers to *Cratylus* when he comments on Humpty Dumpty: "Ever since the issue between *phusis* and *nomos* (nature and law, or custom) was first fully joined in Plato's *Cratylus*, dissension has continued between those who believe that the meaning of words are rooted in the nature of things, and those who see them as a product of human choice and convention" (Heath 1974: 192).

cussed here as something that mediates ideas and arguments on the one hand, but on the other hand covers them like a piece of cloth covering a body. The metaphor of clothes often appears in reflections about the way in which ideas are verbally expressed. Rhetorical means traditionally appear as means of dressing up ideas, thoughts and concepts, and – according to this basic language-reflexive metaphor – the more beautiful or impressive the verbal dress, the more efficient is the argument.

Is there any *deeper* reason of names or of the act of naming itself? Whenever words are regarded as arbitrary signs that depend on conventions, they are modelled as a kind of tags – as something that is added to the surface of ideas and concepts in order to make them identifiable.[15] Especially in British nominalist philosophy, as it is represented by the language concepts of Berkeley and Locke, this way of reflecting the uses of words becomes crucial. From a nominalist perspective, the relationship between ideas and verbal signs has to be regarded as arbitrary: The words are attached to ideas like name tags. Locke regards the ideas as the immediate objects of thought.[16] Words are devices to express and communicate ideas, and they fulfil their function as long as there is a general consent about the correct way of labelling.

All ideas, however, exist prior to and independent of their naming. Locke's language theory explicitly stresses that ideas can be *tagged* or *labelled* appropriately, but also in inadequate ways. Reasonable uses of language are necessarily based on adequate labels, and verbal *labels* can and must sometimes be corrected. Inadequate labels, however, lead onto inappropriate paths of thinking. Berkeley argues analogously to Locke, as far as the function of words is concerned. His argument concentrates on the misunderstandings and false ideas caused by inadequate label uses. Here, Berkeley especially fights deceptive general terms and concepts[17]; he is deeply suspicious of metaphors, although his way of thinking is based on metaphors itself. In Locke's *Essay Concerning Human Understanding* (1690) as well as in Berkeley's *Treatise*

---

15 Siegfried J. Schmidt uses the term "*Etikettmodell*" ["tag model"] in order to characterize Locke's language philosophy (1968: 16). Cf. also Rauter (1970: 15–41, 42–66, 84–96).
16 Cf. John Locke ("Of Human Understanding," 4.1, § 1): "Since the mind, in all its thoughts and reasonings, hath no other immediate object but its own ideas, which it alone does or can contemplate; it is evident, that our knowledge is only conversant about them" ([1823] 1963: 308).
17 Cf. Rauter (1970: 50), referring to Berkeley: "Der einzig sichere Weg zur Erkenntnis ist die unmittelbare Betrachtung der eigenen Ideen. Das größte Hindernis auf dem Wege zur Erkenntnis ist die Sprache." ["The only certain way to cognition is the direct consideration of one's own ideas. The greatest obstacle on this way is language."].

Concerning the Principles of Human Knowledge (1710) several suggestive *surface* metaphors related to words and language occur – as for instance the metaphor of clothes (Berkeley describes the ideas without names as naked)[18] and the curtain metaphor (both Berkeley and Locke suggest the possibility of unveiling concepts beyond words). Using another similar metaphor, Locke compares people who have complex ideas without being able to name them properly, with book sellers who just offer loose paper sheets without a book binding that connects them. Books' covers are another kind of labels, and the lack of such labels stirs confusion of ideas and contents.[19] Both Locke and Berkeley admonish language users to avoid incorrect thinking in the consequence of non-systematic and uncontrolled labelling processes. Most severe warnings are addressed to those whose labels do not denote anything or who do not know what their words mean. In the course of his argument, Locke mentions several examples – one of which is the word "antipathy": the word Alice uses when she suspects that she is going to arrive at the antipodes.[20] (Carroll's use of the word "an-

---

18 Berkeley ("Introduction," § 24): "a man may with greater ease prevent his being imposed on by words. He that knows he has no other than particular ideas, will not puzzle himself in vain to find out and conceive the abstract idea annexed to any name. And he that knows names do not always stand for ideas, will spare himself the labour of looking for ideas, where there are none to be had. It were therefore to be wished that everyone would use his utmost endeavours, to obtain a clear view of the ideas he would consider, separating from them *all that dress and incumbrance of words* which so much contribute to blind the judgment and divide the attention. In vain do we extend our view into the heavens and pry into the entrails of the earth, in vain do we consult the writings of learned men and trace the dark footsteps of antiquity; we need only *draw the curtain of words*, to behold the fairest tree of knowledge, whose fruit is excellent, and within the reach of our hand" ([1710] 1998: 101; my italics).

19 "[H]e that has complex ideas, without particular names for them, would be in no better case than a bookseller, who had in his warehouse volumes that lay there unbound, and *without titles*; which he could therefore make known to others only by showing the loose sheets, and communicate them only by tale. This man is hindered in his discourse for want of words to communicate his complex ideas, which he is therefore forced to make known by an enumeration of the simple ones that compose them; and so is fain often to use twenty words, to express what another man signifies in one" (Locke [1823] 1963: 285–286; "Of Human Understanding," 3.10, § 27; my italics).

20 "To remedy the defects of speech before-mentioned to some degree, and to prevent the inconveniences that follow from them, I imagine the observation of these following rules may be of use, till somebody better able shall judge it worth his while to think more maturely on this matter, and oblige the world with his thoughts on it. [...] First, a man shall take care to use no word without a signification, no name without an idea for which he makes it stand. This rule will not *seem altogether needless to any one who shall take the pains to recollect how often he has met with such words, as instinct, sympathy, and antipathy*, &c. in the discourse of others, so

tipodes" may be regarded as an allusion addressed to readers that are familiar with Locke.)

In both *Alice* novels, surface concepts and language reflection are closely linked. There is a wordplay concerning surfaces to be found quite early in *Through the Looking-Glass*, which does not only refer to material surfaces but also to the superficiality of verbal expressions as they are not based on logic. The Red Queen explains to Alice: "I could show you hills, in comparison with which you'd call that a valley"; and Alice replies: "a hill *ca'n't* be a valley, you know. That would be nonsense –" (Carroll [1996] 1998: 149). Nonsense thus is derived from an improper way of referring to superficies.

Humpty Dumpty is, not by chance, just a surface (a curved one) – and he, who is so proud of his respectable appearance, perishes when this surface breaks, in accordance with the words of a nursery rhyme that anticipates this event. As an egg who reflects about verbal tags as surfaces Humpty Dumpty obviously tries to get behind *surfaces* – and thus violates different rules of language use as they are set up or confirmed by Locke and Berkeley, especially concerning the intended private uses of language. Egocentric and even contradictory, Humpty Dumpty's notions of words and language turn out to be rather *superficial*, thus corresponding to his own superficial existence which is not *grounded* but based on words.

Carroll himself argues in the sense of a *labelling concept* of names, when he writes in *Symbolic Logic*:

> I maintain that any writer of a book is fully authorised in attaching any meaning he likes to any word or phrase he intends to use. If I find an author saying, at the beginning of his book, "Let it be understood that by the word '*black*' I shall always mean '*white*,' and by the word '*white*' I shall always mean '*black*,'" I meekly accept this ruling, however injudicious I may think it. [...] I maintain that every writer may adopt his own rule, provided of course that it is consistent with itself and with the accepted facts of Logic.
>
> (Carroll [1895] 1958: 166; cf. Zirker 2010: 205)

---

made use of, as he might easily conclude, that those that used them had no ideas in their minds to which they applied them; but spoke them only as sounds, which usually served instead of reasons on the like occasions. Not but that these words, and the like, have very proper significations in which they may be used; but there being no natural connexion between any words and any ideas, these, and any other, may be learned by rote, and pronounced or writ by men who have no ideas in their minds to which they have annexed them, and for which they make them stand; which is necessary they should, if men would speak intelligibly even to themselves alone" (Locke [1823] 1963: 293–294; "Of Human Understanding": "Of the Remedies of the foregoing Imperfections and Abuses," 3.11, § 8; my italics).

Obviously, Carroll's interest in the tension between surfaces and depths as well as in the dichotomy of two-dimensional and three-dimensional surface models is motivated by his interest in language and language concepts. Already in the first episode of *Alice's Adventures in Wonderland*, the tag or label model is highlighted: when Alice falls through the rabbit hole, she is passing shelves and stacks, and one of them contains a jar labelled as a container of "marmalade" – but it does not contain marmalade, and thus it represents the idea of *false labels* on the surface (cf. Carroll [1996] 1998: 16). As a metonymy of *denomination* or *designation*, the false label here points to nominalist ideas about the nature and function of verbal expressions – and to the problem connected with nominalism: If words are arbitrary, how can they express *truths*? Carroll repeatedly confronts his protagonist with a typically nominalist problem properly after she has lost the ground under her feet in a literal sense. From now on, Alice will lose *ground* also metaphorically. Her way through the rabbit hole is depicted as a journey through a world of deceptive labels. While Alice is on her way to the *antipodes* (whom she also labels falsely, calling them "antipathies" like the people Locke criticizes) there is more than one reason to reflect upon the relation between names and the denominated ideas – as for instance the experience that sometimes the thinking subject is aware of some *idea* but cannot find the correct word to *label* it.

In the following episodes there are numerous allusions to the tag model as a concept of signifying and modifying the *surface metaphor*. Convention rules processes of *labelling*, and labels are hence unreliable. Alice's adventures are repeatedly centred on the idea that verbal signs are just arbitrary – and, moreover, instable. On different occasions and from different perspectives, Carroll's creatures discuss suggestions of *deeper* meanings. Their dialogues however reveal that there is no *deeper* reason for things to be called the way they are called. As the tragi-comical example of Humpty Dumpty illustrates, the idea of ruling verbal tags as it is related with the idea of their arbitrariness, is both the very epitome of self-confidence – and a tragic illusion.

As several episodes illustrate, there are no *deeper truths* to be gained from the examination of verbal surfaces. Homonyms, for instance, turn out to be the starting points of misunderstanding. Proper names are similarly intricate. On the one hand they are just arbitrary labels – but when somebody forgets his proper name (like Alice; see Chapter 3 in *Through the Looking-Glass*) he or she is in danger of losing the notion of being somebody with an identity. Changing one's name – even if it is only hypothetically – is a most dazzling experience, as Alice finds out when her label eventually seems to be "Mabel" (cf. Carroll, *Alice's Adventures in Wonderland*, Chapter 2: "The Pool of Tears," ([1996] 1998:

25)); and one might suspect that the similarity between "Mabel" and *label* is an intentional pun). Yet convention not only rules the meanings of word tags but also the categories words are submitted to. Here, the conventional distinction between proper names and general terms is crucial, and so is the distinction between positive signs and negative expressions. When a word like "nobody" is interpreted as a proper name, confusion arises – on the one hand. On the other hand, this is one of the miraculous moments in Carroll's world, when an imaginary being is just derived from its name (cf. Carroll, *Through the Looking-Glass*, Chapter 7: "The Lion and the Unicorn" ([1996] 1998: 203–214)). Thus the *superficiality* of verbal tags is both the reason for misunderstanding, disorientation, and failure as well as for inventiveness, creativity, and innovation.

Some quite audacious etymologies in the books are based on sound similarities. If verbal labels are *true* labels indicating to ontological relationships, a "thimble" can become a *symbol* (cf. Zirker 2010: 121), and even the symbol of a *symbol* (Zirker additionally points to the fact that in Alice's reaction to the thimble the word "simply" occurs, which also resembles "symbol"; 2010: 122n45). In another playful arrangement based on the idea of names as *true labels*, Carroll suggests that names can be taken off their bearers; in "the wood [...] where things have no names" (cf. Carroll [1996] 1998: 162), objects *lose* their names, as if names could fall down from the surfaces they usually adhere to. Having lost one's name thus is comparable to being naked – and Bruno's horror in *Sylvie and Bruno* (1889) when he is asked to "give" his name corresponds to this idea (cf. Carroll [1996] 1998: 346; cf. Zirker 2010: 188).

4 Language and *Meta-language* as a Surface Phenomenon

Carroll's Alice is never situated on flat grounds that allow standing stable. She is exposed to dizziness, and especially her attempts to get ground under her feet by understanding how language works, how words *function* even intensify this effect. The positive aspect of such instability is the experience of *dynamic* spaces that do not even allow for a clear distinction between the flat and the spatial. As is said in the motto of *Tristram Shandy* (borrowed from Epictetus), it is not the world of things that produces confusion but the opinions about things.[21]

---

[21] Cf. Sterne (1980: 1): "It is not things that disturb men, but their judgments about things."

With regard to Carroll, one may argue that words cause confusion and that verbally uttered opinions are ambiguous and can be easily mistaken – but things get even worse when opinions about words are exchanged. Beyond the verbal surface there is no *more substantial* reality, but only more surfaces, more tags, tags of tags – and so on, infinitely. Carroll *stages*, as we might say, especially the problem of meta-language in a manner which suggests that we always remain on surfaces. His contribution to the discourse about the impossibility to get beyond language (*Unhintergehbarkeits-Problem*; cf. Wittgenstein 1971; Frank 1989) mainly consists in staging surface adventures. The desire to detect the *deeper reasons*, to go to the *roots*, to get *profound* insights still is virulent, but it gets consistently and regularly disappointed.

Many wordplays and puns in Carroll's books are based on false etymologies. False etymologies suggest that similar names refer to similar or causally linked objects – which is not at all the case in natural languages. Only in artificial languages may it be a ruling principle to *label* objects analogously to their factual relationships. One might say that arguing by false etymologies suggests an identity or at least an ontological coherence between labelled objects and labels – which therefore allows interpreting objects via their labels.

Humpty Dumpty's case illustrates that he who reflects about language is constricted to surfaces – to words and to verbally mediated concepts. And it is mainly this famous episode that foregrounds the continuing desire for motivated signs, for signs that are actually *deeply* connected with their significants. Humpty Dumpty asserts that there are *true* and adequate names – especially when he comments on the reasons why certain words in the Jabberwocky poem have specific meanings –, although on the other hand he claims for himself the right to *label* things according to his own will.[22] The gnat also argues in favour of

---

[22] Cf. Peter Heath's comment on Humpty Dumpty: "Humpty Dumpty is on this point clearly a conventionalist, and to that extent a nominalist, since he believes it is words, and not things, that possess meaning. But he also claims that words mean just what *he* chooses them to mean. He is the master, they the servants; the conventions that govern his employment of them are arbitrarily laid down by himself, and he sees no reason for informing anyone beforehand what his stipulations are to be. His language is not private in the sense of referring only to private objects or in disdaining the use of the ordinary vocabulary, but it is in making word-meaning dependent on private acts of choice. Wittgenstein ([48] § 665, p.18; [49], pp. 34*ff*., 41, 145; see also Pitcher [in Fann], pp. 327–28) persistently assails this view of meaning, whose extremer forms would manifestly be fatal, in practice, to any form of verbal communication. Conventions imply agreement and a willingness to conform with others, though not the opposing folly of attributing word-meanings to a ceremonial compact between language-users. For most purposes, obviously, such meanings are social products, created unwittingly by many genera-

the idea of *motivated* expressions, when he (or she?) refers to beings that react when they are called by their proper names.[23] However, the gnat episode again illustrates the arbitrariness of signs – especially when current and familiar expressions are altered.

5 Word Creatures and Paper Worlds

Although in Carroll's world words and verbal expressions turn out to be obstinate and querulous, from another point of view they sometimes function very well, remarkably well even: Several times characters present themselves as the *offspring* of words, generated by their names or by colloquial expressions ("Wortgeburten"; cf. Hölter and Schmitz-Emans 2009: 10). The mock turtle is an instructive example of this potential of words to let beings emerge, as it is derived from its name that is taken literally here: if turtle soup is made out of turtles, then there must be mock turtles to cook mock turtle soup.[24] Several other creatures in Wonderland and Looking Glass country are similarly produced out of verbal expressions. Partially they emerge from nursery rhymes and other popular songs, sometimes from colloquial expressions – as for instance the Mad Hatter and his friend the March Hare, the Cheshire Cat, the Tweedle brothers. Humpty Dumpty is born from a nursery rhyme ("*Humpty Dumpty sat on a wall: / Humpty Dumpty had a great fall. / All the king's horses and all the King's men /*

---

tions of choice and conformity among earlier users of language. Once they are established, the individual has to accept them *as if* they were part of the natural order, and departs from them only at his peril. Nevertheless (or so Carroll thought) he still has a right of departure, either in creating new words, or in attaching new meanings to old ones; and so long as he exercises this right in sparingly and announces his intention in advance, logicians, at least, can have no quarrel with him (cf. Carroll's *Symbolic Logic*, p. 165, quoted by Gardner, pp. 268–69)" (Heath 1974: 192–193).

23 "'What sort of insects do you rejoice in, where *you* come from?' the Gnat inquired. 'I don't *rejoice* in insects at all,' Alice explained, 'because I'm rather afraid of them – at least the large kinds. But I can tell you the names of some of them.' 'Of course they answer to their names?' the Gnat remarked carelessly. 'I never knew them to do it.' 'What's the use of their having names,' the Gnat said, 'if they won't answer to them?' 'No use to *them*,' said Alice; 'but it's useful to the people that name them, I suppose. If not, why do things have names at all?'" (cf. Carroll, *Through the Looking-Glass*, Chapter 3: "Looking-Glass Insects," [1996] 1998: 158).

24 Mock turtle soup imitates real turtle soup; it is made of veal. Therefore, John Tenniel depicts Carroll's mock turtle with a calf's head and hoofs (cf. Carroll, *Alice's Adventures in Wonderland*, Chapter 9: "The Mock Turtle's Story," [1996] 1998: 92).

Couldn't put Humpty Dumpty in his place again," Carroll [1996] 1998: 192). As further members of Carroll's collection of word breeds we may regard the Bread-and-Butter and the Rocking-Horse-Fly.[25] Derived from words, all these creatures have literally as well as in a metaphorical sense been created on a paper surface. As merely imaginary entities without 'roots' in the reality of natural history, they might be described as verbal surface phenomena. But the paper surface they stem from is not just flat. It is comparable to the paper objects created by Japanese origami artists or to the paper constructions of movable books and pop-up-books, even to paper theatres. Paper art flourished in Victorian culture, and Carroll as a collector of toys and games certainly was familiar with the sometimes most refined paper and book constructions that made flat figures emerge into a third dimension, made them unfold, bend, and move.[26] It may be noted in this context that, among the many works of world literature that have been *staged* by the paper architects of pop-up books in the course of twentieth century and more recently, *Alice in Wonderland* is among the most frequently selected texts.[27] Paper architects and book designers obviously feel familiar with Carroll's paper creatures, and they make them rise from their originally flat book surfaces in most inventive ways. The pop-up-books' constructions themselves programmatically subvert the distinction between two- and three-dimensionality.

Maybe another comparison highlights the special effects of Carroll's word breedings even more clearly: In biology, cytoplasmic pseudopodia are structures at the surface of inferior (non-complex) beings (organisms) that serve as a device of movement – feet that are not really feet but buckles. However: the pseudo-feet fulfil their function – they move and allow movement. Similarly, Carroll's language produces pseudopodia ("Scheinfüßchen"), pseudo-bodies, pseudo-beings, pseudo-worlds that strictly spoken consist of nothing but verbal surfaces.

---

[25] Verbal creatures like them are not simply the product of playful puns. They can, on the contrary, be regarded as an indication to the atavistic but never completely abolished belief in language spell, in words' magic power of evocation and creation.
[26] Cf. Pelachaud (2010).
[27] Cf. for instance as a more recent example Denchfield and Vining (2002).

6 Conclusion

In Carroll's novels, transitions between surfaces and depths as well as between two- and three-dimensional objects play an important role on the level of content (as, for instance, mirror-surfaces open up to imaginary spaces, two-dimensional cards and paper objects act as protagonists etc.). Puns alluding to surfaces and superficial observations are also related to the issue of *dimensionality* and can thus be interpreted as self-reflexive comments about an intradiegetic world, in which the opposition of surface and depth is questioned in more than one sense. Carroll stresses the virtual affinities between the discourse about surfaces and depths, on the one hand, and the poetics of puns and word play on the other: In puns, the verbal *surface* is presented either with the ambition to refer to a deeper meaning (which would correspond to a metaphysical conception of hidden meanings) – or the search for such *deeper sense* is evidently exposed to parody and deconstruction.

Comparing Carroll's interest in curved planes with Lawrence Sterne's fascination for curved lines we observe that in both cases topological structures from conventional geometry are used as a motif as well as a structural model. In both cases there is a self-referential aspect in this reference to geometry: Non-linearity in Sterne's *Tristram Shandy* can be regarded as a structural model of experience as well as of writing, and bending planes both illustrate the situation Alice is confronted with by the world Carroll invented and the way the narrator creates imaginary beings out of seemingly *flat* word labels. Carroll's arrangements concerning flat and curved planes, surfaces that promise a depth beyond and, at the same time, disappoint the quest for deeper structures, are self-reflexive, because they are linked to the reflection about words and language. To speak about language does not mean to leave the playing field – the *plane* defined by words –, but it occurs that this playing field *bends*, curves and opens up to holes.[28]

When words refer to words, and those words refer to other words, and so on, the result may be compared to an accumulation of *labels*: Something new is formed out of small paper planes, not flat, however, but folded, crunched, and screwed up. Such objects at the borderline between two- and three-dimensionality can be regarded as metaphors for the genesis of those beings that are derived from words as from seemingly *flat* labels. In John Tenniel's

---

[28] In this regard the playing field of language use is reflected by Carroll's strange chessboard and by the magic mirror's surface.

drawing of the final scene of *Alice in Wonderland*, Alice throws about the playing cards she is surrounded by, and the flat pieces of paper bend slightly, thus forming a spatial structure (cf. Carroll [1996] 1998: 118). Evidently, flat surfaces create spaces as soon as they behave like three-dimensional entities. Interpreted metaphorically, a text can be regarded as a composition of *flat* verbal tags, but as soon as those tags behave like three-dimensional beings, they build up new *spaces* – worlds made out of words. In Carroll's worlds, language itself *buckles* – similar to a non-Euclidean plane, to a rumpled sheet of paper.

As a mathematician, Carroll prefers to stick to the Euclidean world; as a witness of young non-Euclidean mathematics conquering scientific discourse, however, he is at least acquainted with the new space models he rejects. In a way, it is only consistent that a mathematician, who regards non-Euclidean geometry as a kind of *faked* science, invents imaginary worlds which are shaped by non-Euclidean rules of space. Carroll's texts present themselves as curved surfaces simulating spatiality – and at the same time they reflect about this simulation process as a questionable invention.

In the late nineteenth century, the dichotomy of surface and depth changes its meaning and thus its metaphorical meaning potentials. Nietzsche might be quoted in order to illustrate this process. His critical reflections about language and metaphysics indicate, that *depths* are just *surfaces*, produced by the suggestions of language – and that they are linked with the metaphysical habitude to insinuate *foundations* (cf. Nietzsche [1873] 1969: 309–322). As Gilles Deleuze has pointed out, Carroll contributed efficiently to the new evaluation of surfaces and depths, especially by experimenting with the image of curved planes.[29] Similarly to Nietzsche (and anticipating Wittgenstein), Carroll realizes that there is no *space behind* language itself. It is just language that suggests that there are *deeper spaces* – by producing verbal constructions. In the best case, these verbal creatures turn out to be mobile.

---

29 Cf. Deleuze (1969: 13–21): "deuxième série de paradoxes, des effets de surface." Deleuze interprets Carroll's paradoxes as *surface* phenomena that indicate to a loss of *depth*. According to his perspective, the *Alice* books' episode illustrates a disinterest in *deep* meanings in favour of *superficial* processes. Although Deleuze describes Carrollian imagination by using the distinction between *surface* and *depth* as a guideline, he does not refer to the difference between flat and bended planes (1969: 19–21).

7 References

Abbott, Edwin. [1884] 2006. *Flatlanders: A Romance of Many Dimensions*. Oxford: Oxford University Press.
Berkeley, George. [1710] 1998. *A Treatise Concerning the Principles of Human Knowledge*. Jonathan Dancy (ed.). New York: Oxford University Press.
Blake, Kathleen. 1974. *Play, Games, and Sport: The Literary Works of Lewis Carroll*. Ithaca & London: Cornell University Press.
Carroll, Lewis. [1895] 1958. *Symbolic Logic and The Game of Logic*. Edmund C. Berkeley (ed.) New York: Dover.
Carroll, Lewis. [1879] 1973. *Euclid and His Modern Rivals*. New York: Dover.
Carroll, Lewis. [1996] 1998. *The Complete Illustrated Lewis Carroll*. Ware: Wordsworth Editions.
Deleuze, Gilles. 1969. *Logique du Sens*. Paris: Minuit.
Deleuze, Gilles. 1988. *Le Pli: Leibniz et le Baroque*. Paris: Minuit.
Denchfield, Nick & Alex Vining. 2002. *Alice's Pop-Up Theatre Book: Bring Wonderland to Life! With Six Amazing Pop-Up Scenes and over 30 Press-Out Pieces*. London: Macmillan.
Frank, Manfred. 1989. Wittgensteins Gang in die Dichtung. In Manfred Frank & Gianfranco Soldati, *Wittgenstein: Literat und Philosoph*, 7–72. Pfullingen: Neske.
Genette, Gérard. 1976. *Mimologiques: Voyage en Cratylie*. Paris: Seuil.
Gill, Christopher. 1993. Plato on Falsehood – not Fiction. In Christopher Gill & T. P. Wiseman (eds.), *Lies and Fiction in the Ancient World*, 38–87. Exeter: University of Exeter Press.
Heath, Peter. 1974. *The Philosopher's Alice:* Alice's Adventures in Wonderland *and* Through the Looking-Glass *by Lewis Carroll*. London: Academy Editions.
Holquist, Michael. 1969. What is a Boojum? Nonsense and Modernism. *Yale French Studies* 43. 145–164.
Hölter, Achim & Monika Schmitz-Emans. 2009. Introduction. In Achim Hölter & Monika Schmitz-Emans (eds.), *Wortgeburten: Zu Ehren von Karl Maurer*, 7–14. Heidelberg: Synchron.
Kleinspehn, Thomas. 1997. *Lewis Carroll*. Reinbek: Rowohlt.
Kreutzer, Eberhard. 1984. *Lewis Carroll:* Alice in Wonderland *und* Through the Looking-Glass. Munich: Fink.
Locke, John. [1823] 1963. *The Works of John Locke*, vol. 2. Aalen: Scientia.
Müller, Lothar. 2012. *Weiße Magie: Die Epoche des Papiers*. Munich: Hanser.
Nietzsche, Friedrich. [1873] 1969. Über Wahrheit und Lüge im außermoralischen Sinne. In Karl Schlechta (ed.), *Werke: Friedrich Nietzsche*, vol. 3, 6th edn. Munich: Hanser.
Pelachaud, Gaëlle. 2010. *Livres animés: Du papier au numérique*. Paris: L'Harmattan.
Plato. [1926] 1996. *Cratylus*. London : Heinemann.
Rauter, Herbert. 1970. *Die Sprachauffassung der englischen Vorromantik in ihrer Bedeutung für die Literaturkritik und Dichtungstheorie der Zeit*. Bad Homburg, Berlin & Zürich: Gehlen.
Schmidt, Siegfried J. 1968. *Sprache und Denken als sprachphilosophisches Problem von Locke bis Wittgenstein*. The Hague: Nijhoff.
Spacks, Patricia Meyer. 1961. Logic and Language in *Through the Looking Glass*. *ETC: A Review of General Semantics* 18(4). 91–100.
Sterne, Laurence. 1980. *Tristram Shandy*. Howard Anderson (ed.). New York & London: Norton.
Suerbaum, Ulrich. 1996. *Shakespeares Dramen*. Tübingen & Basel: Francke.

Sutherland, Robert D. 1970. *Language and Lewis Carroll*. The Hague: Mouton de Gruyter.
Taylor, Alexander L. 1952. *The White Knight: A Study of C. L. Dodgson (Lewis Carroll)*. Edinburgh: Oliver & Boyd.
Wittgenstein, Ludwig. 1971. *Philosophische Untersuchungen*. Frankfurt a. M.: Suhrkamp.
Zirker, Angelika. 2010. *Der Pilger als Kind: Spiel, Sprache und Erlösung in Lewis Carrolls Alice-Büchern*. Münster: LIT.

Matthias Bauer
Secret Wordplay and What It May Tell Us

Abstract: This article describes wordplay which does not aim at an immediate, general effect but stays unnoticed for some time and / or by a part of the hearers. Such unobvious and sometimes even secret wordplay has not yet been regarded as a kind of its own, even though it has features and functions that distinguish it from wordplay that is perceived immediately. It is also to be distinguished from related phenomena such as wordplay whose meaning is "unharnessed" (Womack 2002). When secret wordplay is noticed, it is found to enhance the meaning of the text. Whereas open wordplay flouts several maxims belonging to the cooperative principle in communication, the maxims are apparently not flouted by secret wordplay. At the same time, secret wordplay makes us see more clearly the range of features and effects of wordplay in general. For example, it helps us realize that wordplay is a scalar phenomenon. The less obvious a wordplay is, the stronger it must be so as to avoid being contested. When analysing secret wordplay, at least four parameters should be taken into account: its linguistic features (such as homonyms of synonyms, frequently in different languages), its contextual integration (such as its contribution to thematic unity, its communicative functions (such as underscoring the speaker's and the hearer's wit), and its social functions (such as excluding certain hearers). Finally, we see that analysing secret wordplay contributes to the discussion of wider issues, such as the relation of word knowledge and world knowledge in the appreciation of literature.

Keywords: communication in drama, communication in poetry, Edmund Spenser, Emily Dickinson, *Hamlet*, *Henry 5*, homonymy, John Milton, paronomasia, paronymy, Paul Grice, *Romeo and Juliet*, Speaker-hearer interaction, secret wordplay, synonymy, William Congreve, William Shakespeare

1 What Is Secret Wordplay?

Wordplay frequently aims at effects that go along with a certain processing effort: the reader or hearer must notice that there is a play on words intended, must realize its meaning, and will, as a rule, take pleasure in the discovery. Wordplay thus establishes a bond between speaker and hearer: the speaker assumes that the hearer will be able to get it and thus pays his audience a compliment, which is returned by their appreciation and expression of delight. Authors, however, may wish to heighten the pleasure by deferring it, or they may have other reasons for raising the hurdles, turning the play on words into a mystery that is only to be solved by a select, knowledgeable audience.

In this paper, I will be concerned with such unobvious, mysterious or even secret wordplay by focusing on examples mainly from English literature. How is this kind of wordplay brought about? What are its functions? And how can we know, especially when confronted with instances from earlier periods, that the secret nature of the wordplay is the result of a communicative strategy rather than just the outcome of linguistic and cultural change that makes the wordplay go unnoticed? By considering these questions, we may even hope to learn more about wordplay in general. At the same time, secret wordplay shares features with other forms of secrecy in communication, such as the riddle or unexplained allegory (*tota allegoria*).[1] As regards the reader's task of discovery, the secret pun comes very close to a riddle, with the difference that the riddle is, in most cases, exhausted once you have found the solution, whereas the wordplay that you discover opens up a new dimension of meaning. The riddle is a text that exists for its answer[2]; the discovery of secret wordplay exists for the text in which it is made.[3] This distinction also points to a difference between open and secret wordplay: a more or less obvious pun may need very little text (a short sentence may be enough: "An archaeologist's career ended in ruins"; Pollack 2012: 42) but secret wordplay as a rule needs more embedding, and this is why it is especially at home in literary texts.

---

[1] For the relation of wordplay and riddle, see Cook (2006), especially chapter 7 (on Lewis Carroll and the *Alice* books). See also Green and Pepicello (1978). Quilligan maintains that "the generation of narrative structure out of wordplay" (1979: 22) is a defining feature of allegory. Quilligan in fact strives to redefine allegory by a "fundamental shift in emphasis away from our traditional insistence on allegory's distinction between word said and meaning meant, to the simultaneity of the process of signifying multiple meaning" (26). Ambiguity and wordplay are thus to replace "the time-honored definition of allegory" which tends to see allegory disintegrating into "a process of verbal legerdemain designed to hide, rather than to reveal, meaning" (26–27). Quilligan criticizes this tendency but could well have integrated established notions of allegory as the "hidden" expression of meaning with her approach to allegory via puns and "verbal ambidextrousness" (26): when she stresses that the allegory of Despair in Book 1 of Spenser's *Faerie Queene* depends on the punning evocation of "dis-pair" (37), she realizes that "many have seen the Despair episode as a conflict between the teachings of the Old and New Testaments without noticing the pun" (40). Thus the wordplay may be just as hidden as the allegorical meaning.

[2] Apart from possible social communicative functions, of course.

[3] For this reason, riddles can be translated easily, whereas the translation of wordplay is, in most cases, quite difficult.

Let me explain, by means of an example, why I think that there is such a thing as "secret wordplay" and that, even though it may not be categorically different from other kinds of wordplay, it is still something special. Why, for example, is it that Elizabeth's neck, in Edmund Spenser's *Amoretti* 64, smells "lyke to a bounch of Cullambynes [columbines]" (Spenser [1595] 1997: 94)? As Alastair Fowler (1975) has noted, it is not just because columbines are white but also because *collum* means 'neck' (96).[4] We see that such unobvious wordplay may be based on expressions that are not even mentioned in the text, e.g. words in another language which provide the link between different parts of an utterance. In the case of Spenser's poem, the wordplay is semantically fitting but does not add any new denotations to the line. The link between *neck* and *columbine* is underscored by letting the one expression participate in the meaning of the other through wordplay. The evocation of Latinity through combining *neck* and *columbine* may also strengthen thematic coherence, since it serves as an indirect reminder of the fact that the columbine, in classical antiquity, was a plant connected with the goddess of love.[5] The wordplay makes the expression serve, in this poem of praise, not only to show a quality of the admired lady but the attitude and the wit of the speaker (and of the poet); it furthermore invites readers to be delighted by their own wit in making the discovery. This involvement and exposure of qualities by all participants agrees with the way in which the *blason* or beauty catalogue is reduced (or enhanced) to absurdity in this poem, where the various body parts are associated with different smells and the speaker implicitly claims to be able to distinguish, for example, between the smell of the lady's eyes and that of her brows.[6] The interlingual pun thus shows very clearly that the point of the description is the description itself, the playfulness, secrecy and process of discovery that go along with it.

It seems to me that systematic descriptions of wordplay have neglected to consider the place and nature of this kind of "secret wordplay," which also has been given the mock-learned name "paronomasia celata" (Bauer 1995). Jacqueline Henry (2003) distinguishes between wordplay (*calembour*) "*in absentia*" and

---

[4] In his edition of Spenser's *Amoretti and Epithalamion* ([1595] 1997: 197), Larsen expatiates on this in his annotation: "*neck ... bounch of Cullambynes*: an extended etymological pun: 1. *collum* = neck + *bynde* = bunch (*OED* bind 9); but 2. also *columbine*: like a dove (= *columba*) or of the color of a dove's neck (*OED* 3)."

[5] For symbolic meanings of the columbine, see Kandeler and Ullrich (2009).

[6] "Her lips did smell lyke vnto Gillyflowers, / her ruddy cheekes lyke vnto Roses red: / her snowy browes lyke budded Bellamoures, / her louely eyes lyke Pincks but newly spred" (Spenser [1595] 1997: 94, l. 5–8).

"*in praesentia*" (288),[7] which takes cognizance of the fact that the wordplay may be contained in a single plurivalent textual element (*in absentia*) or in the combination of several (*in praesentia*). This distinction, however, does not really tell us much about secret wordplay. We might perhaps assume that secret wordplay is always wordplay *in absentia* but this need not be the case. In the Spenser example, the wordplay is based on the combination of several textual elements (and is therefore "present"), but it is nevertheless "absent" in the sense that we will not notice it unless we switch to Latin. So how do we know that there is a play on words? It seems to me that two conditions must be fulfilled: there must be a semantic, phonetic or graphic plurivalence, which may be translingual, and the textual and / or situational context must warrant that the different forms and meanings are related in a way that may be unexpected and go unnoticed for some time but is still relevant to what the discourse is about. The discovery of that relevance or aptness is part of the game in secret wordplay. (Thus it may be doubted that secret wordplay is possible in nonsense literature, but it may be equally doubted that there is, strictly speaking, a lot of such literature.[8]) This is analogous to a phenomenon such as the Metaphysical Conceit, in which a seemingly far-fetched metaphor may turn out to be particularly appropriate.[9]

We may describe the difference between "open" and "secret" wordplay by referring to Grice's maxims that substantiate the cooperative principle (Grice [1975] 1991). Wordplay that has been noted by the hearer or reader can be described, in most cases, as a flouting of the maxims of relation (be relevant) and manner (be perspicuous, e.g. avoid ambiguity). According to Grice, the flouting of maxims "characteristically gives rise to a *conversational implicature*" (30). In the case of wordplay, the implicature may be that the speaker wants to be deliberately ambiguous (as in *double entendre*).[10] By contrast, in secret wordplay the speaker apparently does *not* flout the maxims, whereas in fact they are being flouted – that is to say, we discover the flouting of the maxims only after we have noticed the wordplay. Accordingly, the conversational implicature is a different one. It is not just delayed but gains the additional feature of unobvi-

---

7 This is taken up by Rabatel in *The Dynamics of Wordplay* 2.
8 For the absence of any coherent meaning would make the discovery of pertinent meanings impossible. But even in texts frequently counted among nonsense literature, such as *Alice in Wonderland* (1865), there is usually a level of coherence or a frame to be discovered in which the wordplay makes sense. See the chapter on "Sprachspiel und Nonsens" by Zirker (2010: 220–264, e.g. 236–237).
9 For a discussion of the appropriateness versus arbitrariness of the conceit, see van Hook (1986). For a general survey, see Johnson (2012).
10 See the contribution by Maik Goth in this volume.

ousness, i.e. becomes much more implicit than ordinary implicatures. In that way, secret wordplay, once it has been noted, creates an awareness of the implicature; it is seen as a reflexion on communication-by-implicature itself.

2 What Is Not Secret Wordplay?

Considering critical views on related forms of wordplay helps us get a better idea of what secret wordplay entails and what it does (and is) not. Womack's study of "Undelivered Meanings" (2002) is most helpful in this respect. The examples and critical reflections he mentions are similar to and yet different from what I am after. Womack discusses "unharnessed meanings" (e.g. 2002: 147) in wordplay, i.e. meanings that are neither promoted by the context nor contribute to the meaning of the text. To Womack these are "unnoticed but poetically effective puns" (146). Apart from the fact that puns are not the only form of wordplay to be taken into consideration, Womack mixes up two different issues here: the question whether the wordplay "reaches our conscious attention" or remains unnoticed (148), and the question whether the meanings connected to the expressions involved are pertinent to the context in which they occur or whether they stay "undelivered, potential, nascent" (148). The secret wordplay with which I am concerned does not, at least not immediately, reach our attention but definitely enhances the meaning of the passage or text in which it occurs.

Womack is interested in the aesthetic effect of wordplay (what he calls "poetically effective") rather than in the integration of its meaning. But there is a problem with this distinction: other than the modes and techniques with which he compares wordplay, namely "the modulations in key and rhythm in a musical composition" (142), or "the patterns of shape, color and light in a painting" (142) which need not have related functions or meanings, wordplay only exists because meanings are joined and played off against each other. In paronomasia, the play on meanings is realized by a play on sounds and their similarity, but it is still a play on meanings. What distinguishes such wordplay from other forms of soundplay, such as rhyme or alliteration, is that the meanings necessarily play a significant role, whereas in rhyme and alliteration the identical sounds may suggest a semantic relationship but need not do so.

Accordingly, let us briefly consider the distinction between "harnessed" and "unharnessed" or "undelivered" meanings discussed by Womack. As an example of "harnessed" meanings, he cites the words of the mortally wounded Mercutio in *Romeo and Juliet*, "Ask for me tomorrow, and you shall find me a grave man" (Shakespeare 2008: 3.1.93–94; Womack 2002: 149). The pun on the noun "grave" is obvious, and the meaning contextually appropriate, since Mercutio is about to die. Nevertheless, Womack claims that Mercutio's "wordplay calls attention to the wit that produced it rather than to some profound connection between tombs and dignity" (Womack 2002: 149). This reminds us of the example from Spenser (and of communication-by-implicature): there is frequently a self-reflexive dimension in wordplay which draws attention to the speaker's disposition. In neither case, however, does this detract from the semantic link. In *Romeo and Juliet*, it actually enhances the profound connection between tombs and being serious and grave: the very words that Mercutio utters show him to be anything but grave while he is alive; only death will bring about this change. To him, living means *not* being "grave".[11]

Womack contrasts the Mercutio example with Hamlet's words after the death of Polonius: "This counsellor / Is now most still, most secret, and most grave, / Who was in life a foolish prating knave" (Shakespeare 2008: 3.4.213–15). As Womack points out, "the context for a pun on *grave* is at least as rich here as in *Romeo and Juliet*" but it "is not harnessed to bring the potential for punning to our conscious attention" (149). Again, it is a bit confusing to find the question of our attention mixed up with the question if the meanings are connected. The two issues may but need not go together. Instead, I suggest we consider briefly why the *Hamlet* expression does not inevitably work as an example of wordplay. I think there is much less of a surprise in it. Mercutio astonishingly maintains his lack of gravity on the brink of its inevitable preponderance. With Polonius, gravity is less surprising, even though Hamlet contrasts his now being most still and secret and grave with his having been "a foolish prating knave." If there is a wordplay, it is based on the repeated use of "most," which points to the absolute stillness, secrecy and gravity of death, three qualities which, in a less absolute fashion, mark the councillor. Polonius possesses them now that he is dead, whereas he was an imperfect councillor before, as he lacked them while he was alive. Furthermore, the reading of "grave" as a noun fits better syntactically in Mercutio's than in Hamlet's utterance.[12] This is not a requirement, and

---

11 Winter-Froemel and Zirker (2015) cite this example as a case of ambiguity produced by the internal vs. external level of dramatic communication (323). While this may be right (trying to be funny may be inappropriate at this point in the play world and the pun might therefore be primarily considered as a moment of comic relief for the audience), I think that the wordplay eminently fits the character within the world of the play – not so much because Mercutio cannot help cracking jokes, but because his play on words is a very serious self-characterization.

12 Leech (1969), cited approvingly in Delabastita (1993), seems to think otherwise, when he writes (cf. Bross 36 in this volume) about Mercutio's pun: "Yet, the strength of such syntactic

Hamlet actually does play on the word just as he plays on the notion of the "secret" councillor – in fact, as soon as Polonius is dead, he starts being jocular. Nevertheless, I would suggest that the less fitting the second meaning is syntactically (or the less similar the forms involved), the stronger the combination of semantic surprise and appropriateness must be (the unexpected link that is then realized to be most fitting) in order to establish wordplay. In that respect, Hamlet's wordplay on "grave" is a rather weak one, but so are all his rather desperate attempts at being witty in this scene. The more secret a wordplay is, the stronger it must be in order to avoid being contested.

3 Scales of Wordplay

Neither of the two passages in *Romeo and Juliet* and *Hamlet* is an example of secret wordplay, but both of them help us to see, together with our first example from Spenser's *Amoretti*, that wordplay is a scalar phenomenon: it may be stronger or weaker, and it may be perceived at once or it may be less obvious, even secret. Both scales are dependent on a number of factors and are interdependent. A play on words may justly be called strong when a fairly wide gap between meanings expressed by the same or similar forms is surprisingly made relevant to the textual or situational context (as in the case of Mercutio); the context – especially, but not only in a literary work – may be manipulated accordingly. The relationship may involve contrast as well, as a recent non-literary example from the British election campaign shows. It is a quip by the London Mayor, Boris Johnson: "Vote Tory, get broadband. Vote Ukip, get Miliband" (Hyde 2015). The basis of this play on words is the (apparently inappropriate) semantic relationship discovered between the two forms *mili-* and

---

constraints must not be overestimated, as considerations of syntactic well-formedness can sometimes be seen to give way under the pressure of other (semantic, non-verbal, etc.) contextual constraints. Using a term from Leech (1969: 211), one may call such wordplay asyntactic" (Delabastita 1993: 71). Leech actually writes about Mercutio's pun: "The sinister meaning of grave hinted at here is that of grave as a noun, although in the given construction 'a grave man,' it can only be an adjective" (Leech 1969: 211). This is of course incorrect. Nominal collocations and compounds including "man" were common even in Shakespeare's time, familiar examples being "bellman," "cellarman," and "waterman" (*Oxford English Dictionary* 2014: "waterman" *n.* 2.a. "A man working on a boat or among boats, *esp.* a boatman (as the licensed wherry-man of London) who plies for hire on a river, etc."). Even though "graveman" is not lexicalized, there is no problem in forming it analogously to the other examples mentioned. Therefore, the syntax of "you shall find me a grave man" is perfectly regular.

milli- (wordplay *in absentia*), the former being part of the Labour leader's name and the latter being a prefix indicating smallness ('a thousandth part'). We read the politician's name as a compound in this way because it is paired with a compound whose first part, "broad," stands in a relation of opposition to the implied meaning 'milli' (wordplay *in praesentia*). The surprise is enhanced by presenting the primary wordplay (*mili-* / *milli-*) only after the seemingly innocuous context has been introduced. Secret wordplay in the sense described above only works, I think, if the play on words is a fairly strong one—only that the surprise is delayed, and the uncovering of the secret is part of it. The Johnson example fulfils the requirement of strength but, in spite of its complexity, is still a rather obvious one, at least as regards its verbal material. It presupposes a certain kind of cultural knowledge (about current issues, about politicians) but it is still not secret. It is not made in such a way as to be recognized only after overcoming a big hurdle. The hurdle is low enough to make hearers jump it (almost) immediately, yet big enough to make us realize the wit of the speaker.

4 Four Parameters of Secret Wordplay

We are beginning to distinguish several parameters for analyzing the textual strategies of secret wordplay. For in order to come to terms with secret wordplay, we must assume that the secrecy is intentional – even though, especially when dealing with examples from the past, we may find it difficult to decide if the unobviousness is deliberate or not. Linguistic and cultural change will have to be taken into account. We have already seen that (1) linguistic features (e.g. similarity of form, syntactic appropriateness) play a decisive role, as does (2) the contextual integration. Both are linked with (3) communicative functions (e.g. in the Spenser example, enhancing the impression of wit; the reflexion on implicature) and with (4) social functions, i.e. with the relation to the hearer or reader, who has to fulfil certain requirements. A special case in this respect is presented by the double (internal and external) communication of fictional texts and especially drama. All these four parameters are interdependent but it may be helpful to focus on each of them individually.

4.1 Linguistic Features

As to the linguistic material, its special nature and arrangement is the primary cause for wordplay going unnoticed. If, however, the second meaning in a pun does not fit syntactically, or the similarity of two forms in paronomasia is but slight, it is all the more imperative that the above-mentioned requirement of appropriateness and surprise be fulfilled. It is no coincidence that unobvious wordplay frequently involves synonymy rather than (or besides) homonymy or paronymy. For in that case the morphological aspect is unproblematic (or deceptively harmless) and still the intended effect of deferral or hurdle-raising may be achieved. A not very secret example is to be found in Shakespeare's *As You Like It*, where Touchstone says to Audrey, "I am here with thee and thy goats as the most capricious poet honest Ovid was among the Goths" (Shakespeare 2008: 3.3.5–6). The paronomasia goats / Goths is the obvious case of wordplay; the slightly more secret one is the explanation why Ovid is capricious: because *capra* means 'goat.' The fact that this case of wordplay reminds us of the columbine / *collum* example above points up the historical distance which may play a role in turning it more secret than it used to be: at a time when Latin was still omnipresent (and the main subject at school), switching from English to Latin even without an injunction to do so was a much more frequent activity than it is today.

But of course Latin was not the only language involved in this technique of unobvious wordplay. An example is Milton's translation of Psalm 88:

> 3 For cloyed with woes and trouble store
>   Surcharged my soul doth lie,
> My life at death's uncheerful door
>   Unto the grave draws nigh.
>
> (Milton 1981: 317, l. 9–12)

This is particularly interesting since the other translations are very different. The Authorized Version, for example, simply has "For my soul is full of troubles: and my life draweth nigh unto the grave" (*The Bible* [1611] 1997: 688, Ps 88.3). Why does Milton introduce "cloyed" and "surcharged" to describe the fullness of the soul, thus adding a graphic image of surfeit? I suggest it is because Milton's brain, as is well known (cf. Hale 1997), constantly worked in several languages at once, which is why *soul* to him evoked the homographic French *soûl*; Cotgrave in his 1611 French-English dictionary has the spelling *saoul* and gives the equivalent (for the adjective) "*Full, glutted, cloyed, saciated, that hath so much of a thing as he is readie to loath it*" ([1611] 1971)[13] *Soul* seems to

---

13 Perhaps John Donne had this in mind when death, in one of his Holy Sonnets ("This is my Play's last Scene"), is called "glutt'nous" and, true to this quality, begins to "unjoint / My body and soul" (Donne 2010: 531).

be especially suited to Anglo-French connections. For example, Gilian West has noted (1998: 156–157) that Shakespeare has quite a preference for associating the soul with the willow, as when Desdemona sings "the poor soul sat sighing, by a sycamore tree / Sing all a green willow" (*Othello* 2008: 4.3.40-41). This is an appropriate association, for the willow is "worne of forlorne Paramours" (Spenser, *The Faerie Queene*, [1590] 1977: I.1). The obvious pun on the sycamore tree (i.e. *sick-amor*, which suggests the meaning 'love-sick,) fits in perfectly. It is furthermore secretly obvious that the willow is such a soulful tree (and herb) because its French name is *saule* (Cotgrave [1611] 1971).

Foreign language expressions, however, are not an absolute requirement in order to produce this kind of unobvious wordplay. Emily Dickinson uses it in an ironical poem about one of the Old Testament stories most irritating to the modern mind, Abraham and Isaac (Johnson no. 1317):

> Abraham to kill him
> Was distinctly told —
> Isaac was an Urchin —
> Abraham was old —
>
> Not a hesitation —
> Abraham complied —
> Flattered by Obeisance
> Tyranny demurred —
>
> Isaac — to his children
> Lived to tell the tale —
> Moral — with a Mastiff
> Manners may prevail.
>
> (Dickinson 1979, vol. 3: 911)

This is of course not a poem that teaches us how to appease unpleasantly large animals. The last lines only make sense if we remember that the generic term (or synonym) for mastiff, dog, is a conventional euphemism (or rather dysphemism) for "God" (cf. Bauer 1995 / 1996).

The examples confirm that, whereas obvious wordplay is based on the juxtaposition of meanings produced by words that sound or look similar, secret wordplay goes one step further in that it combines homonymy or paronomy with synonymy (and similar semantic relationships). This is frequently the reason why it may take a couple of centuries to spot it. In the Dickinson example, we have seen that paronymy (the anagram *dog-god*) is combined with a sort of synonymy (*mastiff-dog*). Frequently the synonymy consists in foreign-language equivalents of the native word, so that either the English homonym of the foreign synonym (as in *columbine* and *collum*) or the English synonym of the foreign homonym (as in *soul / soûl / saule* and *surcharged / willow*) is used. John Florio, in his famous Italian-English dictionary called *A Worlde of Wordes* (1598), defines synonym ("Sinonimo") as a "word of one signification" (Florio [1598] 1972: 373), which is quite striking, for we would rather expect it to be defined as *two* words "of one signification." It seems that Florio chooses to define synonyms in this way in order to mirror his English translation of "Homonimia, when divers things are signified by one word" (163). The notion of "one word" can thus comprise, firstly, words that have the same sense (cf. *Oxford English Dictionary* 2014: "synonym" *n.* 1.) and, secondly, words that have the same "name" or form (cf. *OED* 2014: "homonym" *n.* 1.). This clearly suggests the close conceptual relationship of homonym and synonym at Florio's time.

As regards the way in which language is used in secret wordplay, however, this combination is not the only one. It may also, for example, involve merely conceptual links. The rich tradition of Roman stage wordplay will provide an example. In the opening scene of Plautus's *Cistellaria* (*The Casket Comedy*), the (apparent) courtesan Selenium engages, over breakfast, in witty wordplay with the (actual) courtesan Gymnasium and her mother. Selenium has fallen in love with a young man, a fact that is called by Gymnasium the perfidy of love. In spite of her emotional state, Selenium has resources for a witty rejoinder: "ergo in me peculatum facit" (Plautus 2011: 142, l. 72). The wordplay is not based on homonymy or paronymy or synonymy here but on a conceptual connection: it is not only that Selenium describes love's action as a robbery (*peculatum*). As Auhagen explains (2004: 193), when Amor makes a courtesan fall in love with a particular man, his action is like the embezzlement of public money, for this is what *peculatum* specifically means.[14] The courtesan, who belongs to all, should not become private property. In order to get this wordplay, we must know that *peculatum* combines two concepts: robbery and the public; the notion of the public is shifted from the area of the state to the area of eros without turning

---

14 Cooper ([1578] 1958), s.v. "Peculâtus," gives the English equivalent "Robbery of a common treasurie." A nineteenth-century dictionary, Georges's *Handwörterbuch*, translates the expression from Plautus as an example of figurative [bildlich] usage: "bild., amor in me peculatum fecit, spielt an mir Betrug, Plaut. Cist. 72" (Georges and Georges [1913] 1988, vol. 2: 1529).Thus the lexicographer does not seem to have got the wordplay, or would not admit it for reasons of delicacy, for it is the very point of Selenium's joke that *peculatum* literally refers to a common treasury.

peculum into a metaphor.[15] Hearers of course must know what the occupation of the ladies is.

4.2 Contextual Integration

The example also serves to show – in agreement with Juliet's injunction that conceit should be "more rich in matter than in words" (Shakespeare 2008: 2.5.30) – that secret wordplay is a particularly intricate device of linking matter (i.e. meaning) and words. In particular, it may establish or reinforce coherence in a text which otherwise may seem to consist of disparate elements. My case in point is John Donne's poem "The Canonization," in which the speaker starts by defying the world that apparently interferes with his love; a generalizing "you" is told to mind their own business since the world will not be affected by the speaker's cold or heat anyway, e.g. "Soldiers find wars, [...] / Though she and I do love" (Donne 2010: 151, l. 16–18). At this point we are utterly at a loss about the poem's title; we might even suspect a pun on the title word (just as Shakespeare has Timon of Athens pun on "Religious canons" that are "cruel"; 2008: 4.3.60). But in the third of the five stanzas there is a shift. The lovers who at first were nothing are now anything and everything, "Call us what you will, we are made such by love" (Donne 2010: 151, l. 19); the lovers' power of transformation is so great and so mysterious that they give new meaning to the "phoenix riddle" (23), as they "die and rise the same" (26); the speaker envisages "Us canonized for love." He finally calls upon the addressee to invoke him and his beloved, and, in the last two lines to "beg from above / A pattern of your love" (44–45). This last line has frequently been misunderstood; the most authoritative recent critical and annotated edition, for example, prints it as if it was the lovers who were to beg such a pattern:

> And by these hymns, all shall approve
>   Us canonized for love.
>
> And thus invoke us: 'You, whom reverend love
>   Made one another's hermitage;
> You to whom love was peace that now is rage;
> Who did the whole world's soul extract, and drove
>   Into the glasses of your eyes

---

15 Cf. Knospe (this volume), who deals with the kind of conceptual blending taking place in bilingual wordplay.

>   (So made such mirrors and such spies
>   That they did all to you epitomize)
>   Countries, towns, courts—beg from above
>   A pattern of your love!'
>
>   (Donne 2010: 154–155, l. 35–45)

The quotation marks provided by the editor obscure the sense, for the point is that the speaker and his beloved themselves become such a pattern. If one wishes to add quotation marks, the stanza should look like this:

> And thus invoke us: 'You, whom reverend love
>   Made one another's hermitage;
> You, to whom love was peace, that now is rage;
> Who did the whole world's soul extract, and drove
>   Into the glasses of your eyes;
>   (So made such mirrors and such spies
>   That they did all to you epitomize)
>   Countries, towns, courts.' Beg from above
>   A pattern of your love.

This is made evident through wordplay that obviously has escaped the notice of annotators. "Pattern" is, in the Early Modern Period, still an allograph of "Patron" and meant, at the time, what nowadays is usually called "patron saint"; "A saint to whose intercession and protection a person, place, occupation, etc., is specially entrusted" (*OED* 2014: "patron" *n*. 3.a.).[16] Accordingly, the speaker and his beloved both become models or archetypes of love and they become patron saints of lovers; this double process is epitomized in the play on "pattern," which thus literally encapsulates the outline or "ground-plot" of the poem.[17] The "Canonization" of the title word is taken up again in the last line of the poem.

We become aware of a mutual relationship: the unobvious wordplay both depends on thematic context (in this case, the issue of sainthood) and establishes it (in this case, it makes us see the connection between ideal patterns and sainthood). This double function can be found in other poems by Donne as well, for example in "A Valediction: Forbidding Mourning," in which a half-secret interlingual play on the Latin words *aurora*, *aura* and *aurum*, as well as *spero*,

---

[16] The identity of *pattern* and *patron* can still be seen in Irish English; thus the *OED* (2014) lists the meaning of "patron" 3.c. ("patron day") also under "pattern" *n*. 13.

[17] The expression "imaginative ground-plot" is to be found in Sidney ([1595] 2002: 103).

spiro, spira, sphaera and *spritus,* provides the coherence of the context by which it is suggested (cf. Bauer 1995).

4.3 Communicative Functions

Apart from the functions mentioned above, unobvious wordplay frequently contributes to strategies of indirectness. This may be motivated by politeness; you do not wish to mention something directly but give a hint, hoping that the addressee may understand a critical remark without being offended or realize a compliment without considering it trivial flattery. Martina Bross (2015) has given an example of such a hidden wordplay which makes disagreement visible but does not openly create offence. When Hamlet, responding to his uncle, states that he is (in the spelling of the Second Quarto) "too much in the sonne" (cited in Bross 36), he punningly rejects his uncle's claims of replacing his father, as he does not wish to be placed in the position of a son by his new "father" Claudius (Bross 40). The example deserves special attention for it shows that even quite obvious wordplay (such as the sun / son pun) may become secret in the sense that its specific, unflattering meaning (out of a range of possible meanings that are evoked simultaneously) is not expressly referred to.

You might say that straightforward wordplay could serve that purpose just as well in that you do not say something directly but evoke it through a pun. But that is frequently still too obvious, too direct. An example of how an unobviously punning mixture of compliment and allegation may indeed serve to declare love better than a complimentary platitude is the wooing of Henry and Katherine at the end of Shakespeare's *Henry V*. In this scene, the course of true love does not run quite as smoothly as the English King may have wished. They are having difficulties (or pretend to do so) for the one speaks English and the other French. Thus Henry tells Katherine: "Come, your answer in / broken music – for thy voice is music and thy English broken" (Shakespeare 2008: 5.2.225–226). I think it is not just enough to get the pun here, namely that "broken" is a musical term meaning music arranged for different instruments (*OED* 2014: "broken" *adj.* †15.). The point of the pun is, rather, that "broken" in that sense is a synonym of "consort" (the *OED* 2014 quotes Bacon, "music which we call broken-music or consort-music"), with which it also forms a collocation, "broken consort." In an unspoken pun Henry wishes Katherine to become his consort in the sense of becoming his wife. Of course he also tells her so quite explicitly, but the communicative function of the unobvious wordplay is added, in that it has its very own playful persuasive force.

4.4 Social Functions

Molly Mahood, in her classic study of *Shakespeare's Wordplay*, regards Juliet's words as an example of "unconscious wordplay" (Mahood 1957: 13): "Conceit more rich in matter than in words, / Brags of his substance, not of ornament" (Shakespeare 2008: 2.5.30–31). The fiscal sense of "rich" is enhanced by the context (the ambiguous "matter" and "substance"; Romeo's earlier "dear encounter") while we know that Juliet does not speak of material things. What Mahood therefore means by "unconscious wordplay" is that the *character* at this point does not play on words but Shakespeare does: "The vital wordplay in Shakespeare's writings is that between the characters and their creator, between the primary meaning of words in the context of a person's speech and their secondary meanings as part of the play's underlying pattern of thought" (Mahood 1957: 41). Mahood's term is obviously not the same as secret wordplay, but it is relevant to our discussion. While there may be just a small difference between the two meanings of "rich" involved in the example and the play therefore easy to get, the double communication typical of drama or indeed of almost any literary work of art may turn this play into a difficult one, and we may not find its meaning and purpose obvious.[18]

Dramatists and narrators may play on words behind their characters' backs, so to speak, and even the poet may convey meanings which are different from those intended by his or her speaker or persona. In that case, the wordplay is unobvious or even secret not because the relation of words and their meanings remains hidden but because the ostensible speaker seems largely unaware of it. We can generalize this a bit and say that wordplay may be exclusive as well as unobvious, and that the two features are not necessarily linked, at least not when different levels of communication are involved. In the latter case the wordplay as such may be obvious, but we will have to construct different contexts for the different levels of communication, and we will try and reconcile them, which may not be an easy task. In other cases, however, exclusiveness is brought about by wordplay which is deliberately unobvious to the party who is not to get it. Secret wordplay thus has a social function. You might say that realizing it requires a particular kind of code or knowledge, and for that reason the wordplay acquires a certain degree of secrecy. We find this sort of thing in

---

[18] On the different levels of communication (e.g. interior and exterior communication, but also the levels of experiencing and narrating self in autodiegetic narratives) and the ambiguities triggered by it, see e.g. Bauer, Knape, Koch and Winkler (2010); Winter-Froemel and Zirker (2010, 2015); Bauer (2015).

comedy a lot, especially when there is a dull-witted character who is thus excluded from the fun or who becomes the unknowing victim of the other characters' jollity. In the fourth act of Congreve's *The Way of the World,* Sir Wilfull Witwould has made up his mind to propose to Mrs. Millamant, who of course does not think of taking him seriously. She does not pay attention to him and quotes some lines of poetry to herself:

> MILLAMANT. (*repeating*)
>   I swear it will not do its part
>   Though thou doest thine, employ'st thy power and art.
>   Natural, easy Suckling.
> SIR WILFULL.
>   Anan? Suckling? No such suckling neither, cousin, nor stripling;
>   I thank heaven I'm no minor.
> MILLAMANT.
>   Ah rustic! Ruder than Gothic!
> SIR WILFULL.
>   Well, well, I shall understand your lingo one of these days, cousin;
>   in the mean while I must answer in plain English. (Congreve [1700] 1994: 4.1.85-92)

This is quite ingenious: Sir Wilfull himself creates the wordplay that remains secret to him. As an ignorant country squire he does not know that Millamant quotes from, and refers to, Sir John Suckling, the cavalier poet. He takes her to refer to a suckling, i.e. a young calf or lamb, and rejects the idea of being treated as a minor. We see how the exclusiveness works: Congreve, Millamant, and we, the knowing urban audience, are "in," and Sir Wilfull is "out." Millamant is "in" even though she does not produce the "Suckling" pun herself – she may have anticipated it – because she goes on referring to "Gothic," which Sir Wilful does not get either but we do. "Gothic" takes up the sheep image in that it is an allusion to the goats / Goths paronomasia, which, as noted, suggests the "capricious" poet Ovid in Shakespeare's *As You Like It.*

5 Conclusion and Further Questions

Exclusiveness, we see here, is based on knowledge or the lack of it. In that respect wordplay, secret wordplay in particular, is not very different from allusion, which you do not get if you are ignorant. Yet it is not the same as allusion, for when allusion is involved in wordplay, something is done to it, usually by means of homophony, paronomasia, and the other familiar techniques of wordplay. A rewarding research question results from this, namely what kind of knowledge is involved and what the consequences of this knowledge-involvement may be for the use of wordplay in literary and non-literary utterances. In some ways strong wordplay is always based on some secret, as the semantic link between two forms is mysterious and astonishing, even when the pun itself is not hidden. Thus it is not so easy to construct a meaningful utterance in which you jump casually from "sun" to "son" or vice versa, since the domains of their meanings are pretty far apart. George Herbert, in "The Sonne" ([1633] 2007), links them by providing a Christological context and by including a half-secret pun on the form ("The Sonne[t]"). He presents the knowledge behind the wordplay. Hamlet, with the same pun, counts on the specific knowledge being unequally distributed.

Secret wordplay will give us valuable hints for the kind of knowledge required in understanding wordplay, as it is particularly well suited to show the difference between different kinds of hearers. The hints are directed at principles of coherence in texts, which textual linguistics has described, for example, in terms of frames and scripts; we may also think of discourse topics or of "topics" in the looser general sense of the word, or of isotopy in the semiotic sense.[19] These approaches abstract from the visible or acoustic form of the words and are concerned with semantic features only. By contrast, wordplay is frequently effective because it ignores all those semantic principles of coherence or makes us see coherence where we did not expect it. This is what brings about surprise, laughter, sudden insight. Whereas the meaning-based principles of coherence primarily depend on *world* knowledge (only think of the idea of a communicative frame), the coherence established by wordplay primarily depends on *word* knowledge. It goes without saying that the two belong together but it makes sense to differentiate between two *primarily* relevant kinds of knowledge. And this is even true of secret wordplay when synonymy comes in. You have to know that broken music means consort music in order to realize how Henry gets from one thing to another when he says "broken." You do not even have to know what consort music really is. The differentiation may help us account for a number of things; for the literary scholar, for example, it would be interesting to learn whether the word knowledge required in order to fully appreciate a literary work of art is not more lasting – in spite of language change – than the world knowledge that may be necessary to understand what it is about. In other words, literary texts that significantly depend on forms of wordplay may have a wider and more enduring presence than texts that depend on specialized world

---

19 Cf., e.g., Lötscher (2008). For a concise statement by A. J. Greimas on his notion of "isotopy of discourse," see Parret (1974: 60–61).

knowledge. This is, admittedly, a somewhat speculative hypothesis that would have to be confirmed or refuted by empirical evidence. My suggestion would be to begin with specific genres: the kind of satirical comedy that is full of allusions to political and other facts may turn out to be much more short-lived than comedy based on verbal wit (which may still be replete with factual references but they are only secondary). In any case, secret wordplay, even more so than wordplay in general, tells us, once we have discovered it, about the ability of language to establish patterns of thought and relationships of meaning that will draw the world along with them.

6 References

Auhagen, Ulrike. 2004. Das Hetärenfrühstück (*Cist.* I 1) – Griechisches und Römisches bei Plautus. In Rolf Hartkamp & Florian Hurka (eds.), *Studien zu Plautus' Cistellaria*, 187–210. Tübingen: Narr.

Bauer, Matthias. 1995. *Paronomasia celata* in Donne's "A Valediction: forbidding mourning." *English Literary Renaissance* 25. 97–111.

Bauer, Matthias. 1995/1996. "The Language of Dogs: *Mythos* and *Logos* in Emily Dickinson." *Connotations* 5(2–3). 208–227.

Bauer, Matthias. 2015. Ironie und Ambiguität: Annäherungen aus literaturwissenschaftlicher Sicht. In Nicole Falkenhayner, Monika Fludernik & Julia Steiner (eds.), *Faktuales und fiktionales Erzählen*, 139–158. Würzburg: Ergon.

Bauer, Matthias, Joachim Knape, Peter Koch & Susanne Winkler. 2010. Dimensionen der Ambiguität. *Zeitschrift für Linguistik und Literaturwissenschaft* 158. 7–75.

The Bible: Authorized King James Version with Apocrypha. [1611] 1997. Robert Carroll & Stephen Prickett (eds.). Oxford: Oxford University Press.

Bross, Martina. 2015. "Equivocation will undo us"? Wordplay and Ambiguity in Hamlet's First and Second Line. In Angelika Zirker & Esme Winter-Froemel (eds.), *Wordplay and Metalinguistic/Metadiscursive Reflection. Authors, Contexts, Techniques, and Meta-Reflection* (The Dynamics of Wordplay 1), 25–45. Berlin & Boston: de Gruyter.

Congreve, William. [1700] 1994. *The Way of the World*. Brian Gibbons (ed.). New Mermaids. London: A. & C. Black.

Cooper, Thomas. [1578] 1975. *Thesaurus linguae Romanae et Britannicae*. Repr. Hildesheim: Olms.

Cotgrave, Randall. [1611] 1971. *A Dictionary of the French and English Tongues*. Repr. Amsterdam: Da Capo Press.

Delabastita, Dirk. 1993. *There's a Double Tongue: An Investigation Into the Translation of Shakespeare's Wordplay, with Special Reference to Hamlet*. Amsterdam: Rodopi.

Dickinson, Emily. 1979. *The Poems of Emily Dickinson*. Thomas H. Johnson (ed.), 3 vols. Cambridge, MA: Harvard University Press.

Donne, John. 2010. *The Complete Poems of John Donne: Epigrams, Verse Letters to Friends, Love-Lyrics, Love-Elegies, Satire, Religion Poems, Wedding Celebrations, Verse Epistles to*

Patronesses, Commemorations and Anniversaries. Robin Robbins (ed.). London: Longman.

Florio, John. [1598] 1972. *A Worlde of Wordes*. Repr. Hildesheim: Olms.

Fowler, Alastair. 1975. *Conceitful Thought: The Interpretation of English Renaissance Poems*. Edinburgh: Edinburgh University Press.

Georges, Karl Ernst & Heinrich Georges. [1913] 1988. *Ausführliches lateinisch-deutsches Handwörterbuch*, 2 vols. Hannover: Hahnsche Buchhandlung.

Green, Thomas A. & W. J. Pepicello. 1978. Wit in Riddling: A Linguistic Perspective. *Genre* 11. 1–13.

Grice, Paul. [1975] 1991. Logic and Conversation. In Paul Grice, *Studies in the Way of Words*, 22–40. Harvard: Harvard University Press.

Hale, John K. 1997. *Milton's Languages: The Impact of Multilingualism on Style*. Cambridge: Cambridge University Press.

Henry, Jacqueline. 2003. *La traduction des jeux de mots*. Paris: Presses Sorbonne Nouvelle.

Herbert, George. [1633] 2007. The Sonne. In Helen Wilcox (ed.), *The English poems*, 572–574. Cambridge: Cambridge University Press.

Hyde, Marina. 2015. Boris Johnson: "Vote Tory, get broadband. Vote Ukip, get Miliband." *The Guardian*. http://www.theguardian.com/politics/2015/apr/01/boris-johnson-vote-tory-get-broadband-vote-ukip-get-miliband (23 July 2015).

Johnson, C. 2012. Conceit. In Roland Greene et al. (eds.), *The Princeton Encyclopedia of Poetry and Poetics*, 289–291. Princeton: Princeton University Press.

Kandeler, Riklef & Wolfram R. Ullrich. 2009. Symbolism of Plants: Examples from European-Mediterranean Culture Presented with Biology and History of Art: May: Columbine. *Journal of Experimental Botany* 60(6). 1535–1536.

Leech, Geoffrey N. 1969. *A Linguistic Guide to English Poetry*. London: Longmans.

Lötscher, Andreas. 2008. Textsemantische Ansätze. In Nina Janich (ed.), *Textlinguistik: 15 Einführungen*, 85-111. Tübingen: Narr.

Mahood, M. M. 1957. *Shakespeare's Wordplay*. London: Methuen.

Milton, John. 1981. *Complete Shorter Poems*. John Carey (ed.). London: Longman.

Oxford English Dictionary, 2nd edn. 2014. http://www.oed.com (23 July 2015).

Parret, Herman. 1974. *Discussing Language*. The Hague: Mouton.

Plautus. 2011. *Casina. The Casket Comedy. Curculio. Epidicus. The Two Menaechmuses*. Wolfgang de Melo (ed.). Cambridge, MA: Harvard University Press.

Pollack, John. 2011. *The Pun Also Rises: How the Humble Pun Revolutionized Language, Changed History, and Made Wordplay More Than Some Antics*. New York: Gotham.

Quilligan, Maureen. 1979. *The Language of Allegory: Defining the Genre*. Ithaca: Cornell University Press.

Shakespeare, William. 2008. *The Norton Shakespeare*. Stephen Greenblatt, Walter Cohen & Andrew Gurr (eds.). New York: Norton.

Sidney, Sir Philip. [1595] 2002. *An Apology for Poetry or The Defence of Poesy*. Geoffrey Shepherd & Robert W. Maslen (eds.). Manchester: Manchester University Press.

Spenser, Edmund. [1590, 1596] 1977. *The Faerie Queene*. Albert C. Hamilton (ed.). London: Longman.

Spenser, Edmund. [1595] 1997. *Edmund Spenser's* Amoretti and Epithalamion: *A Critical Edition*. Kenneth J. Larson (ed.). Tempe, AZ: Medieval & Renaissance Texts & Studies.

Spenser, Edmund. 1977. *The Faerie Queene*. A. C. Hamilton (ed.). London: Longman.

Van Hook, J. W. 1986. "Concupiscence of Witt": The Metaphysical Conceit in Baroque Poetics. *Modern Philology* 24(1). 24–38.
West, Gilian. 1998. *A Dictionary of Shakespeare's Semantic Wordplay*. Lewiston: Edwin Mellen Press.
Winter-Froemel, Esme & Angelika Zirker. 2010. Ambiguität in der Sprecher-Hörer-Interaktion: Linguistische und literaturwissenschaftliche Perspektiven. *Zeitschrift für Linguistik und Literaturwissenschaft* 158. 76–97.
Winter-Froemel, Esme & Angelika Zirker. 2015. Ambiguity in Speaker-Hearer Interaction: A Parameter-Based Model of Analysis. In Susanne Winkler (ed.), *Ambiguity: Language and Communication*, 283–339. Berlin: de Gruyter.
Womack, Mark. 2002. Undelivered Meanings: The Aesthetics of Shakespearean Wordplay. In Mark David Rasmussen (ed.), *Renaissance Literature and Its Formal Engagements*, 139–158. New York: Palgrave.
Zirker, Angelika. 2010. *Der Pilger als Kind: Spiel, Sprache und Erlösung in Lewis Carrolls Alice-Büchern*. Münster: LIT.

Appendix

List of Contributions and Abstracts

The Dynamics of Wordplay 1 & 2

The following overview contains all contributions from volumes 1 and 2 of *The Dynamics of Wordplay*. Furthermore, all abstracts from the French contributions in volume 2 are assembled.

Pierre J. L. Arnaud, François Maniez and Vincent Renner: Non-Canonical Proverbial Occurrences and Wordplay: A Corpus Investigation and an Enquiry Into Readers' Perception of Humour and Cleverness

See this volume.

Matthias Bauer: Secret Wordplay and What It May Tell Us

See this volume.

Pauline Beaucé: Wordplay in the Repertory of 18th Century Fairground Theatres in Paris: From Publicity to Satire (Les jeux de mots dans le répertoire des théâtres de la Foire à Paris au XVIIIe siècle: de la publicité à la satire)

The aim of this article is to show how wordplays are a source of interest not only for specialists in literature and linguistics but also for theatre historians, because their study goes beyond the analysis of language. I will take the fairground theatres of Paris to illustrate how the work on puns brings together two approaches of the theatre: the work on texts and the history of performances. Writing for the Fair in the early eighteenth century supposes to write in the context of a generalized war between theatres. Puns, which are part of the comic theatre, create some complicity with an audience who is aware of the fighting. They also presuppose some knowledge shared by all the audience, and inform the theatre historian about the common heritage on the basis of which the entertaining aspect of fairground shows. Whatever the genre represented, three major functions of pun can be found: a satirical function (authors, institutions), a critical function (works through parody) and an advertising function. Among the new forms of entertainment found in the fairs, some will receive more attention: this article first addresses parts made of monologues and jargons before observing the form taken by puns in parts containing vaudeville songs. Finally, dramatic parodies, especially their titles, offer a fruitful field of exploration on the use of puns.

Marc Blancher: From the Author of Wordplay to Authorial Wordplay (De l'auteur de jeux de mots aux jeux de mots d'auteur)

This paper is dealing with the function of humour and wordplay from the point of view of an author of crime novels, of short stories and of "educational crime novels" (German: *Lernkrimis*). The paper tackles two major aspects, the first being the development of the theory of humour from ancient Greece to the twentieth century, including the humour based on character as well as the dichotomy of "high humour," which causes a smile, and "mean humour," which results in laughter, both on an extradiegetic level (story) and on an intradiegetic level (characters). Authors such as Aristotle, Horace, Scarron, Voltaire, Victor Hugo, Henri Bergson and others that have dealt with humour will be addressed. Noticeably, religion often played a fundamental role in theories of humour. A further aspect concerns etymology which establishes a link between the different expressions used to designate forms of wordplay in French: *calembour* (English: pun), which is rather popular, and *jeux de mots* (English: wordplay), which is more highbrow. The focus then turns to the narration of crime novels; this includes narrative deconstruction, which, according to Todorov, is divided into two parts: the history of detection and the history of crime. In fact, the detective novel is frequently associated with a specific method of narration, based on a conundrum, a game and a double-reading: these three elements are analogous to the process of the constructing and understanding of wordplay. Crime-novels and wordplays are thus based upon the same elements. The last section is devoted to the usage of wordplays in crime-novels, including both the mere use in book- or chapter-titles (e.g. as an identity-mark and as a characteristic of the author's culture, which may entail cinema, comic, literature) and the intradiegetic level, when wordplay is used to distinguish comic characters from less comic ones.

Marc Blancher: "Ça est un bon mot!" Or: the (Icono-)Textual Humour of Goscinny ("Ça est un bon mot!" ou l'humour (icono-)textuel à la Goscinny)

This paper is devoted to the most famous French comic series of all time, *Asterix the Gaul* (orig. *Astérix le Gaulois*), first created in 1959 by the writer René Goscinny and the illustrator Albert Uderzo, and focuses on the period during which the two of them worked together, i.e. between 1959 und 1977. One approach to understanding the success of the series is to read it in the light of the theory of double address, which has frequently been applied to this work: young readers will enjoy themselves by discovering the jokes around Obelix and the Romans, particularly the hyperbolized und ridiculed fighting scenes, while adult readers will enjoy themselves on a different level of reading on which the authors are playing with stereotypes about the French and other European cultures and, first and foremost, with words. Wordplay is not only characteristic for the comic series *Asterix*, it also makes the translation of this work into other languages very difficult. In *Asterix*, wordplays can be found on the extradiegetic level (i.e. on the level of the storytelling, as for example in the character-names) as well as on the (intra-)diegetical level (i.e. in the interactions between the characters who frequently use wordplay in their conversations). The first part of this paper deals with occurrences of wordplay on the extradiegetic level, specifically the character-names. The focus then turns to those instances of wordplay which are based upon references to the French culture, including advertisement, history, literature, politics etc. The last section is devoted to the tridimensional aspect of wordplay, when the play with words is no longer merely bidimensional but becomes tridimensional, with a pictorial aspect added that allows for both the construction and the understanding of an allusion.

Martina Bross: "Equivocation will undo us"? Wordplay and Ambiguity in Hamlet's First and Second Line

See this volume.

Federica Di Blasio: *La Disparition* **by Georges Perec and Wordplay: The Ambiguity of the Metatext and the Negotiation of Translation** (*La Disparition* de Georges Perec et les jeux de mots: l'ambiguïté du métatexte et la négociation de la traduction)

In this article, George Perec's novel *La Disparition* (1969) is approached from an ample and heterogeneous perspective that lends the perecquien novel a distinctive and, at the same time, representative role. Although the novel is generally acclaimed for its technical virtuosity, this is usually explained on the basis of the sheer length of the lipogram and not with regard to the variety and multiplicity of wordplay integrated into and evoked by it. The metatext, that is the enigmatic references to the book and its writing as a whole, uses a variety of wordplay by foregrounding the ambiguity proper to certain types of wordplay, for instance in puns and by transgressing the boundaries of the lipogram. In a similar vein, the metatext allows for a multiplication of readings of the text; not only does it influence the reading but also the reproduction of the text in foreign languages. The translation of *La Disparition* offers a new perspective on the perecquien novel: writing and translating are intertwined as the translation is an important issue in the genealogy of the novel and offers possibilities that go beyond the literary play as realized in the text. In a rendering into a foreign language, the translation is a renewal of this play as embedded in the original text: the translator has to find textual equivalents and to negotiate meanings, which includes the loss and the compensation of meaning. This is even true for languages such as English and Italian where the lipogram in itself poses fewer constraints (which is due to the lesser frequency of the lipogramatic letter). Examples from the English version by John Lee's *Vanish'd!* (1989) and the Italian translation by Piero Falchetta, *La Scomparsa* (1995), will reflect on both the variety of strategies used in translation and the character of a literary play that can never quite exhaust its creative and ludic potential.

Ian Duhig: Interview: A Perspective from Practical and Professional Experience – Wordplay in Poetry

See this volume.

Julia Genz: "Il wullte bien, mais il ne puffte pas": From Diglossia to Polyphony in Roger Manderscheid's Novel *Der sechste Himmel* (*Feier a Flam*) ("Il wullte bien, mais il ne puffte pas" – de la polyglossie à la polyphonie dans le roman *Der sechste Himmel* (*feier a flam*) de Roger Manderscheid)

The novel *Der sechste Himmel* (orig. *Feier a Flam*) by the Luxembourgian writer and artist Roger Manderscheid is characterised by its plurilingualism and its wordplays. I wish to examine the interaction of the different languages in the various instances of wordplay and their function in the novel. Charles Ferguson's concept of diglossia, the term polyphony as developed by Mikhail Bakhtin for literary research and its adaptation to linguistics by Oswald Ducrot will support the analysis. With the aid of these concepts, I would like to flesh out how the encounter with different languages and cultures shapes the protagonist's identity and how he assumes responsibility for the narration.

Maik Goth: Double Entendre in Restoration and Early Eighteenth-Century Comedy

See this volume.

Sylvia Jaki: Phraseological Modification and Wordplay: The Case of Lexical Substitution in the Written Press (Détournement phraséologique et jeu de mots: le cas des substitutions lexicales dans la presse écrite)

A popular research topic in phraseology relates to the modification of fixed sequences of words and deals, among others, with the identification of different types of modifications, their functions, and their domains of appearance. In research on verbal humour, it is taken for granted that phraseological modification constitutes a form of pun. Paradoxically, there seems to be hardly any discussion of how this creative use of language actually fits into a theory of verbal humour. In order to fill this gap, this contribution explores to what extent the intentional manipulation of phraseological units is compatible with the definitions of relevant terms in the field of punning and wordplay, for example *jeu de mots* and *jeu de langage*.

In order to shed light on the relation between phraseological modification and punning, the analysis will be restricted to a specific type of manipulation, namely lexical substitution. This type, which is frequently encountered in newspaper headlines, is based on the substitution of one or more lexical elements, such as in *Like a Bat Outta Heaven* (from *like a bat out of hell*). In the presentation and comparison of the different definitions of *jeu de mot* and *jeu de langage*, special emphasis will be put on the *Semantic Script Theory of Humour* (Raskin 1985). These definitions will be linked with the mechanisms and characteristics of lexical substitutions, thereby showing to what extent the latter can be classified as real puns, and in which ways substitutions are more complex.

Johannes Kabatek: Wordplay and Discourse Traditions

See this volume.

Sebastian Knospe: A Cognitive Model for Bilingual Puns

See this volume.

Thomas Kullmann: Wordplay as Courtly Pastime and Social Practice: Shakespeare and Lewis Carroll

See this volume.

Michelle Lecolle: Wordplay and Motivation: An Approach of Linguistic Sensibility (Jeux de mots et motivation: une approche du sentiment linguistique)

This paper is based on the assumption that wordplay makes it possible to reveal the competence, sometimes unconsciously, that speakers possess of a linguistic system and that instances of wordplay thus indirectly exhibit traces of discursive skill and language system competence. The analysis is first based on the distinction (regarding the adjective *epilinguistic* (Culioli 1990 and 1999)) between *savoir épilinguistique* (epilinguistic knowledge), *conscience épilinguistique* (epilinguistic awareness, "which appears in control of correctness, wordplay, etc.") and metalinguistic knowledge. I (further) add 'language awareness' of non-linguist speakers to these notions.

Using this as my starting point, I focus on the phenomena that imply a linguistic motivation, be it real, assumed or invented: as opposed to arbitrariness (Saussure's theory of the sign), one of the characteristics of poetic practice in the broadest sense (including advertising and newspaper headlines) is precisely the way in which, while concentrating on the message, it rediscovers motivation. This search for motivation can be found in a wide range of linguistic phenomena, so that the instances of playful use of language can be compared with other 'serious' ones such as folk etymology, formal neology and even learners' mistakes.

Patricia Oster: "Ne nous tutoyons plus, je t'en prie." Wordplay and the Stakes of Language in Marivaux's Plays ("Ne nous tutoyons plus, je t'en prie." Jeux de mots et enjeu du langage dans le théâtre de Marivaux)

Marivaux was a creator of language and an inventor of neologisms. "Tomber amoureux" ('to fall in love') – his best known neologism – already evokes the surprise at discovering the double meaning of the word *tomber*: does one "fall" into a trap or into an unexpected pleasure? His comedies are based on the double meaning of words and the equivocality of utterances. The plays possess a metalinguistic dimension, for they give rise to profound reflections on language as a system and the stakes at play in the communication between consciousness and the unconscious. Language becomes a screen that functions as a disguise. Long before Freud, Marivaux shows that the unconscious plays with words. In his drama, the lovers do not admit to their repressed desires and hide them behind a veil of connotations. But they find themselves facing an "adversary" who is equally in love and who tries to tear off this veil by turning connotations into denotations. The ambiguity of this game of surprises and hazards is accompanied by a confrontation between verbal and non-verbal language. The semiotics of the body and the semiotics of language oppose each other in an equivocal and ludic dialogue that was termed *marivaudage* by contemporaries. In 2004 Abdellatif Kechiche's film *L'Esquive* (international title: *Games of Love and Chance*) staged such a game of linguistic disguises between *marivaudage* and volubility that foregrounds an extensive metalinguistic reflection.

Alain Rabatel: Substitutive and Cumulative Confronted Points of View in Spoonerisms / *contrepèteries* (*in absentia*) (Points de vue en confrontation substitutifs ou cumulatifs dans les contrepèteries (*in absentia*))

The present article studies the *contrepèterie*, the French version of spoonerisms, a wordplay based on phonemic permutations creating an utterance that plays with taboos according to its carnavalising purpose. Focusing on *contrepèteries in absentia*, which are more frequent than those *in praesentia*, the article first provides an enunciative theoretical framework based on the distinction speaker / enunciator as the sources of the points of view (POV) whose multiplicity raises the question of the enunciative commitment in a ludic context. The article then analyses the structure of spoonerisms, namely the permutations or shiftings of phonemes (or phonemic segments), depending on their positions or combinations. The decoding of associative mechanisms requires the comprehension of numerous phonemic, rhythmic and syntactic equivalences triggered by an active metalinguistic consciousness which is at the service of poetic function and laughter, especially through the complicity implied by the carnavalisation of values and by playing with stereotypes and / or signifiers. Finally, the article examines the enunciative relations between confronted points of view in the case of a non-serious enunciation. The dynamics of spoonerisms actualise them (POV2) in accordance with two types of relations in both their production and their reception. According to the substitution mechanism, the original utterance loses its signification or becomes odd functioning as a mere pretext for the implicit point of view, POV2, which replaces the POV1. According to the cumulative mechanism, POV1, semantically consistent and adequate to the situation, is not rejected although several cues suggest a second reading: the POV2 then manipulates the initial utterance in a more pertinent manner, joining, while prevailing over, the POV1.

Vincent Renner: Lexical Blending as Wordplay

See this volume.

Sheelagh Russell-Brown: The Serious Work of Play: Wordplay in the "Dark Sonnets" of Gerard Manley Hopkins

See this volume.

Jean-François Sablayrolles: Playful Neologisms: A Morphological and Enunciative-Pragmatic Study (Néologismes ludiques: études morphologique et énonciativo-pragmatique)

Naming new objects and new technical and scientific concepts is far from being the only reason for neology. Play on words is another important source. It taps in on particular lexicogenic matrices and shows up in different types of effects in interlocution. From the point of view of morphology, extragrammatical procedures may be called upon, in particular acronymy, but also paronymy, meta-analysis, flexional innovation and others. When regular lexicogenic matrices are involved (suffixation and compounding), the relative frequencies of certain types of elements that enter the word formations differ considerably (hybrids, words or sub-word elements of different registers, etc.). From an enunciative and pragmatic viewpoint, ludic neologisms can appear in different situations (from conversational hapax to neologisms which, for literary and humoristic ones, will spread in the speech community through various stages). They often fulfil other functions as well as that of play on words (teasers, sales pitches, ploys, provocations...), and their life expectancy is variable according to each case.

Svea Schauffler: Wordplay in Subtitled Films – An Audience Study

See this volume.

Monika Schmitz-Emans: Plays around Surfaces and Depths: Transitions between Two- and Three-Dimensionality Reflected by Wordplays and Puns

See this volume.

Laélia Véron: Wordplay and Double Communication in Literary Works: The Example of Balzac's *Comédie humaine* (Jeu de mots et double communication dans l'œuvre littéraire: l'exemple de la *Comédie humaine* de Balzac)

This article focuses on the different functions of puns in Balzac's *La Comédie humaine* and mostly in the novels of Scènes de la vie parisienne. Puns are taken here as any witty, sparkling remark that gives rise to smiles or laughter. Balzacian puns can only be understood through historical and cultural semantics: indeed, the early 19th century was the theatre of a 'crisis of wit,' connected to historical, social and ideological upheavals in French post-revolutionary society. I shall argue that a twofold communication is at stake in Balzacian puns: between characters within the dialogues on the intradiegetic level; and between the narrator and the narratee on the extradiegetic level – these last two categories may, in turns, overlap or differ from those of author and reader. Balzacian puns rely on a fundamental ambiguity: they entail a certain art of distancing, of indirectness that enables characters to express critical, agonistic or even malicious remarks without breaking social conventions. Therefore, puns may constitute a hermeneutic puzzle, as well on the intradiegetic level, for the characters themselves, as on an extradiegetic level, for the reader. This article tackles the role of the narrator's speech in the hermeneutic process of deciphering puns. The role of the narrator goes beyond the mere explanatory role characteristic of an omniscient narrator: Balzac's narrator may clarify, but also label and praise – and sometimes keep quiet. Though puns have above all a pragmatic function on the intradiegetic level, they may take on a meta-poetic dimension on the extradiegetic level. Explaining, not explaining, or going beyond the explanation: all these options allow the narrator to exhibit and decipher the characteristics of a modern society in the process of self-differentiation; but also to serve the autonomy of Balzac's fictional project.

Angelika Zirker and Esme Winter-Froemel: Wordplay and Its Interfaces in Speaker-Hearer Interaction: An Introduction

See this volume.

List of Contributors

The Dynamics of Wordplay 1 & 2

Pierre J. L. Arnaud (Université Lumière Lyon 2)
Pierre J. L. Arnaud is professor emeritus of English linguistics at the Université Lumière, Lyon. Most of his research activity has been devoted to the lexicon in many of its aspects. His current interests include lexical semantics, morphology, phraseology, and metonymy.

Matthias Bauer (Eberhard Karls Universität Tübingen)
Matthias Bauer is professor of English Literature at the Eberhard Karls Universität Tübingen. His fields of teaching and research include Early Modern English literature (Shakespeare and the Metaphysical Poets), 19th century literature (Dickens), literary theory, the language of literature, the theory and practise of explanatory annotation, and religion and literature. He co-chairs (with Sigrid Beck) a project on "Limits of Interpretability" in the Collaborative Research Centre "The Construction of Meaning" (SFB 833), and is the chair of the Graduate Research Training Group "Ambiguity: Production and Perception" (GRK 1808) at Tübingen University.

Pauline Beaucé (Université Bordeaux Montaigne)
Pauline Beaucé holds a PhD in French language and literature; she is an assistant professor at the Bordeaux Montaigne University. Her research focuses on the history of performing arts and particularly on the history of hybrid forms and genres of 18th century drama. She has published a monograph (*Parodies d'opéra au siècle des Lumières* (Presses Universitaires de Rennes, 2013)) and several papers on fairground theatres and musical theatre (opera, *opéra comique*). She has also edited about ten dramatic plays, most recently Rousseau's *Pygmalion* and its parody (Espaces 34, 2012).

Marc Blancher (Eberhard Karls Universität Tübingen)
Marc Blancher, PhD, was born in France in 1981. He has been living and teaching in Germany since 2006, and has been an instructor of French language and cultural studies at Tübingen University since 2009. Blancher studied German

language and culture, Comparative Literature, French as a Foreign Language, Medieval History and Spanish and wrote three master theses on crime literature. In his PhD thesis, he pursues the same topic, concentrating on European crime literature. Additionally, his research focuses on French comics, intercultural studies and humour. Blancher has done extensive work in publishing and in the media as an author of French crime novels, screenplays and short novels, for which he received several prizes.

Martina Bross (Eberhard Karls Universität Tübingen)
Martina Bross is currently completing her doctoral thesis on poetic economy in different versions of Shakespeare's *Hamlet* at Eberhard Karls Universität Tübingen. She is a member of the DFG Research Training Group "Ambiguity – Production and Perception" (GRK 1808). Martina Bross has taught seminars on Shakespeare and Early Modern drama at Tübingen University and is Editorial Assistant for *Connotations: A Journal for Critical Debate*. She has published an article on "Character Writing and the Stage in the Early Seventeenth Century" (with Matthias Bauer; in *Anglistentag 2013 Konstanz: Proceedings*, eds. Silvia Mergenthal and Reingard M. Nischik, 2014).

Federica Di Blasio (University of California, Los Angeles)
Federica Di Blasio studied European Literatures in Italy (Bologna) and France (Tours, Lyon), mainly focusing on the contemporary Italian and French periods. She developed her interest in wordplay working on *La Disparition* by Georges Perec and its translations in Italian and English. In 2015 she obtained an M.A. degree in Comparative and World Literature from the University of Illinois at Urbana-Champaign. She is starting a PhD program in Italian at the University of California at Los Angeles, working on a research project about hospitality in the contemporary Mediterranean region.

Ian Duhig (University of Leeds)
After working with homeless people for fifteen years in England and Northern Ireland, Ian Duhig was made redundant then became a full-time writer. Since then he has held several university fellowships, including servings as International Writer Fellow at Trinity College Dublin. He has written six collections of poetry, most recently *Pandorama* (Picador 2010) and won a Forward Prize, the National Poetry Competition twice and was three times shortlisted for the T. S.

Eliot Prize. A Cholmondeley Award recipient and Fellow of the Royal Society of Literature, Duhig writes in diverse genres and his most recent short story was published in Comma's *The New Uncanny* anthology, which won a Shirley Jackson Award in 2008.

Julia Genz (Eberhard Karls Universität Tübingen and Universität Witten / Herdecke)

Julia Genz is professor of comparative and modern German literature at Tübingen University. From 2010 to 2015 she held various chairs in modern German literature at the universities of Cologne, Witten / Herdecke and Essen. She completed her second book (*Habilitation*) in the field of comparative and modern German literature in 2009. Among her works are a study on discourses of evaluation (*Diskurse der Wertung: Banalität, Trivialität und Kitsch*. Munich 2011) and a volume of essays on *Metamorphoses of (New) Media: On Matters of Semiotics, Discourse and Aesthetics* (Newcastle upon Tyne 2015) and a comparative study on Eichendorff and Balzac (Joseph von Eichendorff "La statue de marbre" et Honoré de Balzac "Le chef-d'œuvre inconnu," in: Claude Paul and Eva Werth (eds.): *Comparatisme et intermédialité: Réflexions littéraires et interculturelles*. Würzburg 2015).

Maik Goth (Ruhr-Universität Bochum)

Maik Goth is a researcher in English literature based at Ruhr-Universität Bochum (Germany), and specializes in Renaissance literature as well as in Restoration and eighteenth-century drama. In addition to various articles and reviews, he has published two monographs: *From Chaucer's Pardoner to Shakespeare's Iago: Aspects of Intermediality in the History of the Vice* (Frankfurt a. M.: Peter Lang, 2009), and *Monsters and the Poetic Imagination in* The Faerie Queene (Manchester: Manchester University Press, 2015). He is currently working on the reception of Terence in English comedy and criticism from the Restoration to the late eighteenth century. Maik Goth is also book reviews editor of *Medievalia et Humanistica* and corresponding editor of *The Spenser Review*.

Sylvia Jaki (Universität Hildesheim)

Sylvia Jaki graduated from the University of Munich, Germany, in 2008. She holds a PhD from the International Doctoral Programme *LIPP* (now *Graduate School Language & Literature Munich, Class of Language*), with a dissertation focussing on phraseological modifications (Jaki, Sylvia. 2014. *Phraseological Substitutions in Newspaper Headlines: "More than meats the eye."* Amsterdam / Philadelphia: John Benjamins). Since 2013, Sylvia Jaki has taught and pursued new research directions at the University of Hildesheim. Her main areas of interest include media language, audiovisual translation, phraseology, verbal humour, and spoken language.

Johannes Kabatek (Universität Zürich)
Johannes Kabatek studied Romance Philology, Political Science and Musicology in Tübingen and Málaga (Spain). He obtained his PhD in 1995 at Tübingen (with a thesis on Language contact in Northwest Spain). He was assistant professor in Paderborn and in Tübingen; 2001-2004 full Professor (chair) in Freiburg (Germany); 2004-2013 full professor (chair) at Tübingen University; since September 2013 he is professor for Ibero-Romance linguistics at the University of Zurich. He was visiting professor in the US, Brazil, Chile, Spain. Kabatek's research areas: Romance linguistics (French, Ibero-Romance Languages); Language contact, minority languages, Medieval Spanish; Galician, Catalan; Brazilian Portuguese; Historical Linguistics; Historical syntax, spoken and written language.

Sebastian Knospe (Ernst Moritz Arndt Universität Greifswald)
Sebastian Knospe is a post-doctoral lecturer and researcher in English linguistics at the University of Greifswald, Germany. His main research fields include contact linguistics, qualitative sociolinguistics and lexicology. In his PhD thesis, published by Peter Lang in 2014, he examines the array of structural forms and the discursive functions involved in language mixing with English in the contemporary German press, considering the complex interconnections between codeswitching, borrowing and processes of word-formation. In his post-doc project, he studies humour and wordplay in English and German, acknowledging cultural differences and convergences that result from increasing trends toward Anglicization visible in different European languages.

Thomas Kullmann (Universität Osnabrück)
Thomas Kullmann is Professor of English Literature at the University of Osnabrück. Currently, his main research interests are Shakespeare and Renaissance Culture; English Children's Fiction, and Images of India in 19th century Britain. His publications include two books on Shakespeare, one on landscape and wea-

ther in the nineteenth-century English novel, and one on English children's and young adults' fiction as well as numerous articles on English Renaissance Literature, Victorian and twentieth-century literature and culture, and children's literature. He also edited two volumes of essays on aspects of English children's fiction.

Michelle Lecolle (Université de Lorraine-Metz)

Michelle Lecolle is Maître de conférences at the University of Lorraine in Metz. Her areas of specialization rely on an approach which brings together semantics and contemporary discourse analysis. She is interested in phenomena related to indirect reference and, more generally, in the complex and intricate determinations governing meaning and the interpretation of nouns in context. She has devoted articles to the lay person's feeling for language, to change in meaning, multiple meanings, and to different types of names: collective nouns, place names, and names of social groups.

François Maniez (Université Lumière Lyon 2)

François Maniez is Professor of English linguistics at the University of Lyon. His research interests include lexicology, neology, noun phrase syntax, translation and corpus linguistics. His research has appeared in journals such as *ASp*, *Meta*, and *Revue Française de Linguistique Appliquée*.

Patricia Oster (Universität des Saarlandes)

Patricia Oster holds the chair for French Literature at Saarland University (since 2003), and she is currently president of the *Université franco-allemande* (elected in 2015). She studied Romance literature and languages as well as comparative literature in Bonn, Toulouse, and Harvard. Patricia Oster obtained her PhD in French Literature and wrote her second book (*Habilitation*) in Romance studies and comparative literary studies in Tübingen. Among her publications are a book on Marivaux (*Marivaux und das Ende der Tragödie*) and a book on the veil in the text in Dante, Petrarca, Tasso, Rousseau, Goethe, Nerval, Proust, and Claude Simon (*Der Schleier im Text*) and many articles on French and Italian literature from the Middle Ages to the present (see the list at http://www.uni-saarland.de/lehrstuhl/oster-stierle/lehrstuhl/prof-dr-oster-stierle.html#c13228 1). She also focusses on intermediality between literature, image and film.

Alain Rabatel (Université de Lyon 1)

Alain Rabatel is a professor of linguistics at Université de Lyon 1. He specializes in enunciation, textual linguistics and (literary, religious and media) discourse analysis, and he is also interested in didactic interaction. He is the author of numerous publications (see the list at (http://icar.univ-lyon2.fr/membres/arabatel). Alain Rabatel first became known for his work on perspective, empathy, polyphony and dialogism in narration. Later he became interested in the relation between indirect argumentation, enunciative effacement and perspective. He also works on tropes and wordplay from the standpoint of confrontation, responsibility and enunciative charge. In the context of this approach, he aims to uncover the diverse pos-itions of co-, over- and under-enunciation at the intersection of cognitive, enunciative and interactional problem sets.

Vincent Renner (Université Lumière Lyon 2)

Vincent Renner is Professor of English linguistics at the University of Lyon. His research interests include word-formation, contact linguistics and contrastive linguistics. Together with François Maniez and Pierre J. L. Arnaud he is co-editor of *Cross-Disciplinary Perspectives on Lexical Blending* (De Gruyter Mouton, 2012). His research has appeared in journals such as *English Studies*, *Morphology*, *Word Structure* and *Neologica*.

Sheelagh Russell-Brown (St. Mary's University)

Sheelagh Russell-Brown is a lecturer in the Department of English at Saint Mary's University in Halifax, Canada, having previously taught for seven years at Townshend International School in the Czech Republic. Dr. Russell-Brown's conference paper continues research that began with her doctoral thesis on the influence of Anglo-Saxon purism on the language of Gerard Manley Hopkins. Her research interests include nineteenth-century and modern British and European literature and culture, and neo-Victorian literature. She has published on memories of the Roma Holocaust, on Havel and Beckett, on Palliser and Dickens (especially on *Hard Times* and mathematical imagery).

Jean-François Sablayrolles (Paris 13 Sorbonne Paris-Cité)

After passing his *agrégation* in Grammar, receiving his doctorate in *Sciences du langage* and obtaining his *habilitation à diriger des recherches* in 2004, Jean-François Sablayrolles has been a Professor of linguistics at Paris 13 Sorbonne

Paris-Cité since 2006, after being *maître de conférences* at Limoges and at Paris 7. He is a member of the Conseil de laboratoire LDI UMR 7187 and in charge of the master 2 recherche COLEDI (ex-SCIL). His research focuses on contemporary French neology, and he has organized two colloquia on linguistic innovation (Limoges 2011) and "la fabrique des mots" (Cerisy 2015). Among his publications are *La Néologie en français contemporain* (Champion, 2000) and *Les néologismes* (with Jean Pruvost, PUF 2003); together with J. Humbley he founded the journal *Neologica* in 2006 (ed. Classiques Garnier).

Svea Schauffler (Hochschule Augsburg)
Svea Schauffler has been a Professor of English Language at the University of Applied Sciences Augsburg in Germany since 2014, after spending several years living and working in the United Kingdom and obtaining a PhD from the University of Sheffield. Originally at home in the field of Applied Linguistics, her main research interests include Audiovisual Translation, Audio Description, and the transfer of linguistic humour.

Monika Schmitz-Emans (Ruhr-Universität Bochum)
Prof. Dr. Monika Schmitz-Emans holds the Chair of Comparative Literature Studies (Allgemeine und Vergleichende Literaturwissenschaft) at Ruhr-Universität Bochum (Germany). After her studies of German literature, Italian language and literature, Philosophy and Pedagogics she finished her doctoral dissertation about Jean Paul (*Schnupftuchsknoten und Sternbild: Jean Pauls Ansätze zu einer Theorie der Sprache*) in 1984, followed by her Habilitation (*Schrift und Abwesenheit: Historische Paradigmen zu einer Poetik der Entzifferung und des Schreibens*), published in 1995. Before and after her habilitation (1992) she taught at the Universities of Bonn, Essen, and Jena; in 1992 she was applied Professor of Modern European Literature (Europäische Literatur der Neuzeit) at the Fern Universität Hagen (distance teaching university). Since 1995 she has been teaching at Bochum. Her research areas include European Literatures from 20th to 21th centuries, Poetics, Literature and the Other Arts. Literature, Images and Visuality.

Laélia Véron (Université Lumière Lyon 2)
Laélia Véron, holds an *agrégation*, has a degree in French language from the ÉNS of Lyon. She is completing a PhD in stylistics (discourse analysis and pragmatics), focusing on the topic of the pun in the *Comédie humaine* by Balzac.

She has published several articles on balzacian works and on the notions of "wit" and "pun." She is contributing to the Balzac dictionary and to the republishing of the *Comédie humaine*. She was a lecturer in France (ÉNS de Lyon, Université d'Orléans) and England (Royal Holloway University) and is currently teaching stylistics in the University of Paris 3. She co-hosts a seminar at the ÉNS of Ulm that studies the links between politics, commitment and literature.

Esme Winter-Froemel (Universität Trier)
Esme Winter-Froemel is Professor of Romance Linguistics at the University of Trier. She studied Romance Languages (French, Spanish, Italian), Comparative Literature and Philosophy at the universities of Tübingen, Nantes and Pisa, and completed her PhD on loanwords and loanword integration in Romance in 2009. In her *Habilitation*, she examined the role of ambiguity in processes of semantic change from indefinite to first person plural meaning (indirectness, reanalysis). Additionally, she has conducted research and taught on wordplay since 2009. She directs the scientific network "The Dynamics of Wordplay: Language Contact, Linguistic Innovation, Speaker-Hearer-Interaction" funded by the German Research Foundation (DFG, 2013–2016). Moreover, she is a member of the Research Training Group (GRK 1808) "Ambiguity: Production and Perception" and a co-leader of project C4 "Phenomena of Ambiguity in the Diachrony of Romance" of the Collaborative Research Centre / SFB 833 "The Construction of Meaning" (both at Tübingen University).

Angelika Zirker (Eberhard Karls Universität Tübingen)
Angelika Zirker is an assistant professor at Tübingen University. She received her PhD in 2010 with a study on Lewis Carroll's *Alice* books (*Der Pilger als Kind: Spiel, Sprache und Erlösung in Lewis Carrolls* Alice-Büchern – *The Pilgrim as Child: Play, Language, and Salvation in Lewis Carroll's* Alice *Books*). In 2015 she completed her second book (*Habilitation*) with *Stages of the Soul in Early Modern Poetry: William Shakespeare and John Donne*. She has been involved in various projects that combine the study of literature and linguistics for some years, including "Limits of Interpretability" (chaired by Matthias Bauer and Sigrid Beck) in the Collaborative Research Centre on "The Construction of Meaning" (SFB 833) at Tübingen as well as the Research Training Group (GRK 1808) on "Ambiguity: Production and Perception," and, with Esme Winter-Froemel, a joint project on "Wordplay in Speaker-Hearer Interaction." She is also one of the editors of *Connotations: A Journal for Critical Debate*.

Index

advertisement 10, 164, 167, 171, 173
allusion 7, 16, 18, 137, 142, 144, 146–7, 150, 153, 163, 175, 200–1, 216, 218, 226, 259, 284, 286
ambiguity 8, 10, 25–45, 57, 60, 107, 163, 221, 247, 272, 283
– in literature 25–45, 72–92, 199–200, 262, 272
– lexical 34
– strategic use of 41, 72–92, 174, 199–200
– structural 25–45
anglicism 161–93
Astérix 215–18
auto-referentiality 1, 222, 265, 273–4

backronymy 120
Bergson, Henri 6, 213
blend 119–33, 138, 161–93
– code blend 161–93
– conceptual blend 161–93
blending 119–33, 161–93
– code blending 164
– conceptual blending 165, 280
– lexical blending 109, 119–33, 161–93
Bühler, Karl 220–25

Carroll, Lewis 59–67, 95, 161, 245–66
– *Alice's Adventures in Wonderland* 59–67, 245–66, 272
– *Letters* 64–65, 250
– *Symbolic Logic* 259
– *Through the Looking-Glass* 61, 245–66
Castiglione, Baldassare 53–56, 61
cleverness 103, 135–59, 162
clipping 119–33
cognitive approach 6, 161–93
– blend space 179
– generic space 180–85
– input space 179, 180–85
Collier, Jeremy 85–87
comics 215–18
communication 48, 136, 146, 185, 223
– everyday communication 1, 10

– external communication 10, 72–92, 274, 276, 283
– in literature 269–86
– internal communication 10, 72–92, 274, 276, 283
– levels of communication 14–18, 25–45, 72–92
– literary communication 10, 49
compound 4, 106–9, 119–33, 161–93, 224, 275–6
– compounding 119–33, 161–93
conceptual 165
Congreve, William
– *Love for Love* 77–8
Coseriu, Eugenio 9, 220–25
courtliness 55, 57, 47–69, 58

Delabastita, Dirk 5, 37, 161, 230, 274
Deleuze, Gilles 247, 266
dialect 99, 101, 106–9, 175
diamorph 172, 177, 181, 183, 188
Dickens, Charles
– *A Tale of Two Cities* 6
Dickinson, Emily 278
dimension 220, 270, 274
– metalinguistic 6, 9
– three-dimensionality 245–66
– two-dimensionality 245–66
disambiguation 25–45, 76, 78–9, 83
discourse tradition 1, 13, 72, 171, 213–28, 270
double entendre 48, 72–92, 272
drama 7, 11, 15, 276, 283
– early modern drama 25–45, 50–53
– Restoration Comedy 72–92
dubbing 232
Duhig, Ian 195–207
Durfey, Thomas
– *A Fond Husband* 76–77
– *The Modern Prophets* 80–81

Farquhar, George
– *The Recruiting Officer* 77
film 167

– animated film 229–43
fraternization 15
Freud, Sigmund 6
function
– ludic 63, 95–114, 124, 129–30, 161
– metalinguistic 9–14, 52, 173, 221–2
– poetic 6, 8, 104, 195–207, 221–3
– pragmatic 15, 61, 146, 223

Genette, Gérard 256
Grice, Paul 11, 48, 272

homonymy 26, 50, 65, 73, 153, 164, 172–3, 176–7, 180, 187–8, 245–66, 277–9
homophony 7–8, 34–41, 48, 53, 62, 73, 127, 164, 172–3, 175, 177, 182, 187, 284
Hopkins, Gerard Manley
– *Dark Sonnets* 95–114
Huizinga, Johan 6, 97–98, 102, 113, 220
humour 5, 11, 52, 72–92, 135–59, 197, 199, 213–28, 229–43

iconicity 202
in absentia 14, 271
in praesentia 272, 276
interdisciplinary approach 1–22
interplay 1–22, 81, 90, 167, 231, 234

Jakobson, Roman 9, 48, 52–3, 220–25
Jonson, Ben 35, 200
– *Cynthia's Revels* 57–8

Locke, John 257–9

mathematics 200, 253
– geometry 247–9, 266
Milton, John 277
Morgan, Edwin
– *Homage to Zukovsky* 199

naming 129, 200, 216–7, 230, 256–7
neologism 108–9, 130
Nietzsche, Friedrich 266

parody 108–9, 219, 265
paronomasia 52, 54, 58, 95–114, 172, 195–207, 271, 273, 277, 284

paronymy 8, 148, 172–3, 175, 180–1, 188, 277–9
performance 99
– linguistic 51, 187
– theatrical 11, 32, 40, 58, 80, 196, 254–5
philosophy
– nominalism 257
phraseologism 136–7, 140, 146, 151, 231, 234
Plato *256*
Plautus
– *Cistellaria* 279
play 51–2, 61, 95–114, 120, 131, 220–1
politeness 61, 282
polyphony 17, 203
polysemy 4, 48, 52, 57, 60, 65, 72–92, 136, 171, 187
proverb 8, 39, 135–59, 217, 227
pun 25–45, 50–2, 55, 58, 61, 63, 72–92, 95–114, 147–8, 151, 161–93, 198, 203, 213, 216, 219, 232, 245–66, 269–86
– bilingual pun 280

Renaissance 25–45, 63, 74, 269–86
riddle 8, 72, 98, 221, 270, 280

satire 89, 91, 136
semantic complexity 122, 128–9, 152–3, 174, 221, 272
Shadwell, Thomas
– *Bury Fair* 74
Shakespeare, William 7, 161, 225, 255, 283
– *As You Like It* 284
– *Hamlet* 50, 274–5, 282, 285
– *Henry V* 52, 282
– *Much Ado About Nothing* 50–3
– *Romeo and Juliet* 7, 273–5, 283
sound 4, 7, 14, 62, 216, 218, 224, 273, 278
– sound effect 106
– sound play 48, 74, 176, 188, 198, 220, 222, 273
speaker-hearer interaction 1–22, 26, 49, 53, 78–80, 89, 91, 131, 146, 185–7, 220, 226, 269
Spenser, Edmund
– *Amoretti* 271
– *The Faerie Queene* 56, 270, 278
spoonerism 14, 221, 225

Steele, Richard
- *The Funeral* 72, 87–90
- *The Lying Lover* 78
Sterne, Lawrence 197
- *Tristram Shandy* 195–207, 261
subtitling 229–43
surfaces 174, 177, 245–66
synonymy 30, 122–3, 143, 277–9, 282, 285

theatre 26, 49, 50–3, 57–8
translation 55, 162, 168, 200, 215–8, 226, 277
- audiovisual translation 229–43

Victorian literature 59–67, 245–66

Wittgenstein, Ludwig 262, 266
word formation 95–114, 119–33, 164, 215–8
wordplay
- comic 4, 50–53, 161–93, 215–9, 229–44, 245–66
- comic wordplay 4
- in drama 25–45, 50–53
- in film 229–43
- in poetry 95–114, 195–207, 223, 269–86
- pragmatic 79
- secret 41–2, 269–86
- serious (*serio ludere*) 8, 105, 113
- wordplay in drama 8
Wycherley, William
- *The Country Wife* 74, 81–6
- *The Plain Dealer* 86

www.ingramcontent.com/pod-product-compliance
Lightning Source LLC
Chambersburg PA
CBHW050103170426
43198CB00014B/2435